Lecture Notes in Computer Science   1987

Edited by G. Goos, J. Hartmanis and J. van Leeuwen

Springer
Berlin
Heidelberg
New York
Barcelona
Hong Kong
London
Milan
Paris
Singapore
Tokyo

Kian-Lee Tan   Michael J. Franklin
John Chi-Shing Lui (Eds.)

Mobile
Data Management

Second International Conference, MDM 2001
Hong Kong, China, January 8-10, 2001
Proceedings

 Springer

Series Editors

Gerhard Goos, Karlsruhe University, Germany
Juris Hartmanis, Cornell University, NY, USA
Jan van Leeuwen, Utrecht University, The Netherlands

Volume Editors

Kian-Lee Tan
School of Computing
Department of Computer Science
3 Science Drive 2, Singapore 117543
E-mail: tankl@comp.nus.edu.sg

Michael J. Franklin
University of California at Berkeley
EECS, Computer Science Division
387 Soda Hall 1776
Berkeley, CA 94720-1776, USA
E-mail: franklin@cs.berkeley.edu

John Chi-Shing Lui
The Chinese University of Hong Kong
Department of Computer Science and Engineering
Shatin, N.T., Hong Kong, China
E-mail: cslui@cse.cuhk.edu.hk

Cataloging-in-Publication Data applied for

Die Deutsche Bibliothek - CIP-Einheitsaufnahme

Mobile data management : second international conference ; proceedings
/ MDM 2001, Hong Kong, China, January 8 - 10, 2001. Kian-Lee Tan ...
(ed.). - Berlin ; Heidelberg ; New York ; Barcelona ; Hong Kong ;
London ; Milan ; Paris ; Singapore ; Tokyo : Springer, 2001
    (Lecture notes in computer science ; Vol. 1987)
    ISBN 3-540-41454-1

CR Subject Classification (1998): C.2, C.5.3, C.3, D.2, H.5, H.4

ISSN 0302-9743
ISBN 3-540-41454-1 Springer-Verlag Berlin Heidelberg New York

Springer-Verlag Berlin Heidelberg New York
a member of BertelsmannSpringer Science+Business Media GmbH
© Springer-Verlag Berlin Heidelberg 2001

Typesetting: Camera-ready by author
Printed on acid-free paper   SPIN 10781983   06/3142   5 4 3 2 1 0

Message from the Conference Chair

The Second International Conference on Mobile Data Management (MDM 2001) is the continuation of the First International Conference on Mobile Data Access (MDA'99), which was also held in Hong Kong. Organizing MDM 2001 was a very rewarding experience for me. It gave me an excellent chance to work with many fine colleagues both inside and outside Hong Kong, and the opportunity to interact with leading companies in the mobile industry.

I am thankful to Mike Franklin of UC Berkeley and John Lui of the Chinese University of Hong Kong for putting together a world-class Program Committee, which worked very hard to bring an excellent technical program to the conference.

MDM 2001 includes an industrial track consisting of both invited and submitted papers. I would like to thank David Cheung of the University of Hong Kong and Wang-Chien Lee of Verizon, USA, for setting the program for the industrial track. Wang-Chien, in particular, is responsible for inviting speakers from the USA. I strongly feel that the interaction between academia and industry is of particular importance in the mobile area since ideas and applications cannot be realized if they do not fit into the mobile infrastructure built by the industry.

I appreciate very much the support of the Hong Kong Polytechnic University for hosting the conference, colleagues in the Department of Computing, namely, Alvin Chan, Hong Va Leong, and Allan Wong, for taking care of every fine detail in the operation of the conference, Kian-Lee Tan of the National University of Singapore for his relentless effort in collecting the manuscripts and meeting the publication deadline, Victor Lee of the City University of Hong Kong and Jeffrey Yu of the Chinese University of Hong Kong for handling the publicity of the conference, and Joseph Fong of the City University of Hong Kong for raising funds for the conference.

Last but not least, the conference would not have been possible without the generous support of our industrial sponsors, which include Hutchison Telecom, Nokia (HK) Ltd., and Oracle (HK) Ltd. At the time of writing, I am still expecting a few more industrial sponsors and invited presentations in the industrial track. Those whom I cannot acknowledge here by name, I would like to thank in advance in anticipation of their support!

November 2000   Dik Lun Lee

Preface

Welcome to the Second International Conference on Mobile Data Management (MDM 2001). The conference serves as a forum for the exchange of technical ideas and research results in the areas of mobility and database management.

This year, we have a very exciting program for MDM 2001. Many quality papers were submitted to the conference. All of the submitted papers were reviewed by at least three PC members. Due to the limitations of the program schedule as well as the desire to organize the conference using a single track format, we selected only 18 papers for full presentation at the conference. As a result many excellent papers could not be accepted.

The papers chosen for presentation span a large range of topics, from network protocol issues up to the semantics of mobile applications. The common theme of all these papers is their recognition of the central role played by data management techniques in the development of the emerging world of mobile and wireless applications.

We have loosely organized these papers into six areas:

1. DATA MANAGEMENT ARCHITECTURES,
2. CONTENT DELIVERY,
3. DATA BROADCASTING,
4. CACHING AND HOARDING,
5. COPING WITH MOVEMENT,
6. NETWORKS AND SYSTEMS ISSUES

In addition to the research track, we have sought to broaden the scope of the conference with an industrial session as well as poster presentations. Overall, the program strikes a comfortable balance between applied and theoretically oriented papers.

We were fortunate to have the help of a large group of renowned and hardworking researchers from around the world, who served on the technical program committee and the organizing committee. Their invaluable efforts in helping put together this technical program are most gratefully acknowledged. We would also like to take this opportunity to thank our keynote speakers.

We are only at the very beginning of what will be an explosion in mobile and wireless applications. These applications present new problems across the range of computer systems, networking, and data management topics. Through this forum, we hope to facilitate the dialog among leading researchers and practitioners in all of these areas, and we look forward to a productive and lively conference.

November 2000

Mike Franklin
John C.S. Lui

The Second International Conference on Mobile Data Management (MDM 2001)

Executive Committee

Honorary Chair: Tharam Singh Dillon (Hong Kong Polytechnic University)

Conference Chair: Dik Lun Lee (Hong Kong University of Science and Technology)

Technical Program: Michael Franklin (University of California, Berkeley)

John Chi-Shing Lui (Chinese University of Hong Kong)

Publicity: Victor Lee (City University of Hong Kong)

Jeffrey Yu (Chinese University of Hong Kong)

Local Arrangement: Alvin Chan (Hong Kong Polytechnic University)

Hong Va Leong (Hong Kong Polytechnic University)

Finance: Allan Wong (Hong Kong Polytechnic University)

Industrial Track: David Cheung (Hong Kong University)

Wang-Chien Lee (GTE Labs, USA)

Publication: Kian-Lee Tan (National University of Singapore)

Fund Raising: Joseph Fong (City University of Hong Kong)

Program Committee

Swarup Acharya	Lucent Bell Labs (USA)
Divyakant Agrawal	UC Santa Barbara (USA)
B.R. Badrinath	Rutgers University (USA)
Daniel Barbara	George Mason University (USA)
Philippe Bonnet	Cornell University (USA)
H.W. Chan	Hong Kong University (Hong Kong)
Panos Chrysanthis	University of Pittsburgh (USA)
Maggie Dunham	Southern Methodist University (USA)
Richard Guy	UCLA (USA)
Nen-Fu Huang	National Tsing Hua University (Taiwan)
Anupam Joshi	University of Maryland Baltimore County (USA)
Peter Keleher	University of Maryland (USA)
Dae Young Kim	Chungnam National University (Korea)
John Kubiatowicz	UC Berkeley (USA)

Victor Lee	City University of Hong Kong (Hong Kong)
Wang-Chien Lee	GTE (USA)
K. S. Leung	Chinese University of Hong Kong (Hong Kong)
Yi-Bing Lin	National Chiao Tung University (Taiwan)
Michael Lyu	Chinese University of Hong Kong (Hong Kong)
K.L. Tan	National University of Singapore (Singapore)
Y.C. Tay	National University of Singapore (Singapore)
Ouri Wolfson	University of Illinios Chicago (USA)
M. H. Wong	Chinese University of Hong Kong (Hong Kong)
Naoaki Yamanaka	NTT Japan (Japan)
Lawrence K. Yeung	City University of Hong Kong (Hong Kong)
Stan Zdonik	Brown University (USA)

Sponsoring Institutions

ACM Hong Kong Chapter
Department of Computing, Hong Kong Polytechnic University
Department of Computer Science, Hong Kong University of Science and Technology
E-Business Technology Institute (ETI), University of Hong Kong

Industrial Sponsors

Hutchison Telecommuications (Hong Kong) Ltd.
Nokia (Hong Kong) Ltd.
Oracle (Hong Kong) Ltd.

Technically Sponsored by

IEEE Technical Committee on Personal Communications

In Cooperation with

ACM SIGMOBILE
IEEE Hong Kong Section Computer Chapter

Table of Contents

Session V: Coping with Movement

Session VI: Networks and Systems Issues

Industrial Papers

Posters

Session I: Data Management Architectures

Towards Sensor Database Systems

Philippe Bonnet, Johannes Gehrke, Praveen Seshadri[1]

Computer Science Department, Upson Hall
Cornell University
Ithaca, NY, 14853 USA
{bonnet,johannes,praveen}@cs.cornell.edu

Abstract. Sensor networks are being widely deployed for measurement, detection and surveillance applications. In these new applications, users issue long-running queries over a combination of stored data and sensor data. Most existing applications rely on a centralized system for collecting sensor data. These systems lack flexibility because data is extracted in a predefined way; also, they do not scale to a large number of devices because large volumes of raw data are transferred regardless of the queries that are submitted. In our new concept of sensor database system, queries dictate which data is extracted from the sensors. In this paper, we define the concept of sensor databases mixing stored data represented as relations and sensor data represented as time series. Each long-running query formulated over a sensor database defines a persistent view, which is maintained during a given time interval. We also describe the design and implementation of the COUGAR sensor database system.

1   Introduction

The widespread deployment of sensors is transforming the physical world into a computing platform. Modern sensors not only respond to physical signals to produce data, they also embed computing and communication capabilities. They are thus able to store, process locally and transfer the data they produce. Still, at the heart of each sensor, a set of signal processing functions transform physical signals such as heat, light, sound, pressure, magnetism, or a particular motion into sensor data, i.e., measurements of physical phenomena as well as detection, classification or tracking of physical objects.

Applications monitor the physical world by querying and analyzing sensor data. Examples of monitoring applications include supervising items in a factory warehouse, gathering information in a disaster area, or organizing vehicle traffic in a large city [6]. Typically, these applications involve a combination of stored data (a list of sensors and their related attributes, such as their location) and sensor data. We call *sensor database* the combination of stored data and sensor data. This paper focuses on sensor query processing – the design, algorithms, and implementations used to run

---

[1] Praveen Seshadri is currently on leave at Microsoft: 3/1102 Microsoft, One Microsoft Way, Redmond, WA. pravse@microsoft.com.

K.-L. Tan et al. (Eds.): MDM 2001, LNCS 1987, pp. 3-14, 2001.

queries over sensor databases. The concepts developed in this paper were developed under the DARPA Sensor Information Technology (SensIT) program [23].

We define a *sensor query* as a query expressed over a sensor database. A typical monitoring scenario involves aggregate queries or correlation queries that give a bird's eye view of the environment as well as queries zooming on a particular region of interest. Representative sensor queries are given below in Example 1.

Example 1 (Factory Warehouse): Each item of a factory warehouse has a stick-on temperature sensor attached to it. Sensors are also attached to walls and embedded in floors and ceilings. Each sensor provides two signal-processing functions: (a) *getTemperature()* returns the measured temperature at regular intervals, and (b) *detectAlarmTemperature(threshold)* returns the temperature whenever it crosses a certain threshold. Each sensor is able to communicate this data and/or to store it locally. The sensor database stores the identifier of all sensors in the warehouse together with their location and is connected to the sensor network. The warehouse manager uses the sensor database to make sure that items do not overheat. Typical queries that are run continuously include:

- Query 1: "Return repeatedly the abnormal temperatures measured by all sensors."
- Query 2: "Every minute, return the temperature measured by all sensors on the third floor".
- Query 3: "Generate a notification whenever two sensors within 5 yards of each other simultaneously measure an abnormal temperature".
- Query 4: "Every five minutes retrieve the maximum temperature measured over the last five minutes".
- Query 5: "Return the average temperature measured on each floor over the last 10 minutes".

These example queries have the following characteristics:

- Monitoring queries are long-running.
- The desired result of a query is typically a series of notifications of system activity (periodic or triggered by special situations).
- Queries need to correlate data produced simultaneously by different sensors.
- Queries need to aggregate sensor data over time windows.
- Most queries contain some condition restricting the set of sensors that are involved (usually geographical conditions).

As in relational databases, queries are easiest to express at the logical level. Queries are formulated regardless of the physical structure or the organization of the sensor network. The actual structure and population of a sensor network may vary over the lifespan of a query.

Clearly, there are similarities with relational database query processing. Indeed, most applications combine sensor data with stored data. However, the features of sensor queries described here do not lend themselves to easy mapping to relational databases and sensor data is different from traditional relational data (since it is not stored in a database server and it varies over time).

There are two approaches for processing sensor queries: the warehousing approach and the distributed approach. The warehousing approach represents the current state-of-the-art. In the warehousing approach, processing of sensor queries and access to the sensor network are separated. (The sensor network is simply used by a data collection mechanism.) The warehousing approach proceeds in two steps. First, data is extracted from the sensor network in a predefined way and is stored in a database located on a unique front-end server. Subsequently, query processing takes place on the centralized database. The warehousing approach is well suited for answering predefined queries over historical data.

The distributed approach has been described by Bonnet et al. in [2][3] and is the focus of this paper. In the distributed approach, the query workload determines the data that should be extracted from sensors. The distributed approach is thus flexible – different queries extract different data from the sensor network – and efficient – only relevant data are extracted from the sensor network. In addition, the distributed approach allows the sensor database system to leverage the computing resources on the sensor nodes: a sensor query can be evaluated at the front-end server, in the sensor network, at the sensors, or at some combination of the three.

In this paper, we describe the design space for a sensor database system and present the choices we have made in the implementation of the Cornell COUGAR system. This paper makes the following contributions:

1. We build on the results of Seshadri et al. [20] to define a data model and long-running queries semantics for sensor databases. A sensor database mixes stored data and sensor data. Stored data are represented as relations while sensor data are represented as time series. Each long-running query defines a persistent view, which is maintained during a given time interval.

2. We describe the design and implementation of the Cornell COUGAR sensor database system. COUGAR extends the Cornell PREDATOR object-relational database system. In COUGAR, each type of sensor is modeled as a new Abstract Data Type (ADT). Signal-processing functions are modeled as ADT functions that return sensor data. Long-running queries are formulated in SQL with little modifications to the language. To support the evaluation of long-running queries, we extended the query execution engine with a new mechanism for the execution of sensor ADT functions. The initial version of this system has been demonstrated at the Intel Computing Continuum Conference [7].

Addressing these two issues is a necessary first step towards a sensor database system. In addition, a sensor database system should account for sensor and communication failures; it should consider sensor data as measurements with an associated uncertainty not as facts; finally, it should be able to establish and run a distributed query execution plan without assuming global knowledge of the sensor network. We believe that these challenging issues can only be addressed once the data model and internal representation issues have been solved.

2   Sensor Database Systems

In this section, we introduce the concepts of sensor databases and sensor queries. We build on existing work by Seshadri et al [20] to define a data model for sensor data and an algebra of operators to formulate sensor queries.

2.1   Sensor Data

A sensor database involves stored data and sensor data. Stored data include the set of sensors that participate in the sensor database together with characteristics of the sensors (e.g., their location) or characteristics of the physical environment. These stored data are best represented as relations. The question is: how to represent sensor data? First, sensor data are generated by signal processing functions. Second, the representation we choose for sensor data should facilitate the formulation of sensor queries (data collection, correlation in time, and aggregates over time windows).

Note that time plays a central role. Possibly, signal processing functions return output repeatedly over time, and each output has a time-stamp. In addition, monitoring queries introduce constraints on the sensor data time-stamps, e.g., Query 3 in Example 1 assumes that the abnormal temperatures are detected either simultaneously or within a certain time interval. Aggregates over time windows, such as in Query 4 and 5, reference time explicitly.

Given these constraints, we represent sensor data as time series. Our representation of sensor time series is based on the sequence model introduced by Seshadri et al. [20]. Informally, a sequence is defined as a 3-tuple containing a set of records R, a countable totally ordered domain O (called ordering domain – the elements of the ordering domain are referred to as positions) and an ordering of R by O. An ordering of a set of records R by an ordering domain O is defined as a relation between O and R, so that every record in R is associated with some position in O. Sequence operators are n-ary mappings on sequences; they operate on a given number of input sequences producing a unique output sequence. All sequence operators can be composed. Sequence operators include: select, project, compose (natural join on the position), and aggregates over a set of positions. Because of space limitation, we refer the reader to Bonnet et al. [4] for a formal definition of sensor time series

We represent sensor data as a time series with the following properties:
1. The set of records corresponds to the outputs of a signal processing function over time.
2. The ordering domain is a discrete time scale, i.e. a set of time quantum; to each time quantum corresponds a position. In the rest of the paper, we use natural numbers as the time-series ordering domain. Each natural number represents the number of time units elapsed between a given origin and any (discrete) point in time. We assume that clocks are synchronized and thus all sensors share the same time scale.
3. All outputs of the signal processing function that are generated during a time quantum are associated to the same position p. Note that in case a sensor does not generate events during the time quantum associated to a position, the Null record is associated to that position.
4. Whenever a signal processing function produces an output, the base sequence is updated at the position corresponding to the production time. Updates to sensor time series thus occur in increasing position order.

2.2   Sensor Queries

Sensor queries involve stored data and sensor data, i.e. relations and sequences. We define a sensor query as an acyclic graph of relational and sequence operators. The inputs of a relational operator are base relations or the output of another relational operator; the inputs of a sequence operator are base sequences or the output of another sequence operator. Thus relations are manipulated using relational operators and sequences are manipulated using sequence operators. We have defined two other operators that combine relations and sequences: (a) a projection operator that takes a sequence as input and outputs a relation by projecting out the position attribute in the sequence, and (b) a cross product operator that takes as input a relation and a sequence and outputs a sequence by performing a position-wise cross product.

Sensor queries are long running. To each sensor query is associated a time interval of the form $[O, O + T]$ where O is the time at which the query is submitted and T is the number of time quantums (possibly 0) during which the query is running.

During the span of a long-running query, relations and sensor sequences might be updated. An update to a relation R can be an insert, a delete, or modifications of a record in R. An update to a sensor sequence S is the insertion of a new record associated to a position greater than or equal to all the undefined positions in S (see Section 3.1.1). Concretely, each sensor inserts incrementally the set of records produced by a signal processing function at the position corresponding to the production time.

A sensor query defines a view that is persistent during its associated time interval. This persistent view is maintained to reflect the updates on the sensor database. In particular, the view is maintained to reflect the updates that are repeatedly performed on sensor time series.

Jagadish et al. [13] showed that persistent views over relations and sequences can be maintained incrementally without accessing the complete sequences, given restrictions on the updates that are permitted on relations and sequences, and given restrictions on the algebra used to compose queries. Informally, persistent views can be maintained incrementally if updates occur in increasing position order and if the algebra used to compose queries does not allow sequences to be combined using any relational operators. Both conditions hold in our concept of a sensor database.

3 The COUGAR Sensor Database System

In this section, we discuss the representation of sensor data, as well as the formulation and evaluation of sensor queries in the initial version of COUGAR. We discuss the limitations of this system and the conclusions that we have drawn.

We have introduced in Section 2 the concept of a sensor database. We took a set of design decisions when implementing this model in the COUGAR system. We distinguish between the decisions we took concerning:
1. User representation: How are sensors and signal processing functions modeled in the database schema? How are queries formulated?
2. Internal representation: How is sensor data represented within the database components that perform query processing? How are sensor queries evaluated to provide the semantics of long-running queries?

3.1 User Representation

In COUGAR, signal-processing functions are represented as Abstract Data Type (ADT) functions. Today's object-relational databases support ADTs that provide controlled access to encapsulated data through a well-defined set of functions [21]. We create a sensor ADT for all sensors of a same type (e.g., temperature sensors, seismic sensors). The public interface of a sensor ADT corresponds to the specific signal-processing functions supported by a type of sensor. An ADT object in the database corresponds to a physical sensor in the real world.

Signal-processing functions are modeled as scalar functions. Repeated outputs of an active signal processing functions are not explicitly modeled as sequences but as the result of successive executions of a scalar function during the span of a long-running query. This decision induced some limitation. For example, as we will see below, queries containing explicit time constraints (such as aggregates over time windows) cannot be expressed.

Sensor queries are formulated in SQL with little modifications to the language. The 'FROM' clause of a sensor query includes a relation whose schema contains a sensor ADT attribute (i.e., a collection of sensors). Expressions over sensor ADTs can be included in the 'SELECT' or in the 'WHERE' clause of a sensor query.

The queries we introduced in Section 1 are formulated in COUGAR as follows. The simplified schema of the sensor database contains one relation *Sensors(loc POINT, floor INT, s SENSORNODE)*, where *loc* contains the location of the sensor, *floor* denotes the floor where the sensor is located in the data warehouse and *s* represents a sensor node. *SENSORNODE* is a sensor ADT that supports the methods *getTemp()* and *detectAlarmTemp(threshold)*, where *threshold* is the temperature above which abnormal temperatures are returned. Both ADT functions return temperature represented as float.

- Query 1: "Return repeatedly the abnormal temperatures measured by all sensors"
  SELECT Sensors.s.detectAlarmTemp(100)
  FROM Sensors
  WHERE $every();
  The expression *$every()* is introduced as a syntactical construct to indicate that the query is long-running.
- Query 2: "Every minute, return the temperature measured by all sensors on the third floor".
  SELECT Sensors.s.getTemp()
  FROM Sensors
  WHERE Sensors.floor = 3 AND $every(60);
  The expression *$every()* takes as argument the time in seconds between successive outputs of the sensor ADT functions in the query.
- Query3: "Generate a notification whenever two sensors within 5 yards of each other measure simultaneously an abnormal temperature".
  SELECT R1s.detectAlarmTemp(100), R2.s. detectAlarmTemp (100)
  FROM Sensors R1, Sensors R2
  WHERE $SQRT($SQR(R1.loc.x – R2.loc.x) + $SQR(R1.loc.y – R2.loc.y)) < 5
  *   AND R1.s > R2.s AND $every();*
  This formulation assumes that the system incorporates an equality condition on the time at which the temperatures are obtained from both sensors.

Query 4 and 5 cannot be expressed in our initial version of COUGAR because aggregates over time windows are not supported.

3.2   Internal Representation

Query processing takes place partly on a database front-end. The query execution engine on the database front-end includes a mechanism for interacting with remote sensors. On each sensor a lightweight query execution engine is responsible for executing signal processing functions and sending data back to the front-end.

In COUGAR, we assume that there are no modifications to the stored data during the execution of a long-running query. Strict two-phase locking on the database front-end ensures that this assumption holds.

The initial version of COUGAR does not consider a long-running query as a persistent view; the system only computes the incremental results that could be used to maintain such a view. These incremental results are obtained by evaluating sensor ADT functions repeatedly and by combining the outputs they produce over time with stored data.

The execution of Sensor ADT functions is the central element of sensor queries execution. In the rest of the section, we show why the traditional execution of ADT functions (which is explained below) is inappropriate for sensor queries and we present the mechanisms we have implemented in COUGAR to evaluate sensor ADT functions.

Problems with the Traditional ADT Functions Execution

In most object-relational database systems, ADT functions are used to form expressions together with constants and variables. When an expression containing an ADT function is evaluated, a (local) function is called to obtain its return value. It is assumed that this return value is readily available on-demand. As for client-side ADT functions [15], this assumption does not hold in a sensor database for the following reasons:

1. Scalar sensor ADT functions incur high latency due to their location or because they are asynchronous;
2. When evaluating long-running queries, sensor ADT functions return multiple outputs.

To illustrate these problems, let us consider Query 1 in our example. One possible execution plan for Query 1 would be the following. For each temperature sensor in the relation R, the scalar function detectAlarmTemp(100) is applied.

There is a serious flaw in this execution. First, the function *detectAlarmTemp (100)* is asynchronous, i.e. it returns its output after an arbitrary amount of time. While the system is requesting an abnormal temperature on the first sensor of the relation R, the other temperature sensors have not been yet been contacted. It may very well be that some temperature sensors could have detected temperatures greater than 100 while the system is blocked waiting for the output of one particular function.

Second, during the span of a long-running query, *detectAlarmTemp (100)* might return multiple outputs. The evaluation plan presented above scans relation R once and thus does not respect the semantics of long running queries we have introduced in Section 2.

Virtual Relations

To overcome the problems outlined in the previous paragraph, we introduced a relational operator to model the execution of sensor ADT functions. This relational operator is a variant of a join between the relation that contains the sensor ADT attribute and the sensor ADT function represented in a tabular form. We call the tabular representation of a function a virtual relation.

A virtual relation is a tabular representation of a method. A record in a virtual relation (called a virtual record) contains the input arguments and the output argument of the method it is associated with.[2] Such relations are called virtual because they are not actually materialized, as opposed to base relations, which are defined in the database schema.

If a method M takes m arguments, then the schema of its associated virtual relation has m+3 attributes, where the first attribute corresponds to the unique identifier of a device (i.e., the identifier of an actual device ADT object), attributes 2 to m+1 correspond to the input arguments of M, attribute m+2 corresponds to the output value of M and attribute m+3 is a time stamp corresponding to the point in time at which the output value is obtained. In our example Query 1, the virtual relation *VRdetectAlarmTemp* is defined for the Sensor ADT function *detectAlarmTemp()*. Since this function takes one input arguments, the virtual relation has four attributes: *SensorId, Temp, Value, and TimeStamp, i.e.*, the identifier of the Sensor device that produces the data *SensorId*, the input threshold temperature *Temp*, the *Value* of the measured temperature and the associated *TimeStamp*.

We observe the following:

- A virtual relation is append-only: New records are appended to a virtual relation when the associated signal processing function returns a result. Records in a virtual relation are never updated or deleted.
- A virtual relation is naturally partitioned across all devices represented by the same sensor ADT: A virtual relation is associated to a sensor ADT function, to each sensors of these type is associated a fragment of the virtual relation. The virtual relation is the union of all these fragments.

The latter observation has an interesting consequence: a device database is internally represented as a distributed database. Virtual relations are partitioned across a set of devices. Base relations are stored on the database front-end. Distributed query processing techniques are not implemented in the initial version of COUGAR; their design and integration is the main goal of COUGAR V2 that we are currently implementing.

Query Execution Plan

Virtual relations appear in the query execution plan at the same level as base relations. Base relations are accessed through (indexed) scans. Each virtual relation fragment is accessed on sensors using a virtual scan. A virtual scan incorporates in the query execution plan the propagation mechanism necessary to support long-running queries.

Our notion of virtual scan over a virtual relation fragment is similar to the fetch_wait cursor over an active relation in the Alert database system [19]. A fetch_wait cursor provides a blocking read behavior. This fetch_wait cursor returns new records as they are inserted in the active relation and blocks when all records have been returned. A classical cursor would just terminate when all records currently in the relation have been returned.

---

[2] We assume without loss of generality that a device function has exactly one return value; an extension to the general case is straightforward.

The join between a base relation and a virtual relation is basically a nested loop with a pipelined access to the virtual scans that encapsulate the execution of the sensor ADT function. (Note that we make the simplifying assumption that arguments to the sensor ADT functions are constants.) Indeed, the sensor ADT function is applied with identical parameters on all sensors involved in the query. The algorithm is presented below.

In: Base relation R, sensor ADT function f
Out: join between relation R and virtual relation associated to f
Initialize virtual scans for the virtual relation fragments associated to f on all sensors involved in the query
FOREVER DO
  Get next output from the sensor virtual scan
  Find a matching sensor id in the base relation R
  If match is found then return record
END DO

The incremental results produced by a virtual join are directly transmitted to the client, or they are pipelined to the root of the execution plan (as the outer child in a nested loop join for instance)[3]. Consequently, queries with relational aggregates or 'ORDER BY' clauses do not return an incremental result. Indeed, such queries require an operator to accumulate all the results produced by its children. With such operators no incremental results are produced before the query is stopped.

3.3   Conclusions

Here are the conclusions that we have drawn from our experience with the initial version of COUGAR:

1. Representing stored data as relations with an ADT attribute representing sensors and sensor data as the output of ADT functions is a natural way of representing a sensor database.
2. Virtual joins are an effective way of executing ADT functions that do not return a value in a timely fashion (because they are often asynchronous, because they generally incur high latency or because they return multiple values over time).
3. Representing all signal processing functions as scalar functions fails to capture the ordering of sensor data in time. As a result, queries involving aggregates over time windows or correlations are difficult to express. This problem has previously been identified in the context of financial data [22].

4   Related Work

Two representative projects that build wireless sensor network infrastructures are the WINS project at UCLA [18] and the Smart Dust project at UC Berkeley [14]. The COUGAR system is implemented on top of the WINS infrastructure.

The goals of the DataSpace project at Rutgers University are quite similar to the goals of a sensor database system [9]. Imielinski et al. recognized the advantages of

---

[3] Note that queries with sensor ADT functions applied on more than one collection of sensors require that the join between two virtual joins is a double-pipelined join.

the distributed approach over the warehousing approach for querying physical devices. In a DataSpace, devices that encapsulate data can be queried, monitored and controlled. Network primitives are developed to guarantee that only relevant devices are contacted when a query is evaluated. We are currently integrating COUGAR with similar networking primitives, i.e., the Declarative Routing Protocol developed at MIT-LL [5], and the SCADDS diffusion-based routing developed at ISI [10]. Other related projects include the TELEGRAPH project at UC Berkeley [1], which studies adaptive query processing techniques, and the SAGRES project at the University of Washington [11], which explores the use of data integration techniques in the context of device networks.

The environment of a sensor network with computing power at each node resembles a mobile computing environment [8]. Sensors differ from mobile hosts in that sensors only serve external requests but do not initiate requests themselves. Also, recent work on indexing moving objects, e.g. [17], is relevant in such environments. The techniques proposed however assume a centralized warehousing approach.

Our definition of sensor queries bears similarities with the definition of continuous queries [23]. Continuous queries are defined over append-only relations with time-stamps. For each continuous query, an incremental query is defined to retrieve all answers obtained in an interval of t seconds. The incremental query is issued repeatedly, every t seconds, and the union of the answers it provides constitute the answer to the continuous query. Instead of being used to maintain a persistent view, incremental results are directly returned to users. The answers returned by the initial prototype of COUGAR respect the continuous queries semantics.

Time series can be manipulated in object-relational systems such as Oracle [16] or in array database systems such as KDB [12]. These systems do not support the execution of long-running queries over sequences.

5   Conclusion

We believe that sensor database systems are a promising new field for database research. We described a data model and long-running query semantics for sensor database systems where stored data are represented as relations and sensor data are represented as sequences. The version of the Cornell COUGAR system that we presented is a first effort towards such a sensor database system. The second version of COUGAR [4] improves on the initial prototype in that sequences are explicitly represented. This allows for more expressive sensor queries. In particular, queries containing aggregates over time windows can be expressed.

This first generation of the Cornell COUGAR systems showed much promise for providing flexible and scalable access to large collections of sensors. It helped us identify a set of challenging issues that we are addressing with our ongoing research:

- Due to the large scale of a sensor network, it is highly probable that some of the sensors and some of the communication links will fail at some point during the processing of a long-running query. We are studying how sensor database systems can adjust to communication failures and return a more accurate answer at the cost of increased response time and resource usage.
- Sensor data are measurements not facts. Sensor values can be thought of as drawn from a continuous distribution, e.g. a normal distribution. We are working on a data model and an associated algebra for representing and manipulating continuous distributions.

* Because of the large scale and dynamic nature of a sensor network, we cannot assume that a centralized optimizer maintains global knowledge and thus precise meta-information about the whole network. We are studying how to maintain meta-data in a decentralized way and how to utilize this information to devise good query plans.

Acknowledgements
We would like to thank Tobias Mayr and Raoul Bhoedjiang who helped debug earlier versions of this paper. This paper benefited from interactions with the SensIT community. In particular, Bill Kaiser provided valuable information concerning the Sensoria WINS network. Tok Wee Hyong has implemented most of the sequence ADT extension for COUGAR V2. Joe Hellerstein suggested the relevance of sequences for sensor databases. This work is sponsored by the Defense Advanced Research Projects Agency (DARPA) and Air Force Research Laboratory, Air Force Material Command, USAF, under agreement number F-30602-99-0528 and by the National Science Foundation under Grant No. EIA 97-03470

References

1.   Ron Avnur, Joseph M. Hellerstein: Eddies: Continuously Adaptive Query Processing. SIGMOD Conference 2000: 261-272

2.   Ph. Bonnet, P.Seshadri. Device Database Systems. Proceedings of the International Conference on Data Engineering ICDE'99, San Diego, CA, March, 2000.

3.   Ph.Bonnet, J.Gehrke, P.Seshadri. Querying the Physical World. IEEE Personal Communications. Special Issue "Networking the Physical World". October 2000.

4.   Ph.Bonnet, J.Gehrke, P.Seshadri. Towards Sensor Database Systems. Cornell CS Technical Report TR2000-1819. October 2000

5.   D.Coffin, D.Van Hook, S.McGarry, S.Kolek. Declarative AdHoc Sensor. SPIE Integrated Command Environments. 2000.

6.   D.Estrin, R.Govindan, J.Heidemann (Editors): Embedding the Internet. CACM 43(5) (2000)

7.   The Intel Computing Continuum Conference, San Francisco, May, 2000. http://www.intel.com/intel/cccon/

8.   Tomasz Imielinski, B. R. Badrinath: Data Management for Mobile Computing. SIGMOD Record 22(1): 34-39 (1993)

9.   Tomasz Imielinski, Samir Goel: DataSpace - Querying and Monitoring Deeply Networked Collections in Physical Space. MobiDE 1999: 44-51

10.   C.Intanagonwiwat, R.Govindan, D.Estrin. Directed Diffusion: A Scalable and Robust Communication Paradigm for Sensor Networks. Mobicom'00.

11.   Z. G. Ives, A. Y. Levy, J. Madhavan, R. Pottinger, S. Saroiu, I. Tatarinov, S. Betzler, Q. Chen, E. Jaslikowska, J. Su, W. Tak and T.Yeung: Self-Organizing Data Sharing Communities with SAGRES. SIGMOD Conference 2000: 582

12.   Kx Systems Home Page: http://www.kx.com.

13.   H. V. Jagadish, Inderpal Singh Mumick, Abraham Silberschatz: View Maintenance Issues for the Chronicle Data Model. PODS 1995: 113-124

14.   J. M. Kahn, R. H. Katz and K. S. J. Pister, "Mobile Networking for Smart Dust", ACM/IEEE Intl. Conf. on Mobile Computing and Networking (MobiCom 99), Seattle, WA, August 17-19, 1999

15.   Tobias Mayr and Praveen Seshadri: Client-Site Query Extensions. In Proceedings of the ACM SIGMOD Conference 1999, Philadelphia, PA, June 1999.

16.   Oracle8™ Time Series Data Cartridge. 1998. http://www.oracle.com/

17.   Dieter Pfoser, Christian S. Jensen, Yannis Theodoridis: Novel Approaches in Query Processing for Moving Objects. VLDB 2000:

18.   G.Pottie, W. Kaiser: Wireless Integrated Network Sensors (WINS): Principles and Approach. CACM 43(5) (2000)

19.   U. Schreier, H. Pirahesh, R. Agrawal, C. Mohan: Alert: An Architecture for Transforming a Passive DBMS into an Active DBMS. VLDB 1991: 469-478

20.   Praveen Seshadri, Miron Livny, Raghu Ramakrishnan: SEQ: A Model for Sequence Databases. ICDE 1995: 232-239

21.   P. Seshadri. Enhanced Abstract Data Types in Object-Relational Databases. VLDB Journal 7(3): 130-140 (1998).

22.   D.Shasha: Time Series in Finance: The Array Database Approach. 1998. http://cs.nyu.edu/shasha/papers/jagtalk.html

23.   D.Tennenhouse: Proactive Computing. CACM 43(5) (2000)

24.   Douglas B. Terry, David Goldberg, David Nichols, Brian M. Oki: Continuous Queries over Append-Only Databases. SIGMOD Conference 1992: 321-330

An Architecture for the Effective Support of Adaptive Context-Aware Applications

Christos Efstratiou, Keith Cheverst, Nigel Davies and Adrian Friday

Distributed Multimedia Research Group, Department of Computing, Lancaster University,
Bailrigg, Lancaster, LA1 4YR U.K.
e-mail: most@comp.lancs.ac.uk

Abstract. Mobile applications are required to operate in environments characterised by change. More specifically, the availability of resources and services may change significantly during a typical period of system operation. As a consequence, adaptive mobile applications need to be capable of adapting to these changes to ensure they offer the best possible level of service to the user. Our experiences of developing and evaluating adaptive context-aware applications in mobile environments has led us to believe that existing architectures fail to provide the necessary support for such applications. In this paper, we discuss the shortcomings of existing approaches and present work on our own architecture that has been designed to meet the key requirements of context-aware adaptive applications.

1   Introduction

Mobile applications are required to operate in environments that change. Specifically, the availability of resources and services may change significantly and frequently during typical system operation [8,11]. As a consequence, mobile applications need to be capable of adapting to these changes to ensure they offer the best possible level of service to the user [11]. While early research focused on applications which adapted to changes in network characteristics, there is now increasing interest in applications that adapt to general environmental and contextual triggers such as changes in a system's physical location, e.g. the GUIDE system [2,3] which supplies users with information tailored to their current location.

Current adaptive mobile applications are built using one of two approaches: either the adaptation is performed by the system which underpins the application (in an attempt to make transparent the effects of mobility) or, the application itself monitors and adapts to change. In some cases, these approaches are combined as, for example, in the MOST system [8] where the middleware platform adapts the operation of the network protocol in the face of changes in QoS and, additionally, reports these changes to the application to enable application level adaptation. However, in the general case, it has been demonstrated that maintaining transparency in the face of mobility is not practical and that it is difficult for a system to adapt without support from the application.

Careful examination of current approaches to supporting adaptation reveals two important facts. Firstly, support for adaptation is often fragmented with a range of

K.-L. Tan et al. (Eds.): MDM 2001, LNCS 1987, pp. 15-26, 2001.
© Springer-Verlag Berlin Heidelberg 2001

mechanisms being used to notify applications of changes in different environmental and contextual attributes [4]. Secondly, there is a lack of mechanisms that support coordination of adaptive behaviour across the whole system, according to user requirements. In this paper, we explore the requirements for, and our research into creating, a unified architecture. It can support multiple contextual attributes coupled with a user driven adaptation control mechanism. The benefits of such an approach are clearly illustrated using a set of real-world examples.

2   Drawbacks of Current Approaches

Mobile systems need to be capable of adapting to a wide range of attributes such as network bandwidth, location, power etc. In general, current mobile systems provide support for adaptive applications by notifying applications when certain 'interesting' changes in attributes occur, e.g. bandwidth falls below some specified minimum threshold. It is then the responsibility of the application to adapt in an appropriate way, e.g. by reducing its bandwidth requirements. However, this approach can be shown to lead to inefficient solutions because of the lack of support for enabling coordination between the adaptation policies of multiple applications that may co-exist on the same system. In the following scenarios, we illustrate the kind of problems that could occur as a result of relying upon a simplistic notification based approach and isolated, uncoordinated, application adaptation.

2.1   Scenarios

The Need for Coordinated Application Adaptation for Power Management. This scenario illustrates the need for coordination in order to achieve efficient power management on a mobile system. One existing approach for handling power management, i.e. the ACPI [1] model, is to enable the operating system to switch hardware resources into low power mode when not in use, e.g. spinning down the hard-disk. This approach requires that applications leave hardware resources in an idle state for sufficient periods of time to make the transition between idle and active states worthwhile. Although this approach is suitable when only one application is running on a mobile device, the approach can prove ineffective when multiple applications or system services are sharing hardware resources. In more detail, the lack of coordinated access to hardware resources can result in poor utilisation of the shared resource and therefore sub-optimum power management. For example, consider the case of multiple applications that implement an auto-save feature. In the absence of any coordination between applications each application may choose to checkpoint its state to the disk at an arbitrary time, without considering the state of the disk (i.e. spinning or sleeping). In contrast, if applications are able to coordinate their access to the hard-disk then access to the disk can be clustered, allowing longer periods of inactivity. This latter approach is clearly more power efficient than the situation in which usage of the hard-disk is completely arbitrary and uncoordinated.

The Problem of Conflicting Adaptation. In this scenario, we illustrate the potential problems that can occur in a system that utilises separate adaptation mechanisms for different attributes. We consider a hypothetical mobile system which utilises two independent adaptation mechanisms, one for managing power and the other for managing network bandwidth. The two mechanisms can conflict with one another as the following example illustrates. If the system needs to reduce power consumption, the power management mechanism will request those applications that are utilising network bandwidth to postpone their usage of the network device in order to place the network device in to sleep mode. As a consequence of applications postponing their use of the network, the available network bandwidth increases. However, the network adaptation mechanism will detect this unused bandwidth and notify applications to utilise the spare bandwidth. In this way, the request to utilise available bandwidth is in direct conflict with the request to postpone network usage.

This example highlights the problem of relying on independent and uncoordinated adaptation mechanisms. Clearly, coordination or harmonisation is required in order to detect and avoid potentially conflicting adaptation mechanisms. In the example presented, the instruction given to applications to utilise more bandwidth should have been withheld if conserving power was the system's primary goal.

Utilising Alternative Location Sensing Mechanisms. This scenario considers the case of supporting multiple services for providing similar contextual information. In this case, we consider a location aware system that is capable of sensing its current location through two different mechanisms: a local GPS device and using beaconing in a cell-based wireless network. Using the latter mechanism, the system can identify the current cell in which it operates and thus specify its location. Both mechanisms deal with the same problem but they both have different characteristics. The GPS mechanism is typically the more accurate (accuracy in the region of 5m) but does require extra power to operate. Alternatively, the network-based solution is generally less accurate (depending on the size of a cell, e.g. approximately 200m for WaveLAN). However, the fact that the network device is already in use by the system for communications means that the addition power consumption required for identifying the location of the base-station would be minimal.

It follows that the mobile system would select to use the GPS based solution if accurate location information was required and concern over additional power usage was not an important issue. Alternatively, if the lifetime of the system's batteries (and therefore operation) was more important than achieving greater location accuracy then the network location mechanism would be the more appropriate mechanism. The adaptive strategy that would be most appropriate depends on both the user's requirements and the context of other attributes, such as power. In order for the system to make such decisions there is a basic requirement for system-wide adaptation policies. Without such policies, coordinated adaptation on the use of alternative context retrieval mechanisms is difficult because each application relies on a single mechanism without being able to identify the implications of its operation on other system resources and, consequently, other applications.

3   Analysis

Multiple Attributes. The previous scenarios illustrated a number of potential problems with current approaches to developing adaptive context-aware mobile systems. In this section, we generalise on these findings to present a critique of existing mobile systems and their suitability for supporting adaptive applications.

Based on the ideas of ubiquitous computing [20] future mobile systems should be able to discover changes in both the user and system environment and adapt to these changes. Current context-aware applications handle context in an improvised fashion. Application developers usually bundle the application with specific mechanisms for accessing context. However, this approach does not allow coordinated adaptation on context changes leading to the problems presented. Dey [5] has addressed this problem and suggested a general platform to support context-aware application. Our belief is that though a general platform for supporting context-aware application is necessary, this platform should also be capable of addressing the problems of coordinated adaptation.

The situation is complicated still further by the fact that the adaptive behaviour triggered by one attribute can cause side-effects on other attributes. These side-effects could, in-turn, trigger adaptation requests to other applications that result in conflicting actions (as illustrated in the conflicting adaptation scenario in section 2.1.2). Moreover, current research [4,6,7,12,13] has identified the need to provide adaptation solutions based on the combination of different attributes.

Existing architectures do not provide the necessary support to enable programmers to construct applications, which can adapt to multiple attributes and identify and cope with conflicts in adaptation strategies.

Adaptation Mechanism. Current mobile systems supporting adaptive applications tend to rely heavily on integrating QoS feedback and adaptation with network bindings. Examining the architecture of such systems allows us to identify a framework for analysing the architectural model of existing adaptive systems. The framework comprises two layers, the upper application layer and the lower representing the adaptation support platform. Between these two layers we can identify four distinct flows of control and information (see figure 1).

Flow A. Represents the requirements set by the application concerning the resources or attributes supported by the underlying infrastructure. For example, in the case of network adaptation this flow could represent the application's network QoS requirements.

Flow B. Represents the ability of the application to control the functionality of the underlying infrastructure. In the case of accessing a GPS device this could represent, for example, the control of the device by the application.

Flow C. Represents an information flow from the platform to the application. This could be used, for example, as a notification mechanism to inform the application when certain requirements cannot be met. Such notification could then trigger the application to adapt.

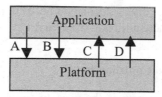

Fig. 1. Directed flows between applications and platform

Flow D. Represents the ability of the underlying platform to actually control the operation of the application. More specifically, this flow represents an explicit request from the system for the application to perform a specific adaptive behaviour. For example, the application might be requested to reduce its demand for network bandwidth or disk usage.

Consideration of this framework enables a classification of current systems according to the types of flows supported. For example, network based adaptive systems such as BAYOU [18], Odyssey [16], MOST [8] and Rover [10] support flows A and C.

Context aware applications like GUIDE [2,3], Stick-e Notes [17] and Cyberguide [14] are based on flows B and C. In more detail, for these applications, flow B represents the access to the various context-sensors while flow C represents the information flowing from the sensors to the application.

According to our knowledge no platform supporting context-aware adaptation provides a flow of control from the platform to the application. Indeed, although examples of systems providing this type of flow can be found in the distributed systems community, e.g. ISIS-META [15], it should be noted that these systems consider only network triggered adaptation.

4   Architectural Requirements

The previous sections have described the limitations of current approaches for supporting adaptive mobile applications. In particular, these approaches do not provide appropriate support to enable applications to adapt to multiple attributes in an efficient and coordinated way. This section considers a set of requirements that could be used to develop an appropriate architecture for supporting adaptive mobile applications.

4.1   Supporting a Common Space for an Extensible Set of Attributes

The first key requirement of the architecture is to provide a common space for handling the adaptation attributes used by the system. It is important that new attributes can be introduced into the system as and when they become important, e.g. the cost of specific services for mobile users or information about human physiology for wearable computers. The fact that new contextual attributes for triggering adaptation can arise implies that:

- the set of attributes that can trigger adaptation needs to be extensible,
- the characteristics of all these attributes may vary.

4.2 Application Control and Coordination

A second architectural requirement is the need to support the control of adaptative behaviour across all components involved in the interaction. As described earlier, one of the main limitations of current approaches is that applications themselves are responsible for triggering an adaptive mechanism when the underling infrastructure notifies them about any changes. In order to support flexible and coordinated adaptation there is a requirement for the triggering of adaptation on a system-wide level. Given this approach, the decision about when and how an application should adapt is pushed into an external entity, with cross-application knowledge, while the adaptive behaviour is still a part of the application's characteristics.

4.3 Support for System Wide Adaptation Policies

A further requirement is to support the notion of system-wide adaptation policies. More specifically, such policies should enable a mobile system to operate differently given the current context and the requirements of the user.

The specification of adaptation policies should be goal-oriented. Two kinds of goals can be identified:

1. effects on resources. The policy specifies a specific aim for the use a specific resource. Example policies include reducing the required network bandwidth and maximising the duration of operation of the system.
2. effects on applications. The policy specifies the mode of operation for specific applications. Example policies include defining priorities on applications which determine the order in which they are allocated resources and maximising the duration of operation of the system while having a specific application operating with full functionality.

5. Architecture

5.1 Structure of the Platform

We propose that future mobile adaptive applications should adopt an architecture in which mechanisms and policies are decoupled and, furthermore, mechanisms can be exposed and externalised in order to enable control by independent entities. Our architecture has been designed to address these requirements.

Figure 2 shows the relationship between the main components of the architecture of our proposed platform. The basic functionality of the architecture is two-fold, namely: the discovery and control of services offering contextual information and the coordination of adaptive behaviour of the system based on changes in context. More specifically, the platform discovers available context information in the system's environment and manipulates the contextual information in the *context database*. Context aware applications expose their adaptive mechanism to the platform by registering with the *application database*. The *adaptation control* driven by *adaptation policies* (as specified by the user) coordinates the coexisting applications according to changes in context.

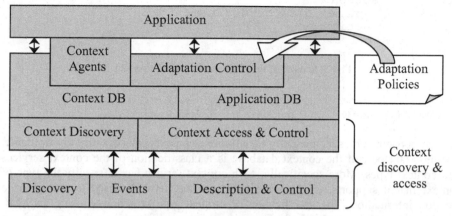

Fig. 2. The overall architecture of the system

All communications between the main components of the architecture are performed using HTTP as the transport protocol and XML to represent the format of the messages. The reason for this decision was based on the fact that these technologies support the lightweight integration of distributed components. Other alternatives, such as CORBA and RMI, are too heavyweight, and would require additional infrastructure, i.e. an ORB or RMI daemon respectively.

5.2 Context Discovery and Access

This part of our architecture is responsible for locating services that provide contextual information. These services can either be sensors embedded within the system (e.g. a body temperature sensor) or services in the surrounding environment (e.g. active devices in the user's environment). In a mobile environment the availability of context information can change rapidly. Thus, it is important to be able to discover context services when they are available and receive notification when they are not. For this reason, a considerable part of the architecture is based on the UPnP architecture [19]. In more detail, the mechanism for discovering available context services is based on services advertising themselves (using multicasting) to any interested context-aware applications.

Once a service is discovered the platform retrieves the XML description of the device, an abbreviated example of which is shown figure 3. The XML description provides the access points for sending control messages to the object and subscribing for event notifications. In addition, it defines the types of messages that can be sent to the service and the types of information that the service can offer. Given this information, the platform is capable of using the service and receiving notification events when the state of the service changes.

```
<service>
  <category> Location </category>
  <type> GPS </type>
  <action>
    <name> getXCoord </name>
  </action>
</service>
```

Fig. 3. Sample of the XML definition of a service

5.3 Context Database

This component serves as a registry for all those context services currently available. An important part of the context database is a classification of the context services into context types. More specifically, each context service has to specify the type of context that it supports, e.g both the GPS and the network based locator provide location information. The specification of context type is achieved using an XML template that defines the kind of information this type offers. Using this approach, an application can retrieve the specific contextual data in a way that is decoupled from the service used for acquiring the data.

This method of hiding the actual mechanism for retrieving contextual information, allows the platform to coordinate the access to context for different application. Moreover it offers our platform with the potential to switch between different services of the same type depending upon the predefined adaptation policies that have been specified.

5.4 Application Database

The application database serves as a repository for the adaptation mechanisms of all applications running on the system. The application developer is responsible for actually implementing the adaptive behaviour of his/her application. In addition, the application developer is also responsible for exposing this behaviour to the platform by ensuring that the application registers all of its adaptation mechanisms with the application database.

The description of the adaptation mechanisms should specify the type of context that can trigger this mechanism. This information is used by the adaptation control in order to coordinate the triggering of the applications based on changes in context. In figure 4, we illustrate an example of the information that may be provided by an application in XML, concerning its adaptive functionality.

5.5 Context Agents

A context agent is a piece of code that can be plugged into the platform in order to perform the application specific manipulation of contextual information.

```
<application>
  <name> WebBrowser </name>
```

```
<adaptationMode>
  <name> lowBand </name>
  <trigger>
    <context> availableBand </context>
    <condition> lessThan-9600 </condition>
  </trigger>
</adaptationMode>
</application>
```

Fig. 4. Sample of the XML definition of application's operation modes. The XML based description provides the different operational modes of the application, coupled with the contextual trigger that would make the application switch into that mode.

A common case of context manipulation is the combination of primitive context information for constructing a complex type of contextual data. For example, a context agent plugged into the platform can combine location data and current time in order to provide location-and-time tracking information similar to the data used by the Stick-e Note system [17].

To present even more clearly the operation of a context agent we will present an example based on the GUIDE system [2, 3]. The GUIDE system is a mobile electronic context-aware tourist guide. As part of its functionality it provides information about tourist attractions in HTML format, triggered by the location of the user. In order to introduce the GUIDE system into our platform we need to split the application into two parts: an ordinary web-browser and a location-triggered HTTP proxy. The HTTP proxy operates as a context agent which is plugged into the platform and has direct access to the location information provided by the platform. Triggered by changes in location, the agent can request the appropriate HTML data from the content server.

The key motivation behind introducing the notion of context agents is to enable the developer to distinguish the functionality of the application from the acquisition and manipulation of context data. Importantly, this allows context agents to be used for integrating non-context-aware applications (like an ordinary web browser) into a context-aware system.

5.6 Adaptation Control

This module is responsible for monitoring the status of contextual triggers and making decisions about the behaviour of the platform and the applications. The decision taking procedure is based on a set of adaptation policies specified by the user. These adaptation policies are specified by defining priorities both among the applications running on the system and among the resources of the system. This prioritisation represents the importance of these entities according to the user needs.

The adaptation control is further divided into two sub-modules: *internal adaptation* and *external adaptation as* explained below.

Internal adaptation. This module coordinates the context monitors that are required for all applications running on the system and coordinates potential adaptation within the platform itself.   The adaptation actions that can be performed on context acquisition are tightly coupled with the context classification that has been described earlier (in section 5.3). Context services are clustered into context types according to the type of information they provide. For example, a GPS device and a network based location mechanism would be members of the same type of context, i.e. location. Both these mechanisms can provide similar types of information but have different specifications and different requirements. When the system gets into a state whereby one of the two mechanisms is favoured (according to the adaptation policies specified by the user) then the platform will switch to the mechanism that is preferred (as illustrated in figure 5).

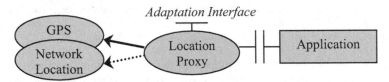

Fig. 5. Internal adaptation: switching between different location mechanisms.

In the example discussed, all applications that require location information do so via the location proxy object. Thus, the actual mechanism for retrieving contextual information is hidden from the application. This transparent access to context enables the platform to switch between mechanisms without affecting the applications involved. To illustrate this, consider the example described in section 2.1.4 and a scenario in which it is crucial to reduce the aggregate level of power consumption. In such a scenario, the platform could reduce power consumption by switching off the GPS device, and using the network locator in order to retrieve location information.

External adaptation. This module is responsible for coordinating the adaptive behaviour of the applications running on the system. Its operation is driven by both a set of adaptation policies defined by the user and the XML description of each application specifying its various operation modes (as described in section 5.4). Recall that the XML description of each operation mode is marked according to its effect on resource utilisation (e.g. power, network) and the use of context services. The adaptation control module can use this information in order to decide which operation mode has to be triggered under each potential set of circumstances. In more detail, when resources (power, network, etc.) become unavailable the adaptation control picks the adaptation mechanism with the lowest resource requirements.

In order to clarify this approach, consider the following example (which is illustrated in figure 6). Two adaptive applications run on a mobile device: a web browser and a video player. The adaptation policies specified by the user define priorities between the applications and the resources (such that the lower the number the greater the priority). The adaptation control module is aware of the adaptive modes that these applications can support by accessing the application database. It also knows the status of all the contextual data that is available on the system. When any of the contextual triggers reach a value that triggers a reaction by the system, the adaptation control has to decide which adaptation mechanism should be invoked. In the example presented, both power and available bandwidth are low. However, the adaptation control would choose to overcome the power problem, because the user has specified that power is the most important resource. Note that enabling the user to specify priorities has in this case enabled the platform to overcome an area of potential conflict (as highlighted in section 2.1.2).

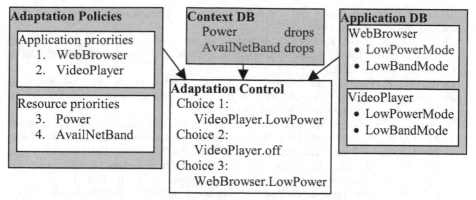

Fig. 6. External adaptation: making adaptation choices according to adaptation policies

In order to decide which application to invoke, the adaptation control component checks the prioritisation of the applications and picks the application that is less important to the user (i.e. the video player). The appropriate adaptation mode would then be triggered causing the video player to switch to low power mode. If the reduction in power resulting from this action is insufficient then the adaptation control component would proceed with the next course of action, i.e. turning off the video player and triggering the web browser to enter low power mode.

6. Conclusions

In this paper, we have argued that existing architectural approaches for supporting adaptive mobile applications have a number of shortcomings. Furthermore, analysis of these shortcomings has led to the identification of a set of architectural requirements. Namely: support for a common contextual space, mechanisms to support co-ordinated adaptations between multiple adaptive applications and support for user defined adaptation policies. We have also described the architecture of our platform, which has been designed to meet these requirements and which enables mobile systems to extend their awareness of all relevant contexts that might affect overall system adaptation policies. Fundamental to our approach is the idea of having system-wide decision making policies that consider the most efficient adaptation outcome from a number of possible adaptations. This is achieved by requiring the applications to provide information about themselves, their adaptation mechanisms, and the contextual triggers that can affect their behaviour.

References

1. Advanced Configuration and Power Interface Specification, Revision 1.0, Intel/Microsoft/Toshiba (1999).
2. Cheverst, K., N. Davies, K. Mitchell, A. Friday.: Experiences of Developing and Deploying a Context-Aware Tourist Guide: The GUIDE Project. In: Proc. of MOBICOM'2000, Boston, ACM Press (2000)
3. Davies N., K. Cheverst, K. Mitchell, A. Friday.: Caches in the Air: Disseminating Information in the Guide System. In: Proc. of the 2nd IEEE Workshop on Mobile Computing Systems and Applications (WMCSA '99) (1999)
4. Davies N., A. Friday, S. Wade, G. Blair.: L^2imbo: A Distributed Systems Platform for Mobile Computing. In: ACM Mobile Networks and Applications (MONET), Special Issue on Protocols and Software Paradigms of Mobile Networks, 3(2) (1998) 143-156
5. Dey A., Abowd G., Salber D.: A Context-Based Infrastructure for Smart Environments. In: Proc. of the 2000 Conference on Human Factors in Computing Systems (2000)
6. Elis C.: The Case for Higher-Level Power Management. In: Proc. of HotOS (1999)
7. Flinn J., M. Satyanarayanan.: PowerScope: A Tool for Profiling the Energy Usage of Mobile Applications. In: Proc. of the Second IEEE Workshop on Mobile Computing Systems and Applications (1999)
8. Friday A., N. Davies, G. Blair, K. Cheverst.: Developing Adaptive Applications: The MOST Experience. In: Journal of Integrated Computer-Aided Engineering, 6(2) 143- 157
9. Goland, Y., Cai T., Leach P., Gu Y., Albright S.: Simple Service Discovery Protocol, Version 1.03. IETF Internet-Draft. http://www.ietf.org/internet-drafts/draft-cai-ssdp-v1-03.txt
10. Joseph A., J. Tauber, F. Kaashoek.: Mobile Computing with the Rover Toolkit. In: IEEE Transactions on Computers: Special issue on Mobile Computing, 43(3), (1997)
11. Katz R.: Adaptation and Mobility in Wirless Information Systems. In: IEEE Personal Communications, 1(1) (1994) 6-17
12. Kravets R., P. Krishnan.: Application-Driven Power Management for Mobile Communication. In: Fourth ACM International Conference on Mobile Computing and Networking (MOBICOM '98) (1998)
13. Kunz T., J. Black.: An Architecture for Adaptive Mobile Applications. In: Proc. of the 11th International Conference on Wireless Communications (Wireless '99) (1999)
14. Long, S., R. Kooper, G.D. Abowd, C.G. Atkeson.: Rapid Prototyping of Mobile Context-Aware Applications: The Cyberguide Case Study. In: Proc. of the 2nd ACM International Conference on Mobile Computing (MOBICOM) (1996)
15. Marzullo K., R. Cooper, M. Wood, K. Birman.: Tools for Distributed Application Management. In: IEEE Computer, 24(8) (1991) 42-51
16. Noble B., M. Satyanarayanan, D. Narayanan, J. E. Tilton, J. Flinn, K. Walker.: Agile Application-Aware Adaptation for Mobility. In: Proc of the 16th ACM Symposium on Operating System Principles (1997)
17. Pascoe J.: The Stick-e Note Architecture: Extending the Interface Beyond the User. In: Proc. of the International Conference on Intelligent User Interfaces (1997)
18. Terry D. B., M. Theimer, K. Petersen A. J. Demers.: Managing Update Conflicts in Bayou, a Weakly Connected Replicated Storage System. In: Proc of the 15th ACM Symposium on Operating System Principles (1995)
19. Universal Plug and Play Device Architecture, Version 0.91, Microsoft Corporation, March 2000. http://www.upnp.org/download/UPnP_Device_Architecture.mht
20. Weiser M.: Some Computer Science Issues in Ubiquitous Computing. In: Communications of the ACM, 6(7) (1993) 75-84

Event Engine for Adaptive Mobile Computing

Shiow-yang Wu   H.S. Cinatit Chao

Department of Computer Science and Information Engineering
National Dong Hwa University
Hualien, Taiwan, R.O.C.
E-mail: showyang@csie.ndhu.edu.tw

Abstract. To cope with the highly resource constrained and dynamically changing mobile computing environment, we propose an architecture which employs an active event engine to detect current resource and environment status, inform registered applications about status changes, and provide a suite of actions for application adaptation. Preliminary implementation and evaluation results demonstrate that the event engine can successfully detect the registered events and invoke application specified actions to bring the system to a desired state.

1 Introduction

The operating condition of a mobile host is constantly subject to resource availability and environment variability such as changing *mobile support stations*, connection status, as well as terrain and weather. Effective information services in such a demanding environment is undoubtedly a great challenge to information system designers [2,3,11]. Our goal is to develop enabling technologies for building effective information systems in mobile computing environment.

To cope with the problem of change, a mobile application must first be aware of the change before proper action can be taken. We propose an architecture for application adaptation based on an active event engine for application awareness. The availability of resources on a mobile host and the status changes in the operating environment are modeled as events. Applications can register events of interest to be notified when the events occur. The event engine keeps monitoring the resource and environment status for the detection of registered events. Once the events occur, all registered applications of the corresponding events are notified for possible adaptive actions. Applications can either choose from a suite of predefined actions provided by our framework or supply customized actions for application adaptation. Being resource and environment aware, an application can easily optimize its operating mode and execution strategy to better utilize available resources and to cope with the changing environment. The relationship between the event engine, applications and the operating system on a mobile host is depicted in Figure 1. As a summary, the main contributions of this paper are:

– An architecture for adaptive mobile computing based on active event engine.

K.-L. Tan et al. (Eds.): MDM 2001, LNCS 1987, pp. 27–38, 2001.

- An event language for specifying events of interest.
- API for applications to interact with the event engine.
- Change detection and event triggering mechanism for monitoring resource and environment status.
- A suite of responsive actions for application adaptation.

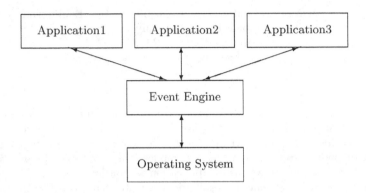

Fig. 1. The event engine, applications, and the operating system.

The rest of the paper is organized as follows. Section 2 provides a background survey of related issues and research work. Section 3 presents the event classification and event language for the applications to specify events of interest. Section 4 describes the structure and operation of our event engine which is central to the proposed architecture. Preliminary implementation and evaluation results presented in Section 5 demonstrate the feasibility of our framework toward the construction of highly adaptive mobile information systems. Section 6 concludes the paper.

2   Related Work

The need for intelligent adaptation is considered essential for mobile data management [9,16]. Similar ideas have been discussed under terms like context-aware [14], application-aware [13], environment-directed [17], and adaptive [8] information systems. Various techniques on dynamic power adaptation have been proposed for mobile computers [1,7]. In general, the decision on when and how to adapt can be made by either the underlying system (*application-transparent adaptation*) or the application programs (*application-aware adaptation*) [12]. Application-transparent implies that no change is needed to existing applications which also means no application-specific feature can be exploited. On the other hand, the performance and flexibility offered by the application-aware adaptation may very well come with higher complexity and software development cost. The approach we propose in this paper is inspired by the work on active database systems which successfully augment traditional database systems with the capability of actively responding to changes [10,18]. More specifically, we provide event modeling, specification, registration, and detection mechanisms, as well as proper actions for intelligent adaptation, which offers an active framework toward the construction of effective mobile information systems. Our framework is different from other event engine work such as [6,15] in that our event modeling and triggering mechanisms have been specially tailored for mobile computing environment for which, as far as we know, no other similar system exists.

3   The Event Language

The events in an active data base system represent any change to the database itself or the way it is being used. We model changes to the resource availability and environment status as events. Events in our system can be *primitive* or *composite* [4,5]. A primitive event is to model a certain level of change on a single source (such as disk capacity, free memory, bandwidth, etc.). Primitive events can be combined using *event operators* to form composite events. We classify the events of interest in a mobile environment into *resource events*, *mobility events*, and *environment events* as depicted in Figure 2.

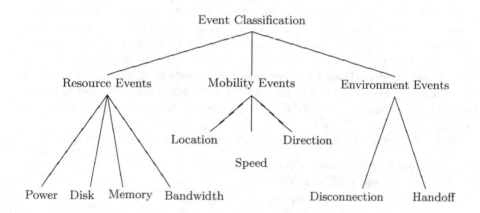

Fig. 2. Event Classification.

Resource events model the change in resource availability on a mobile host. An application must be aware of the current resource status in order to better utilize the usually limited resources. In particular, we have identified the available disk space, free memory, battery power, and the wireless bandwidth level as the primary resources for monitoring and detection. For disk space, we monitor the free disk space left on the hard drive in MB. For memory, we measure both the available free memory space in MB and in percentage with respect to the total memory on the mobile host. Similarly for the battery power, we monitor the estimated power left in seconds remaining as well as in percentage with respect to the fully charged battery. For bandwidth, we measure the current level in Kb/second to enable the applications to be aware of the connection quality and status.

Mobility events are related to the change in position of the mobile host under consideration. This is a unique characteristic in mobile computing which has no direct counterpart in traditional distributed computing environment. We propose to monitor the current position, speed, and direction as three key parameters for representing the mobile host's current mobility status. As a first step, we use the current cell ID within which the mobile host resides as its current position. The speed is represented as km/second or as symbolic levels such as low, medium, and high. The direction is the current direction of movement of the mobile host. This is especially useful in conjunction with speed to estimate the mobility pattern of the mobile host in the near future.

Environment events are changes to the operating environment that are expected to have significant effect on the mobile host. We have identified disconnection and handoff as the two most distinctive state changes to monitor for the mobile client. This allows applications to take preventive actions in response to these changes.

Resource, mobility, and environment events are primitive events since each event of the above types is detected directly from status change of a single source. Primitive events alone are not expressive enough to express various situations of interest. We therefore provide *event operators* to combine primitive events into composite events. To simplify our system design and implementation, we provide only the AND and OR operators for combining events. For example, the composite event "E1 AND E2" occurs only when both E1 and E2 occur. Similarly, the composite event "E1 OR E2" occurs when any one of the events occurs.

Primitive events are specified using the following three formats:

ON <event_type> <op> <value> <unit>
ON <event_type> LEVEL <level>
ON <environment_event_type>

where <event_type> is the name of a resource or mobility event. <op> is a relational operator such as >, <, = etc. <value> and <unit> are used together to specify the exact value threshold to be detected by the event engine. The second form allows user-defined symbolic levels to represent value ranges of interest. The third form is used to denote environment events for which only the occurrences of the events are of interest.

Some examples should make the event specification formats clear. The resource event

"ON Bandwidth < 100 kbps"

will be triggered whenever the current wireless bandwidth goes down below 100 kbps. Similarly, the mobility event

"ON Speed LEVEL high"

will be triggered if the current speed of the mobile host reaches a level defined by the user as high. Take another example, the environment event

"ON Disconnection"

will be triggered if the mobile host is disconnected from the server.

Primitive events as specified above can be further combined using the event operators to form composite events. For example, the event

ON Disk < 100 mb AND ON Handoff

will be triggered only when both the free disk space is low and the mobile host is in the handoff process.

Any application can register its events of interest to the event engine. Events specified by applications must be carefully managed to reduce redundancy and improve efficiency. For such purposes, registered events are organized into an *event forest* as depicted in Figure 3. All primitive events are at the leaf nodes. Others are either OR nodes or AND nodes. Applications registered for the same event(s) can share the same event node(s). We keep the application's ID and the associated actions with the event node(s) that the application registered. These nodes are depicted as shaded nodes in the figure. The event forest is used by the event engine for managing registered events as well as for event triggering to be discussed in the next section.

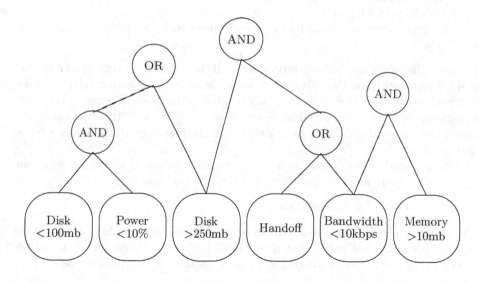

Fig. 3. The Event Forest.

4   The Event Engine

The event engine plays the central role in our adaptive mobile computing framework. It consists of an *event register*, a *change detector*, an *event detector*, and an *action activator* as depicted in Figure 4. Applications register their events of interest through the event register which then classifies the events and builds the event forest as described in the previous section. The change detector is responsible for detecting changes on the resource or environment status that are of interest to the registered applications. The event detector periodically compares the status changes with registered events to determine if any event(s) occurs. Once a registered event occurs, the action activator triggers the associated actions to respond to the changes. The process of event detection and action triggering is done by marking and traversing the event forest as follows:

- On each event detection period, all leaf nodes are checked first to determine if any primitive event occurs. A leaf node is marked if the corresponding event occurs.
- For each marked node, if there are application IDs stored with it, the action activator is invoked to inform the applications about the event occurrence and to trigger the corresponding registered actions.
- Once a marked node is processed, it is unmarked to prevent unnecessary repeated triggering. The marker is then passed upward to its parent.
- An OR node is considered marked if it receives at least one marker from any of its children. An AND node is considered marked if it has received markers from all its children.
- The process repeats until no more node need to be processed in the event forest.

We note that if an application terminates, all its records are removed from the event forest such that the subsequent event detection and action triggering do not perform wasted work on applications that are no longer exist. From the experience of our preliminary implementation to be discussed in Section 5, we found the above approach to be a simple yet efficient way of managing events and actions.

For applications to specify proper actions to respond to status changes, we also provide a simple action specification format as follows.

DO <action> [<parameters>]

The <action> is the name of a built-in or user-defined action. An action can be invoked with optional parameters if required. For example, the following action instructs the event engine to trigger a power suspend action to save the energy.

DO power_suspend

And the action that follows directs the event engine to trigger a save action to protect valuable file.

DO save C:\DOC\budget.doc

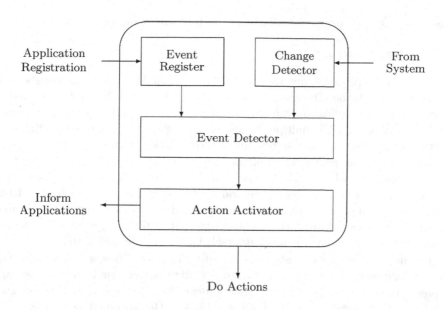

Fig. 4. The Event Engine.

5   Implementation and Evaluation

To evaluate the feasibility and performance of our approach, we have finished a preliminary implementation of the event engine that handles resource events. The event engine is implemented on a Windows98 based PC platform using MFC and experimented on a Pentium 266 notebook. As a first step, we have developed an event engine API for the applications to register events of interest and the actions to respond. The API is in a function format that can be invoked in any C/C++ application program.

   Registration(*APid, Event, Action*)

The *APid* is a unique identifier to represent the application that are registering. Both *Event* and *Action* are character strings to specify the event to be detected and the associated actions to perform once the event occurs. To simplify the implementation, we adopt a prefix notation for specifying composite events. For example, the event

   ON Disk < 20mb AND ON Power < 10%

is specified as

   "AND (disk < 20 mb) (power < 10 %)"

The action is also specified similarly as the following example.

```
"(power_suspend)"
```

Whenever an application invokes the **Registration** API, the event register immediately records the ID, events, actions, and incorporates them into the current event forest. An application can register multiple event-action pairs by invoking the **Registration** API multiple times. Once registered, the event engine will start detecting the specified events for the application immediately.

To evaluate the performance of the event engine, we develop a simple text editor application which registers events and actions with the event engine. We then conduct a series of experiments on each resource event type to see if the event engine can successfully detect the specified events and trigger the desired actions. We are also interested in observing that, after invoking responsive actions, how fast the system can adjust itself to reach a desired state.

The first set of experiments is on the effectiveness of power adaptation. For each experiment, the editor application registers power event on a percentage of power remained on the battery and requests for the triggering of power suspension action once the power level goes below the specified percentage. We then measure how long the mobile host lasts from power on till power exhausted completely. The result depicted in Figure 5 demonstrates that power suspension is quite effective in keeping the mobile host on. For example, if the action is activated when power level goes below 40%, the mobile host can last for more than 5 hours.

The second experiment is on memory adaptation. In order to control the memory usage, the experiment follows a sequence of steps that mimics a typical operation by opening a number of applications, one of which is our editor application which registers a memory event to trigger adaptive actions when the memory usage goes above 54MB. The actions are to close the system tray first, and then clear the clipboard. The sequence of steps are as follows.

1. Start the Windows98 and the System Monitor.
2. Start up the File Manager.
3. Open the editor application.
4. Copy a number of text and image files.
5. Open the ACDSee32 graphic application.
6. When the memory usage goes above 54MB, trigger the action to close the system tray first.
7. Then clear the clipboard.

The Windows98 System Monitor is activated to display the memory usage on the screen for recording. Figure 6 demonstrates the result as displayed on the System Monitor. It is quite clear from the figure that once the physical memory usage goes above 54MB, the event engine immediately triggers the adaptive actions which quickly bring the system back to a state where the memory usage is below 50MB.

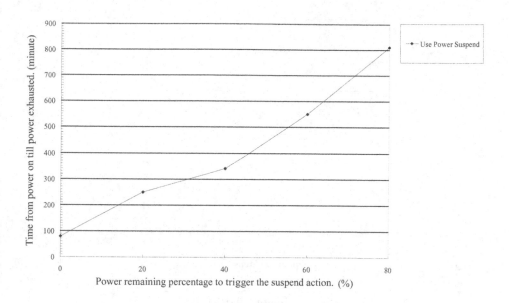

Fig. 5. Power Adaptation.

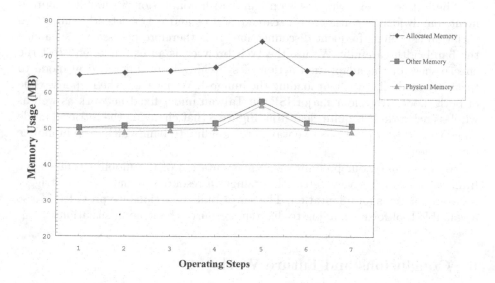

Fig. 6. Memory Adaptation.

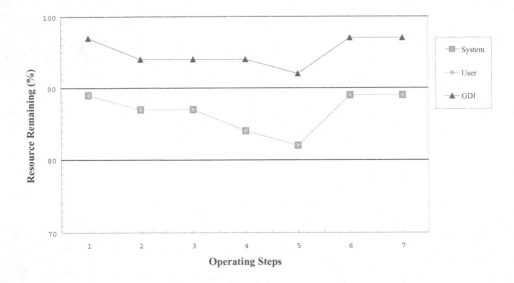

Fig. 7. Memory Adaptation.

Figure 7 displays the change in resource availability along each operating steps. We can observe the significant increase in available resources after the event engine triggers the adaptive actions.

The last set of experiments is on bandwidth adaptation. In mobile environment, bandwidth is considered a scarce resource and is consistently subject to variation as well as frequent disconnection. It is therefore necessary to manage the bandwidth carefully. We use the Web browser as an example, and test the effectiveness of the adaptation action of switching from full retrieval mode to text only mode (i.e. without loading the images). We measure the response time of both modes from four major ISPs in Taiwan under fixed network as well as wireless network. It is quite clear from Figure 8 that changing the retrieval mode on a Web browser is an effective way of responding to bandwidth drop in mobile environment.

As a summary, our preliminary implementation of the mobile event engine framework can effectively detect the change in resource availability and trigger registered actions for adaptation. The set of built-in actions we provided is also a valuable tool for responding to different resource challenging situations.

6   Conclusions and Future Work

We have proposed an event-driven architecture and implemented a mobile event engine to detect resource and environment status for mobile application pro-

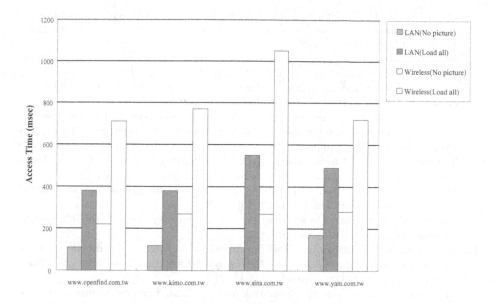

Fig. 8. Bandwidth Adaptation.

grams and to trigger responsive actions when application specified events occur. Evaluation results demonstrate that our approach is quite effective as a mechanism for building adaptive applications. The work reported in this paper is part of a modular framework for adaptive mobile information management [19,20]. The framework integrates an event engine and a rule system to facilitate intelligent adaptation in mobile environment. We are now in the stage of system integration and testing. We plan to apply our technology to turn a Web browser an adaptive application such that it can automatically adjust its browsing strategy in the constantly changing mobile environment.

Acknowledgments

This work was supported in part by National Science Council under project number NSC 88-2213-E-259-001.

References

1. Fred Douglis, P. Krishnan, and Brian Bershad. Adaptive disk spin-down policies for mobile computers. *Computing Systems*, 8(4):381–413, Fall 1995.   28
2. D. Duchamp. Issues in wireless mobile computing. In *3rd IEEE Workshop on Workstation Operating Systems*, pages 2–10, Key Biscayne, Florida, U.S., 1992. IEEE Computer Society Press.   27
3. G. Forman and J. Zahorjan. The challenges of mobile computing. *IEEE Computer*, 27(6):38–47, April 1994.   27

4. Stella Gatziu, K. R. Dittrich, and O. Shmueli. Composite event specification in active database : Model and implementation. Technical report, AT&T Bell Lab., Murray Hill, New Jersey, 1992. 29

5. N. H. Gehani and H. V. Jagadish. Event specification in an active object-oriented database. Technical report, University Zurich, Switzerland, 1993. 29

6. Andreas Geppert and Dimitrios Tombros. Event-based distributed workflow execution with EvE. In *Middleware'98*, pages 427–442, 1998. 29

7. David P. Helmbold, Darrell D. E. Long, Tracey L. Sconyers, and Bruce Sherrod. Adaptive disk spin-down for mobile computers. *Mobile Networks and Applications (MONET) Journal*, to appear. 28

8. T. Imielinski and S. Vishwanathan. Adaptive wireless information systems. Technical report, Department of Computer Science, Rutgers University, 1994. 28

9. R. H. Katz. Adaptation and mobility in wireless information systems. *IEEE Personal Communications*, 1(1):6–17, 1994. 28

10. Norman W. Paton and Oscar Díaz. Active database systems. *ACM Computing Surveys*, 31(1):63–103, March 1999. 28

11. E. Pitoura and B. Bhargava. Building information systems for mobile environments. In *Third International Conference on Information and Knowledge Management*, pages 371–378, November 1994. 27

12. M. Satyanarayanan. Mobile information access. *IEEE Personal Communications*, 3(1), February 1996. 28

13. M. Satyanarayanan, B. Noble, P. Kumar, and M. Price. Application-aware adaptation for mobile computing. *Operating System Review*, 29, January 1995. 28

14. B. Schilit, N. Adams, and R. Want. Context-aware mobile applications. In *IEEE Workshop on Mobile Computing Systems and Applications*, Santa Cruz, CA, U.S., December 1994. 28

15. James Vera, Louis Perrochon, and David C. Luckham. Event-based execution architectures for dynamic software systems. In *Proceedings of the First Working IFIP Conf. on Software Architectur*, 1999. 29

16. T. Watson. Application design for wireless computing. In *IEEE Workshop on Mobile Computing Systems and Applications*, Santa Cruz, CA, U.S., December 1994. 28

17. G. Welling and B. R. Badrinath. Mobjects: Programming support for environment directed application policies in mobile computing. In *ECOOP'95 Workshop on Mobility and Replication*, August 1995. 28

18. J. Widom and S. Ceri. *Active Database Systems: Triggers and Rules for Advanced Database Processing*. Morgan Kaufmann, San Francisco, California, 1996. 28

19. Shiow-yang Wu and Chun-Shun Chang. An active database framework for adaptive mobile data access. In *Workshop on Mobile Data Access, 17th International Conference on Conceptual Modeling, Singapore*, 1998. 37

20. Shiow-yang Wu and Shih-Hsun Ho. Active rule system for adaptive mobile data access. In *MDA'99: 1st International Conference on Mobile Data Access, Hong Kong*, 1999. 37

Session II: Content Delivery

Adaptive Delivery of Multimedia Data in Heterogeneous and Mobile Environments

Mqhele Nzama, Alexander Ng, and Arkady Zaslavsky

900 Dandenong Road, Caulfield East 3145, Melbourne, Australia

{mnzama, nalex, azaslavs}@broncho.ct.monash.edu.au

Abstract. This paper discusses the sources of variability in heterogeneous and mobile networks that make it difficult for traditional applications to work properly. The problems associated with delivering multimedia content to clients of varying capabilities are also investigated. Adaptivity is presented as a tool to extend the lifetime of critical applications as well as a technique to meet client device variability. To this end we have developed prototypes for the mobile environments that aim to reduce dependency on scarce resources. The adaptation space framework is used to provide a flexible and consistent design strategy.

1 Introduction

The design of adaptive applications is driven by one main inspiration, to give the best service possible under a given set of conditions [1]. This design philosophy is not new with robust systems, re-configurable systems and evolving systems considered to be a variation of adaptive systems [7], [8], [9]. Designing for adaptivity means designing for change; change in the availability of resources and demands placed on them. The sources of changes in an application's operational environment are further discussed in Section 2.

Applications need a minimum set of resources to sustain a specified level of service. Traditional applications assume that the demands on the resources are either static or that resources are available at the time that they are requested. If it turns out that this assumption is violated, then the utility of the application drops to zero altogether. The idea behind adaptivity is that the quality of service (QoS) provided to an application depends on the level at which the operational environment is able to supply the required resources. When a reduction in the supply of resources occurs the application does not 'die' altogether but instead, it gives service that is commensurate with the levels of available resources.

The service given by an application can be defined in terms of a set of functions carried out by the application or accessible to the user. An application needs a set of resources to carry out a specific task, and the QoS is a measure of the level at which resource requirements are met by the operational environment. QoS has dimensions that include timeliness, volume and reliability and these translate to environmental attributes such as latency (or delay), jitter, throughput, and bit error rates [10].

K.-L. Tan et al. (Eds.): MDM 2001, LNCS 1987, pp. 41-52, 2001.

2   The Environment

The support environment of networking applications typically consists of underlying communications and client hardware. Adaptive applications are required to deal with variability in resources that are directly related to the communications and hardware.

Heterogeneous networks [2], [7] have variable performance that mainly arises from technology and traffic factors. The link capacities range from 64 Kbps to 155 Mbps and more for ISDN, LANs, FDDI and ATM technologies. The networks also consist of various communication and processing components of different speeds and that use different protocols.   Many networks such as the original Internet use best-effort approach and that makes it hard if not impossible to guarantee a certain level of performance. Network faults and load variability often result in congestion that shows up as delay, and increased error rate. It is noted that even contention-free, dedicated links may suffer performance degradations when used with TCP/IP algorithm that requires positive acknowledgement [3]. The maximum transmission rate in such a case is independent of the physical link's capacity to carry the data but is limited by the delay. This problem is called the *bandwidth * delay limit* [3] and is of particular importance to networks with variable delay such as the Internet.

Mobile networks [14], [15], [17], [18] are increasingly becoming an extension to existing networks giving a further dimension of variability. The mobile environment [12] is popularly characterised as turbulent because of its underlying physics.   Its performance can change drastically in space and time, sometimes within a short time interval or small degree of movement. In some areas the mobile infrastructure overlays fixed networks [12] so that geographic coverage depends on the level of deployment.

Client hardware on the other hand consists of a wide range of devices ranging from PDAs to high-end workstations each with different multimedia-related capabilities. Mobile clients are by design poorer in resources than their fixed counterparts arising from the design goal to achieve low power consumption, lightweight and small physical size [15]. In spite of these differences, the clients are expected to access the same information and this requires applying some content adaptation schemes.

3   Adaptation Techniques

Traditional applications are structured to follow *the all or nothing law* since they tend to assume full availability of required resources. The goal of adaptivity is to design applications that respond dynamically and continuously to their environment. This makes it possible for the performance of applications to scale up and to degrade gracefully under deteriorating conditions. The ability to respond to detected changes in the environment results in extended lifetimes and economic viability of adaptive applications. Particularly in the mobile environment, adaptivity is a necessary precondition since the inherently instability means that the QoS cannot be realistically fixed nor maintained beyond certain time intervals [1]. An environment that supports adaptive applications benefits from the relaxed QoS negotiation and resource management, however, at increased cost and additional complexity.

3.1   The Basic Mechanisms of Adaptation

The problem of adaptation is presented in [1], who defines two spaces: the performance space, P, and resource space, R. P is dimensioned along user-oriented QoS parameters such as play-out quality, response time, etc. R on the other hand is dimensioned along resource characteristics of the support environment that includes CPU power, memory, bandwidth, jitter, loss rates, etc. We can define the acceptance region AR of P as the region in which the application is considered to be working properly. Formally, "for a given application class without adaptation there exist a mapping $M:P \Rightarrow R$ that maps AR onto region B in R. Introducing adaptation changes M so that AR now maps onto a larger region A that would normally include B" [1]. Effective adaptation inflates the region A towards the limit of application usability.

3.2   Adaptation Support at Data and Communications Levels

Adaptation is centred on secure and timely delivery of data objects. Multimedia applications are gaining popularity because of the expressive power of multimedia [10], [11], [13]. Since multimedia covers all types of data with their associated delivery constraint, they can benefit from adaptive approaches. There are several communications and data based strategies that can be employed to achieve this goal. How can data be structured to support adaptation?

- *intelligent data* can be created by wrapping code around the data object for autonomous response to changing network conditions. For example, congestion could force the data object to drop its non-critical data in order to guarantee its timely delivery by matching its size to the prevailing network conditions. Such an approach requires adherence to standards in data formulation and infrastructure.
- *hierarchical/progressive data* coding allows applications to receive the quality of data commensurate with network resources. The data object is encoded in multiple scans arranged in successive order of refinement. The first scan encodes a rough but recognisable version of the object (e.g. image). In the case of images, the first image scan is sent quickly and successive scans refine the image to a given quality.
- *compression* is used to reduce the size of a data object while retaining the quality of the original object. Images tend to consume large bandwidth on a network because of their size. Conventional loss-less compression techniques for images have modest ratios ranging from two to three [3]. The success of lossy reduction techniques are demonstrated by the wide use of JPEG, MPEG and similar standards [6], [10] which give much higher compression for multimedia data with little degradation from the user's perceptive.
- *layered encoding* is based on distributing media as multiple streams [2], [4]. The layered steams provide cumulative information such that receiving more steams provides the application with better media quality. The layers are arranged to be independent or hierarchical. In hierarchical layers, the decoding of higher layers relies on having properly decoded all lower layers hence it is unsuitable for the unpredictable mobile environment.
- *scaling* is used to reduce the data size by selecting an appropriate quantasation level that in turn gives corresponding a coarseness in the final data object.

Examples include the JPEG algorithm for images while audio exists at different qualities ranging from stereo CD-quality to mono low-quality sound.

- *reduction* techniques destructively change the data object. For example frame packets or non-critical data can be dropped to ease congestion.
- *transforming* changes the data object from one format into another for transmission or storage. For example speech technology enables transformations between speech and text.
- *Simulcasting* is a communication feature that simultaneously sends data as independent streams to receiver groups of different bandwidth requirements. The clients subscribe to an appropriate group according to their support network.

Combining communication strategies with data coding strategies achieves greater efficiency in the use of network resources such as in the application presented in [2]. Out of the realisation that multimedia data needs to be adapted to diverse client devices in addition to network-centric conditions, [23] developed an InfoPyramid framework that makes it possible to describe multimedia content in different modalities, resolutions, multiple abstractions and methods to manipulate, translate, transform and generate data (Fig.1).

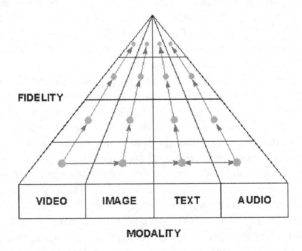

Fig. 1. Information pyramid multimedia content

4   Formal Adaptation Framework For Multimedia Content

Multimedia systems have generated a lot of interest in adaptation mechanisms as indicated by developments in QoS frameworks. Applications tailored to continue to offer service despite loss of resources (reflected by degraded QoS) or limited capabilities of the target devices (device heterogeneity) must adapt. Most of the work looks at strategies to manage quality of service, typically performing a trade-off between quality of service and quality of content. Such trade-off can be considered to be a survivable adaptation whose aim is to reduce resource consumption when resources are scarce or need to be freed for other important applications. Adaptation presents numerous modes of operation, and the set of possible combinations of adaptation modes can get complex. We see adaptation spaces as a useful theoretical tool in the design and description of adaptive systems that enables us to [25]:

- identify different operational modes and environmental parameters to monitor;
- define a framework to reason about alternative strategies and selection criteria;
- provide a theoretical basis to enhance confidence during design and promote thorough understanding of the system's operation under various conditions;
- integrate with other adaptation frameworks such as the InfoPyramid to identify possible granularities of adaptation along link and client capabilities.

The role of adaptation spaces is to provide a formalism to navigate among combinations of adaptive behaviour. This approach enables us to reason about various alternatives and gives confidence that all alternative strategies have been considered.

An adaptation space is a collection of alternative configurations called adaptation cases. An adaptation case takes various forms that include independent software modules that accomplish similar functionality, variants of code within software modules that accomplish the same task, selection of different parameters during configuration and exhibiting different behaviour under different conditions.

Each adaptation case is characterised by a *use condition*, a predicate that must be true to instigate its use. The use condition is expressed in terms of the environmental variables in which the adaptation space operates thereby providing a convenient way to identify and define the relevant environmental parameters. In addition, each case has a *set of properties*, which define the conditions that will hold if that adaptation case is selected. Such properties of a case capture its behaviour, and this provides a convenient way to define an adaptation strategy or policy of adaptation. Typically, properties of interest are enabled functionality, resource use, precision, and accuracy of representation of a multimedia object or data.

4.1   Formal Implementation and Manipulation of Adaptation Spaces

An implementation of an adaptation space requires the provision of a mechanism to verify that the use conditions hold for the current case, and means to switch to another case if they do not. There is also a need for a policy that specifies how to select one case among the cases when multiple cases are enabled according to the use condition. The selection policies should reflect preferences for the provided properties in a case, restrictions on movement between adaptation cases and associated costs of moving to a particular case. Costs considerations include computational overheads in moving from one case to another, initialising states, refreshing data structures/caches, etc.

Formally, an adaptation space is a set of adaptation cases, partially ordered by the relation "more specialised than" [25]. Case A is more specialised than Case B if the use condition of Case A is logically implied by the use conditions in Case B i.e. the use conditions of Case B are a subset of the use conditions of Case A represented as $a \supseteq b$. A complete adaptation space can be computed by taking the power set $r(S)$ of all individual predicates that form a set S. The set is infinite if one of the predicates is continuous. Being also lattice structured, not all cases are of interest so that the selected adaptation space may only cover a subset of conceivable configurations.

Cases can be manipulated by the *meet* and *join* operations in order to simplify, combine and prune implementations. The meet operation of two cases in the lattice provides a new case that *generalises* the two cases, and its use conditions is the intersection of the use conditions of the two cases i.e. *Case C = Case A meet Case B* $\Leftrightarrow$ $c = a \cap b$. Similarly the join of two cases results in a new case that *specialises* the two cases, and its use conditions is the union of the use conditions of the two cases *(Case C = Case A JOIN Case B $\Leftrightarrow c = a \cup b$)*.

Implementing an adaptive system consists of mapping an adaptation space to a set of implementations. The process is done algorithmically as described in [25]. The final transition diagram indicates allowable system degradation paths as the resources change or as the device capabilities differ depending on the design scope problem.

In this case, part of the information pyramid is used as a basis to carry out the algorithm (Fig. 2). Adaptation case navigation is usually based on user preferences and some quality specification, properties than can be derived from the information pyramid. Audio data can be related to the required bandwidth for its transmission by the applied sampling rate, number of bits per sample and the number of channels supported. For documents, different levels of summarization can be applied.

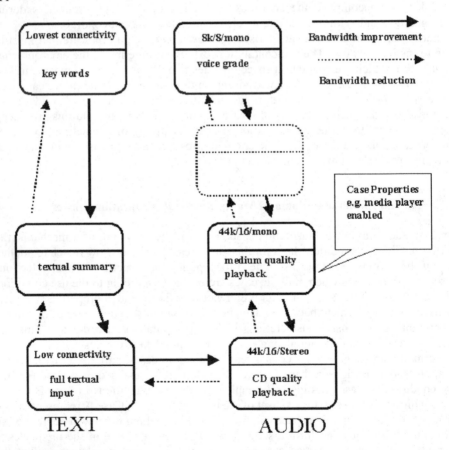

Fig. 2. An adaptive system implementation for text and audio

5   Design Principles and Goals

This section describes the design principles for implementing adaptation. The specific issues and questions to be addressed are presented.

5.1   Design Principles

Can some applications benefit from data transformation technologies? Information can be presented at various levels of fidelity as well as formats or modalities. Transcoding is the process of changing information from one format into another. For example, speech encoding and synthesis technologies allow transformation of text to speech and vice versa. The extra degree if freedom in the design of adaptive applications may prove invaluable in meeting variable network resources as well as different client capabilities. Adaptive applications that employ this approach are therefore able to continue operating under otherwise prohibitive conditions. This approach is readily applicable to the development of critical applications such as emergency where information has to reach its destination at all costs.

Can computational opportunity be used on the client side? The time interval during which the CPU waits for the delivery of data translates to a waste of computational cycles. Such wastage is particularly pronounced in powerful clients and multiprocessors machines, which are gaining wider applicability. Any approach that fully utilises this computational opportunity makes it possible to reduce dependency on the scarce network resources by sending smaller data objects over the network, which can later be reconstructed on the client machine. It is envisaged that the use of computational opportunity will gain greater attention as processing power becomes relatively less scarce than bandwidth

5.2   Design Goals

The first and most important goal of the prototypes is to reduce reliance on variable and scarce resources within the mobile environment, such as bandwidth. The second goal is to demonstrate the use of data transformation techniques with multimedia data. This raises challenges in how to deal with real-time encoding and decoding as well as synchronisation aspects of multimedia. Successful development of such a framework proves its viability that can even be extended to other forms of multimedia content. The bandwidth is chosen as a resource to which to adapt as mobile clients are normally faced with fluctuating bandwidth. Other resources constraints such as power consumption could be used instead as demonstrated in [5]. The third goal is to operate within a formal framework based on sound engineering and software principles.

In this design, we have considered that information content can be mapped directly onto client capabilities and vice versa (Fig. 3). It is noted that client capabilities and multimedia content form similar hierarchies that readily conform to adaptation cases and the concept of specialisation. The initial lattice of adaptation space is generated from the use conditions of interest. Within the lattice we are guaranteed substitutional-ability of all cases less specialised than the current case based on the implication of a use condition of a more-specialised case to a less-specialised case. For example, a high-end workstation is expected to have all the multimedia features of those devices below it in the hierarchy (e.g. palmtop devices). Similar reasoning holds for multimedia content. We are guaranteed that all more specialised cases than the current will provide more desirable properties. In both cases applications can survive by adapting to a less specialised case, and thrive by adapting to a more specialised case.

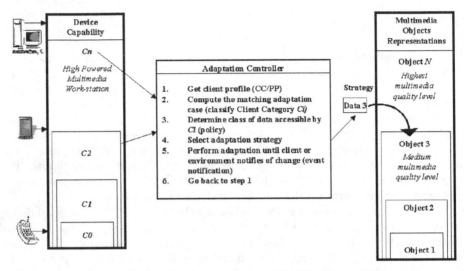

Fig. 3. Adaptation space based on the information pyramid and device capabilities

The adaptation controller performs a mapping between the device capabilities or resources and the multimedia content that can be supported. Event based mechanisms are used to communicate the changes in the environment. Each event notification carries with it information that the adaptation controller uses to derive its mapping. Event based notification is considered an appropriate and efficient strategy [24].

6   Prototype Design

The implementation is based on two approaches, real-time and static multimedia content.

6.1 Real-time Multimedia

The first approach deals with a real-time multimedia audio conferencing application [16], [17] (Fig. 4). A client communicates with a server via a wireless link. The server dispatches voice conferencing content in two formats depending on network conditions and client capabilities. It is assumed that the client has speech conversion capabilities. The adaptation space consists of two cases, sampled audio when the network conditions suit and audio transcoding when the bandwidth is prohibitive for audio content. The adaptation mechanism uses speech recognition to convert speech to text, which is then represented by a Voice Markup Language (VoiceXML) [21], an efficient format for delivery over low bandwidth links. VoiceXML multimedia content is decrypted and played back on the mobile client to emulate natural speech. The challenge is to preserve some of the characteristics of the original speech such as tone, volume, and synchronisation using the mark up language.

VoiceXML [21] is expected to yield an open and broadly applicable voice mark up language standard. The expected features will support development of sophisticated interactive voice services as well as provide speech driven interfaces to all types end users. Such features include handling telephony input and output, automatic speech recognition support, audio recording, ability to play recordings (such as WAV files), speech synthesis from textual input, conferencing and other management features.

Our interest in VoiceXML is guided by its ability to create and describe multimedia object. Speech input can be sampled, converted into text, and its description together with its synchronisation features packaged using VoiceXML. The resulting multimedia object is a description of the original object (substantially smaller) and therefore requires fewer resources to communicate. This approach is radically different from *streaming* in that the actual multimedia objects is not transmitted, but rather its description instead. This raises interesting issues such as how to deal with synchronisation of discrete multimedia objects than need to be decoded to emulate the original input. It is also noted that in this approach the resources space is changed completely. For example speech synthesis and recognition trades computational resources for bandwidth.

Speech recognition and synthesis is carried out using Java speech APIs based on IBM's Via Voice product [19]. The implementation relies heavily on the accuracy of the speech to text conversion, which in turn depends on the physical environment of the user. An important parameter to be included in composing the adaptation space is therefore the background noise.

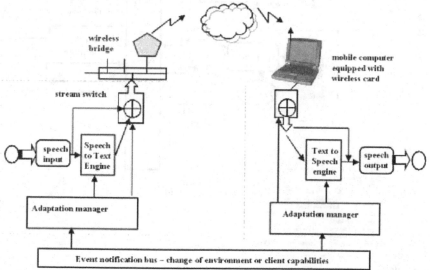

Fig. 4. System layout of prototype to demonstrate real-time adaptive multimedia delivery

6.2 Static Multimedia Content

The second approach transcodes multimedia content based on client capabilities, user preferences and link quality (Fig. 5). On first establishing a connection, the system has to recognise the mobile client's preferences and capabilities. The client's capabilities are communicated via an HTTP request through a Composite Capability Preference Profile (CC/PP). The CC/PP is a standard framework under development by W3C (World Wide Web Consortium) [22] employed in adaptation and delivery purposes. The request is next passed to the web server for content fetching and handed back to the proxy for adaptation. In the latter process, both context and network conditions are factored in before content can undergo adaptation. Information gathered through CC/PP and the network agent allows adaptation of data for best delivery and display. Device and preference checks are included with the detection and selection of data types. For example the adaptation policy can be implemented via XML based on client profiles and device characteristics. This can be used as a basis to scale the data to meet device and environmental constraints.

The prototypes have been implemented and presently their performance proves that this type of adaptation is viable. In addition, the concept of adaptation space framework provides a consistent basis in which the implementation was based. There is still a question of accuracy in the recognition of free-form speech. The real-time multimedia prototype shows marked improvement in the speech recognition time and accuracy when the vocabulary is constrained. The static-media prototype still needs refinement to cater for different types of devices. Another area that needs refinement is the levels of granularity supported by the multimedia objects from a web server.

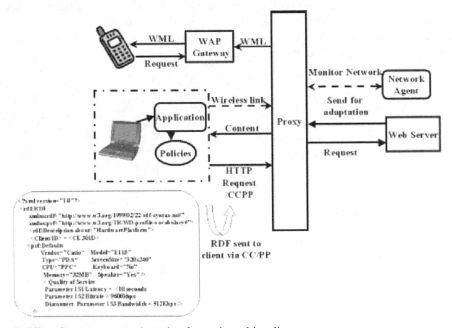

Fig. 5. Client-Server content adaptation for static multimedia

These prototypes form a basis for further work that includes defining and selecting a degradation path at design or run-time, performance measurement of adaptive schemes, predictive schemes and other heuristics for adaptation and finally the use of formalisms to define a framework of adaptivity. This work is further inspired by the realisation [20], [21] that the bandwidth in a wireless system is perhaps the most precious and scarce resource of the whole communication system, and should be used wisely. The popularity of multimedia with the convenience of mobile computing indicates that while the design of future wireless systems will support a wide range of applications with diverse bandwidth requirements, multimedia content also needs to be structured to meet a diverse range of client capabilities. Applications will also have to adjust to customised QoS parameters on a per call and/or service basis, an approach that will enable users to select a level of service according to a pricing plan.

7 Conclusion

Adaptivity is a tool to maintain acceptable performance during unpredictable and uncontrollable QoS variations that arise from heterogeneity and the mobile environment. The goal of adaptivity can be achieved by focusing on data and communication techniques. Greater adaptivity can be achieved by using methods that conserve network resources (e.g. bandwidth) and fully utilising the computational opportunity presented by the client computers. We are developing prototypes that aim to demonstrate that multimedia data manipulation is a feasible approach to extend the operational range of some applications. We take advantage of the fact that digital data has the desirable ability to represent different media as objects that can be manipulated in a flexible manner. In addition, device dependency adaptation has to be factored in.

References

1. J. Gecsei, "Adaptation in Distributed Multimedia Systems," *IEEE Multimedia*, April - June 1997, pp. 58 - 66.
2. A. Banerjea, "Heterogeneous Networking," *IEEE Multimedia,* April-June 1997, 84 - 87.
3. G. R. Thoma and L. R. Long "Compressing and Transmitting Visible H uman Images," *IEEE Multimedia*, April - June 1997, 36 - 45.
4. T. M. Parks, D. A. Kassay and C. J. Weinstein, "Security Implications of Adaptive Multimedia Distribution," *Presented at the IEEE International Communications Conference*, Vancouver, Canada, June 1999, http://www.ll.mit.edu/IST/pubs/icc99-parks/icc99.ps
5. T. Lan, A. H. Tewfik, "Adaptive Low Power Multimedia Wireless Communications," *in Proc. IEEE Signal Processing Society 1997 Workshop on Multimedia Signal Processing*, June 23 - 25, Princeton, New Jersey, USA, http://www.ee.umn.edu/users/tsehu-a/mmsp97/paper6.html.
6. J. Hunter, V. Witana and M. Antoniades, "A Review of Video Streaming over the Internet," August 1997, http://archive.dstc.edu.au/RDU/staff/jane-hunter/video-streaming.html (last modified 24-Jun-1999).

7. Marathon Technologies Corp, "An Introduction to Robust Sytems," http://www.geneous-solutions.ch/marathon/en/white_paper.htm (last modified 30-Jul-1998).
8. Robust Distributed Systems for Real-Time Applications, http://alpha.ece.ucsb.edu/pro-ject_totem.html
9. J. E. Moreira and V. K. Naik "Dynamic resource management on distributed systems using reconfigurable applications," *IBM Journal of Research & Development* http://www.research.ibm.com/journal/rd/413/moreira.html (last modified 22-Apr-1999)
10. G. Blair, and J. Stefani, *Open Distributed Processing and Multimedia*, Addison-Wesley, Harlow, England, 1997
11. N. A. Davies and J. R. Nocol, "A Technological Perspective On Multimedia Computing," *Computer Communications,* Vol 14. No. 5, 1992.
12. R. H. Katz, and E. R. Brewer, *The Case For wireless Overlay Networks* in (editors) Imielinski, T. and Korth, H.F., Mobile Computing, Kluwer Academic Publishers, Boston, 1996.
13. Steinmetz, R. and Nahrstedt, K. *Multimedia: Computing, Communications & Applications*, Prentince Hall, New Jersey, 1995.
14. M. Umehira, M. Nakura, H. Sato and A. Hashimoto, "ATM Wireless for Mobile Multimedia: Concept and Architecture," *IEEE Personal Communications*, Vol 3. No. 5. October 1996.
15. N. J. Muller, *Wireless Data Networking*, Artech House INC, Boston, 1995.
16. Aironet, "Aironet Wireless Communicatons Inc," http://www.aironet.com, June 1999.
17. A. Hills, and D. B. Johnson, "Wireless Data Network Infrastructure at Carnegie Mellon University," *IEEE Personal Communications*, Vol 3. No. 1, Feb 1996.
18. I. Brodsky, Wireless: Revolution in Personal Telecommunications, Artech House, Boston, 1995
19. IBM, ViaVoice, http://www.software.ibm.com/speech/.
20. D. A. Levine, I. F. Akyildiz, and M. Naghshineh, "A Resource Estimation and Call Admission Algorithm for Wireless Multimedia Networks," *IEEE/ACM Transactions on Networking,*, Vol 5. No. 1, Feb 1997.
21. IBM Alphaworks – VoiceXML. (http://www.alphaworks.ibm.com/tech/voicexml)
22. World Wide Web Consortium (W3C). http://www.w3.org/TR/NOTE-CCPPexchange
23. R. Mohan, J. R. Smith and C. Li, "Adapting Multimedia Internet Content for Universal Access", IBM T.J. Research Center, NY 10598, 1999.
24. C. E. Perkins, "Mobile networking in the Internet," *Mobile Networks and Applications*, Vol 3. pp 319-334, 1998
25. C. Cowan, L. Delcambre, A. L. Meur, L. Liu, D. Maire, D. McNamee, M. Miller, C. Pu, P. Wagle and J. Walpole, " Adaptation Space: Surviving Non-Maskable Failures", Technical Report, Department of Computer Science and Engineering, Oregon Graduate Institute of Science and Technology, 1998 ftp://cse.ogi.edu/pub/tech-reports/1998/98-013.ps.gz

Effects and Performance of Content Negotiation Based on CC/PP

Kinuko Yasuda[1], Takuya Asada[2], and Tatsuya Hagino[1,2]

[1] Keio University, Endo 5322, Fujisawa, Kanagawa, 252–8520, JAPAN,
{kinuko,hagino}@tom.sfc.keio.ac.jp
[2] W3C Keio, Endo 5322, Fujisawa, Kanagawa, 252–8520, JAPAN,
asada@w3.org

Abstract. We describe our investigation of the effectiveness of Web content negotiation using CC/PP. CC/PP is a proposed specification on a user-side content negotiation framework to comply with various clients. CC/PP is based on common technologies such as XML and HTTP extension and is expected to provide a generic content negotiation solution, but neither its performance nor effectiveness has ever been shown. We have implemented a CC/PP capable Web browser and a CC/PP proxy, and measured the performance of CC/PP and various different settings. The result shows that the use of *indirect reference* and abbreviating *profile-diff*s have good improvements on retrieval time when the client connection is as narrow as cellular phones. When the connection is faster than that, the use of *inline encoding* would be better provided that the profile size is less than a certain threshold, in our tests, approximately one-tenth the value of effective bandwidth of the client connection. The observed traffic with content conversion by CC/PP was smaller than the case without CC/PP for all tested environments, and the retrieval time is better or comparable for cellular phone clients. The result confirms that CC/PP is an effective solution for general content negotiation.

1 Introduction

As World Wide Web includes wide range of clients, a general mechanism for content negotiation is demanded in order to provide suitable contents for each one. Particularly, the appearance of new types of Web clients, such as Web-capable cellular phones which have only small displays and limited resources or Web-capable appliances which have only interfaces devices such as microphones and speakers, have dramatically changed the common image of Web clients.

CC/PP (Composite Capability/Preference Profiles) [1] and CC/PP Exchange Protocol [2] are new specifications for user side content negotiation. They are now being proposed in W3C[1] and IETF[2], and also are being incorporated in WAP (Wireless Application Protocol) architecture [7]. CC/PP (and its exchange protocol) is expected to provide a general content negotiation solution because

---

[1] World Wide Web Consortium (http://www.w3.org/)
[2] Internet Engineering Task Force (http://www.ietf.org/)

K.-L. Tan et al. (Eds.): MDM 2001, LNCS 1987, pp. 53–64, 2001.
© Springer-Verlag Berlin Heidelberg 2001

of its inherent openness. The openness mainly comes from the use of common technologies like XML (Extensible Markup Language) [5], full compatibility with HTTP/1.1 [10], and allowing of multiple sources to provide capability/preference profiles. However, currently many things are left unspecified about handling CC/PP on Web. Also there has so far been no evaluation of CC/PP based on implementation, though CC/PP has some trade-offs to be discussed. For example, the use of XML is expected to encourage the adoption of CC/PP, but it is also anticipated degrading network performance because of its verbosity.

This paper is intended to reveal the performance and effectiveness of CC/PP. We have developed a mobile Web browser and a CC/PP proxy by which CC/PP's overhead and merits are measured. The rest of this paper is organized as follows: section 2 introduces a brief summary of CC/PP specification and explains the design and implementation of our prototype. Section 3 describes the setting of experiments for performance evaluation. In section 4, we show the results of the experiments and give some discussions. Finally, we conclude the paper in section 5.

2   Design and Implementation

2.1   Overview of the CC/PP Specification

We begin this section by giving a brief summary of CC/PP specifications. More details can be found in the W3C notes and working drafts of the specifications [1,2,3,4].

The framework proposed in the specification consists of four types of network nodes: *CC/PP clients*, *CC/PP repositories*, *CC/PP proxies*, and *CC/PP servers*. These nodes exchange *CC/PP profiles* which describe user agent capabilities (with respect to both hardware and software) and user preferences in XML format for content negotiation. Each node has following roles:

CC/PP Client: A web client that is the original compositor of a CC/PP profile. When a CC/PP client sends a HTTP request to a server, it appends a CC/PP profile (or a URI to a CC/PP repository) to the request header. It also appends a difference between original profiles and newer ones to the request when some capabilities or preferences are changed from the original profile: e.g., a speaker is turned off during the session. Such difference is called *profile-diff*.

CC/PP Repository: A server that stores the user agent profile or profile segments persistently in a form that may be referenced by and incorporated into a profile. A CC/PP repository is typically a Web server that provides CC/PP profiles or profile segments in response to HTTP requests. A CC/PP client can send the URI as an *indirect reference* to the profile on the repository instead of sending the whole profile data *inline*.

CC/PP Proxy: An intermediate node that locates between client and server. A CC/PP proxy receives HTTP requests, recognizes CC/PP profiles, and forwards that requests toward the origin server. It also receives the response from the origin server and forwards it to the requesting client. In providing its forwarding functions, the proxy may modify either the request or response in order to provide suitable content negotiation functionalities (e. g., generating `Accept` header fields from the profile).

CC/PP Server: A Web server that may perform dynamic *content generation* or *content selection* when it responds the request in order to comply with the provided profile.

2.2   Overview of the Prototype

We have designed an experimental CC/PP system that consists of a CC/PP capable mobile browser which can emulate multiple hardware capabilities and a CC/PP proxy which converts Web contents to fit the provided profiles (figure 1). The reason why we do not place a CC/PP capable server in the system is that we wanted to preserve the possibility to use existing real Web servers and contents for the evaluation. Figure 1 shows the overall structure of the system.

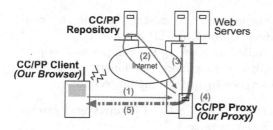

Fig. 1. The outline of CC/PP operation is as follows: (1) The CC/PP client sends an HTTP request piggybacked with its CC/PP profile. (2) The CC/PP proxy intercepts the request and parses the CC/PP profile. If there is an *indirect reference* to an external CC/PP profile, the proxy retrieves the profile from the indicated CC/PP repository. (3) The CC/PP proxy forwards the request to the server. (4) The CC/PP proxy receives the Web content from the server and converts it to fit the provided CC/PP profiles. (5) The CC/PP proxy forwards the converted content to the CC/PP client.

2.3   The Proxy

Our CC/PP proxy provides the functionality of content conversion by using the provided CC/PP profiles. In the initial specifications [1,2], there has been no explicit notion about the functionality of CC/PP proxies. However, the solution such as generating `Accept` header fields from the profile seems clearly insufficient, therefore we have decided to implement a CC/PP proxy which converts the content by using the provided profiles. In the newer specification [4], there are explanation about content conversion proxies. The newer specification also

Table 1. Conversion Functionalities of Our Proxy

Name	Description
Image format conversion	Converts image formats between GIF, JPEG and PNG
Color reduction	Reduces color depth to 8bits, 4bits, 2bits and 1bits
Image size reduction	Reduces the size of images
HTML conversion	Converts HTML to valid HTML or to XHTML-Basic [8]
Char-code conversion	Converts Japanese character codes

describes how to provide capabilities for conversion proxies to advertise their conversion capabilities, though our proxy has not supported it yet.

There have been a lot of Web proxies which convert the Web contents in order to adopt the contents to various network and client environment. Most of previous proxies such as [12,13] assume the existence of specific network path to enable content conversion, and others such as [11] force users to tune how the proxies should convert contents. Compared with those previous attempts, the key advantages of our CC/PP approach are:

– Enabling best-effort content conversions on the existing Internet by constructing the service on the common protocol, HTTP extension.
– Avoiding troubles to tune their profiles by allowing the composition of profiles originating from multiple sources (e.g. vendors, developers, users, etc).
– Encouraging the adoption of the proxies by using common technologies.

Our proxy implements basic functionalities as a CC/PP proxy and several content conversion functionalities as listed in table 1.

2.4   The Mobile Browser

Our mobile browser implements a simple hardware emulator and a compositor of CC/PP profiles, in addition to basic functionalities as an ordinary Web browser.

Users can dynamically change several parameters to set hardware capabilities, software capabilities and user preferences. Then the browser generates *profile-diffs* to the default CC/PP profiles corresponding to the parameters. Some parameters can be set interactively via GUI, and others can be set as command-line options.

3   Test Setup

In this section, we describe the setting of experiments for performance evaluation.

3.1   Test Machine Environment

New types of Web clients such as cellular phones could have very different machine environment as compared with existing clients. However, we decided to

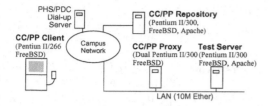

Fig. 2. Test environment. Each machine is connected to a campus network which is also connected to the Internet. A dial-up server for cellular phones is also located in the campus network. There are 4 hops from the segment which the CC/PP proxy is located to the dial-up server and to the CC/PP repository respectively.

Table 2. Connection between Client and Proxy

Connection	Bandwidth	Latency (RTT)
Wireless LAN (IEEE802.11b, Low)	High (1Mbps)	Low (4~10ms)
Wireless LAN (IEEE802.11b, Std)	High (2Mbps)	Low (4~10ms)
Cellular Phone (PHS/PIAFS [14])	Medium (64Kbps)	High (220~260ms)
Cellular Phone (PDC)	Low (9600bps)	High (500~600ms)

use ordinary PCs for the test since we mainly focus on the network performance of CC/PP. The tested environment is shown in figure 2.

Between the CC/PP client and the CC/PP proxy, we have set up four types of connection as shown in table 2.

3.2   Test Web Sites

We also measured the performance of content conversion by CC/PP in the Internet by using 50 real Web sites. Test sites are chosen from a list of most referred Web sites at Saitama University[3]. The summary information of test sites are shown in table 3.

For the test of content conversion, we used two CC/PP profiles totaling about 600 bytes which consists of the 250 bytes software capability profile and 350 bytes hardware capability profile.

4   Performance Evaluation

4.1   Basic Performance of CC/PP

In order to evaluate the basic performance of CC/PP and examine the optimal settings, we have compared the retrieval time between with *inline encoding* and

---

[3] We used the statistics data from Jan. to Dec. 1999 of
http://www.saitama-u.ac.jp/squid_stats/.

Table 3. Summary of Tested Sites

# of embedded images	2~62
# of requests	3~65
Total size of embedded images (Kbytes)	1.54~134.4
Total size (Kbytes)	2.18~231.9
# of hops to the server	10~30
RTT to the server (msec)	6~210

with *indirect reference*, with cache and without cache, and with normal *profile-diffs* and with abbreviated *profile-diffs*.

Effects of Indirect Reference *Indirect reference* is considered as an optimization technique to enhance network performance despite the verbosity of XML. While using *indirect reference* saves the traffic between client and proxy, the amount of the whole network traffic can be, without caching mechanisms, larger than the case using *inline encoding*. Therefore, the use of *indirect reference* is thought as a kind of trade-off problem and the effects of *indirect reference* depends on the network condition.

We have investigated the optimal point to switch from *indirect reference* to *inline encoding* by comparing the elapsed time under four types of network environment (table 2). Figure 3 and figure 4 shows the time elapsed to retrieve a zero-size document without profile cache.

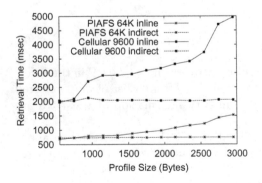

Fig. 3. Comparison between *inline encoding* and *indirect reference* for low bandwidth connections. The horizontal axis indicates the size of CC/PP profiles of the client and the vertical axis indicates the retrieval time for the zero-size document. In the case of PIAFS, a threshold can be found at the 800 bytes of profile size.

The result shows that *indirect reference* is essential in the case where the connection between client and proxy is as narrow as 9600bps cellular phones

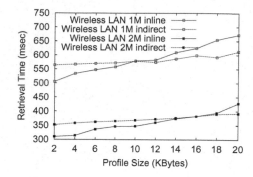

Fig. 4. Comparison between *inline encoding* and *indirect reference* for high bandwidth connections. The horizontal axis indicates the size of CC/PP profiles of the client and the vertical axis indicates the retrieval time for the zero-size document. In the case of 1M mode, a threshold can be found at the 10KB of profile size. In the case of 2M mode, also a threshold exists around 16KB.

regardless of the profile size. Other cases (PIAFS and Wireless LAN) show existence of threshold at which we should switch from *inline encoding* to *indirect reference*. To roughly conclude, in our test environment, the threshold is approximately $B \times 0.1$ bytes, where B is for the value of effective bandwidth B bytes per second of the client connection.

Effects of Profile Cache Each CC/PP profile can be cached at CC/PP proxies or CC/PP servers independently in order to reduce overhead to retrieve it from external CC/PP repositories. We have investigated the performance effects of profile cache by comparing the elapsed time with various sizes of profiles. We also tested effects of cache in another setting: the CC/PP server case by running the CC/PP proxy in **server** mode (i. e., the CC/PP proxy acts as a Web server). Figure 5 shows the measured result. Each value is measured with Wireless LAN 2Mbps connection.

The result shows that the cache has a little improvements on the measured retrieval time in the normal proxy case. On the other hand, in the case at CC/PP server, existence of profile cache has a big impact on the measured time. This is probably because that, when the indicated profile is cached locally, the CC/PP server needs not perform any network operations until it sends back the response to the client. Furthermore, if both the profile and the desired content are cached in the local memory, no blocking operations are performed on the request. Therefore, profile cache at CC/PP servers have the possibilities to achieve better performance than the cache at proxies in the optimal case.

The real-world performance will depend on the condition of the repository; for example, if the indicated CC/PP repository is very popular one and is always

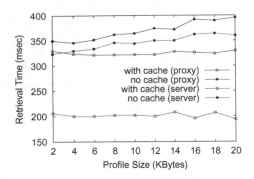

Fig. 5. Effects of profile cache. Values labeled `proxy` means that we tested with the normal Web server (Apache), the CC/PP proxy (our proxy with/without cache) and the CC/PP client (our browser). Values labeled `server` means that we tested with the CC/PP capable Web server (our proxy in server mode) and the CC/PP client (our browser). Each value labeled `with cache` does not include any cache miss cases.

crowded, using the profile cache would have more visible effects on the elapsed time improvements.

Effects of Abbreviation of Profile-Diff CC/PP is intended to provide lightweight exchange mechanism that permits the client to avoid re-sending the elements of the CC/PP profiles that have not changed since the last time the information was transmitted. The mechanism of *profile-diff* is introduced in order to meet this requirement. In usual cases, sending only differences changed since the last time as *profile-diff*s will be far more effective than re-sending the whole CC/PP profiles. However, since each *profile-diff* can also be verbose, the total amount of *profile-diff*s could become very large as the number of *profile-diff*s becomes large.

In order to avoid making the request size large, we have investigated the possibility of abbreviation of *profile-diff*s. For example, if we have following two *profile-diff*s,

```
99-Profile-Diff-1: <?xml version="1.0"?><RDF xmlns="http://www.w3.org
/TR/1999/PR-rdf-syntax-19990105#" xmlns:PRF="http://www.w3.org/TR/WD-
profile-vocabulary#"><Description ID="HardwarePlatform" PRF:ScreenSiz
e="220x220x24" /></RDF>
99-Profile-Diff-2: <?xml version="1.0"?><RDF xmlns="http://www.w3.org
/TR/1999/PR-rdf-syntax-19990105#" xmlns:PRF="http://www.w3.org/TR/WD-
profile-vocabulary#"><Description ID="HardwarePlatform" PRF:Speaker=N
o" /></RDF>
```

we could consider another expression of it as following:

```
99-Profile-Diff-1: <?xml version="1.0"?><RDF xmlns="http://www.w3.org
/TR/1999/PR-rdf-syntax-19990105#" xmlns:PRF="http://www.w3.org/TR/WD-
profile-vocabulary#"><Description ID="HardwarePlatform" PRF:ScreenSiz
e="220x220x24" PRF:Speaker=No" /></RDF>
```

By adopting such abbreviation technique, we can dramatically reduce the total amount of *profile-diffs*. However, to abbreviate in this fashion, clients should dynamically combine and generate a new *profile-diff* from multiple *profile-diffs*. In addition, clients should take care about the length of combined *profile-diffs*, because some older proxy and server implementations may not properly support such very long header-field.

We have measured the retrieval time with both normal *profile-diffs* and abbreviated ones. Figure 6 shows the result of the measurement. The result shows that the abbreviation of *profile-diffs* will be desirable when the connection to the proxy is as slow as cellular phones, while abbreviation shows few improvements when the connection is fast. Also we found that sending whole CC/PP profiles as *inline encoding* will be better than sending normal *profile-diffs* provided that the number of *profile-diffs* is larger than three, because the total size becomes larger than that of normal *profile-diffs* in normal cases.

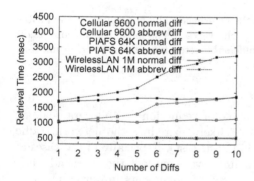

Fig. 6. Effects of *diff* abbreviation.

4.2   Effects of Content Conversion using CC/PP

Traffic Saving In order to compare between the CC/PP overhead and the savings by content conversion, we measured the network traffic for retrieval tests for 50 Web sites using 15 combinations of five types of color reduction (`color` (no conversions), `gray256` (8bits grayscale), `gray16` (4bits grayscale), `gray4` (2bits grayscale), and `mono` (monochrome)) and three types of image size reduction (`full` (no conversions), `240x320` (240×320), and `110x110` (110×110)).

The result shows that, for all cases, the measured traffic using CC/PP was smaller than the traffic without CC/PP (the case of **no conversions**). Figure 7 shows how the merit by content conversion changed as the size of embedded images varied. Notice that the figure only compares the conversions for color reduction, because image size reduction showed few impacts on saving traffics in our tests.

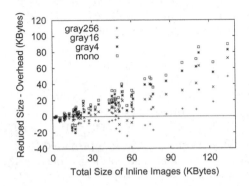

Fig. 7. Conversion Merit against the CC/PP Overhead: The horizontal axis indicates the total size of embedded inline images and the vertical axis indicates the conversion merit (the amount of CC/PP overhead traffic subtracted from the amount of network savings obtained by content conversion).

When the client user-agent needs the color reduction to 4bits grayscale or less, the content conversion using CC/PP likely to reduce the network traffic at a high probability (86% of documents in our test). Especially in the cases of monochrome and 2bits grayscale, the saving always exceeds the overhead when the image size is larger than 20 Kbytes (88% of documents in our test). As a result, the content conversion using CC/PP is effective in terms of traffic saving, especially in the case where the client's display capability is 4bits grayscale or less.

Retrieval Time Saving Also we have measured effectiveness of content conversion in terms of retrieval time saving. For the test, we set up a test Web server and a document which have 10 Kbytes texts and GIF images totaling from 0 Kbytes to 140 Kbytes. Figure 8 shows the result.

The result shows that when the connection is as fast as Wireless LAN, the retrieval time with proxy is worse than that without proxy for all cases. However, in the case of PIAFS (64K in the figure), the retrieval time with proxy is comparable provided that with the color reduction to monochrome. In the case of PDC cellular phones (9600 in the figure), the reduction to 4bits grayscale or

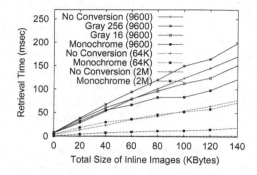

Fig. 8. Conversion merit on retrieval time against the CC/PP overhead. From the observation of real Web sites, the distribution of image sizes used for the test is: 70% of images are 1KB, 20% of images are 5KB, and others are 10KB and 20KB.

less can achieve better performance when the total size of images are larger than 60 Kbytes.

5   Conclusion and Future Work

This paper is intended to investigate the performance and the optimal settings of CC/PP for content negotiation. For the actual evaluation of CC/PP, we have implemented a mobile browser which generates and sends its CC/PP profiles and a CC/PP proxy which converts Web contents by using the provided CC/PP profiles.

The measured performance shows that the use of *indirect reference* dramatically improves the performance in the case where the connection between client and proxy is as narrow as 9600bps PDC cellular phones. The abbreviation of *profile-diffs* had also a great improvement when the connection is slow, though abbreviation would incur some implementation problems. On the other hand, with faster connections than PDC cellular phones (but slower than the connection between the proxy and the repository), the use of *inline encoding* will outperform provided that the profile size is less than a certain threshold, in our test environment, approximately $B \times 0.1$ where B is for the value of effective bandwidth B bytes per second of the client connection. When the connection is as fast as Wireless LAN, use of *indirect reference* improves the performance only if the profilie size is larger than 10 Kbytes. However, normally the profile will not exceed 10 Kbytes (especially if some kind of compaction technique is adopted), therefore, without cache mechanisms, it would be questionable that introducing *indirect reference* improves the performance when the connection speed is fast.

With profile cache, *indirect reference* will perform better for all cases, though the effect of profile cache at CC/PP proxy has not shown significant improvement in our tests. Our test also shows the profile cache at CC/PP server found more valuable than that at CC/PP proxy.

We have also investigated whether content conversion using CC/PP enhances the network performance despite CC/PP overhead caused by its verbosity. Though our proxy is still prototype and is not tuned properly, the observed traffic was smaller than the case without CC/PP for all tested environment, and the retrieval time with CC/PP is better or comparable in the case with cellular phones. The result confirms that CC/PP is an effective solution for general content conversion.

We are currently considering our CC/PP proxy to incorporate new specifications [4] so that it can advertise and chain a profile of its behavior to the downstream client or proxy. We are also examining the compaction of CC/PP profile to avoid the verbosity of XML using binary XML [9].

References

1. Reynolds, F., Hjelm, J., Dawkins, S. and S. Singhal: Composite Capability/Preference Profiles (CC/PP): A user side framework for content negotiation, W3C Note (1999). 53, 54, 55
2. Ohto, H., Hjelm, J.: CC/PP exchange protocol based on HTTP Extension Framework, W3C Note (1999), also appeared as Internet Draft (2000). 53, 54, 55
3. Nilsson, M., Hjelm, J., Ohto, H.: Composite Capabilities/Preference Profiles: Requirements and Architecture, W3C Working Draft (2000). 54
4. Reynolds, F., Woodrow, C., Ohto, H.: Composite Capabilities/Preference Profiles: Structure, W3C Working Draft (2000). 54, 55, 64
5. Bray, T., Paoli, J., Sperberg-McQueen, C. M.: Extensible Markup Language (XML) 1.0, W3C Recommendation (1998). 54
6. Frystyk, H., Leach, J. and Lawrence, S.: An HTTP Extension Framework, RFC 2774, (2000).
7. WAP Forum: *WAGUAPROF Version10 – Wireless Application Group User Agent Profile Specification*, WAP Forum (1999). 53
8. M. Ishikawa, S. Matsui, P. Stark, and T. Yamakami: XHTML Basic, W3C Working Draft (2000). 56
9. Martin, B. and Jano, B.: WAP Binary XML Content Format, W3C Note, (1999). 64
10. Fielding, R., Gettys, J., Mogul, J., Frystyk, H., Masinter, L., Leach, J. and Berners-Lee, T.: Hypertext Transfer Protocol – HTTP/1.1, RFC 2616 (1999). 54
11. Spyglass, *Spyglass Prism 3.0*, Spyglass., http://www.spyglass.com/. 56
12. Fox, A., Goldberg, I., Gribble, S. D., Lee, D. C., Polito, A., Brewer, E. A.: In *Proceedings of Middleware 98*, Experience With Top Gun Wingman: A Proxy-Based Graphical Web Browser for the 3Com PalmPilot, The Lake District, Springer (1998). 56
13. Barett, R., Maglio, P.: Intermediaries: New Places for Producing and Manipulating Web Content, In *Proceedings of the 7th International WWW Conference*, Brisbane, Elsevier Science B. V. (1998). 56
14. Personal Handyphone System, http://www.nttdocomo.com/p_s/. 57

Design and Implementation of an Information Announcement Toolkit for Mobile Computers

S. Tagashira *, K. Saisho **, and A. Fukuda

Graduate School of Information Science
Nara Institute of Science and Technology
8916-5, Takayama, Ikoma, Nara, Japan.

Abstract. We design and implement an information announcement basic software toolkit that realizes a new using style in mobile computing. This style regards a mobile computer as a server as well as a client. The proposed toolkit has two features. One is that the toolkit can solve problems such as disconnections and narrow network bandwidth. The other is that the toolkit allows a wide variety of legacy network applications designed for stationary environments to be adapted to mobile environments easily and smoothly. In this paper, we design an information announcement toolkit that supports the construction of information announcement systems from mobile computers. In addition, through implementing server applications on the toolkit, we show that the system works well and gives useful environment to clients.

1 Introduction

A mobile computer has become popular because of the advance in packaging and low power technologies. Users can carry it and do their jobs anywhere. A mobile computer is usually used to keep, generate, and modify personal information. Thus, the latest personal information usually exists on a mobile computer. On the other hand, with the advance of the network environment, a mobile computer can be connected to a network at any place using various communication vehicles. Therefore, the mobile computer can make full use of a distributed environment. In distributed environments, a computer can obtain information on other computers through networks. The Internet is worldwide distributed environment. By using the Internet, a great deal of beneficial information can be distributed all over the world.

Many studies [1,2] on mobile computing have been done. Under these studies, however, mobile computers only play the role of getting some information from computers connected to fixed networks. That is, these studies regard a mobile computer as a client or an intelligent terminal. In order to wide application fields

---

* Presently with Dept. of Electrical Engineering, Faculty of Engineering, Hiroshima University.
** Presently with Dept. of Reliability-based Information Systems Engineering, Faculty of Engineering, Kagawa University.

K.-L. Tan et al. (Eds.): MDM 2001, LNCS 1987, pp. 65–76, 2001.
© Springer-Verlag Berlin Heidelberg 2001

of mobile computing, it is important that a mobile computer plays the role of a server as well as a client; an information announcement system from mobile computer. If a mobile computer can announce information from any place, the latest personal information on the mobile computer can be provided. Moreover, it is possible to construct live broadcasting systems from the outside and handy phones through a network very easily.

In order to realize an information announcement system on mobile computers, many issues have to be solved. The typical issues are as follows:

- The underlying network condition in a mobile environment changes such as connections and disconnections frequently.
- The low quality network such as a wireless communication one is usually used in mobile environments.
- Legacy applications are not designed for mobile environments.

Even for the above situations, a software system on mobile computers have to provide stable services. This paper proposes an information announcement system in mobile environments and a software toolkit that supports the construction of the system. The proposed toolkit has the following features.

- In order to address the above issues in mobile environments, the toolkit provides three mechanisms: (1) providing stable services under any network condition such as connections and disconnections, (2) automatically limiting announcing information to effectively use a given network bandwidth, and announcing in order of priority of the information, and (3) using a well-suited protocol for a type of transferring information and an environment.
- The toolkit allows a wide variety of legacy network applications designed for stationary environments to be adapted to mobile environments easily and smoothly.

This paper designs and implements the toolkit. In addition, we show that two applications, a web system and an Internet TV telephone system, are constructed on the toolkit as examples, and the applications can be adapted to the mobile environment with little programming overhead by using the toolkit.

2   Information Announcement from Mobile Computers

2.1   Motivation

Many useful network applications in stationary environments have been developed. Since most of them are designed for fully connected, high speed, and low latency network environment, we cannot use the applications in mobile environments. In addition, since the applications are distributed with binary format, we cannot modify them. Therefore, the system that makes the applications available in mobile environments without modification is required. Our purpose is to design and implement a software system, a toolkit, which allows the following applications to be implemented in a mobile environment easily.

Web system in mobile environments A mobile computer can announce information with a web system. A mobile computer can announce not only text information, but also many types of information such as sounds and images. A substitute server prepared by the system keeps copy of information on a mobile computer. The substitute server can announce the copy on behalf of the mobile computer during its disconnection period.

Handy phone system on the Internet An Internet telephone system is adapted to mobile environments. The system can be extended to handy phone system. During disconnection period, an answering machine replies on behalf of the mobile computer.

2.2   Issues of Announcing Information in Mobile Environments

Some issues occur in announcing information from mobile computers. We discuss the issues and the facilities required to address them.

(1) Management of network connectivity Disconnections of a mobile computer from a network occur due to an empty battery energy or a physical disconnection. When a mobile computer is disconnected, a service from the mobile computer is intermitted because the communication with the mobile computer is unavailable. A mobile computer is frequently disconnected for long periods. In addition, a mobile computer can be connected to a network using a variety of communication vehicles. The differences among the hardware characteristics of the vehicles influence the bandwidth and latency. For example, wired communication vehicle has enough bandwidth for announcing information (strong connectivity). Wireless communication vehicle has insufficient bandwidth, and the communication is often interrupted by noise (weak connectivity). The proposed system needs to have the facility that manages the network connectivity.

(2) Auxiliary processing according to network connectivity When   a mobile computer is disconnected, a service from the mobile computer is intermitted. A substitute service on a stationary host is needed instead of the original service from the mobile computer. The proposed system needs to have the facility that can provide suitable services for the network connectivity.

(3) Efficient utilization of network bandwidth The communication with a mobile computer becomes unstable frequently even when the mobile computer is connected to a network. If the given network bandwidth is narrow, the system needs to have the flexible communication method considering a communication area, a type of data, and an objective of an application to utilize the network bandwidth effectively. Examples of the situation are as follows.

(a) In a wide area network, the packet loss rate is high. In this case, the TCP based communication is suitable. A resume facility is added in order to guarantee the communication.

(b) In a local area network, the packet loss rate is low. In this case, the UDP based communication is suitable. A resume facility and a retransmission facility are added to avoid the overhead in TCP.

(c) In case of transmitting real-time data as MPEG movies, the UDP based communication is also suitable because of low latency. A time-stamps facility for synchronization and a parity packet facility [3] to recover lost packet without retransmission, are added to the communication protocol.

(d) In case of transmitting the same data type in (c), choice of communication methods depends on objectives of applications. For example, another application can focus on quality in transmitting MPEG movies.

(4) Control of simultaneous announcing information If multiple applications announce information concurrently, the total traffic exceeds the upper limit of the performance of a mobile computer and the network bandwidth. In this case, the system needs to have the facility that can control the number of simultaneous announcing information. Moreover, high priority has to be given to the application that transmits time-constraint data.

2.3   Related Work

In order to adapt applications to mobile environments, many system softwares have been proposed.

The paper [4] has proposed the system providing the facility which keeps the appropriate quality of data for mobile environments. The system adopts the application-aware adaptation method with which the system administrates a load of the network and the performance of a mobile computer, and notifies applications of the load. The applications lower the appropriate quality of data for the load by using each application-dependent method. Disconnections of mobile computers is, however, not considered.

Indirect transport layer protocol [5,6], which supports a wide variety of applications in a low quality network, was proposed. Disconnected operations target short and medium term disconnections. Mechanisms for handling disconnections are provided by the system to be used by a wide variety of applications. However, mechanisms for handling long-term disconnections in these systems cannot adapt to the system that regards a mobile computer as a server.

The Coda file system [1,2] and Rover [7] employed other approaches for disconnected operations. In the Coda file system, disconnection handling is based on caching of files on a mobile computer expected to be used during disconnection. The system can handle disconnections operations for only the file system and cannot support a wide variety of applications. Rover can provide disconnected operations for any type of application. The study regards a mobile computer as a client rather than as a server. The proposed system regards a mobile computer as a server as well as a client, and can provide the facility that adapts a wide variety of applications to a mobile environment.

It is important for our system to provide disconnected operations from a viewpoint of not only a client but also a server for a mobile computer. In our previous work [8], we have constructed an information announcement system

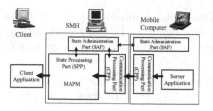

Fig. 1. Structure of Information Announcement System.

from a mobile computer. The system can support only disconnected operations. The quality of communication and a wide variety of applications, however, are not considered. In this paper, the proposed system solves the problems in mobile environments and aims at realizing an information announcement system from mobile computers dealing with network connectivity. The system allows many kinds of applications to be adapted to mobile environments smoothly.

3   Design of Information Announcement System

In this section, we design an information announcement system and an information announcement toolkit with which network applications including legacy ones can be easily implemented. We explain an information announcement system for mobile computers. Figure 1 shows the overview of our system. The proposed toolkit has the following features.

- The toolkit can solve the issues in mobile environments described in Section 2.2.
- The toolkit allows a wide variety of legacy network applications designed for stationary environments to be adapted to mobile environments easily and smoothly.

In order to implement legacy network applications in mobile environments without modification, the system adopts a similar model to a client-server model which is popular for them. In this model, an application server runs on a mobile computer. A SMH (System Management Host) as a stationary host is located at a fixed network between a server as a mobile computer and clients in order to manage mobile computers.

3.1   Software Architecture Model

We adopt the above model to our information announcement system because the model has the following advantages compared with a centralized control model in which information on a mobile computer is stored on a stationary host and provided by it.

- In a centralized control model, announcing information is restricted because of the stationary host's facilities. In the model, announcing information can be unrestricted because mobile computers can directly announce their own information.
- The model allows our system to be available in ad-hoc network, because a facility of announcing information by itself is installed in a mobile computer.

3.2   Structure of Information Announcement System

The information announcement system consists of the toolkit, a MAPM (Mobile Application Processing Module), and a legacy client-server application. The mesh area in Figure 1 shows the proposed toolkit for announcing information. Application developers only prepare a MAPM which can cope with any network connectivity of a mobile computer. A SMH consists of three parts: State Administration Part, State Processing Part, and Communication Processing Part.

State Administration Part (SAP)   In order to address the issue (1) described in Section 2.2, this part manages network connectivity of a mobile computer. This part consists of two parts put into a SMH and a mobile computer. Both parts cooperate each other in deciding a connectivity state which is described in Section 3.3.

State Processing Part (SPP)   In order to address the issue (2) described in Section 2.2, this part performs a suitable auxiliary processing for a connectivity state of a mobile computer. This part is partitioned into the application independent part and an application dependent part. We call the application dependent part MAPM. In order to adapt a legacy application to mobile environments, its developers only create a MAPM for it.

Communication Processing Part (CPP)   In order to address the issue (3) and (4) described in Section 2.2, this parts provide the following two facilities.

Flexible Application Protocol (FAP)
In order to effectively announce information under the narrow network bandwidth between a SMH and a mobile computer, this protocol realizes a well-suited communication method for the objective of an application. **FAP** consists of protocol modules. A protocol module can cope with a variety of conditions on mobile environments. An application can decide a combination of modules and make use of a well-suited protocol for its objective.

Connection Control Mechanism (CCM)
In order for excessive announcing information to be limited, the number of connections in announcing information is controlled automatically. The control mechanism is provided by connection control mechanism [9] described in Section 3.4.

When a SMH gets a request for a mobile computer from a client, the SMH gets a connectivity state of the mobile computer from **SAP**. The SMH performs the auxiliary processing specified in a MAPM which was prepared in advance.

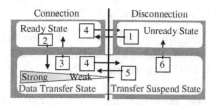

Fig. 2. Connectivity States.

For example, when a state is the connection state, the request is relayed to a server application on the mobile computer by **SPP**. The client can get data provided from the mobile computer through **CPP**. If the quality of communication becomes low, **SAP** detects the change of the quality and updates the state. **CPP** decreases the number of connections to reject a new request or suspend a current connection. As the quality becomes lower, **SAP** makes transition from connections into disconnections. **SPP** replies to a request on behalf of the mobile computer.

3.3 Connectivity State

The information announcement toolkit administrates a state of network connectivity for a mobile computer by using connectivity states as shown in Figure 2. In order to manage the quality of the communication depending on the communication condition and the distance from an access point, the states represent not only the connection state and the disconnection state, but also the quality of the communication.

1. Unready State
   This state means that a mobile computer is disconnected from a network. A mobile computer cannot provide any service to clients.
2. Ready State
   This state means that a mobile computer is connected to a network. A mobile computer waits for a request from clients.
3. Data Transfer State
   This state means that a mobile computer is sending data to clients. The attribute of this state includes the communication quality.
4. Transfer Suspend State
   This state means that transfer data is suspended. Transition only from Data Transfer State to Transfer Suspend State is available.

Transfer Suspend State is introduced. The reason is that the system can deal with temporary disconnections of a mobile computer. When a mobile computer is disconnected and immediately reconnected to a network, the system can recover the suspended communication.

3.4   Connection Control Mechanism (CCM)

In order to maximize throughput of the communication with a mobile computer and satisfy the required throughput of transmitting real-time data, this mechanism controls connections of the communication using the parameter on Data Transfer State.

By using multiple connections simultaneously, total elapsed time of transferring data is expected to be reduced because the protocol overhead of each connection, such as open connections, waiting for acknowledgment, and multiplex I/O may be reduced. Individual elapsed time, however, becomes longer with multiple connections since the allocated bandwidth of a connection becomes narrower. This also affects transferring real-time information. Thus, the deadline of transferring real-time information cannot be guaranteed. When the number of connections is less than the optimum number, the total throughput decreases. In order to make the best use of the narrow bandwidth and obtain efficient throughput, this mechanism can keep the optimum number of connections.

In addition, information is set to have priority. The priority of real-time information and frequently accessed information is high in order to keep the deadline. Lower priority information is provided during little traffic term or idle term

We adopt the mechanism that controls the number of connections for communication, because the mechanism is available for many kinds of communication vehicles and many kinds of network protocols such as TCP/IP.

4   Implementation of Information Announcement Toolkit

We describe the implementing of **SAP**, **SPP**, and **CPP** in this section.

4.1   State Administration Part (SAP)

When unexpected disconnections occur, the system cannot keep the coherency between network connectivity and the connectivity state the system manages. The incoherency influences providing stable services. For examples, a SMH has the connection state as connectivity states, even if a mobile computer is physically disconnected from a network. In this situation, the SMH waits for a reply from a mobile computer. There is an opposite situation that a SMH has the disconnection state as connectivity states, even if a mobile computer is physically connected to a network. In this case, the SMH performs a disconnection processing. **SAP** works toward avoiding the incoherency.

When a mobile computer starts to communicate with its own SMH, **SAP** on the mobile computer sends a connection message to the partner on the SMH. The partner replies a ACK message. **SAP** on the SMH periodically sends a check messages to check the connection of the mobile computer. **SAP** on the mobile computer replies a ACK message to the partner on the SMH. **SAP** on the SMH measures RTT (Round Trip Time), keeps its average, and manages the parameter of the communication throughput.

Table 1. List of Entry Points

connect_c2m	Process in Ready State is specified.
	This function is used to communicate between a client and a mobile.
connect_m2c	Process in Ready State is specified.
	This function is used to communicate between a mobile and a client.
suspend	Processing in Transfer Suspend State is specified.
reconnect	Processing, when a mobile computer is reconnected, is specified
disconnect	Processing in Unready state is specified.

Figure 2 shows transition of connectivity states. Here, α and β shows the number of the loss of ACK messages. α is decided by the toolkit and β is given by an application. The initial state is Unready State.

1. When **SAP** on a SMH receives a connection message, the state is Ready State.
2. A SMH relays a request from a client to a mobile computer. When transferring information between the SMH and the mobile computer starts, it makes the transition to Data Transfer State.
3. When all transactions with clients are completed, it makes the transition back to Ready State.
4. When there is no response to a check messages out of average RTT, the number of the loss is counted up. When there is a response within average RTT, the number of the loss is set to be zero. If the number is more than α times, the current state changes. If the current state is Data Transfer State, it makes the transition to Transfer Suspend State. If the current state is Ready State, it makes the transition to Unready State.
5. When there is a response, it makes the transition back to Data Transfer State.
6. When the number of the loss is more than β times, it makes the transition back to Unready State.

4.2   State Processing Part (SPP)

SPP gets a connectivity state of a mobile computer from **SAP** and performs an auxiliary processing according to the state. The processing is specified in a MAPM for each application. A MAPM is embedded into the system as Dynamic Loadable Module. A MAPM provides the entry points as shown in Table 1. Getting a request from a client, **SPP** calls the MAPM entry according to the state.

4.3   Communication Processing Part (CPP)

CPP provides **FAP** and **CCM**. Figure 3 shows **CPP** in detail. APS in the figure shows a server application. **CPP** consists of CCP (Communication Control

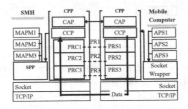

Fig. 3. Structure of Communication Processing Part

Part), CAP (Connections Administration Part), and PR modules. **FAP** consists of PR modules that have a specified API. A PR consists of a PRS (PR on a mobile computer) and a PRC (PR on a SMH). In order to realize a suitable protocol for mobile environments, PR modules encapsule a packet in the communication between a mobile computer and a SMH. Socket Wrapper is introduced to encapsule a packet. Socket Wrapper Part provides the same API as that is usually used in network programming [10]. A packet for the communication from an application is hooked by Socket Wrapper Part and passed to CCP. CCP passes the packet to PRSs. PRSs encapsule the packet and send it to PRCs. PRCs receive the packet and passes it to a MAPM.

SAP administrates the throughput between a mobile computer and a SMH. CAP controls communications for applications in order to maximize the throughput of communication with a mobile computer.

5   Evaluation

We evaluate the proposed toolkit through constructing a web system and an Internet TV telephone system as applications on it. The softwares on a mobile computer and a client are implemented on Windows98/NT. A SMH is implemented on FreeBSD. Socket library on Windows is provided by wsock32.dll. The original library is replaced with a toolkit library provided by the toolkit.

Web System

We realize a web system for mobile computers with the toolkit. When a mobile computer is connected with a network, information is directly announced from the mobile computer and copies of the information are created on a SMH. When a mobile computer is disconnected from a network, the SMH announces the copies of the information on behalf of the mobile computer.

Figure 4 shows the structure of the system. A web server software runs on a mobile computer and a client makes use of a browser software. The system prepares PR_resume as **FAP**. PR_resume can present the function that can resume a suspended communication.

We compare the system using the toolkit (say X system) with the system proposed in [8] (say Y system) by program code size. The Y system is implemented for mobile environments by adding program codes to the original web

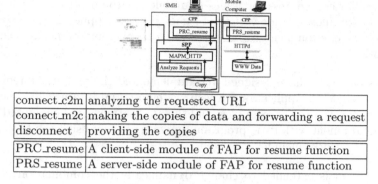

connect_c2m	analyzing the requested URL
connect_m2c	making the copies of data and forwarding a request
disconnect	providing the copies
PRC_resume	A client-side module of FAP for resume function
PRS_resume	A server-side module of FAP for resume function

Fig. 4. Sample Application: Web System

system developed for stationary computers. In the Y system, the added code size is 2930 lines at a stationary host and 4655 lines at a mobile computer. In the X system, the required code size is 346 lines. The ratio is approximately 5% in the code size. In the Y system, application developers also have to understand the whole code of a web system. On the other hand, in X system, they only focus on the entry points for a MAPM to construct an application.

Thus, application softwares developed for stationary computers can be adapted to the mobile environment with little programming overhead by using the toolkit

Internet TV Telephone System

We construct an Internet TV telephone system on mobile computers with the toolkit. The application can provide an uni-directional transmission from a mobile computer to the other mobile computer. To prepare a server software on each computer can make the interactive system.

When a mobile computer is connected to a network, a SMH relays the communication of movies and sounds from a mobile computer to a client. When the SMH detects Suspend State in the connectivity state of the mobile computer, the SMH notifies the prepared message for Suspend State by a MAPM to the client. When the connectivity state of the mobile computer is Unready State, the SMH can work as a simple answering machine. The added code size is 200 lines to implement this application.

6   Conclusion

In this paper, we have proposed the information announcement system for mobile computers. We have described the issues in announcing information from mobile computers and the facilities required to address them. The information announcement system can realize the facilities, and a software toolkit can support the construction of the system. The proposed toolkit has the following features.

- The toolkit can address the issues in mobile environments.
- The toolkit allows a wide variety of legacy network applications designed for stationary environments to be adapted to mobile environments easily and smoothly.

In this paper, we have designed and implemented the toolkit. Moreover, we have shown that two applications, a web system and an Internet TV telephone system, are constructed as examples, and the applications can be adapted to the mobile environment with little programming overhead by using the toolkit.

The future works include:

- The system is extended to change dynamically the combination of **FAP** according communication environments, and
- Various applications are applied to the system. We realize the system that allows particular applications to be adapted to mobile environments.

References

1. J. J. Kistler and M. Satyanarayanan, Disconnected Operation in the Coda File System, Operating System Review, Vol.25, No.5, pp.213-225, 1991. 65, 68
2. J. J. Kistler, Disconnected Operation in a Distributed File System, ACM Distinguished Theses, 1996. 65, 68
3. K. Saisho, Highly Reliable Multimedia Data Transmission with Redundancy, Advanced Database Systems for Integration of Media and User Environments '98 , Ed. Y.Kambayashi et al., World Scientific, pp.61–65, 1998. 68
4. B. D. Noble, M. Satyanarayanan, D. Narayanan, J. E. Tilton, J. Flinn, and K. R. Walker, Agile Application-Aware Adaptation for Mobility, Proc. the 16th ACM Symposium on Operating System Principles, pp.276–287, 1997. 68
5. A. V. Bakre, Design and Implementation of Indirect Protocols for Mobile Wireless environments, Ph.D. Thesis, Rutgers University, 1996. 68
6. A. V. Bakre and B. R. Badrinath, Indirect Transport Layer Protocols for Mobile Wireless Environment, Mobile Computing, Kluwer Academic Publishers, pp.229–252, 1996. 68
7. A. D. Joseph, J. A. Tauber, and M. F. Kaashoek, Mobile Computing with the Rover Toolkit, IEEE Trans. Computers, Special issue on Mobile Computing, Vol. 46, No. 3, pp.337–352, 1997. 68
8. S. Tagashira, K. Nagatomo, K. Saisho, and A. Fukuda, Design and Evaluation of a Mobile Information Announcement System Using WWW, Proc. the IEEE Third Int'l Works. on Systems Management (SMW'98), pp.38–47, 1998. 68, 74
9. S. Tagashira, F. Inada, K. Saisho, and A. Fukuda, Design and Evaluation of an Information Announcement Mechanism for Mobile Computers, Proc. the First Int'l Conf. on Mobile Data Access (MDA'99), pp.135–145, 1999. 70
10. W. R. Stevens, UNIX Network Programming, Prentice Hall PTR, Vol.1, Second Edition, 1998. 74

Session III: Data Broadcasting

High Performance Data Broadcasting: A Comprehensive Systems' Perspective

Peter Triantafillou, R. Harpantidou, M. Paterakis

Dept. of Computer Engineering
Technical University of Crete

peter@ced.tuc.gr
roula@telecom.tuc.gr
pateraki@telecom.tuc.gr

Abstract. Broadcast scheduling algorithms have received a lot of attention recently, since they are important for supporting mobile/ubiquitous computing. However, a comprehensive system's perspective towards the development of high performance broadcast servers is very much lacking. With this paper we attempt to fill this gap. We contribute four novel scheduling algorithms that ensure the proper interplay between broadcast and disk scheduling in order to attain high performance. We study comprehensively the performance of the broadcast server, as it consists of the broadcast scheduling and the disk scheduling, algorithms. Our results show that the contributed algorithms outperform the algorithms, which currently define the state of the art. Furthermore, one of our algorithms is shown to enjoy considerably higher performance, under all values of the problem and system parameters (such as the skew of access distributions, the system load, the data object sizes, cache- and disk-intensive workloads, etc.). An important conclusion of this study is that broadcast scheduling algorithms have only a small effect on the overall broadcast system performance, a fact that necessitates the refocusing of related research.

1. Introduction

Mobile computing and wireless networks are quickly evolving technologies that are making ubiquitous computing a reality. As the population of portable wireless computers increases, mechanisms for the efficient transmission of information to such wireless clients are of significant interest. Such mechanisms could be used by a satellite or a base station to disseminate information of common interest. Many emerging applications involve the dissemination of data to large populations of clients. Examples of such dissemination-oriented applications include information dispersal systems for volatile time-sensitive information such as stock prices and weather conditions, news distribution systems, traffic information systems, electronic newsletters, software distribution, hospital information systems, public safety applications, and entertainment delivery.

K.-L. Tan et al. (Eds.): MDM 2001, LNCS 1987, pp. 79-90, 2001.

Many of the dissemination-oriented applications we mention above, have data access characteristics that differ significantly from the traditional notion of client-server applications as embodied in navigational web browsing technology. A fairly limited amount of data is distributed from a small number of sources to a huge client population (potentially many millions) that have overlapping interests, meaning that any particular data item is likely to be distributed to many clients. Data broadcasting is considered to be an efficient way, in terms of bandwidth and energy, for the distribution of such information for both wireless and wired communication environments and has been extensively studied (see [11], [12], [14] and [15]). Furthermore, broadcast transmission compared to traditional unicast can be much more efficient for disseminating information, because unicast by having to transmit every data item, often identical, at least once for every client who requests it, creates scalability problems as the client population increases. Thus, the main advantage of broadcast delivery is its scalability: it is independent of the number of clients the system is serving. Much of the communication technology that has enabled large-scale dissemination supports broadcast, and in some cases, is primarily intended for broadcast use. For instance, direct broadcast satellite providers, and cable television companies (through the use of high-bandwidth cable modems) are now, or will soon be, capable of supporting multi-megabit per second data broadcast. Intel has also been broadcasting data along with normal TV signals, [9].

1.1 Related Work

The problem of determining an efficient broadcast schedule for information distribution systems has been extensively studied in the past ([1], [2], [3], [4], [5], [10], [11], [12], and [14]). In [1] the authors propose the RxW scheduling algorithm which calculates the product of the number of outstanding Requests (R), times the Wait time (W) of the oldest outstanding request for all data items corresponding to the requests pending in the broadcast server queue. The data item with the highest product value is chosen for broadcast. Therefore, RxW broadcasts a data item either because it is very popular (high R value) or because it has at least one long-outstanding request. It provides a balanced treatment of requests for both popular (hot) and not-so-popular (cold) items.

In [2], Acharya and Muthukrishman, study the scheduling problem arising in on-demand environments for applications with data requests of varying sizes and they introduce an alternative to the response time of a requests metric- the stretch of a request, which seems better suited to variable-sized data items. They present an algorithm called MAX based on the criteria of optimizing the worst case stretch of individual requests. In [3] and [16] memory is assumed available at each user. The management of this memory was considered in order to reduce the mismatch between the push-based broadcast schedule and the user's access pattern. In [4], the authors consider the problem of scheduling the data broadcast such that the access latency experienced by the users is minimized. Push-based and pull-based systems are considered. In [5], algorithms for determining broadcast schedules in asymmetric environments that minimize the wait time are considered. Variations of those algorithms for environments subject to errors, and systems where different clients may listen to different number of broadcast channels are also considered.

1.2 Problem Formulation and System Model

The abundance of dissemination-based applications caused the rapid development of scheduling algorithms for data broadcast. All such algorithms attempt to select which item to broadcast in order to improve performance. The root implicit or explicit assumption of existing scheduling algorithms is that the data items are immediately available in the broadcast servers' main memory, (see [1], [2], [4], [5], [10], and the references therein). This assumption ignores the fact that in many cases data items must be retrieved from secondary storage before they can be broadcasted. They also typically ignore the existence of the broadcast server's cache and the related cache management issues. By ignoring these issues, such scheduling algorithms when used in real systems can cause significant degradation of the broadcast efficiency, or at the very least the reported results, regarding the efficiency of proposed broadcast scheduling algorithms are misleading. In our paper, we take into account the fact that broadcast scheduling, disk scheduling, and cache management algorithms affect the performance of each other and the overall performance of the broadcast server.

With this paper we put forward a comprehensive study from a systems' viewpoint of the problem of pull-based broadcast scheduling. We consider a broadcast server with the architecture shown in Figure 1. All newly generated client requests enter into the broadcast server queue. The requests may need service from the disk server or alternatively, when cache memory exists, the data items may be found in the cache (i.e., they had been retrieved earlier from disk) and they are forwarded directly to the transmitters' queue. From the transmitters' queue all data items are transmitted through the communication channel, reaching the clients that had made the corresponding requests. When a data item is broadcasted, all requests for the particular data item are satisfied simultaneously regardless of the time of their arrival.

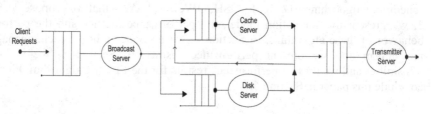

Fig. 1. Broadcast Server Architecture

The system we study consists of a large and possibly time varying client population that requests data items from an information source equipped with a data broadcasting capability. Clients use two independent networks for communicating with the server: an uplink channel for sending requests to the server, and a "listen only" downlink channel for receiving data from the server. When a client needs a data item (e.g., a database object) that cannot be found locally, it sends a request for the item to the server. Client requests are queued up (if necessary) at the broadcast server upon arrival. Requests that correspond to the same item are grouped together forming a multi-request. In the remainder of the paper, we refer to such multi-requests as requests.

We make the following assumption. First, we assume, for simplicity reasons only, that data items are of fixed-length (e.g., database objects). Second, we assume that clients continuously monitor the broadcast channel after they send a request to the server and we do not consider the effects of transmission errors, so that all clients waiting for a data item receive it when is broadcasted by the server. We ignore the delay for sending requests via the client-to-server uplink, which we expect to be small compared to the latency of obtaining broadcast items from moderately or heavily loaded servers.

1.3 Overview of Contributions

Our study is comprehensive in that it considers the interplay between the broadcast scheduling algorithm and the disk scheduling algorith. The contributions are:

- We propose mechanisms that ensure the required interplay of the above algorithms in order to ensure high performance. These mechanisms consist of four novel scheduling algorithms.
- We show that without such mechanisms the algorithms for broadcast scheduling found in the literature can be of little practical use.
- We conduct a detailed performance study: we quantify the expected performance under different values of the problem parameters and we identify the critical mechanisms that limit performance under different configurations.

1.4 The Remainder of the Paper

The remainder of the paper is organized as follows. In Section 2, we describe the scheduling algorithms ADoRe, FLUSH, OWeiST, RxW/S that we propose. In Section 3, we present the simulation model, the performance metrics and the performance behavior of these algorithms. In Section 4, we introduce a novel cache management mechanism and we present performance results. In Section 5, we include the transmitter and we present performance results for the FLUSH algorithm. Finally, we conclude this paper in Section 6.

2. Broadcast and Disk Scheduling Algorithms

The broadcast scheduling algorithm that we have chosen is the exhaustive RxW algorithm, which appears to be a practical, low-overhead scalable scheme that requires no a-priori advanced knowledge (such as the access probabilities of items), [1]. Our group has performed performance studies comparing RxW with other algorithms (e.g., the algorithms in [2], and [5]), and we have found it to have the best performance. These are the reasons we have chosen it as broadcast scheduling algorithm.

For the disk scheduling we selected the C-LOOK algorithm [18], unless stated otherwise. The C-LOOK algorithm sorts data items to be retrieved from the disk in ascending order of their cylinder position on the disk. The read-write head is only moved as far as the last request in each direction. It services requests from the service queue as it reaches each cylinder, until there are no requests in the current direction. Then, it immediately returns to the first requested item of the other end, without servicing any requests on the return trip, and repeats the process.

In this section, we disregard the existence of a cache and we assume that each requested data item must be retrieved from the secondary storage. This is done for two reasons: first in order to measure the impact of the disk system in the performance of the server, and second, because in applications where the data items will be very large and the distribution of the requests to data items will not be skewed, the cache will have little impact. Furthermore, in some system configurations the cache size might be quite small (e.g., as an extreme example, consider a broadcast server on a network attached disk which has a cache size that is a negligible percentage of the database size).

2.1 Combining Separate Broadcast and Disk Scheduling Algorithms

The first of the algorithms we present below extend and combine the RxW broadcast scheduling algorithm with a disk scheduling algorithm through various mechanisms. In the literature ([1]), RxW is described as being applied after the transmission of the previously selected item from the broadcast queue has been completed. The second uses FCFS, as broadcast scheduling algorithm. The algorithms depend on the C-LOOK disk scheduling algorithm.

2.1.1 The ADoRe Algorithm: Active Disk on Requests
The ADoRe is a fairly simple algorithm. When the disk becomes idle, K or fewer requests (corresponding to the case when the broadcast queue does not contain K requests) are directed from the broadcast server queue to the disk scheduler queue to be served. If there are more than K outstanding requests in the broadcast server queue, the RxW algorithm is applied and a group of K requests with the highest RxW values are directed to the disk queue.

A straightforward implementation of the RxW algorithm would imply that each time it is called the broadcast scheduling algorithm forwards a single request to the disk system and once the item is retrieved and broadcasted, RxW is called again to pick the next item, and so on. This, obviously, results in poor disk system performance. The ADoRe algorithm attempts to avoid this shortcoming by using RxW to select a group of K requests. The parameter K allows the formation of groups of requests, in contrast to the straightforward implementation of the RxW algorithm mentioned before. Intuitively, the ADoRe algorithm tries to keep the disk system as highly utilized as possible, while on the other hand it tries to reduce the average disk service time by forwarding a group of requests to be served on which the disk scheduling algorithm seek optimization will produce better results. For example, a C-LOOK sweep with 10 requests served (i.e., when K=10) will take less time than running the RxW algorithm 10 times picking one request at a time and giving it to the disk. Therefore, if K equals to 1 the ADoRe algorithm resembles the straightforward implementation of the RxW algorithm since it directs one request from the broadcast server queue by applying the RxW algorithm, to the disk server queue every time the broadcasting of the previously selected data item is completed.

2.1.2 The FLUSH Algorithm

The requests in the disk queue are served using the C-LOOK algorithm. The FLUSH algorithm manipulates differently the requests on the broadcast server. Every time the disk finishes the service of a single request, all the requests in the broadcast server queue are flushed to the disk server and incorporated into the C-LOOK lists.

2.2 Amalgamating Broadcast and Disk Scheduling Algorithms

The amalgamated algorithms combine information available at the broadcast server and at the disk server.

2.2.1 The OWeiST Algorithm: Optimal Weighted Service Time

The OWeiST algorithm attempts to improve performance in two ways. First, it exploits information available at the broadcast server and at the disk server. Second, it employs a different disk scheduling algorithm, which for larger groups of requests, introduces further optimizations.

According to the OWeiST algorithm whenever the disk becomes idle, K or fewer requests as in the AdoRe algorithm, are being selected from the broadcast queue and forwarded to the disk queue. The service of the requests is being carried out in such order that the sum of the products R times Disk Service Time of the requests is kept minimum. The operation of the algorithm is as follows. We maintain a graph of K requests. The edge connecting two requests r_i and r_j has a label $R_j x S_j$ where R_j is the number of requests in the broadcast queue for item j and S_j represents the disk access cost to access item j, given that the previously retrieved item from the disk was item i. The disk access cost contains both the seek time from the cylinder of item i to the cylinder of item j, plus the rotational delay necessary to access item j once the disk head is positioned on j's cylinder, plus the time to retrieve item j from the disk. The algorithm computes all possible permutations for the K requests and selects the optimal permutation that gives the smallest total weighted cost. Note that, obviously, this is analogous to computing a solution to the Traveling Salesman Problem (TSP). However, by bounding the value of the parameter K we can control the overhead involved in computing the optimal service schedule. Notice that, when K equals 1 OWeiST is identical to ADoRe with K equal to 1.

2.2.2 The RxW/S algorithm

We also propose the amalgamated algorithm RxW/S, where S is the disk service time, which takes into account information of the broadcast scheduling algorithm (i.e., R and W for every requested data item) and the disk service overhead. It is an one step algorithm, which is being activated whenever the disk becomes idle and selects a request from the broadcast queue to be serviced from the disk. The selected request, is the one that has the higher value of the fraction (RxW)/S. In this algorithm there is no grouping of requests because requests are directed to the disk one at a time. The selection of the data item to be broadcasted, favors items of high RxW value and low disk access times.

3. Performance Study

The performance of the algorithms has been studied through simulation. The simulations were executed on a Pentium II PC, 400MHz. Each run simulates the transmission of one million data items. We observed, that by simulating 1,000,000 transmitted data items, we were able to estimate with accuracy the steady-state algorithms performance.

Table 1 shows the parameter setting for the simulated disk system. We assume that the database consists of 10,000 16KB (or alternatively 200KB data items).

Disk Characteristics	
Cylinders	6,900
Surfaces	12
Sector Size	512
Revolution Speed	10,000 RPM
Number of Zones	20
Average Transfer Rate	12 MBps

Table 1.

3.1 Simulation Model

We developed a model, as depicted in Figure 1. We used a Request Generator, which generates a stream of requests according to a Poisson arrival process. The request arrival rates we used in our simulations vary between 10 and 500 requests per second.

Requests are generated from the Request Generator and then they enter the broadcast server queue. By the application of the algorithms in section 3, requests are directed to the disk server queue where the corresponding data items are retrieved from disk and are then forwarded to the transmitters' queue (see paragraph 3.3), or in the presence of cache memory the data items that are located in the cache are sent directly to the transmitters' queue (see paragraph 4.2). When a cache exists, all the data that are forwarded to the transmitters' queue are first moved from disk to the cache (provided that they are not already located in the cache). The transmitter conveys all the data items to the clients through the channel link. Finally, the statistics collector records all relevant statistics in order to measure the performance.

In our simulation, it is assumed that the request probabilities of all data items follow a Zipf distribution. The Zipf distribution may be expressed as follows:

$$p_i = c\,(1/i)^\theta, \quad 1 \le i \le M \tag{1}$$

where $c = 1/\sum_{i=1}^{M}(1/i)^{\theta}$ is a normalizing factor, and θ is a parameter referred to as the

access skew coefficient. The distribution becomes increasingly "skewed" as θ increases, [5], [6]. We will report results for two values for θ; $\theta = 0$ (uniform distribution), and $\theta = 1.17$ (highly skewed access distribution).

3.2 Performance Metrics

In client-server information systems, the user response time, namely the time between the arrival of the request at the broadcast server and its service, is one of the most important factors for evaluating the systems' performance. A metric that gives an overall view of the response time of all clients in the system is the mean response time. As is remarked in [6], it is natural in the real world some users' demand patterns to completely differ from the overall demand pattern and their own response time may be much worse than the overall mean. In this paper, we address this problem by adopting as a performance metric an *index of fairness* that always lies between 0 and 1, [7]. We have chosen this metric over the square coefficient of variation since the fairness index is a further normalization giving a number between 0 and 1. This boundedness aids intuitive understanding of the fairness index. For example, an algorithm with a fairness index of 0.10 means that it is unfair to 90% of the users, and an algorithm with a fairness index of 0.90 means that is fair to 90% of the users. The fairness index, if n contending users are in the system such that the response time of the request of the ith user is denoted by x_i, is defined as follows:

$$f(x) = \frac{[E[x]]^2}{E[x^2]} = \frac{\left[\sum_{i=1}^{n} x_i\right]^2}{n\sum_{i=1}^{n} x_i^2} \quad , \quad x_i \geq 0 \qquad (2)$$

where x is the random variable denoting the response time of a client's request. We have also considered the ratio of the standard deviation to the mean response time of a request, (i.e., the square root of the square coefficient of variation), as an additional fairness indicator.

3.3 Performance Results

The results we present below are only a small indicative sample of the results we have obtained since we cannot present them all, due to the space limitations. We conducted a number of experiments under different combinations of the arrival rate, the grouping parameter K (for algorithms ADoRe and OWeiST), and the access skew coefficient θ. The two primary performance metrics, the mean response time and the fairness index, are plotted versus λ, for different values of the parameter K. The CPU overhead for the RxW algorithm and for calculating the optimal permutation of the OWeiST algorithm is not included in the mean response time results[1]

Figures 2 through 5, present the results under the assumptions of no cache memory available and of infinite broadcast channel speed. The response time of a

---

[1] The CPU time (overhead) of the application of the RxW algorithm on the broadcast server queue was estimated to be less than 1ms and the corresponding time for the disk scheduling mechanism of the OweiST algorithm for figuring out the optimal permutations when K equals 5 was estimated to be approximately 1ms. These estimations were based on experiments executed a Pentium II PC, 400MHz.

client's request corresponds to the time between the arrival of the request at the server and the retrieval of the corresponding data item from the disk.

Figures 2 through 4 present the mean response time of the proposed scheduling algorithms, ADoRe, FLUSH, OWeiST, and RxW/S. As we mentioned in section 2, the ADoRe algorithm with K equal to 1 resembles the RxW algorithm. Figure 2, presents the mean response time (in milliseconds) versus the arrival rate •, for •=1.17, 16KB data item size, and K=1 (which means that each group of the requests contains 1 element). We observe that as the aggregate request arrival rate increases beyond 50 (•>50), the mean response time of the ADoRe, and the OWeiST is sharply increased, reaching the value of 590ms for arrival rate •=120 requests/sec. On the contrary, the mean response time is maintained low for the FLUSH, and the RxW/S algorithms, with mean response time values less than 130ms for the RxW/S and less than 100ms for the FLUSH, with arrival rate •=120 requests/sec. This demonstrates that the latter two algorithms perform considerably better. The same trend is observed for 200KB data item size, as is shown in Figure 3. The difference in the mean response time is due to the retrieval time from the disk of the 200KB data item, which is a multiple of the corresponding time of the 16KB data items.

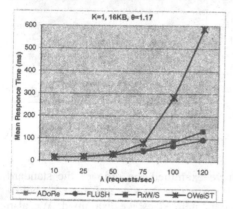

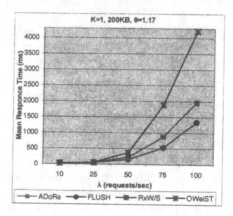

Fig. 2.   Fig. 3.

In Figure 4 the value of K increases to 5 and we notice similar behavior. Notice that K refers only to ADoRe and OWeiST algorithms, while the curves of FLUSH and RxW/S are the same as in Figure 2. OWeiST performs much better than before, and the mean response time is similar to that of the FLUSH and the RxW/S for all • values examined. This improvement of the OWeiST was expected, since its optimization (i.e., the calculation of the shortest path for visiting all K data items on the disk in accordance to their popularity) introduces greater benefits as K increases. ADoRe with K equal to 5 performs slightly better than with K equal to 1, because the RxW algorithm forwards a group of requests to the disk and not just one at a time.

The improved performance of FLUSH over the other three algorithms, as • increases, shown in Figures 2 through 4 was expected since FLUSH forwards requests to the disk server as they arrive, increasing the number of requests that are waiting to be serviced in the disk queue. This gives the disk scheduling algorithm (C-LOOK) the chance to further optimize the disk access time. The OweiST algorithm cannot do that since given the NP-Completeness of calculating the optimal schedule, the disk system queue must be relatively small. The critical observation is that the broadcast server must keep the disk server as busy as possible and this outweighs in importance any improvement from the other disk scheduling algorithms.

Figure 5 shows the fairness index plotted versus the request arrival rate λ for the case of 16KB data item size, and K equal to 1. We observe that FLUSH and RxW/S have a fairness index above 70% even for increased arrival rates, while the fairness indices of ADoRe and OWeiST drop abruptly. Even for 200KB data item sizes (due to lack of space these results are not shown), FLUSH maintains a fairness index around 70% when the fairness indices of the other algorithms drop well below 50%.

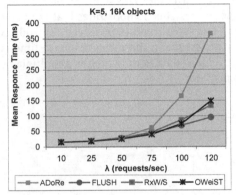
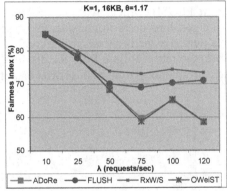

Fig. 4.   Fig. 5.

As an additional fairness metric we have examined the ratio of the standard deviation to the mean response time. FLUSH maintains the value of this ratio below 0.7 for all values of the arrival rate, and data item sizes we examined. We also simulated the demand for data items using the Uniform distribution (θ=0). As expected, the mean response time of all algorithms for θ=0, increases rapidly with arrival rate increases (compared to the results in Figures 2, 3, and 4). This is due to the decreasing possibility of serving more than one client by a single broadcast. FLUSH, however, continues to perform best and has a fairness index above 65%.

4. Contributions and Concluding Remarks

Looking at related work for broadcasting scheduling, one can find several interesting algorithms for deciding which data item to pick for broadcasting. However, all these algorithms make the (implicit or explicit) assumption that the chosen data item is immediately available to the transmitter for broadcasting. In a real system this obviously does not hold. This fact begs the question of how all the basic system components of a broadcast server's system infrastructure should interact in order to build high performance broadcast servers. With this paper we attempt to address this question. We put forward a comprehensive study from a system's viewpoint of the problem of broadcast scheduling. Our study is comprehensive in that it considers the interplay between the broadcast scheduling algorithms, the disk scheduling algorithms, and the cache management algorithms.

We study the interplay between broadcast and disk scheduling algorithms, which will be the critical performance issue in applications and system configurations where the impact of caches will be secondary. We propose four novel scheduling algorithms, the ADoRe, FLUSH, OWeiST, and RxW/S classified under two categories: those that combine separate broadcast and disk scheduling algorithms and those that amalgamate the information available at the broadcast queue and at the disk queue, producing a single scheduling criterion. We study their performance in terms of mean response time and their fairness under different values of the problem parameters (system load, access distributions, object sizes, etc.).

The major conclusions of this work are:

In environments where the broadcast server depends heavily on the disk system, (i.e., it is disk-intensive as opposed to cache-intensive) the critical issue is to design mechanisms which ensure that the server keeps the disk system highly utilized and allowing the disk scheduling algorithm to perform its optimizations. Our results show that our FLUSH algorithm can outperform significantly other mechanisms, which are based on either more efficient disk scheduling algorithms or on algorithms based on combining information at the broadcast and the disk queues.

Our performance study has shown that the proposed algorithms namely, ADoRE, FLUSH, OWeiST, and RxW/S can achieve significantly better performance than that of the RxW algorithm (as it is straightforwardly implemented using the ADoRe (K=1) mechanism) under a large variation of the values of the basic problem parameters (e.g., access skew distribution, system load, object sizes, cache or disk intensive workloads etc.). Furthermore, our results show that FLUSH, consistently outperforms all others under all the above workload and system parameters, while being fair.

A conclusion worthy of special notice is that we have actually found that "efficient" broadcast scheduling algorithms found in the literature have a negligible impact. Specifically, if instead of employing the RxW algorithm at the broadcast queue we employed FCFS scheduling the difference in the overall performance of the broadcast system would barely be noticeable. Notice that, in the FLUSH algorithm, every time we have an arrival, it is passed to the disk system. Viewed differently, this implies that FLUSH essentially uses a FCFS scheduling at the broadcast queue. This conclusion is a strong indication that the main attention of most related research efforts needs to be refocused.

References

[1] D. Aksoy, M. Franklin, "Scheduling for Large-Scale On-Demand Data Broadcasting", Proc. IEEE InfoCom Conf., San Francisco, CA, 1998.
[2] S. Acharya, S. Muthukrishnan, "Scheduling On-demand Broadcasts New Metrics and Algortihms", Proc. ACM/IEEE Int. Conf. MobiCom '98, Dallas,October 1998.
[3] C. J. Su, and L. Tassiulas, "Joint Broadcast Scheduling and User's Cache Management for Efficient Information Delivery", Int. Conf. MobiCom '98, Dallas,October 1998.

[4] C.-J. Su and L. Tassiulas, "Broadcast Scheduling for Information Distribution", Proc. IEEE INFOCOM Conf.,CA, 1997.

[5] N. H. Vaidya and S. Hammed, "Data Broadcast in Asymmetric Wireless Environment", Proc. of Workshop on Satellite-based Information (WOSBIS), New York, November 1996.

[6] S. Jiang and N.H. Vaidya, "Response Time in Data Broadcast Systems: Mean, Variance and Trade-Off ", Proc. of Workshop on Satellite-based Information (WOSBIS), Texas, October 1998.

[7] R. Jain, D-M. Chiu, W.R Hawe, "A Quantitative Measure of Fairness and Discrimination for Resource allocation in Shared Computer Systems", DEC-TR-301, September 1984.

[8] E.J. O'Neil, P.E. O' Neil and G. Weikum, "An Optimality Proof of the LRU-K Page Replacement Algorithm", Journal of the ACM, Vol. 46, January 1999.

[9] Intel Corporation, Intel Intercast Technology, http://www.intercast.com, 1997.

[10] S. Acharya, M. Franklin, S. Zdonik, "Balancing Push and Pull for Data Broadcast", Proc. ACM SIGMOD Conf., Tuscon, Arizona, May 1997.

[11] K. Stathatos, N. Rousopoulos, and J.S. Baras, "Adaptive Data Broadcast in Hybric Networks", in Proc. VLDB, 1997.

[12] H. Dykeman, M. H. Ammar, and J. Wong, "Scheduling algorithms for videotext systems under broadcast delivery", in Proc. International Conference of Communications, pages 1847-1851, 1996.

[13] M. H. Ammar and J. W. Wong, "On the Optimality of Cyclic Transmission in Teletext Systems", IEEE Transaction on Communication, COM-35(1):68-73, January 1987.

[14] S. Acharya, M. Franklin, S. Zdonik, "Dissemination-based Data Delivery Using Broadcast Disks", IEEE Personal Communications, 2(6), 1995.

[15] J. W. Wong, "Broadcast Delivery", in Proc. of IEEE, pp. 1566-1577, December 1988.

[16] M. H. Ammar, "Response Time ina a Teletext System: an Individual User's Perspective", IEEE Trans. On Communications, COM-35(11):1159-1170, November 1987.

[17] R. Alonso, D. Barbara, H. Garcia-Molina, "Data Caching Issues in an Information Retrieval System", TODS 15(3):359-384(1990).

[18] B.L. Worthington, G.R. Ganger, and Y. Patt, "Scheduling algorithms for modern disk drivers", in Proc. of the 1994 ACM SIGMETRICS Conf., pages 241-251.

Optimized Scheduling on Broadcast Disks

Jeong-Hyon Hwang, SungHo Cho, and Chong-Sun Hwang

Dept. of Computer Science and Engineering,
Korea University, 5-Ga, Anam-Dong, SungBuk-Gu, Seoul, South Korea
{jhhwang, zoch, hwang}@disys.korea.ac.kr

Abstract. Since the advent of wireless networks and portable computing devices, push-based data delivery has been discussed as an attractive communication framework for wireless environments. This paper focuses on the way of scheduling that leads to the minimum access delay for a hierarchical push-based data broadcast mechanism. This mechanism, called "Broadcast Disks", partitions data items into a number of logical disks spinning at different speeds and superimposes the disks on a single broadcast channel. In this paper, we mathematically model the Broadcast Disks program generation and suggest concrete design principles for deciding (a) *how many disks to use,* (b) *how to segment data items into disks based on the user access patterns,* and (c) *how to determine the relative spinning speeds for disks* in order to minimize the *average access delay.* In addition, we present our simulation study that substantiates the optimality of the suggested algorithms with detailed analyses.

1 Introduction

This paper explores the problem of optimal broadcast program generation for a push-based repetitive data broadcast model called "Broadcast Disks" [1, 3, 9]. In the model, the server is assumed to have knowledge of the client requirements beforehand and to emphasize the most popular data items by broadcasting them frequently.

Since the Broadcast Disks approach partitions data items into a number of logical disks spinning at different speeds of rotation based on the access probabilities of data items, our research focuses on these three issues:

- In order to minimize the average access delay, *how many disks should be used?*
- Given a number of disks, *how many data items with similar access probabilities* should be assigned to each disk?
- For given broadcast disks, how to choose *the relative frequency (spinning speed)* for each broadcast disk?

The problem of schedule design for broadcast information distribution systems has been widely studied in the past [2, 3, 4, 5, 9]. In [4, 5], Ammar and Wong, using a stochastic Markov Decision Process (MDP) formulation, concluded that the optimal schedule for a push-based broadcast system will be periodic. They also proposed that, in the absence of a cache, the optimal bandwidth

K.-L. Tan et al. (Eds.): MDM 2001, LNCS 1987, pp. 91–104, 2001.

for each data item is proportional to the square root of its access probability. In contrast to the researches that studied scheduling policies for pull-based systems [2, 3], Nitin H. Vaidya and Sohail Hameed presented an approach that attempts to minimize the average access time for push-based asymmetric environments [9]. Even though our approach bears some similarities to theirs, there are differences as follows:

- Their bucketing algorithm segments data items with similar access probabilities into a number of buckets by paying too much attention to the probabilities of the most and the least popular items. To the contrary, by finding the optimal disk segmentation based on the overall pattern of user popularity, our GS (Growing Segments) algorithm outperforms the bucketing algorithm significantly.
- Their proof on the optimality was developed under an assumption that the average access delay must have a minimum value. However, we didn't impose any assumption on the average access delay.

The remainder of this paper is structured as follows. In Section 2, we present our mathematical modeling and proofs on the optimailty of broadcast program generation. Section 3 introduces our algorithms for finding the optimal multi-disk segmentation and the optimal disk frequencies and Section 4 describes the simulation model and analyzes the experimental results derived from the model. Finally, Section 5 presents our conclusions.

2   Mathematical Modeling

In this section, we present our mathematical study on the Broadcast Disks program generation. Due to page limitation, most of the proofs are not included. For more detail, refer to [10].

Let database $\mathcal{D}$ consist of n pages (data items of a uniform and fixed length). I.e.,

$$\mathcal{D} = \{x_1, \ x_2, \ \ldots, \ x_n\} \tag{1}$$

where each x_i denotes a page in the database. Here, it is assumed that the pages are ordered from most popular to least popular and each page is assigned its rank according to its position in the order. Note that the rank of the most popular page is 1. Let $R = (0, n]$.

Definition 1. *If $(a, b]$ is a half-open interval defined on R, a set of points*

$$P = \{r_0, \ r_1, \ldots, r_N\},$$

satisfying the inequalities

$$a = r_0 < r_1 < \ldots < r_{N-1} < r_N = b,$$

is called a partition of $(a, b]$. The interval $(r_{k-1}, r_k]$ is called the kth subinterval of P and we write $n_k = r_k - r_{k-1}$, so that

$$\sum_{k=1}^{n} n_k = b - a.$$

Definition 2. *Let $p_{rank}(r)$ and $r(x)$ denote the access probability of the data item whose rank is r and the rank of a page x, respectively. Then, the access probability of a page x, $p(x)$, is defined by*

$$p(x) = p_{rank}(r(x)). \tag{2}$$

Definition 3. *Let $P = \{r_0, r_1, \ldots, r_N\}$ be a partition of $R = (0, n]$. Then, for each i such that $1 \le i \le N$, the kth broadcast disk D_k is defined as follows:*

$$D_k = \{x \in \mathcal{D} \mid r(x) \in (r_{k-1}, r_k]\}. \tag{3}$$

Note that each disk D_k is defined on the subinterval $(r_{k-1}, r_k]$ and it has n_k data pages.

Lemma 1. *The set of Broadcast disks $\{D_i\}_{i=1,\ldots,N}$ satisfies the following properties:*

1. *$D_i \cap D_j = \emptyset$ for all i, j $(i \ne j)$*
2. *$\mathcal{D} = \cup_{i=1,\ldots,N} D_i$*

Definition 4. *Let $freq(x)$ denote the frequency of a page x. Note that, for all $x \in D_k$,*

$$freq(x) = f_k \tag{4}$$

where f_k denotes the frequency of Disk D_k.

Definition 5. *The Major Cycle of the broadcast, say C, is defined by*

$$C = \sum_{x \in \mathcal{D}} freq(x). \tag{5}$$

Lemma 2. *The Major Cycle of the broadcast, C, satisfies this following property:*

$$C = \sum_{i=1}^{N} n_i f_i. \tag{6}$$

Definition 6. *For a page $x \in \mathcal{D}$, the expected delay of x, $\omega(x)$, is defined by*

$$\omega(x) = \frac{C}{2 \cdot freq(x)}. \tag{7}$$

Definition 7. *The expected delay for page requests (ω) is calculated by multiplying the probability of access with the expected delay for each page and summing the results. I.e.,*

$$\omega = \sum_{x \in \mathcal{D}} p(x) \cdot \omega(x). \tag{8}$$

Lemma 3. *Let B_i be the sum of the access probabilities of pages in Disk D_i. I.e.,*

$$B_i = \sum_{x \in D_i} p(x). \tag{9}$$

Then, B_i can be expressed as

$$B_i = \sum_{i=r_{i-1}+1}^{r_i} p_{rank}(i). \tag{10}$$

Lemma 4. *The expected delay w is expressed as*

$$\omega = \frac{C}{2} \sum_{i=1}^{N} \frac{B_i}{f_i}. \tag{11}$$

Theorem 1. *Given $\{D_i\}_{i=1,\dots,N}$, the expected delay ω has the minimum value*

$$\omega_{min} = \frac{1}{2} \left(\sum_{i=1}^{N} \sqrt{n_i B_i} \right)^2 \tag{12}$$

when each f_i, the frequency of Disk D_i, is proportional to $\sqrt{\frac{B_i}{n_i}}$, i.e., for all f_i ($1 \le i \le N$),

$$f_i = k \sqrt{\frac{B_i}{n_i}} \text{ for some fixed value } k \ (k > 0)$$

where B_i is the sum of the access probabilities of pages in Disk D_i, and n_i is the number of pages in Disk D_i.

Proof. As Lemma 4 states, the expected delay ω satisfies

$$\omega = \frac{C}{2} \sum_{i=1}^{N} \frac{B_i}{f_i}.$$

Since $C = \sum_{i=1}^{N} n_i f_i$ by (6), we have

$$\omega = \frac{1}{2} \left(\sum_{i=1}^{N} n_i f_i \right) \left(\sum_{i=1}^{N} \frac{B_i}{f_i} \right)$$

$$= \frac{1}{2} \sum_{1 \le i,\, j \le N} n_i f_i \frac{B_j}{f_j}$$

$$= \frac{1}{2} \sum_{i=1}^{N} n_i B_i + \frac{1}{2} \sum_{1 \le i \ne j \le N} n_i f_i \frac{B_j}{f_j}$$

$$= \frac{1}{2} \sum_{i=1}^{N} n_i B_i + \frac{1}{2} \sum_{1 \le i < j \le N} \left(n_i f_i \frac{B_j}{f_j} + n_j f_j \frac{B_i}{f_i} \right).$$

Using the fact that for two variables x and y, the arithmetic mean $(\frac{x+y}{2})$ is always greater than the geometric mean $(\sqrt{xy})$ except when x and y are equal[1], we have

$$n_i f_i \frac{B_j}{f_j} + n_j f_j \frac{B_i}{f_i} \ge 2\sqrt{n_i n_j B_i B_j} \text{ for each } i,\ j\ (i < j). \tag{13}$$

The equality in (13) holds when

$$n_i f_i \frac{B_j}{f_j} = n_j f_j \frac{B_i}{f_i}. \tag{14}$$

In addition,

$$n_i f_i \frac{B_j}{f_j} = n_j f_j \frac{B_i}{f_i} \Leftrightarrow f_i^2 \frac{B_j}{n_j} = f_j^2 \frac{B_i}{n_i} \Leftrightarrow f_i^2 : f_j^2 = \frac{B_i}{n_i} : \frac{B_j}{n_j} \Leftrightarrow f_i : f_j = \sqrt{\frac{B_i}{n_i}} : \sqrt{\frac{B_j}{n_j}}.$$

Therefore, when each f_i is proportional to $\sqrt{\frac{B_i}{n_i}}$ (i.e., for all f_i $(1 \le i \le N)$, $f_i = k\sqrt{\frac{B_i}{n_i}}$ for some fixed value k $(k > 0)$), since $n_i f_i \frac{B_j}{f_j} + n_j f_j \frac{B_i}{f_i}$ has the minimum value $2\sqrt{n_i n_j B_i B_j}$ for every $i,\ j$ $(i < j)$, the minimum value of the expected delay ω_{min} is expressed as follows:

$$\omega_{min} = \frac{1}{2} \sum_{i=1}^{N} n_i B_i + \frac{1}{2} \sum_{1 \le i < j \le N} 2\sqrt{n_i n_j B_i B_j}$$

$$= \frac{1}{2} \left(\sum_{i=1}^{N} \sqrt{n_i B_i} \right)^2.$$

3 Algorithms

3.1 Optimal Multidisk Segmentation

In this section, we design an algorithm that determines the number of pages for each disk based on the data access pattern in a way that minimizes the average access delay. This algorithm, called "GS (Growing Segments)" is stated in Figure 1.

---

[1] In this case, the two means are equal

```
function minDelay(Partition (r₀, r₁, ···, rₙ)) {
    for i = 1 to N {
        nᵢ = rᵢ − rᵢ₋₁;
        Bᵢ = Σ_{r=rᵢ₋₁}^{rᵢ} p_rank(r);
    }
    return ½ ( Σ_{i=1}^{N} √(nᵢBᵢ) )² ;
}
```

$$n_i = r_i - r_{i-1};$$
$$B_i = \sum_{r=r_{i-1}}^{r_i} p_{rank}(r);$$
$$\text{return } \frac{1}{2}\left(\sum_{i=1}^{N} \sqrt{n_i B_i} \right)^2;$$

```
function GS(Rank start, Rank end, int N) {
/* getNextIncrement(): returns an appropriate value for the next increment. */

    increment=getNextIncrement();
    r₀ = start;
    for i = 1 to N /* initial setup of (r₀, r₁, ···, rₙ) */
        rᵢ = rᵢ₋₁+increment;
    while(rₙ < end) do {
        increment = getNextIncrement();
        for i = 1 to N {
            p₀ = r₀;
            for k = 1 to N
                if (k ≥ i) pₖ = rₖ+increment;
                else pₖ = rₖ;
            Pᵢ = (p₀, p₁, ···, pₙ);
        }
        Find a partition (r₀, r₁, ···, rₙ) among Pᵢs such that
        minDelay(r₀, r₁, ···, rₙ)=min {minDelay(Pₖ)} for k = 1, 2, ···, N .
    }
    return (r₀, r₁, ···, rₙ);
}
```

Fig. 1. GS Algorithm

Basically, minDelay() returns the minimum expected delay for a given partition $(r_0, r_1, \cdots, r_N)$ (for more detail, see Theorem 1) and GS suggests a partition as the optimal one after taking three parameters into account: the start point of rank (*start*), the end point of rank (*end*), and the number of disks (N). Initially, GS sets up the initial rank partition that starts with the rank *start* and has N segments whose sizes are of the default increment value. For $i = 1, 2, \cdots, N$, it generates a new partition P_i whose segments are of the same size of those of the initial partition except for the ith segment. The ith segment is larger than the corresponding segment of the initial partition by the increment value. Then, the algorithm chooses the partition whose minimum expected delay is the smallest among the generated partitions. The same procedure is applied over and over until the "growing segments" cover the whole pages ($r_N = end$). As Figure 1 shows, GS allows substantial flexibility in determining the increment value at each step by calling getNextIncrement(). Not to mention, the way of deciding the next increment value will heavily affect the performance of the algorithm.

3.2   Selection of Optimal Disk Frequencies

Now, we present an algorithm that returns a list of integer disk frequencies for a given partition. As Figure 2 shows, for $i = 1, 2, \cdots, N$, the OIDF (Optimal Integer Disk Frequencies) algorithm sets n_i and B_i as minDelay() does and assigns the square root of $\frac{B_i}{n_i}$ to f_i as Theorem 1 states. Then, the algorithm adjusts f_is to make $f_N = 1$ by setting each f_i to the integer value closest to $\frac{f_i}{f_N}$, for $i = 1, 2, \cdots, N - 1$. Finally, OIDF returns the resulting frequencies. In contrast to this OIDF algorithm, assigning f_N to some integer greater than 1 may result in a little bit shorter access delay. However, in this case, the period of the broadcast program will be much larger. Since period is important for providing correct semantics for updates (e.g. as was done in Datacycle) [1, 6], we determined to set f_N to 1 so as to make the period as short as possible.

```
function OIDF(Partition (r₀, r₁, ⋯, r_N)) {
    for i = 1 to N {
        nᵢ = rᵢ − rᵢ₋₁;
        Bᵢ = Σ_{r=rᵢ₋₁}^{rᵢ} p_rank(r);
        fᵢ = √(Bᵢ/nᵢ);
    }
    for i = 1 to N − 1    /* adjust fᵢs to make f_N = 1 */
        fᵢ = ⌊fᵢ/f_N + .5⌋;
    f_N = 1;
    return (f₁, f₂, ⋯, f_N);
}
```

Fig. 2. OIDF Algorithm

4   Simulation Study

4.1   Modeling a Broadcast Disks Environment

This section addresses the simulation model that we constructed using SimJava 1.2 [8]. The structure of our simulation environment was affected by the previous simulation environments in [1, 7]. The simulator models a single server that continuously broadcasts pages and a great number of clients that continuously access pages from the broadcast. The parameters of our simulator are summarized in Table 1. In our simulation study, the main performance metric is *broadcast unit* which is the time required to broadcast a single page.

Table 1. Parameter Description

$AccessRange$	Number of pages in range accessed by clients
θ	Zipf distribution skewness parameter
$ThinkTime$	Time between client page accesses
$DBSize$	Number of distinct pages
N	Number of disks
n_i	Size of disk D_i (in pages)
f_i	Relative frequency for disk D_i
$NClients$	Number of clients in the system
$increment$	Increment for segment expansion in GS

Client Model Each client is composed of two modules, namely the *Query Generator* and the *Page Receiver*. The *Query Generator* runs a continuous loop that randomly requests a page according to a specified distribution. Pages to access are chosen from the range 1 to *AccessRange*, which is a subset of the pages that are broadcast. All pages outside this range have a zero probability of access at the client. Within the range the page access probabilities are assumed to follow a Zipf distribution [1, 11], with page 1 being the most frequently accessed, and page *AccessRange* being the least frequently accessed. The Zipf distribution adopts a parameter θ to model the degree of skewness of page accesses by assuming the probability of accessing a page numbered r to be proportional to $(1/r)^{\theta}$ as in [1]. Parameter θ is called the *access skew coefficient* and can vary from zero to one. In short, the distribution becomes increasingly "skewed" as θ increases. Once the *Query Generator* requests a page, the *Page Receiver* waits for the page to arrive on the broadcast. When the requested page arrives, the *Query Generator* makes the next request after waiting $ThinkTime$ broadcast units of time.

Server Model The server is composed of two parts: the *Database* and the *Broadcast Manager*. The *Broadcast Manager* broadcasts pages in the range of 1 to *DBSize*, where $DBSize \geq AccessRange$. The structure of the broadcast program is described by several parameters. N denotes the number of disks in the multidisk program and the disks are numbered D_1 (fastest) to D_N (slowest). For $i = 1, 2, \cdots, N$, n_i is the number of pages assigned to each disk D_i and the sum of n_i over all i is equal to the *DBSize*. The relative frequency f_i for each disk D_i has only one restriction that it must be a positive integer. In addition to those parameters that describe the server resource and the structure of the broadcast programs, parameters *NClients* and *increment* denote the number of clients in the system configuration and the increment value for the next segment expansion in the GS algorithm, respectively.

4.2   Experimental Results

Table 2 shows the parameter settings adopted in our simulation study. Throughout the experiments, both the server database size (*DBSize*) and the client access range (*AccessRange*) were varied from 500 pages to 10000 pages. Those pages were assumed to follow a Zipf distribution ($\theta = 0.95$) as in [1, 7] and the server broadcast them to 5000 clients. The *increment* value for the GS algorithm was set to 1 for the finest segment expansion granularity. We chose the three-disk broadcast configuration (i.e., N was set to 3) in all experiments except for the final experiment, where we explored the effect of the number of disks on the average and worst-case responsiveness by varying N from 2 to 10.

Table 2. Parameter Settings

DBSize	500, 1000, 2500, 5000, 7500, 10000
AccessRange	500, 1000, 2500, 5000, 7500, 10000
θ	.95
NClients	5000
N	3 (except Experiment 4)
n_i	set automatically by GS
f_i	set automatically by OIDF
ThinkTime	2.0
increment	1

Experiment 1: Optimality of GS As described in Figure 1, the GS (Growing Segments) algorithm suggests a rank partition after repeatedly expanding the segment that leads to the minimal access delay among N segments at each step until the union of segments covers the whole pages.

In this section, we show the simulation results that verify the optimality of GS. Given N, when GS returns a partition $P = (R_0, R_1, \cdots, R_N)$, the simulator examines the average access delay for five test partitions: P and four slightly changed partitions. For partition $P = (R_0, R_1, \cdots, R_N)$, the test rank partitions are generated depending on a modification parameter δ as follows:

$$\text{Test rank partition } P_\delta = (r_0, r_1, \cdots r_N) \tag{15}$$

where $r_i = \lfloor R_0 + (\frac{R_i - R_0}{R_N - R_0})^{1+\delta}(R_N - R_0) + .5 \rfloor$ for $i = 1, 2, \cdots, N$. Note that $r_0 = R_0$ and $r_N = R_N$ for any δ. In addition, if $\delta = 0$, then $r_i = R_i$ for $i = 1, 2, \cdots, N$ (i.e., $P_0 = P$). We are to show that the average access delay for $P_0 = P$ is the smallest. The values used for δ in our simulation are -0.2, -0.1, 0.0, 0.1, and 0.2. For example, when $N = 3$ and $DBSize=1000$, algorithm GS returns partition $P = (0, 22, 205, 1000)$ and the resulting test rank partitions are $P_{-0.2} = (0, 47, 281, 1000)$, $P_{-0.1} = (0, 32, 240, 1000)$, $P_{0.0} = (0, 22, 205, 1000) = P$, $P_{0.1} = (0, 15, 174, 1000)$, and $P_{0.2} = (0, 10, 149, 1000)$.

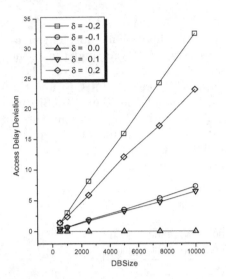
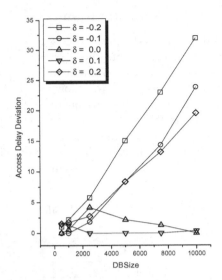

Fig. 3. Multidisk Segmentation with Ideal Frequencies

Fig. 4. Multidisk Segmentation with Integer Frequencies

In the first experiment, in order to precisely investigate the effectiveness of GS, we eliminated the effect of approximating the disk frequencies to integer values (See OIDF in Figure 1). I.e., the disk frequency f_i for each disk D_i does not take an integer value but an ideal real value proportional to $\sqrt{\frac{B_i}{n_i}}$. Figure 3 depicts the differences among the access delays of the five test partitions in terms of *access delay deviation* with varying $DBSize$. The x-axis in the figure represents $DBSize$ and the y-axis represents the access delay deviation. The access delay deviation for partition P_{test} is defined by $minDelay(P_{test}) - min\{minDelay(P_\delta)\}_{\delta=-0.2, -0.1, 0.0, 0.1, 0.2}$, where $minDelay(P_{test})$ denotes the minimum access delay for partition P_{test}. For example, when $N = 3$ and $DBSize = 1000$, the minimum access delays for $P_{-0.2} = (0, 47, 281, 1000)$, $P_{-0.1} = (0, 32, 240, 1000)$, $P_{0.0} = (0, 22, 205, 1000)$, $P_{0.1} = (0, 15, 174, 1000)$, and $P_{0.2} = (0, 10, 149, 1000)$ are 305.069, 302.708, 302.057, 302.692, and 304.42, respectively (Note that the access delay for $P_{0.0}$ is the smallest). Therefore, the access delay deviation for partition $P_{0.2}$ is $304.42 - 302.057 = 2.363$. It should be noted that the access delay deviation for partition $P_{0.0}$ is always 0. It means that, ideally, the partition returned by GS is optimal for any $DBSize$.

However, in order to practically generate broadcast programs, the relative frequency for each disk must be a positive integer. Figure 4 shows the experiment results when integer values are assigned to the disk frequencies by rounding ideal real disk frequencies to the closest integers. In Figure 4, the access delay deviation for partition $P_{0.0}$ is not always 0 (i.e., in some cases, the average access delay for other partitions is less than that of the partition suggested by GS). It means

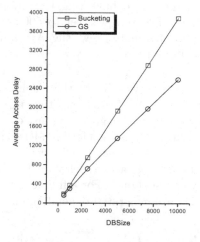
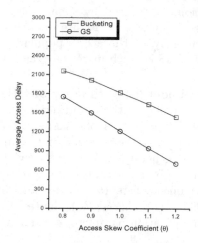

Fig. 5. GS vs. Bucketing with varying *DBSize*

Fig. 6. GS vs. Bucketing with varying θ

that, sometimes, the GS algorithm does not return the optimal rank partition for actual program generation even though the difference is small. This kind of anomaly occurs in spite of the correct behaviour of GS because OIDF forces the ideal disk frequencies to be approximated to the nearest integers during disk frequency determination. In addition, the lines in the figure are irregular for the same reason. This observation implies that using a new version of GS that returns an approximately optimal partition while incurring much less computational overhead may be more desirable than trying to find the optimal partition by strictly expanding a segment by 1 at each step.

Experiment 2: GS vs. Bucketing In [9], Nitin H. Vaidya and Sohial Hameed have presented a heuristic to determine the membership of items to buckets which correspond to broadcast disks. Their heuristic for determining the membership of an item i to a bucket B_j is as follows: Let A_{min} and A_{max} denote the minimum and maximum values of $\sqrt{p_i}$, respectively, where p_i is the access probability of i. Let $\delta = A_{max} - A_{min}$. If, for item i, $\sqrt{p_i} = A_{min}$, then item i is placed in bucket B_1. Any other item i is placed in bucket B_j ($1 \leq j \leq N$) if $(j-1)\delta/k < (\sqrt{p_i} - A_{min}) < (j\delta/k)$. However, their bucketing algorithm has a shortcoming that the algorithm concentrates too much on the probabilities of the most and least popular items.

Figure 5 summarizes our experiment on the performance of GS and bucketing with varying *DBSize* when $\theta = 0.95$. As the figure shows, GS algorithm outperforms bucketing significantly for any *DBSize*. Interestingly, the difference between access delays for two algorithms was increased as *DBSize* increases. In addition, we verified by simulation that GS is superior to bucketing for any access skewness (See Figure 6). In this experiment, *DBSize* was set to 5000. Conclusively, as the access popularity pattern becomes more skew, the access delay of GS is much more shortened than that of bucketing.

Experiment 3: Optimality of OIDF In this section, we present the results of our simulation that substantiate the optimality of OIDF. In this experiment, when N (the number of disks) and *DBSize* (the number of pages to be broadcast) are given, the rank partition returned by algorithm GS is used for broadcast program generation. As in the previous experiment on GS, once OIDF returns the list of frequencies, the simulator examines the average access delay for five test frequency lists: the optimal and four slightly changed ones. For a frequency list $FL = (F_1, F_2, \cdots, F_N)$, the test frequency lists are generated depending on the modification parameter δ as follows:

$$\text{Test frequency list } FL_\delta = (f_1, f_2, \cdots f_N) \tag{16}$$

where $f_N = 1$ and $f_i = \lfloor F_i^{1+\delta} + .5 \rfloor$ for $i = 1, 2, \cdots, N - 1$. Note that if $\delta = 0$, then $f_i = F_i$ for $i = 1, 2, \cdots, N$ (i.e., $FL_0 = FL$). The values used for δ in this experiment are -0.2, -0.1, 0.0, 0.1, and 0.2.

Figure 7 plots the differences among the access delays for the five test cases with varying *DBSize*. Note that the access delay deviation for $FL_{0.0}$ is always 0. I.e., the frequency list returned by the OIDF algorithm is optimal for any *DBSize*.

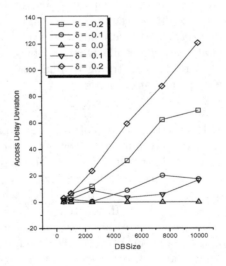

Fig. 7. Selection of Disk Frequencies

Experiment 4: Number of Disks The final goal of our simulation study is to study the effect of the number of disks in broadcast program on the access delay and the period of broadcast. In this experiment, when N (the number of disks) and $DBSize$ (the number of pages to be broadcast) are determined, the rank partition returned by GS and the resulting frequency list returned by OIDF are used. Then, the simulator examines the average access delay and the broadcast period for the generated broadcast program.

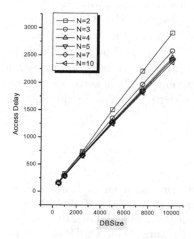
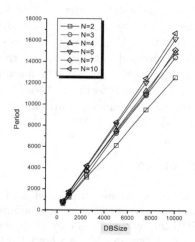

Fig. 8. Number of Disks and Acc. Delay   **Fig. 9.** Number of Disks and Period

For $N = 2, 3, 4, 5, 7, 10$, Figures 8 and 9 plot the average access delay and the broadcast period with varying $DBSize$, respectively. The simulation results show that as the number of disks (N) increases, the average access delay tends to decrease in contrast to the mostly increasing broadcast period. In other words, the more disks the broadcast program has, the more the "average responsiveness" improves regardless of the declining "worst-case responsiveness". Besides, Figure 8 shows that, in terms of average access delay, much improvement is not expected by superimposing more than 4 disks on the broadcast channel.

5   Conclusion

This paper explores the problem of optimal broadcast program generation for a hierarchical data broadcast framework called "Broadcast Disks". In order to answer the problem, we mathematically modeled the program generation mechanism and suggested concrete design principles for deciding (a) *how many disks to use*, (b) *how to segment items with similar access probabilities into disks*, and (c) *how to determine the relative spinning speeds for disks* for the *minimal average access delay*. Contributions of this paper are as follows:

- We developed a mathematical model on the optimality of broadcast program generation.
- Based on our mathematical foundation, we suggested algorithms for finding the optimal multidisk segmentation and disk frequency selection: namely GS (Growing Segments) and OIDF (Optimal Integer Disk Frequencies). By showing that the average access delay for the broadcast program structured by GS and OIDF is the smallest for all experimental cases, we substantiated the optimality of our algorithms. In addition, we showed that GS outperforms "bucketing" significantly for any database size and any access skewness.
- We addressed our analyses on the number of disks: 1) The more disks the broadcast program has, the more the "average responsiveness" improves, in contrast to the declining "worst-case responsiveness". 2) In terms of average access delay, much improvement is not expected by increasing the number of disks beyond 4.

References

1. Acharya, S., Alonso, R., Franklin, M., Zdonik, S.: Broadcast Disks: Data management for asymmetric communications evironments. Proc. of the 1995 ACM SIGMOD International Conference on Management of Data. (1995) 199–210
2. Demet Aksoy and Michael Franklin: Scheduling for Large-Scale On-Demand Data Broadcasting. Proc. of 1998 IEEE INFOCOM. (1998) 651–659
3. Acharya, S., Muthukrishman, S.: Scheduling On-demand Broadcasts: New Metrics and Algorithms. Proc. of MOBICOM '98 (1998) 43–54
4. Ammar, M., Wong, J.: The Design of Teletex Broadcast Cycles. Performance Evaluation 5(4). (1985) 235–242
5. Ammar, M., Wong, J.: On the optimality of cyclic transmission in Teletext systems. IEEE Transactions on Communications 35(1). (1987) 68–73.
6. Bowen, T., Gopal, G., Herman, G., Hickey, T., Lee, K., Mansfield, W., Raitz, J., Weinrib, A.: The Datacycle Architecture. CACM 35(12). (1992)
7. Qinglong Hu, Dik L. Lee, Wang-chien Lee: Dynamic Data Delivery in Wireless Communication Environments. ER'98.
8. http://www.dcs.ed.ac.uk/home/hase/SimJava/
9. Nitin H. Vaidya, Sohail Hameed: Scheduling data broadcast in asymmetric communication environments. ACM Wireless Networks 5. (1999) 171–182
10. Jeong-Hyon Hwang: On the Optimality of Broadcast Disks Program Generation. Master's Thesis. Korea Univ. (2000)
11. Almeida, V., Bestavros, A., Crovella, M., Oliveira, A. D.: Characterizing reference locality in the WWW. PDIS. (1996) 92–103

Optimistic Scheduling Algorithm for Mobile Transactions based on Reordering

SungSuk Kim, Chong-Sun Hwang[1], HeonChang Yu[2], and SangKeun Lee[3]

[1] Dept. of Computer Science and Engineering, Korea University
5-1, Anam-dong, Seongbuk-Ku, Seoul 136-701, Korea
{sskim, hwang}@disys.korea.ac.kr,
[2] Dept. of Computer Science Education, Korea University
yuhc@comedu.korea.ac.kr,
[3] Institute of Industrial Science, The University of Tokyo, Japan
lsk@tkl.iis.u-tokyo.ac.jp

Abstract. In this paper, we propose transaction processing algorithms in the broadcast environment. We take an optimistic approach for mobile transactions because (a) it needs a small number of messages for maintaining transactional consistency, and (b) it can make good use of broadcasting facilities from the servers. The more data conflicts occur, however, the more mobile transactions may be aborted. Thus, we accept reordering technique to reduce the number of aborted transactions; that is, whenever any kind of conflict is found from broadcast information, the system determine the operation orders without violating transactional consistency, not just aborting the mobile transactions unconditionally. The proposed algorithms - *O-Post* algorithm for update transaction and *O-Pre* algorithm for read-only transaction - do not need much information from the server while resulting in serializable executions. Finally, we also evaluate the performance behavior through simulation study

1 Introduction

Rapid advances in computer software/hardware and wireless network technologies have led to the development of mobile computing system. In this environment, mobile users retrieve information with a portable computer. The issues related with efficient information dissemination from the data server to a large volume of mobile clients has been the one of major research areas.

Broadcast disks[1] are a form of data dissemination systems. The server continuously and repeatedly pushes all data objects in the databases. The mobile clients view this broadcast as a disk and can read the values of data objects being broadcast. A periodic broadcast program is constructed to schedule the broadcast of data objects cyclically according to certain popularity criteria. Some extra broadcast slots in each broadcast cycle can be used to broadcast additional information such as the control information described below in our algorithms.

Generally, the performance for transaction processing systems highly depends on the underlying scheduling algorithms. Although data management in broadcast environments receives a lot of attention in these years, however, there are

K.-L. Tan et al. (Eds.): MDM 2001, LNCS 1987, pp. 105–117, 2001.
© Springer-Verlag Berlin Heidelberg 2001

only a few studies on transaction processing. In [13], they proposed two protocols, F-Matrix and R-Matrix for mobile read-only transactions. Although the F-Matrix shows better performance, it suffers from high overhead in terms of expensive computation and high bandwidth requirement for additional control information for consistency check. Also, they develop a new correctness criterion for transaction processing but it weakens serializability.

In [11], [12], a number of broadcast methods were introduced to guarantee correctness of read-only transactions. The multiversion broadcast approach pushes a number of versions for each data object along with the version. This method increases considerably the size of the broadcast cycle and accordingly response time. Moreover, the serialization order is fixed at the beginning of the read-only transaction. It is too restrictive and lacks flexibility. For the conflict serializability method, both the mobile clients and the server have to maintain a copy of the serialization graph for conflict checking. It incurs high overhead to maintain the serialization graph.

In this paper, we suggest new transaction processing algorithms. We choose optimistic technique because it needs a small number of messages during executing transactions. If optimistic scheduling algorithm utilizes broadcast information, it is possible to check whether the executing transactions until that time is correct or not. However, the more data conflicts occur, the more mobile transactions may be aborted. Thus, we also accept reordering technique to reduce the number of aborted transactions; that is, whenever any kind of conflict is found, the system determines the conflict operations order without violating transactional consistency, not just aborting the mobile transactions unconditionally.

The proposed algorithms - *O-Post* algorithm for update transaction and *O-Pre* algorithm for read-only transaction - do not need much information from the server to maintain the consistency and also maintain the serializability as the correctness criterion for transaction processing. The effects of various parameters on the overall performance are carefully studied with our experiments. The main contributions of our research is as following:

1. Because the proposed algorithms decrease the number of aborted transactions, mobile clients can make good use of limited resources.
2. The server's overhead can be reduced considerably because the most part of the responsibility for executing transactions is transferred to clients. Thus, the server can be a scalable system.

The remainder of this paper is organized as follows. Section 2 gives a brief overview for system model and the notion for reordering. Section 3 describes the basic algorithms and Section 4 describes related issues, say maintaining cache data. Section 5 describes the simulation model developed for the evaluation of the proposed algorithms and presents a set of experiment results. Finally, section 6 concludes the paper.

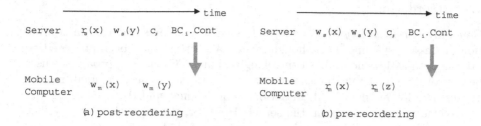

Fig. 1. examples for reordering

2   Motivation - the Notion of Reordering

2.1   System Model

Mobile computing systems are generally composed of three important parts: data server, mobile support station(MSS), mobile computer.

Data servers maintain data objects and process mobile transactions. The detailed issues related with transaction processing will be explained in the section 3. Moreover, servers periodically and repeatedly broadcasts data objects to a large mobile clients population. We assume that servers push all data objects during one cycle. That is, all data items in one cycle are in consistent state. The smallest logical unit of broadcast is called *bucket*. The first bucket of broadcast BC_i ($i \geq 1$), has a serial number i, which means that servers will start to send the $(i+1)$th periodic broadcast. Before broadcasting data object, servers will allocate some buckets for useful information, which is called $BC_i.Cont$, and send them first. The buckets contain the following information, which were collected during the last cycle:

$$BC_i.Cont = \{ Update, \ Commit, \ Abort \}$$

Update   : the identifiers of data objects updated by committed transactions
Commit : the identifiers of committed transactions
Abort   : the identifiers of aborted transactions

Mobile support stations(*MSS*) are located between data servers and mobile clients and do a role of relaying messages. Since the issues related with user's mobility are not main concerns in this paper, we assume that *MSS*s do not play an important role in our system.

The mobile clients view broadcast as a disk. Data operations are executed in optimistic manner based on data objects being broadcast. If they receive $BC_i.Cont$ while executing transactions, they examine the correctness according to some criteria. To simplify the system model, we assume that there is only one data server.

2.2 Reordering

Generally, *serializability(SR)* is adopted as the correctness criterion in transaction processing systems [4]. Although several algorithms have been proposed, we take an optimistic concurrency control algorithm(OCC). This approach seems to be appropriate in the mobile environment, because (a) it needs a small number of messages for maintaining transactional consistency, and (b) it can make use of broadcasting facilities from the server. However, the more the data conflicts occur, the more mobile transactions may be aborted. Therefore, we also accept a *reordering* technique to reduce the number of aborted transactions.

In this paper, we classify the conflict type into *w-w, w-r,* and *r-w. a-b conflict* means that the transaction which was committed in the server executed *a* operation, a mobile transaction executed *b* operation, and *a* conflicts with *b*. If a mobile transaction finds conflicts from $BC_i.Cont$, it will determine whether it should be aborted or not. Now, we will explain them in detail in the next subsection.

Update Transaction - *Post-Reordering* If *w-w* or *r-w* conflicts are found for a mobile transaction T_m, we will apply *Post-Reordering*. Consider the fig.1-(a):

The fact that T_s accessed data object x, y and committed in the server will be shown through $BC_i.Cont$. (In the detailed algorithm, the data objects read by T_s does not be sent. see below.) At the same time, T_m executed two update operations, which occur conflicts with the operations of T_s. When *r-w* or *w-w* conflicts are found, we can determine that the operations of T_s were executed first and then the write operations of T_m are executed considering data semantics. That is, if we consider the final states of the data objects, the result is the same as the decision. Therefore, we can ignore *r-w* or *w-w* conflicts, because the committed transactions in the server never depend on the updated data by T_m.

Definition 1. *If a mobile computer finds r-w or w-w conflicts from $BC_i.Cont$, it determines that the committed transactions in the server were executed before the mobile transaction. We call it Post-Reordering.*

Although *Post-Reordering* is applied to current mobile updated transactions, it has no effect on them (see also 3.1). Therefore, we can ignore the process of checking the occurrence of *r-w* or *w-w* conflicts. However, in case of *w-r* conflict, it may violate the transactional consistency among them. As a consequence, if *w-r* conflicts are found, the mobile transactions should be aborted. The server only need to send the set of updated data objects.

Lemma 1. *The Post-Reordering for $r - w$ or $w - w$ conflicts does not violate serializability*

Proof. Let us assume that *r-w* or *w-w* conflicts between T_m and $T_{si}(i \geq 1)$ have occurred after a mobile computer received control information, $BC_j.Cont$. If *w-r* conflict are found, T_m is aborted. $r-w$ or $w-w$ conflicts are concerned with write operations, $w_m(x)$, of T_m. Since T_{si} has been committed and they would never depend on the result of write operations of T_m, we can determine the conflict order as $T_{si} \to T_m$. After that, the occurrence of $r-w$ or $w-w$ conflicts, if any, also have the same ordering. Therefore the result of Post-Reordering does not violate SR. □

Read-Only Transaction - *Pre-Reordering* Unconditional abort due to w-r *conflict* in Post-Reordering may cost too much if most of transactions are read-only such as stock trading, weather information or traffic updates, etc. Therefore, whenever w-r conflict occurs for read-only transactions, we will apply *Pre-Reordering*. Consider the fig.1-(b):

In the figure, a mobile transaction T_m reads a data object x. However, the data object x was already updated by the committed transaction $T_{si}(i \geq 1)$ during the same period. When T_m listens to next period $BC_i.Cont$, it will find w-r conflict. Considering the data semantics, we can easily determine the conflict order as $T_m \to T_{si}$. That is, instead of just aborting T_m, we determine that the read operation was executed before write operations. After that, we have to execute the remaining operations in pessimistic manner not to violate the decision. Of course, the transaction should be aborted if any of the remaining operations may violate the pre-reordered semantics.

Definition 2. *If w-r conflict occurs, we determine that read operations of a mobile transaction happens before the write operations of committed transactions in the server. We call it Pre-Reordering.*

Lemma 2. *The Pre-Reordering does not violate serializabilty*

Proof. w-r conflicts are related with one or more committed update transactions, $T_{si}(i \geq 1)$ during the last period. The fact that the *Pre-Reordering* is not correct means that T_m has read the data objects which were updated by T_{si}. However, the broadcast program is generated periodically and the updated data objects will be shown only when next period broadcast starts. As a result, although w-r conflicts are found, the conflict order can be determined as pre-reordering. □

3 Optimistic Scheduling Algorithms

3.1 Optimistic Algorithm Based on Post-Reordering: *O-Post*

mobile computer's algorithm The operations of T_m are executed optimistically. When a mobile computer listens to $BC_i.Cont$, it only check the occurrence of w-r conflict; if found, it aborts T_m; otherwise, it continues to execute the remaining operations. After all data operations are executed, it has to send a commit request to the server with the following *MobileData* and waits for the result:

$$MobileData = \{\ T_{id}, ReadSet, WriteSet, BC\_id\ \}$$

T_{id} : Transaction identifier
$ReadSet$: The set of data objects which T_m has read
$WriteSet$: The set of data objects and its new value which T_m has updated
BC_id : The identifier of broadcast which T_m has received recently

From the next period $BC_i.Cont$, it can obtain the result of commit request. BC_id should be maintained to prepare against the difference between the period that the transaction sends the commit request and the server starts to check the validation for it. That is, there may be some $BC_i.Cont$ which the mobile transaction didn't listen to after sent the commit request due to the network delay and the validation processing delay. Algorithm 1 summarizes the mobile computer's algorithm.

Algorithm 1. the *O-Post* algorithm for mobile computers

◇ when receives a $r(x)$ (or $w(x, new\_value)$)
  - execute it from broadcast data
  - $ReadSet$ (or $WriteSet$) $\leftarrow x$ (or (x, new_value)).
◇ when receives a commit request
  - send the commit request with $MobileData$ and then wait.
◇ when receives $BC_i.Cont$
  if (T_m is active) /* check for the occurrence of w-r conflicts */
    - $S \leftarrow ReadSet \cap BC_i.Cont.Update.$
    - if ($S \neq null$) abort T_m;
      else $BC\_id \leftarrow i.$
  else /* when it waits for the result of commit request */
    - if ($BC_i.Cont.Commit \ni T_m.T_{id}$) commit T_m;
      else if ($BC_i.Cont.Abort \ni T_m.T_{id}$) abort T_m;
      else wait for $BC_{i+1}.Cont$

Server's algorithm The server performs the following functions:

- processing the commit requests for mobile update transactions
- collecting the necessary information for the next period control information
- broadcasting both control information and all data objects

In the server, there is one system queue for commit requests. When a request arrives, it will be enqueued and then be served in FIFO mode. When the request is dequeued, the server only check the occurrence of w-r conflict between T_m and the transactions which were committed but does not transferred to clients. That is, the server has to consider all the transactions, T_{si} ($i \geq 0$), which were committed after $MobileData.BC\_id$. The result will be added on next period control information.

Theorem 1. *Every history H generated by O-Post algorithm is serializable*

Proof. T_m is only compared with the committed transactions T_{si} ($i \geq 0$). If w-r conflicts are occurred, T_m is aborted. If r-w or w-w conflicts are found, they are post-reordered($T_{si} \rightarrow T_m$). Therefore, the history H generated by *O-Post* algorithm has no cycle; the history is always serializable.   □

3.2   Optimistic Algorithm Based on Pre-Reordering: *O-Pre*

mobile computer's algorithm When $w\text{-}r$ conflicts are occurred between T_m and T_{si} $(i \geq 1)$, we can determine that read operations are executed before update operations $(T_m \rightarrow T_{si})$.

Once T_m is *Pre-Reordered*, the remaining operations are executed in pessimistic manner. First of all, the mobile computer has to maintain $BC_i.Cont.Update$ into *UpdateList* for the remaining read operations. When a read operation $r(x)$ of the remaining operations is submitted, the mobile computer checked whether data x is an element of *UpdateList*; if so, T_m is aborted. This is to prevent the incorrect result which may be generated if the read operation is executed. For *O-Pre* algorithm, each mobile computer should maintain the following information:

$$MobileData = \{ T_{id}, ReadSet, UpdateList \}$$

T_{id} : transaction identifier
$ReadSet$: the set of data objects which T_m has read
$UpdateList$: Data objects which contain the $BC_i.Cont.Update$

UpdateList will be maintained only after the transaction was pre-reordered. Algorithm 2 summarizes the *O-Pre* algorithm for mobile read-only transactions.

Algorithm 2. the *O-Pre* algorithm for mobile computers

$\diamondsuit$ when receives a $r(x)$
    if no $w\text{-}r$ conflict occurred
        - execute $r(x)$ from broadcast data; $ReadSet \leftarrow x$
    else /* if the transaction was already pre-reordered */
        if $(x \in UpdateList)$ abort T_m
        else   execute $r(x)$; $ReadSet \leftarrow x$
$\diamondsuit$ when receives a commit request
    - commit it unconditionally
$\diamondsuit$ when receives $BC_i.Cont$
    if no $w\text{-}r$ conflict occurred
        $S \leftarrow ReadSet \cap BC_i.Update$
        if $(S \neq NULL)$ /* pre-reordering */
            $UpdateList \leftarrow UpdateList \cup BC_i.Cont.Update$
    else $UpdateList \leftarrow UpdateList \cup BC_i.Cont.Update$

As shown in the algorithm, once pre-reordered, no check for $w\text{-}r$ conflicts is needed. To explain the reason, let's assume that another $w\text{-}r$ conflicts occurred after pre-reordered. However, the decision for conflicts is similar with the previous conflicts, which does not violate the concept of pre-reordering. Of course, if the operation is related with the data objects which are the elements of *UpdateList*, T_m is aborted. Therefore, the conflict check can be omitted.

Read-only transactions can commit without contacting with the server. This is because the pre-reordering does not violate SR(Lemma 2) and the remaining operations are executed to preserve the serializability (Theorem 2).

server's algorithm Unlike *O-Post* algorithm, the server only needs to broadcast the control information and data objects.

Theorem 2. *Every history H generated by O-Pre algorithm is serializable*

Proof. If *w-r* conflict is found, the conflicts order is determined as $T_m \rightarrow T_{si}$ ($i \geq 1$) according to *pre-reordering*. After that, let's assume that another edge, $T_{sj} \rightarrow T_m$ is added into history H. At the server, all update transactions are committed in order of validation. Therefore, the new edge is added since T_{sj} was committed after pre-reordered and T_m has read the data objects which T_{sj} has updated. However, T_m can detect such conflicts by executing the remaining operations in pessimistic manner and then, will be aborted. As a consequence, the history H generated by *O-Pre* algorithm has no cycle; the history is always serializable.   □

4   Related Issues

4.1   Cache Data

Client caching reduces not only the latency but also the span of transactions, since transactions find data of interest in their local cache and thus need to access the broadcast channel for a smaller number of cycles. To maintain cache data consistent, $BC_i.Cont$ information can be very useful. The accessed data are stored into local cache and the replacement policy is LRU(Least Recently Used). If the value of cached data becomes stale, we simply assume that a form of autoprefetching is applied [2].

For data operations of mobile transactions, T_m, when it will access cache data, it can do it unconditionally. It is because that the consistency check for cache data can be delayed until next periodic $BC_i.Cont$. Of course, whenever T_m listens to $BC_i.Cont$, it has to check the consistency of cache data. The rest part of the algorithms are the same as section 3.

4.2   Disconnections

One key aspect of the mobile computing systems is the ability to deal with disconnection. There are many research efforts to cope with this problem [?], many of which are based on optimistic replication schemes and reconciliation.

In this section, we would just extend our algorithms so that the transactions can continue their remaining operations although the system has been disconnected and reconnected. To cope with disconnection, the server has to maintain the control information for the previous N period ($BC_i.Cont$ = the array [1..N] of {*Update, Commit, Abort*}); N periods turns out the tolerable period. After reconnection, clients first have to check how long they are disconnect. If they are in tolerable range, they have to check all control information which they did not listen to.

5   Experiment

5.1   Simulation Model

In this section, we aim at studying the performance of our algorithms for broadcast environments. The performance model is similar to the one presented in [1]. The server periodically broadcasts all data objects(1 to $NumOfData$). For simplicity, we assume that broadcast model is flat; that is, the server broadcasts all data objects just one time during one cycle. We also assume that there is one queue for validation in the server. When a mobile update transaction completed all data operations, the commit request is delivered to the server and then enqueued; they are processed in FIFO mode. The client accesses data objects within the range of $ReadRange$ and $WriteRange$ which are the subset of the broadcast data objects ($ReadRange, WriteRange \leq NumOfData$). The first data object for each range is selected at random. Within this range, the access probabilities follow a $Zipf$ distribution with a parameter $theta$ to model non-uniform access. Access patterns become increasingly skewed as $theta$ increases. The clients stays for $ThinkTime$ units and then executes the next data operation (we set time unit as the time needed for mobile transaction to read one data object from broadcast).

There are N mobile clients executing update transactions. Each transaction has 12 data operations. Parameter $ReadWrite$ means the rate for write operation per transaction; that is, the value of 40, for example, means that 40% are write operations. Table 1 summarizes the parameters and the default values are set. In the experiment, we don't consider the effect of disconnection.

Table 1. parameter setting

parameter	value	meaning
NumOfData	1000	total number of data in the server
CacheSize	50	the size of local cache
Bandwidth	10^6	total bandwidth of the broadcast channel
DataUnit	500	the size of each data object
Theta(θ)	5	zipf distribution parameter
ReadRange	300	access range for read operation
WriteRange	300	access range for read operation
ThinkTime	10	time between operations in broadcast units
RestartTime	10	time between aborts and restart
ReadTime	1	execution time for read operation - time unit
WriteTime	3	execution time for write operation
BCCheckTime	3	the time for validation when receive $BC.Cont$

After setting the relevant parameters, we implemented the simulator. In the experiments, we compare our algorithms both with Invalidation-Only method in case of update transaction. In case of read-only transaction, Invalidation-Only method, Multiversion method are considered [12]. Note that Invalidation-Only method does not consider update transactions. However, we choose it since its environment is very similar to ours. For the experiment, we change Invalidation-Only method a little; namely, clients executes update transactions optimistically. When all operations are completed, it also requests commit for the server, which validates the request identically with *O-Post* algorithm. For Multiversion method, mobile computers maintain cache data and also accept the same form of autoprefetching.

Per each mobile client, 100 transactions are executed per client and the average value is taken from the result. Both abort rate and response time are measured to compare the performance. In case of abort rate, the value of 10, for example, means that 10 % of the transactions are aborted more than one time.

5.2   Experimental Result

We choose two main experiment components to compare the performance for update transaction. The first is the number of clients. Each client executes the update transactions. Therefore, the probability of the occurrence of conflicts will be higher as the number of clients increases. The second one is the number of write operation per transaction. We assume that each update transaction executes 12 data operations. In addition to both components, we may consider various parameters such as hot spot data, local interest data, disconnection, and so on which have an effect on the performance. However, due to the limitation of the space of the paper, we will not touch those factors.

Figure 2, 3 show the comparative results obtained by executing update transactions. Abort rate, n, means that n % among total transactions in a client are aborted more than once. In case of (a), the performance is evaluated with respect to the number of clients and the number of write operation is 3. In case of (b), while the number of clients is fixed ($= 40$), the number of write operation per transaction varies. As the value in both parameters increases, many data objects are updated, thereby resulting in higher conflict rate. Figure 2 shows that proposed *O-Post* algorithm less sensitive to the parameter than Invalidation-Only algorithm. In particular, while almost transactions in Invalidation-Only are aborted more than once under high conflict rate, several transactions in O-Post can continue the remaining operations without being aborted. If our algorithm makes use of cache data, the transaction span decreases and therefore, abort rate is lower because the transaction listens to a fewer *BC.Cont*.

Since response time means the passed time from the start of transaction until the commit, the frequent abort makes worse the response time. In figure 3, the reason that performance differences between algorithms is relatively lower in case of (a) than (b) is paradoxically higher abort rate of Invalidation-Only method; that is, many transactions are aborted frequently, and therefore the number of updated data is small.

The point to note for update transaction is that *O-Post* algorithm is not very sensitive to the number of write operation. This is because the algorithm does

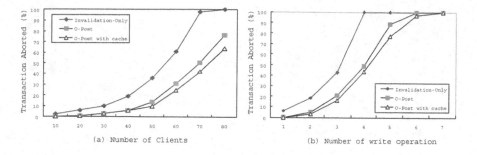

Fig. 2. Abort rate for update transaction

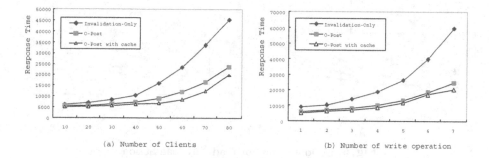

Fig. 3. response time for update transaction

not have an effect on the conflicts which occur due to write operations of mobile transaction.

Figure 4, 5 relate with read-only transaction. To compare the performance for read-only transaction, we changed the two parameters: (a) the number of updated data object during one cycle and (b) the number of data operation per transaction. For the case of (a), we assume that each transaction executes 10 read operations. Since read-only transaction does not interfere with each other and the result for updated transaction is shown until next period, we consider just one mobile client and one server in this experiment. The performance is compared with Invalidation-Only algorithm and Multiversion algorithm [11],[12]. Basic Multiversion method is used and 3 old versions are transmitted.

The results of Invalidation-Only algorithm is similar to those for update transaction. However, Multiversion shows opposite results for abort rate and response time. Since the server sends multiple version, the algorithm maintains abort rate low. Since the size of broadcast disk considerably increases, response time justly makes worse. While *O-Pre* shows comparatively low abort rate, the response time can be approved highly. This result can obtain due to the following reasons: comparatively low abort rate is obtained from reordering and the size of broadcast rarely increases, thereby improving response time. In particular,

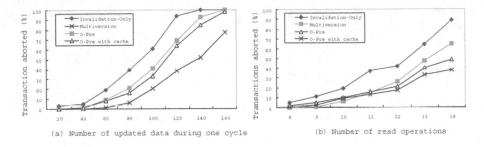

Fig. 4. Abort rate for read-only transaction

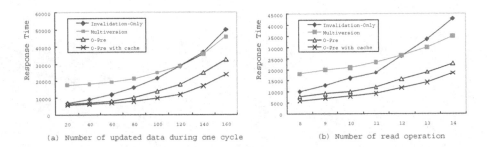

Fig. 5. response time for read-only transaction

O-Pre algorithm shares in benefits of cache data than *O-Post* algorithm since it can commit read-only transactions without contacting with the server.

6   Conclusion and Future Work

We presented two scheduling algorithms- *O-Post* and *O-Pre*- in the broadcast environments. These algorithms are highly based on the optimistic technique. We also accept a reordering technique to reduce the number of aborted transactions, which utilizes the transactional consistency.

By using our algorithms, the server side and the client side can have the virtue as following:

1. Because the proposed algorithms decrease the number of aborted transactions, mobile clients can make good use of limited resources.
2. The server's overhead can be reduced considerably because the most part of the responsibility for executing transactions is transferred to clients. Thus, the server can be a scalable system.

However, as shown in the simulation results, our algorithms cannot be free from high abort rate. That is, due to optimistic execution, a lot of transactions must be aborted in spite of applying reordering technique as conflicts occur more frequently. Therefore we have to devise another algorithms which overcome the above limitation.

In addition, we simply assume that the broadcast from the server is flat disk model[1]. In practice, the organization of broadcast disk deeply affects the performance for transaction processing in the broadcast-based systems. Therefore, we should analyze the properties of broadcast disk.

References

1. S.Acharya, R.Alonso, M.Franklin, and S.Zdonik.: Broadcast Disks: Data Management for Asymmetric Communications Environments. *Proceedings of the ACM SIGMOD Conference on Management of Data*, pp. 199-210, 1995. 105, 113, 117
2. S.Acharya, M.Franklin, and S.Zdonik.: Disseminating Updates on Broadcast Disks. *Proceedings of 22nd International conference on Very Large DataBases*, 1996. 112
3. D.Barbara.: Certification Reports: Supporting Transactions in Wireless Systems. *Proceedings of the 17th IEEE International Conference on Distributed Computing Systems*, pp. 466-473, 1997.
4. P. A. Bernstein, V.Hadzilacos, and N.Goodman.: *Concurrency Control and Recovery in Database Systems*. Addison Wesley, Reading, Massachusetts, 1987. 108
5. D. Barbara and T. Imielinski.: Sleepers and Workaholics: Caching Strategies in Mobile Environments. *Proceedings of the ACM SIGMOD Conference on Management of Data*, pp. 1-12, 1994.
6. M.H. Dunham and A. Helal.: Mobile Computing and Databases: Anything New? *ACM SIGMOD Record*, Vol. 24, No. 4, pp. 5-9, 1995.
7. Q. Hu, W-C. Lee and D.L.Lee.: Indexing Techniques for Wireless Data Broadcast under Data Clustering and Scheduling. *Proceedings of International Conference on Information and Knowledge Management*, pp. 351-358, 1999.
8. P. Lie, P. Ammann and S. Jahodia.: Incorporating Transactions Semantics to Reduce Reprocessing Overhead in Replicated Mobile Data Application *Proceedings of the International Conference on Distributed Computing Systems*, pp. 414-423, 1999.
9. Y. Lee and S. Moon.: Commit-Reordering Validation Scheme for Transaction Scheduling in Client-Server Based Teleputing Systems: COREV. *Proceedings of the International Conference on Information and Knowledge Management*, pp. 59-66. 1997.
10. S.H. Phatak and B.R. Badrinath.: Conflict Resolution and Reconciliation in Disconnected Databases *10th International Workshop on Database and Expert Systems Applications*, pp. 1-6, 1999.
11. E. Pitoura and P. Chrysanthis.: Exploiting Versions for Handling Updates in Broadcast Disks. *Proceedings of the International Conference on Very Large Data Bases*, pp. 114-125, 1999. 106, 115
12. E. Pitoura and P. Chrysanthis.: Scalable Processing of Read-Only Transactions in Broadcast Push. *Proceedings of the 19th IEEE International Conference on Distributed Computing system*, pp. 432-441, 1999. 106, 114, 115
13. J.Shanmugasundaram, A.Nithrakashyap, R.Sivasankaran, and K.Ramamritham.: Efficient Concurrency Control for Broadcast Environments *Proceedings of the ACM SIGMOD Conference on Management of Data*, pp. 85-96, 1999. 106

Session IV: Caching and Hoarding

Bandwidth-Conserving Cache Validation Schemes in a Mobile Database System*

Hyunchul Kang and Sangmin Lim

Department of Computer Sci. & Eng., Chung-Ang University, Seoul, 156-756, Korea
{hckang,smlim}@rose.cse.cau.ac.kr

Abstract. In a mobile dabase system, *caching* at a mobile host could conserve the limited wireless bandwidth while reducing the query response time, and yet *cache consistency* needs to be maintained. The basic cache consistency scheme is for the server to periodically broadcast an *invalidation report* that identifies the updated data objects so that the mobile hosts may purge the stale data objects from their caches. In case that long period of disconnection prevents a reconnecting mobile host from guaranteeing validity of its cache based solely on the invalidation report received, the mobile host could request the server to check validity of its cache. In this paper, we propose a set of new *cache validation schemes* that can efficiently conserve the bandwidth both in cache validation and query processing afterwards. The performance of our schemes is evaluated through the detailed simulation experiments.

1 Introduction

Thanks to advance of wireless communication technology, users are now able to get data service not just at the fixed location on the wired network but at any place in the wireless network environment [2]. Fig. 1 depicts a generic architecture of the mobile computing environment. There are two types of hosts: *fixed* and *mobile*. The fixed ones are connected to the wired communication network and some of them called *MSS (Mobile Support Station)* are equipped with the wireless communication interface to communicate with the mobile hosts. Each MSS (the server) covers a certain physical area called a *cell* employing some wireless communication technology, and communicates with the mobile hosts within the cell through wireless channels. A mobile host can move within a cell or among the cells while maintaining its network connection.

One characteristic of the mobile computing environment is that the network bandwidth of a wireless channel is very limited compared to that in the wired network environment. As such, *caching* whereby the frequently accessed data objects are brought into the non-volatile memory of the mobile host is one of the core mobile data management technologies, and has been widely investigated. Caching could result in reduction of query response time, conservation of the network bandwidth, and thus, of the battery of the mobile host, and

---

* This work was supported by the Chung-Ang University Research Grants in 2000.

K.-L. Tan et al. (Eds.): MDM 2001, LNCS 1987, pp. 121–130, 2001.
© Springer-Verlag Berlin Heidelberg 2001

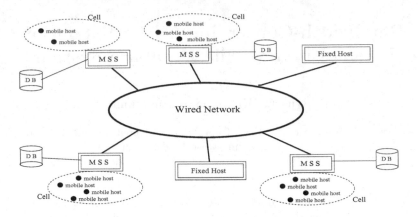

Fig. 1. Mobile Computing Environment

yet incurs the overhead of *cache consistency maintenance*, requiring the efficient cache consistency schemes. In [1], the cache consistency schemes with the *stateless* server that are employing the *invalidation report* were proposed. The server periodically broadcasts to all the mobile hosts in the cell the invalidation report which identifies which data objects were updated at the server and their last update timestamps. The mobile hosts listen to the report and purge the stale data objects from their caches by comparing the update timestamps.

The basic problem with the above approach is the *disconnection* of the mobile hosts from the network. The network connectivity of the mobile computing environment is not so stable as in the wired network counterpart, sometimes disconnecting the active mobile hosts from the network. Besides, the battery life of the mobile hosts is also not long enough, and to conserve the battery, the mobile hosts often operate in a doze mode or are completely turned off. As such, the mobile host could miss the invalidation report because of disconnection, and cannot guarantee validity of its cache when it reconnects, forced to discard the entire cache. Since the entire cache was invalidated, the forthcoming queries will experience bulk of cache misses, incurring costly bandwidth consumption which could have been avoided.

[5] investigates the alternative approach where instead of invalidating the entire cache in such a case, the mobile host contacts the server through the uplink channel to request for the server to validate its cache. There is a performance tradeoff in the cache validation approach in terms of bandwidth requirement. The process of cache validation requires the bandwidth. In return for that, the forthcoming queries referencing those objects retained in the cache could conserve the bandwidth.

In this paper, we propose a set of new cache validation schemes called *2PCV (2 Phase Cache Validation)*, *1PCV (1 Phase Cache Validation)*, and *BCV (Broadcast Cache Validation)* that can efficiently conserve the bandwidth both in the process of checking cache validity and in query processing afterwards.

The rest of this paper is organized as follows: Section 2 reviews the previous cache consistency schemes in the mobile database system. Section 3 proposes three new cache validation schemes. Section 4 presents the results of performance evaluation. Finally concluding remarks are in Section 5.

2 Previous Cache Consistency Schemes

In this section, the cache consistency schemes in the literature directly related to this paper are reviewed. In those schemes, it is assumed that the database is fully replicated at each server (MSS) connected to the wired network, and the timestamp of the last update for each data object in the database are maintained. The mobile hosts are to perform queries only, and the update transactions are executed only at the server. The data object referenced by a query is retrieved from the cache, and if cache miss occurs, the corresponding data object with its most recent update timestamp is requested to the server to be cached. For cache consistency, the server periodically broadcasts the invalidation report. In case that a mobile host wakes up from a long period of disconnection and the invalidation report received is of no use in guaranteeing validity of the cache, either the entire cache is dropped or some cache validation scheme is employed to retain as many valid data objects as possible.

2.1 Schemes TS, AT, and BS

A series of steps repeated by a mobile host in the cache consistency schemes, called *TS (Broadcasting Timestamps)* and *AT (Amnesic Terminals)*, proposed in [1] are as follows:

1. Listen to the next invalidation report.
2. If cache validity can be guaranteed with the invalidation report received, delete the stale data objects from the cache and go to step 4.
3. Drop the entire cache.
4. Process all the pending queries submitted before the current invalidation report is received.
5. Record the timestamp of the current invalidation report.

Scheme AT [1] is similar to TS except that the server broadcasts only the identifiers of the data objects that were updated since the last invalidation report. Thus, AT reduces the bandwidth consumption in broadcasting compared to TS but the mobile host which misses at least one invalidation report is forced to discard the entire cache.

[3] addresses the problem of optimizing the invalidation report size, proposing the scheme called *BS (Bit-Sequences)*. The basic technique in BS is called *bit-sequence naming* which employs a sequence of N bits where N is the number of data objects in the database. Each bit represents a data object in the database, and indicates the update status of the corresponding data object. As such, the naming space for N objects is reduced to N bits from $NlogN$ bits. Such a bit sequence and the timestamp information comprise the invalidation report to conserve the bandwidth while maintaining the cache invalidation effectiveness.

2.2   Schemes SCC, SGC, and GCORE

[5] investigates the cache validation schemes called *SCC (Simple Checking Caching)* and *SGC (Simple Grouping Caching)*, and proposes a scheme called *GCORE (Grouping with Cold Update Set Retention)*. In these schemes, a reconnecting mobile host first listens to the next invalidation report. If cache validity can be guaranteed with the invalidation report received, the mobile host is already in the *normal operating mode*, deleting the stale data objects from the cache, processing queries, and listening to the next invalidation report and so on. Otherwise, it deletes the data objects identified as stale according to the current invalidation report from the cache, and then for the rest of the data objects in the cache, it contacts the server through the uplink channel to verify their validity. After cache validation is done, the mobile host enters the normal operating mode.

In SCC, the mobile host sends the server the identifiers of all the data objects in its cache and the timestamp of the invalidation report it has received most recently. Then, the server notifies to the mobile host which objects are still valid and which are now obsolete by comparing the timestamp sent with the timestamps of the data objects. In doing so, a *bit vector* where each bit indicates the update status of the corresponding data object could be used to conserve the bandwidth.

SCC usually consumes quite a large amount of bandwidth because the identifiers of all the data objects in the cache are sent to the server. To alleviate bandwidth requirement, in SGC, cache validation is done at the group level. The database is partitioned into groups according to some rules so that each data object is mapped to a unique group. The mobile host sends the server the identifiers of the groups represented in its cache instead of the data object identifiers. Then, the server informs the mobile host of groups' validity, and the mobile host deletes all the data objects that belong to the invalid groups from its cache.

Although SGC can considerably conserve the bandwidth compared to SCC, there is the *false invalidation* problem with SGC, the phenomenon where the valid data object is invalidated from the cache just because it belongs to an invalid group. False invalidation of a data object eventually incurs bandwidth consumption if the query that references it is processed, requesting the server to send it back to the mobile host.

To overcome the limitation of SGC, GCORE tries to avoid invalidating the invalid group in its entirety. It considers the fact that the database consists of the *hot update set* and the *cold update set*. The former represents the set of data objects frequently updated at the server while the latter is the set of data objects rarely updated. The data objects of the hot update set are to be often invalidated if they are cached. As such, for an invalid group, instead of invalidating the entire group, GCORE could retain the data objects of the cold update set if all the updated objects (most likely belong to the hot update set) have been included in the most recently broadcasted invalidation report [5]. Although GCORE could salvage more data objects in the cache than SGC, it requires the server to maintain the history of data object updates done over the *invalidation broadcast window* longer than that in TS of [1], and to maintain the group update history for each group. Besides, GCORE could still suffer from false invalidation and might have to drop the entire cache in case that the mobile host wakes up after a long period of disconnection.

3   Bandwidth-Conserving Cache Validation Schemes

As we have seen in the previous sections, a basic problem with the conventional cache validation schemes is that bandwidth requirement could be high either in the cache verification process or in query processing afterwards. This problem gets more apparent as the number of data objects cached into the mobile host increases. Another problem with cache validation is that the contention on the wireless channels could be quite severe if a number of mobile hosts try to validate their caches almost at the same time. Such a case could be observed when the daily work begins in the morning, for example. In this section, we propose three new cache validation schemes that can efficiently deal with these problems in order to conserve the bandwidth.

When a reconnecting mobile host needs to check the validity of its cache with the server, SCC described in [5] should not be employed because its bandwidth requirement is too high. Rather, some grouping-based scheme should be used. However, SGC is prone to falsely invalidate the cache, resulting in high bandwidth consumption in later query processing. As such, a new cache validation scheme that is *grouping-based but avoids false invalidation* is desired.

When the reconnecting mobile hosts try to validate their caches, they first have to acquire the wireless channels. If the number of the reconnecting mobile hosts is far more than the number of available channels, the delay of cache validation at each mobile host could be quite long because of the severe contention on the channels with limited bandwidth. Besides, the bandwidth consumed by the server to reply to each of the mobile hosts separately with information on the validity of the cache gets very high. In such a situation, it could be more efficient for the server to *broadcast* the validity information through the broadcast channel to all the mobile hosts in the cell. The rationale behind such broadcasting is that most of the mobile hosts in the cell might have cached considerable amount of common data objects, say the hot data objects. As such, a new cache validation scheme that *incorporates broadcasting* deserves investigation.

3.1   Message Types and Data Structures

The messages transmitted between the server and the mobile hosts for cache consistency are in Table 1, where *Type*, *OID*, *GID*, and *MHID* denote the message type, the data object identifier, the group identifier, and the mobile host identifier, respectively.

IR is the invalidation report periodically broadcasted by the server. It consists of (timestamp, OID-list) pairs, and identifies the data objects updated in the

Table 1. Message types and Data Structures

Type		Data Structure
Broadcasted Invalidation Report (IR)		Type, $(T_i, \text{OID}, \text{OID}, \ldots)$, $\ldots, (T_{i-k+1}, \text{OID}, \text{OID}, \ldots)$
Request of Data Object (Req_D)		Type, OID
Data Object (D)		Type, Data Object
Request of Invalidation Report (Req_IR)	Req_IR_o	Type, T_l, (OID, OID, …)
	Req_IR_g	Type, T_l, (GID, GID, …)
Requested Invalidation Report (RIR)	RIR_o	Type, (OID, OID, …)
	RIR_g	Type, (GID, GID, …)
Request of Validation Report (Req_VR)	Req_IR_o	Type, T_l, (OID, OID, …)
	Req_VR_g	Type, T_l, (GID, GID, …)
Validation Report (VR)	VR_o	Type, $MHID$, T_l, (OID, OID, …)
	VR_g	Type, T_l, T_c, (GID, GID, …)

last k broadcast intervals. That is, the size of the invalidation broadcast window is w which equals to kL seconds where IR is broadcasted every L seconds at times $T_i = iL$. The first (timestamp, OID-list) pair of IR broadcasted at T_i is $(T_i, OID, OID, \ldots)$ where $OIDs$ are the identifiers of the data objects updated in the time interval $[T_{i-1}, T_i]$. Similarly, the last (timestamp, OID-list) pair of IR broadcasted at T_i is $(T_{i-k+1}, OID, OID, \ldots)$ where $OIDs$ are the identifiers of the data objects updated in the time interval $[T_{i-k}, T_{i-k+1}]$.

Req_D is the message for the mobile host to send to the server at cache miss to request (and cache) the missed data object, and D is the response of the server to Req_D, sending the requested data to the mobile host.

Both Req_IR and Req_VR are the messages for the mobile host to send to the server to request information on the validity of its cache, where those data objects whose validity needs to be checked could be delivered either with the list of data object identifiers or with the list of group identifiers. Req_IR_o (Req_VR_o) denotes the former case while Req_IR_g (Req_VR_g) denotes the latter. Req_IR and Req_VR are the messages equivalent to each other in terms of the purpose and contents, and yet the server's response to each message is different (see below). T_l denotes the timestamp of the most recent IR the mobile host has received, informing the server of the mobile host's disconnection point.

RIR and VR are the responses of the server to the messages Req_IR and Req_VR, respectively. RIR is the message to identify the data objects that are now invalid at the cache, whereas VR is the message to identify the data objects that are still valid at the cache. Another important difference between the two messages is that RIR is to be sent only to the mobile host which sent the server the corresponding Req_IR message, while VR is broadcasted to all the mobile hosts in the cell not just to the mobile host which sent the server the corresponding Req_VR message. T_l of VR is the very timestamp which the mobile host sent to the server in Req_VR, indicating the mobile host's disconnection point. T_l and the current time, which is more specifically the time when the most recent IR was broadcasted by the server, specify the time interval during which the data objects listed in VR have not been updated. $MHID$ of VR is to indicate which mobile host has requested this VR. It is necessary because VR is broadcasted. As in Req_IR and Req_VR, the data objects to be purged from the cache (RIR) and the data objects to be retained in the cache (VR) could be sent to the mobile host either with the list of data object identifiers or with the list of group identifiers. RIR_o (VR_o) denotes the former case while RIR_g (VR_g) denotes the latter.

3.2   Cache Validation Schemes Avoiding False Invalidation

In this section, two cache validation schemes are proposed that are grouping-based but avoid false invalidation.

2 Phase Cache Validation *2 Phase Cache Validation* (*2PCV*, hereafter) could be more efficient than both SCC and SGC. It allows the mobile host to retain as many valid data objects as SCC would retain without sending the entire list of identifiers of data objects in its cache. Besides, contrary to SGC, it does not falsely invalidate the cache.

In 2PCV, a mobile host checks validity of its cache with the server in two phases. In the first phase, the mobile host sends the server the identifiers of the groups represented in its cache with the timestamp of the most recent invalidation report it has received. Then, the server replies to the mobile host, sending the obsolete group identifiers. After this phase, the mobile host could retain as many valid data objects as SGC could. In the second phase, the mobile host sends to the server the identifiers of the data objects that belong to the groups identified as obsolete in the first phase. Then, the server replies to the mobile host, sending the obsolete data object identifiers. After this phase, the mobile host now retains as many valid data objects as SCC could.

1 Phase Cache Validation The disadvantage of 2PCV is that the mobile host needs to send to and receive from the server messages in two phases, consuming the bandwidth in both phases. If the number of groups whose validity need be checked is large or if the number of data objects that belong to the groups identified as obsolete is large, performance of 2PCV is expected to be poor because of high bandwidth requirement. As such, a false invalidation-free scheme that conducts cache validation in one phase is desirable. Such a 1 phase cache validation (*1PCV*, hereafter) could be realized as follows:

When the server receives from the mobile host the identifiers of the groups represented in the cache with the timestamp of the most recent invalidation report the mobile host has received, the server replies to the mobile host with the data object identifiers, *not the group identifiers*, for those data objects that belong to the groups whose identifiers were received and are now stale in the cache.

1PCV is a scheme that downgrades the granularity of the identifiers transmitted between the server and the mobile hosts. The disadvantage of 1PCV is that the server may possibly send the mobile host the irrelevant information as well, that is, the identifiers of the data objects that belong to the obsolete group but not cached there. Despite that, if the update ratio is not high, 1PCV could be an efficient scheme, conserving the bandwidth.

3.3   Broadcast Cache Validation

In this section, a cache validation scheme called *Broadcast Cache Validation* (*BCV*, hereafter) that features the broadcast by the server is proposed. BCV is effective when the number of available channels is far less than the number of reconnecting mobile hosts that are supposed to validate their caches, competing for the channels that might hardly be allocated.

When the contention on the channels is severe, the mobile host that is to validate its cache is very likely to suffer from possibly unpredictable long delays. To resolve the problem while conducting cache validation, BCV works as follows:

The mobile host first initializes *Req_VR* message by listing the identifiers of all the cached data objects whose validity status is not known. Then, while it is waiting for a channel, instead of doing nothing, it listens to the broadcasted *VR*s, which other mobile hosts have requested with the *Req_VR* messages, in order to remove the identifiers of the data objects whose validity is certified from its *Req_VR* message. Such validity certification is possible because *VR* identifies (1) a time interval $[a, b]$ where $a = T_l$ of *VR* and b is the current time (more specifically, the time of the most recent *IR* broadcasted by the server) and (2) the data objects that are not updated in that interval (refer to Section 3.1 and Table 1), and because each mobile host maintains the timestamp (i.e., T_l) of the last *IR* it has received. As such, the mobile host waiting for a channel could reduce the size of its *Req_VR* message, resulting in the reduction of bandwidth consumption eventually when a channel is allocated. This reduction could be significant if most of the reconnecting mobile hosts have cached a large set of common data objects.

4   Performance Evaluation

The performance of the schemes proposed in this paper is evaluated through a set of detailed simulation experiments. Our simulator consists of two subsystems: the mobile host and the server communicating with each other through the *Communication Managers*. The server is modeled with the *Transaction Generator*, the *Invalidation Report Broadcaster*, the *Update Log Manager*, the *Data Object/Group Validity Checker*, and the *Data Object Manager*, whereas the mobile host is modeled with the *Query Generator*, the *Cache Validation Processor*,

Table 2. Simulation Parameters

Parameter	Description	Setting
DatabaseSize	size of the database at the server	100,000 objects
CacheSize	size of the cache at a mobile host	5,000 objects
ObjectSize	size of an object	256 bytes
GroupSize	size of a group	100 objects
IDSize	size of an identifier	64 bits
TimestampSize	size of a timestamp	64 bits
UplinkBandwidth	bandwidth allocated between a mobile host and the server	1.2 KBytes/sec
DownlinkBandwidth	bandwidth allocated for broadcasting by the server	1.2 KBytes/sec
BroadcastInterval	interval between two consecutive IRs	20 sec
w	invalidation broadcast window	10 IR intervals
TranArrRate	arrival rate of update transactions at the server	0.01 Xactions/sec
UpdObjPerTran	average number of objects updated by a transaction	5 objects
HotUpdRegRatio	ratio of hot update region size to database size	0.1
HotUpdProb	probability of updating the hot update region	0.9
QueryArrRate	arrival rate of queries at the mobile host	0.1 query/sec
RefObjPerQuery	average number of objects referenced by a query	20
DisconnectProb	probability of mobile host being disconnected after processing a query	0.1
DisconnectTime	average time for disconnection	700 sec
ChannelCompete	channel competition as the number of mobile hosts per channel	$1 \sim 150$

the *Query Processor*, the *Query Queue*, the *Cache Manager*, and the *Connection Status Manager*. Our simulator was implemented in Visual C++ 6.0 with C++SIM [4], a simulation library for C++, in Windows NT 4.0.

4.1 Performance Metric and Simulation Parameters

There is a tradeoff in terms of bandwidth consumption between the cache verification process and query processing afterwards. As such, the performance metric is defined as the sum of bandwidth consumption both in the cache verification process and in query processing afterwards. The simulation parameters are summarized in Table 2. The baseline parameter settings are in Table 2, which are sustained throughout our experiments unless stated otherwise.

4.2   Experimental Results

Fig. 2 ~ Fig. 7 show the bandwidth consumption in the schemes compared with respect to some varying parameters. The summary of the experimental results is as follows:

1. As the group size, the size of the hot update region of the database, or the object size increases, performance of our 2PCV and 1PCV that are false invalidation free did not degrade, while that of the conventional SGC scheme which suffers from false invalidation degraded considerably.
2. Performance comparison between the proposed 2PCV and 1PCV shows that if the cache size is small and the update frequency at the server is high, 2PCV outperforms 1PCV. Otherwise, 1PCV is superior to 2PCV.
3. BCV is the best scheme under the severe contention on the uplink channels by the reconnecting mobile hosts. However, when the contention is not so severe, BCV performs poorly.

5   Concluding Remarks

Some further works currently under way on cache validation include the followings: First, further performance enhancement could be possible in our 2PCV and 1PCV by optimizing the size of the server's response to the mobile host's request of cache verification. Seconly, the update propagation, whereby the stale data objects are not dropped from the cache but replaced with the up-to-date copies propagated from the server, could be adopted to further conserve the bandwidth in our schemes. Thirdly, the process of cache validation could be interleaved with query processing, reducing the query response time while not consuming the additional bandwidth.

References

1. Barbara, D. and Imielinski, T.: Sleepers and Workaholics : Caching Strategies in Mobile Environments. Proc. ACM SIGMOD Int'l Conf. on Management of Data (1994) 1–12   122, 123, 123, 125
2. Barbara, D.: Mobile Computing and Databases - A Survey. IEEE Transactions on Knowledge and Data Engineering **11(1)** Jan./Feb. (1999) 108–117   121
3. Jing, J. et al: Bit-Sequences: An Adaptive Cache Invalidation Method in Mobile Client/Server Environments. ACM/Baltzer Mobile Networks and Applications **2(2)** (1997)   123
4. Little, M. and McCue, D.: Construction and Use of a Simulation Package in C++. Technical Report 437, Department of Computing Science, University of Newcastle upon Tyne, Jul. (1993)   129
5. Wu, K. et al: Energy-Efficient Caching for Wireless Mobile Computing. Proc. IEEE Int'l Conf. on Data Eng. (1996) 336–343   122, 124, 124, 125

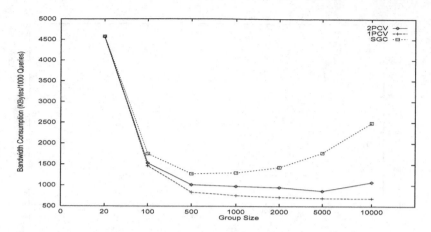

Fig. 2. Bandwidth Consumption vs. Group Size

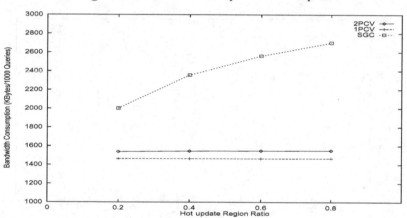

Fig. 3. Bandwidth Consumption vs. Size of Hot Update Region

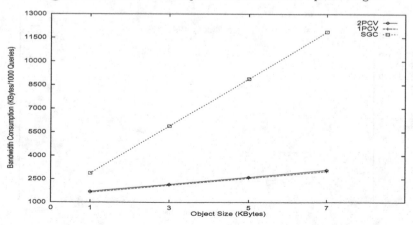

Fig. 4. Bandwidth Consumption vs. Object Size

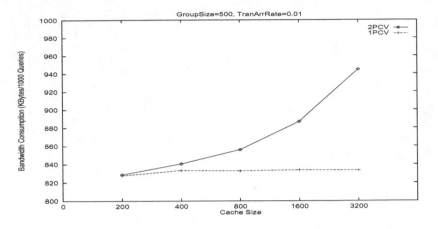

Fig. 5. Bandwidth Consumption vs. Cache Size

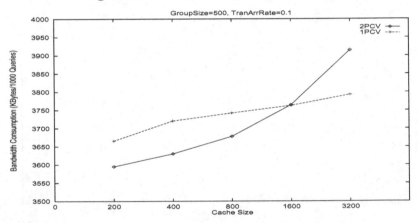

Fig. 6. Bandwidth Consumption vs. Cache Size

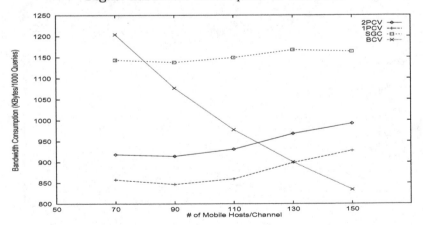

Fig. 7. Bandwidth Consumption vs. # of Mobile Hosts/Channel

Quasi-consistency and Caching with Broadcast Disks

Rashmi Srinivasa   and   Sang H. Son

Department of Computer Science
University of Virginia
Charlottesville, VA
{rashmi, son}@cs.virginia.edu

Abstract. The challenges ensuing from the asymmetric communication capabilities of mobile environments have led to an increased interest in broadcast-based data dissemination. Among the concurrency control (CC) techniques for transactional clients in broadcast environments, BCC-TI has been shown to be more efficient than a traditional technique [1]. We propose two ways of improving CC performance in broadcast environments: caching and a weaker consistency criterion. We demonstrate that caching improves query response time in BCC-TI. We propose a new CC technique called Quasi-TI that enforces a correctness criterion called quasi-consistency [2] — useful when serializability is too expensive to enforce. We introduce a new caching scheme (PIT) and study its effects on Quasi-TI's performance. Through simulation, we demonstrate the benefits of the proposed techniques.

1   Introduction

In asymmetric communication environments, server-to-client capacity is greater than client-to-server capacity, because of physical attributes (e.g. mobile systems with cellular uplinks) or workload characteristics (e.g. a very large number of clients). Transmission by mobile systems over the air is monetarily expensive due to limited bandwidth [3]. In such environments, pull-based techniques are ineffective, and data dissemination techniques like broadcast disks are popular [4, 5, 6, 7, 8, 9, 10, 11]. Many applications in broadcast environments involve a large number of read-only transactions. In information dispersal systems for stock or auction data, numerous speculators read prices frequently, making efficient query processing essential. Many systems have real-time constraints too (e.g. deadlines to avoid financial loss).

CC techniques have been proposed for transactional clients in broadcast environments. Broadcast CC using Timestamp Interval (BCC-TI) achieves serializability more efficiently than a traditional technique [1]. We explore two ways of improving CC performance in broadcast environments: a weaker consistency criterion, and caching. We propose a new CC technique called Quasi-TI that uses timestamp intervals. Quasi-TI guarantees a weaker consistency criterion (quasi-consistency [2]), which allows a controlled amount of imprecision in the data read by a query. Quasi-TI results in lower query response times than BCC-TI. We propose a new caching scheme (PIT) and study the effects of caching on Quasi-TI and BCC-TI.

K.-L. Tan et al. (Eds.): MDM 2001, LNCS 1987, pp. 133-144, 2001.

2   Related Work

Broadcast-based data dissemination has been studied extensively over a few years [3, 12, 14]. In a broadcast disk model, the server broadcasts all objects in its database in a *broadcast cycle* and the cycle is executed repeatedly. Clients can read the values of the objects as they are broadcast. The model can be that of a flat disk or of multiple disks. The multiple disk model has been extended to allow updates at the server [12].

Typical applications in broadcast environments have clients that execute read-only transactions (queries), and a server that executes update transactions. Datacycle [13] supports transactions, guaranteeing serializability. CC techniques that exploit the semantics of read-only transactions are proposed in [1, 15]. In [15], different queries can observe different orders of update transactions. Quasi-consistency differs from this correctness criterion in that it allows a query to specify the amount and type of imprecision it can tolerate. The BCC-TI [1] scheme guarantees serializability using dynamic adjustment of timestamp intervals [16], and works as follows. During each broadcast cycle, the server stores information on update transactions that committed in that cycle, building a control information table (CIT). The server broadcasts the CIT in the next cycle. At clients, every query has a timestamp interval that is used to record the temporary serialization order induced during execution. When a query reads an object or a CIT, its timestamp interval is adjusted to reflect dependencies between the query and committed update transactions. If the interval becomes invalid (lower bound ≥ upper bound), a non-serializable execution is detected and the query is aborted. BCC-TI has been compared to optimistic CC with forward validation adapted to broadcast environments, and performance gains have been shown [1]. Broadcast methods for queries in [3, 17] do not consider real-time constraints.

Semantic-based consistency criteria that are weaker than serializability are presented in [2], in the context of caching data at clients in information retrieval systems in order to improve query response time. In order to reduce the overhead of keeping cache copies consistent, applications allow cache copies to diverge from the central server copy in a controlled manner. Quasi-caching is a technique that allows such controlled divergence. Examples of quasi-caching constraint types include:
1. *arithmetic*: based on difference in values of cache copy and central copy.
2. *version*: based on number of changes between cached and central copies.
3. *delay*: based on time by which cache copy lags behind central copy.
Quasi-caching would be appropriate for a stock trading application. A user interested in stock prices of chemical companies may be satisfied if she reads prices that are within 5% of the true prices (*arithmetic* constraint). On an update, the server decides whether to propagate the value, based on the client's tolerable imprecision level. Propagation-overhead is cut and flexibility in scheduling propagation increases.

3   Quasi-consistency in Broadcast Environments

We propose a new CC technique for broadcast environments called Quasi-consistent Timestamp Intervals (Quasi-TI) based on quasi-caching constraints. Enforcing quasi-consistency instead of serializability can reduce aborts. Consider a query Q that has read some objects, and requires some more objects before it can commit. If an update transaction U modifies one of the objects that Q has read and then commits, it may be impossible to guarantee serializability by ordering either Q after U or U after Q; so Q must be aborted. But if U's modifications leave objects within an imprecision level that Q can tolerate, Q will not be aborted. Let Q_1 be a query at a mobile client, that reads the stock prices of X and Y. Q_1 can tolerate imprecision of up to \$2.50 in the values it reads. U_2 and U_3 are update transactions at the server, and update X by \$3 and \$1 respectively. U_4 is an update transaction that updates Y by \$5. Consider the following events, where r=read, w=write, and c=commit.

Time	8	11	14	16	20
Operations	$w_2(X)\, c_2$	$r_1(X)$	$w_3(X)\, c_3$	$w_4(Y)\, c_4$	$r_1(Y)$

If we enforce serializability, Q_1 proceeds as follows. Q_1 starts with a timestamp interval of $(0, \infty)$. At time 11 when Q_1 reads X, the lower bound of its timestamp interval becomes 8 (last update time of X), because Q_1 must be ordered after U_2 to achieve a serializable execution. At time 14 when X is updated by U_3, the upper bound of Q_1's timestamp interval becomes 14 as Q_1 must be ordered before U_3. At time 20 when Q_1 reads Y, the lower bound becomes 16 (last update time of Y), as Q_1 must be ordered after U_4. Since the lower bound > the upper bound, Q_1 is aborted.

If we take advantage of Q_1's tolerable imprecision and enforce quasi-consistency, the sequence of events changes. At time 11, when Q_1 reads X, the lower bound of its interval becomes 8 (last update time of X), as Q_1 must be ordered after U_2. At time 14 when X is updated by U_3, Q_1 can ignore the update and still hold a sufficiently precise value of X. The upper bound remains at ∞. At time 20, when Q_1 reads Y, the lower bound becomes 16 (last update time of Y), as Q_1 must be ordered after U_4. As Q_1's timestamp interval is valid, Q_1 commits. This illustrates that a quasi-consistent system can potentially reduce aborts and perform better than a serializable system.

3.1   Server Algorithm

The server stores a database of objects. Update transactions execute at the server and update the values of the objects. Let U be an update transaction, and WS(U) the *write set* of U (set of objects that U modifies). When U commits, the server assigns TS(U) (the *timestamp* of U) to be the current time. For every object d, the server maintains WTS(d), the largest timestamp of a transaction that has modified d and committed. In a broadcast cycle, the server broadcasts every database object d with WTS(d). Periodically, the server broadcasts a control information table (CIT) containing information about recently-committed update transactions, so that clients can check the validity of outstanding queries. When a transaction U commits, the server:

1. Sets TS(U) to the current time.
2. Copies TS(U) into WTS(d), for all d in WS(U).
3. Records TS(U) and WS(U) in the CIT.

The CIT is broadcast at least once (and possibly multiple times) every broadcast cycle. This allows a client to detect conflicts at an early stage and abort invalidated queries. Every time the server broadcasts the CIT, it resets the CIT to an empty table.

3.2   Client Algorithm

Queries execute at mobile clients. Before a query starts execution, it optionally specifies its *quasi-consistency limits*: how much inconsistency the query can tolerate. This information is specified in three forms: [1] imprecision in value of any object: *ImpLimit(Q)*; [2] number of version lags between read version and latest version of an object: *VersionLagLimit(Q)*; [3] time lag between read version and latest version: *TimeLagLimit(Q)*. If any of these limits is exceeded before Q commits, Q is aborted. If Q does not specify one of these limits, it is assumed that Q does not care about the inconsistency introduced in that form. Consider an application where any update can modify d by at most 1.0. If Q can tolerate an imprecision of 3.0 in d, Q can leave ImpLimit unspecified and specify a VersionLagLimit of 3 to ensure correctness.

When a client starts executing query Q, it assigns a timestamp interval of $(0, \infty)$ to Q. Let LB(Q) and UB(Q) be the lower and upper bounds of this interval. When Q requests a read, the client adds the request to the list of objects to be read off the air. The client reads only those objects that are requested by its queries, and also reads every CIT. For every object d that Q reads, Q stores the value of d, WTS(d), and a running estimate (versionLag[d]) of the number of versions by which Q's copy of d lags. When Q reads an object or a CIT, Q's quasi-consistency limits are checked. Q's timestamp interval is adjusted only if its quasi-consistency limits make it necessary to reflect the serialization order induced between Q and committed update transactions. If the timestamp interval becomes invalid, Q is aborted and restarted.

When a requested object d is broadcast, the client reads d's value and WTS(d). For every query Q that requested the read, the client checks Q's validity as follows:
1. Store the value of d and WTS(d), and set versionLag[d] to zero.
2. Set LB(Q) to max (LB(Q), WTS(d)).
3. If LB(Q) $\geq$ UB(Q), then abort and restart Q.
In other words, the timestamp interval of Q is set to reflect the fact that Q must be ordered after the last transaction that modified d. When a CIT is broadcast, the client checks the validity of each outstanding query Q as follows:
1. For every d that has been read by Q and has since been written by a transaction U in the CIT, versionLag[d] is incremented by the number of such transactions U. If versionLag[d] > VersionLagLimit(Q), then UB(Q) is set to min (UB(Q), TS(U)). If LB(Q) $\geq$ UB(Q), then Q is restarted.
2. For every d that has been read by Q and has since been written by a transaction U in the CIT, the time difference between TS(U) and the read time of d (WTS(d)) is calculated. If this difference exceeds TimeLagLimit(Q), then UB(Q) is set to min (UB(Q), WTS(U)). If LB(Q) $\geq$ UB(Q), then Q is restarted.
3. If ImpLimit(Q) is 0, UB(Q) is set to min (UB(Q), TS(U)) for all U in the CIT that have updated an object d read by Q. If LB(Q) $\geq$ UB(Q), then Q is restarted.
4. If ImpLimit(Q) > 0, the actual imprecision must be checked the next time the object is broadcast. Therefore, a reread request is enqueued for every such object.
If U leaves objects read by Q within imprecision limits tolerable by Q, then Q does not adjust its timestamp interval in order to serialize after U. But if Q must be ordered after U, Q's interval is adjusted to reflect this order, and Q is aborted if the resulting order is unserializable.

Requests for a reread of object d are processed when the server broadcasts d. For every query Q that requested a reread of d, the client checks Q's validity as follows:
1. Calculate difference between previously read value of d and new value of d.
2. If difference exceeds ImpLimit(Q), then set UB(Q) to min (UB(Q), WTS(d)).
3. If LB(Q) $\geq$ UB(Q), then restart Q.

4   Caching

Without caching, a client waits an average of half a broadcast cycle to read an object. Caching can improve performance by reducing this waiting time. First, we describe the P-caching (P=Probability-of-access) scheme, where a client caches objects that it will access with a high probability. If the set of queries at a client is static, access probabilities can be computed in the beginning. If the set of queries is dynamic or unknown, the client can keep a running estimate of the access probability per object.

4.1   P-Caching

In P-caching, the entry for a cached copy c consists of the value of the object (val[c]), its timestamp (TS[c]), the version lag that the copy has accumulated (versionLag[c]) and the time lag accumulated (timeLag[c]). The changes to the client's algorithm are as follows. When a query Q requests a read, the client checks if there is a cached copy of the object. If there is a copy (c), the client does the following:
1. If versionLag[c] and timeLag[c] are both zero, then Q uses the cached copy c.
2. If ImpLimit(Q) is unspecified, and versionLag[c] < VersionLagLimit(Q), and timeLag[c] < TimeLagLimit(Q), then Q uses the cached copy c. Otherwise, Q waits and reads the object the next time the object is broadcast.

When a requested object is broadcast, the client checks if a copy of the object already exists in its cache. If a copy exists, the value and timestamp of the cache entry are updated, and the versionLag and timeLag of the entry are reset to zero. If a copy does not exist, the object is inserted into the cache if there is an available cache slot. If no slot is available, the cache entry with the lowest P-value (probability of access) is selected as a victim to be replaced by the new object.

Every time a CIT is broadcast, the client checks if it has cached copies of any of the modified objects. For every such copy c, timeLag[c] is set to (TS(U) - TS(c)), where U is the last transaction that modified the object. versionLag[c] is incremented by the number of transactions that have updated the object since the last CIT.

4.2   PIT Caching

P-caching uses the criterion of probability of access to decide which objects to cache. In a quasi-consistent system, another criterion becomes important: the tightness of the consistency constraints of a query. The *constraint tightness* of a query is inversely proportional to the amount of imprecision it allows in ImpLimit, VersionLagLimit and TimeLagLimit. Intuitively, if an object is read by queries with very tight consistency constraints, then caching the object is not very useful because queries may have to read the object off the air anyway, to obtain sufficient precision.

We introduce a new caching scheme PIT (Probability-of-access Inverse constraint-Tightness). Every cached object has a PIT value stored with it. An object's PIT value is the access probability of the object divided by the maximum of the constraint tightness values of the queries that have read the object. During cache replacement, the victim cache entry is selected to be the one that has the lowest PIT value.

5   Performance Evaluation

We simulated a flat broadcast disk with one server and one client. The client accesses only a subset (ClientObj) of the objects that the server broadcasts, modelling the fact that the server is serving other clients. HotObjects among a total of ServerObj are very frequently updated (with probability HotProb). The simulation runs in units of *bit times* (1 bit time = time to broadcast one bit. We assume that the network delivers objects in FIFO order. Each object is of size ObjectSize bits. An update transaction commits at the server every UpdArrive Kbit time

Table 1. Baseline Parameters

Parameter	Value	Parameter	Value
ServerObj	600	HotObjects	200
ClientObj	300	ClientHotObj	100
ObjectSize	8000	UpdArrive	100
QryArrive	132	ThinkTime	64
MinUpdSize	3	MaxUpdSize	4
MinQrySize	3	MaxQrySize	4
MinSlack	2.0	MaxSlack	8.0
CITcycle	100	CacheSize	100
AvgImp	30.0	AvgVLag	6
AvgTLag	3000	HotProb	70
PercNoImp	0	MaxValChange	5.0

units. Update transaction size is uniformly distributed between MinUpdSize and MaxUpdSize. An update can change the value of an object by ≤ MaxValChange units. The server broadcasts a CIT after every CITcycle objects. For the client, there are ClientHotObj hot objects. The probability of reading hot objects is HotProb. No attempt was made to match up hot spots at server and client. A query arrives every QryArrive Kbit time units, and submits a read every ThinkTime Kbit time units. Query size is uniformly distributed in [MinQrySize, MaxQrySize]. Queries specify ImpLimit, VersionLagLimit and TimeLagLimit when they arrive. These limits are chosen from uniform distributions centred around AvgImp, AvgVLag and AvgTLag. PercNoImp percent of the queries leave ImpLimit unspecified. A query can read objects from a cache of size CacheSize objects. A query is allowed to use a cached copy only if it is known that the copy is sufficiently accurate, given the query's quasi-constraints. A query is aborted if objects that it has read become too stale before it commits. An aborted query is restarted and run until it commits, even if it has missed its deadline (soft real-time transaction). We simulate a restart by starting a new query. The deadline is (current time + slack factor * predicted execution time), where slack factor is uniformly distributed in [MinSlack, MaxSlack]. Performance metrics are average query response time, percentage of queries restarted and percentage of queries that missed deadlines.

5.1   Experiment 1: P-Caching in BCC-TI

We ran BCC-TI with no caching and with P-caching, and compared response times and miss rates. Imprecision limits are set to zero to enforce serializability. Fig. 1a shows average query response time for different arrival rates of update transactions.

Fig. 1. Effect of Caching on BCC-TI

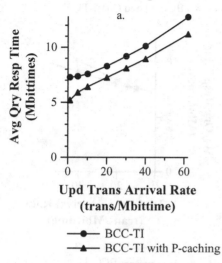

The response time increases as updates become more frequent, since more and more queries are aborted due to object copies becoming stale. When caching is used, the average wait time for a read is reduced since the query can use a cached copy instead of having to wait for the next broadcast of an object. Moreover, the earlier a query completes execution, the less likely it is to abort due to its copies becoming stale. Fig. 1a shows that caching is most useful when updates are rare. The improvement in response time is about 28.5% at the lowest update arrival rates, and about 12.2% at the highest update arrival rate. As updates become more frequent, caching becomes less beneficial, because cache entries are frequently invalidated. The reduction in response time is reflected in a decreased deadline miss rate (Fig. 1b). Fig. 1c shows the average response time of a query, given different cache sizes. As the cache size increases, more objects can be stored in the cache, and it is more likely that a query will find a cached copy of the object. Caching is most effective at the maximum cache size (when all the objects accessed by the client are cached), reducing the average query response time by up to 64% at an update arrival time of 100 Kbit time units.

5.2   Experiment 2: Quasi-TI compared to BCC-TI

BCC-TI enforces serializability, while Quasi-TI enforces quasi-consistency. Quasi-consistency can reduce the number of aborts because a query's semantics may allow it to ignore updates to previously-read data, within certain tolerable limits. Reducing aborts reduces the average response time because fewer queries have to be restarted.

Fig. 2. Effect of Update Arrival Rate on BCC-TI and Quasi-TI

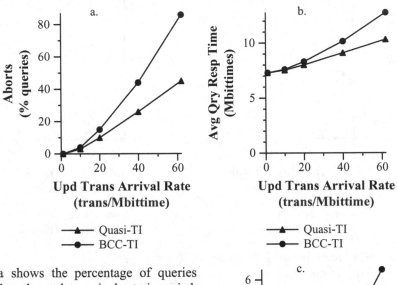

Fig. 2a shows the percentage of queries aborted as the update arrival rate is varied. As updates become more frequent, aborts in BCC-TI increase rapidly, while aborts in Quasi-TI increases less rapidly. As a result of the increased aborts, the average response time increases more rapidly for BCC-TI than for Quasi-TI (Fig. 2b). The UpdArrivTime used for this experiment is 25 Kbit time units. Quasi-TI's response time grows very slowly because queries stay within tolerable imprecision limits even when objects that they have read are updated. The reduction in the percentage of aborts by Quasi-TI is up to 41%, and the resulting improvement in response time of Quasi-TI as compared to BCC-TI is up to 19.2%. The decrease in query response time manifests itself as a reduced deadline miss rate (Fig. 2c).

The looser the consistency constraints of queries, the less likely it is that the queries will be aborted. Fig. 3a shows percentage of queries restarted as the looseness of consistency constraints is varied. The looser the constraints, the higher the values of AvgImp, AvgVLag and AvgTLag. A looseness of zero represents BCC-TI. As constraints become looser, aborts decrease, reducing query response time, letting Quasi-TI outperform BCC-TI by up to a 21.6% reduction in response time (Fig. 3b).

Fig. 3. Effect of Constraint Looseness on BCC-TI and Quasi-TI

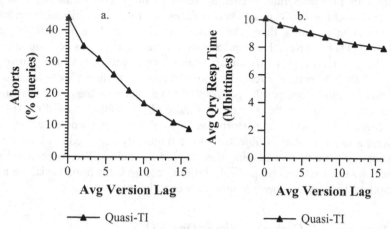

—▲— Quasi-TI   —▲— Quasi-TI

5.3   Experiment 3: Caching in Quasi-TI

In this experiment, we studied caching effects on Quasi-TI. Recall that in addition to P-caching, a new scheme called PIT-caching becomes appropriate for Quasi-TI. We ran Quasi-TI without caching, and then with P-caching and PIT-caching, and compared the average query response time and deadline miss rate. Caching benefits Quasi-TI if consistency constraints are loose and there are a significant number of queries which don't care about the imprecision in object values.

Fig. 4. Performance of Caching in Quasi-TI

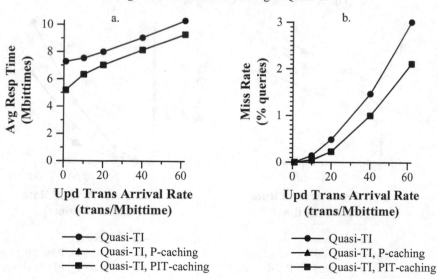

—●— Quasi-TI   —●— Quasi-TI
—▲— Quasi-TI, P-caching   —▲— Quasi-TI, P-caching
—■— Quasi-TI, PIT-caching   —■— Quasi-TI, PIT-caching

The PercNoImp used from now on is 50, and UpdArrivTime is 25. Fig. 4a shows query response time as update transaction arrival rate is increased. The difference between P-caching and PIT-caching is very small and not apparent in the graphs for response time and miss rate. P-caching reduces the response time of Quasi-TI by 28.7% (PIT-caching by 28.6%) when updates are rare. With frequent updates, the improvement in response time goes down to 9.7% for P-caching (9.8% for PIT-caching). This is because at high update rates, more cache copies become invalid, and queries have to read objects off the air. The average wait time to read an object off the air is half a broadcast cycle. The longer execution time makes an abort more likely, and an abort implies a longer response time because the query is restarted. A long response time means that the query is more likely to miss its deadline (Fig. 4b).

P-caching and PIT-caching perform similarly. PIT-caching would perform better if there were a large number of objects that are frequently accessed but have such tight consistency constraints that caching them would be useless. We conjectured that our workload did not have this property. In order to confirm this hypothesis, we modified our workload to have the above property for experiment 4.

5.4   Experiment 4: Caching in Biased Quasi-TI

In order to confirm the above hypothesis, we modified our workload so that the most-frequently-read objects had the tightest consistency constraints, that is, tolerable imprecision limits of zero. We ran Quasi-TI without caching, with P-caching and with PIT-caching, on this modified (biased) workload. Fig. 5a shows query response time as update transaction arrival rate increases. PIT-caching now outperforms P-caching by 23-28%, due to the fact that objects cached in P-caching become invalidated frequently, while PIT-caching selects objects that have loose consistency constraints and that are therefore less frequently invalidated.

Fig. 5. Performance of Caching in Biased Quasi-TI

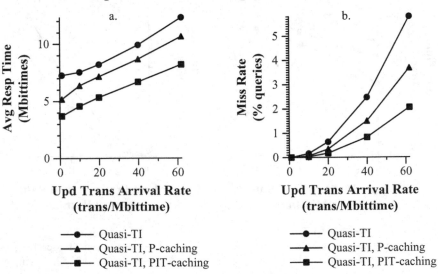

The frequent invalidation of cache entries in P-caching has two implications: [1] Queries don't often find usable cached copies. [2] Even when queries are able to use cached copies, they may be aborted due to the copy becoming invalid. The benefits of PIT-caching are tempered by the fact that the objects that it caches are not accessed frequently. The improvement in response time is reflected in the miss rate (Fig. 5b).

5.5   Experiment 5: Effect of Object Size

As object size increases, the length of the broadcast cycle increases. Therefore the average wait time for a read becomes higher, increasing the query span. A longer query span implies a higher probability of data conflict and hence a higher abort probability. Therefore, the average response time (in BCC-TI and Quasi-TI) increases with object size. The deadline miss ratio in both techniques also increases, because it is more difficult for a query to meet its deadline after an abort. BCC-TI is slightly more sensitive to object size than Quasi-TI because Quasi-TI has fewer aborts and restarts than BCC-TI. The performance of BCC-TI and Quasi-TI for different object sizes are shown in terms of average response time (Fig. 6a) and deadline miss rate (Fig. 6b). The difference in average response time of the two schemes varies from 10.6% at small object sizes to about 15% at larger object sizes.

Fig. 6. Effect of Object Size

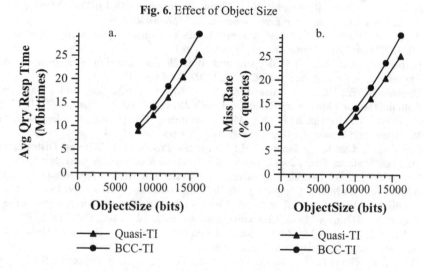

6   Conclusions

We have presented a new CC technique for asymmetric communication environments (Quasi-TI), which allows queries to specify semantic consistency constraints and enforces these constraints. Quasi-TI can result in fewer aborts, a lower query response time and a lower deadline miss rate than BCC-TI. Through simulation, we have demonstrated the benefits of caching for BCC-TI and Quasi-TI. We have presented a new caching scheme, PIT-caching, for quasi-consistent systems. BCC-TI benefits from P-caching when updates are rare and the cache is large. Quasi-TI outperforms BCC-TI, especially when updates are frequent and consistency constraints are loose. Caching benefits Quasi-TI when consistency constraints are loose and a significant number of queries leave their tolerable imprecision in object values unspecified. PIT-caching outperforms P-caching when many frequently-accessed objects have tight consistency constraints. We plan to extend this work to multiple broadcast disks and study broadcast-frequency-based caching. Prefetching objects into the cache is an interesting issue. We plan to run extensive tests with different workloads and study the effect of matching hot spots at server and client. Finally, we would like to explore other caching schemes.

References

1. Lee V., Son S. H., Lam K.: On the Performance of Transaction Processing in Broadcast Environments, *Int Conf on Mobile Data Access (MDA'99)*, Hong Kong, Dec 1999
2. Alonso R., Barbara D., Garcia-Molina H.: Data Caching Issues in an Information Retrieval System, *ACM Transactions on Database Systems (TODS), 15/ 3*, Sep 1990
3. Pitoura E., Bhargava B.: Building Information Systems for Mobile Environments, *Proc of the 3rd Int Conf on Information and Knowledge Management*, pp 371-378, 1994
4. Acharya S., Alonso R., Franklin M., Zdonik S.: Broadcast Disks: Data Management for Asymmetric Communication Environments, *ACM SIGMOD*, 1995
5. Alonso R., Korth H.: Database Systems Issues in Nomadic Computing, *Proc of ACM SIGMOD Conf*, Washington DC, pp 388-392, 1993
6. Barbara D., Imielinski T.: Sleepers and Workaholics: Caching Strategies in Mobile Environments, *Proc of the 1994 ACM SIGMOD Conf*, pp 1-12, 1994
7. Dunham M. H., Helal A., Balakrishnan S.: A Mobile Transaction Model that Captures Both the Data and Movement Behavior, *Mobile Networks and Applications (2)*, 1997
8. Imielinski T., Badrinath B. R:, Mobile Wireless Computing: Challenges in Data Management, *Communications of the ACM 37/10*, pp 18-28, 1994
9. Lee V. C. S., Lam K. Y., Tsang W. H.: Transaction Processing in Wireless Distr Real-Time Database Systems, *Proc 10th Euromicro Workshop on Real Time Systems*, Jun 1998
10. Shekar S., Liu D.: Genesis and Advanced Traveler Information Systems (ATIS): Killer Applications for Mobile Computing, *MOBIDATA Workshop*, New Jersey, 1994
11. Zdonik S., Alonso R., Franklin M., Acharya S.: Are Disks in the Air Just Pie in the Sky, *Proc of Workshop on Mobile Computing Systems and Applications*, California, 1994
12. Acharya S., Franklin M., Zdonik S.: Disseminating Updates on Broadcast Disks, *Proc of the 22nd VLDB Conf*, Bombay, India, 1996
13. Herman G., Gopel G., Lee K. C., Weinrib A.: The Datacycle Architecture for Very High Throughput Database Systems, *Proc of ACM SIGMOD Conf*, pp 97-103, 1987
14. Imielinski T., Viswanathan S., Badrinath B. R.: Energy Efficient Indexing on Air, *Proc of ACM SIGMOD Conf*, May 1994
15. Shanmugasundaram J., Nithrakashyap A., Sivasankaran R., Ramamritham K.: Efficient Concurrency Control for Broadcast Environments, *ACM SIGMOD*, 1999
16. Lee J., Son S. H.: Using Dynamic Adjustment of Serialization Order for Real-Time Database Systems, *Proc 14th IEEE Real-Time Systems Symposium*, pp 66-75, 1993
17. Pitoura E., Chrysanthis P. K.: Scalable Processing of Read-Only Transactions in Broadcast Push, *Proc 19th IEEE Int Conf on Distributed Computing Systems*, 1999

A Map-Based Hoarding Mechanism
for Location-Dependent Information

Uwe Kubach and Kurt Rothermel

Institute of Parallel and Distributed High-Performance Systems (IPVR),
University of Stuttgart, Breitwiesenstr. 20-22, 70565 Stuttgart, Germany
Uwe.Kubach@informatik.uni-stuttgart.de

Abstract. In mobile environments, information systems are often accessed through wireless WANs. Thus the users often have to cope with difficulties such as low bandwidth, high delay, and frequent disconnections. Hoarding is an efficient method to overcome these difficulties. The idea is to transfer information, which is probably needed by the user in the near future, in advance, so that it is already stored on the user's mobile device when it is actually accessed. In this paper, we present a location-aware hoarding mechanism that is based on the use of wireless LANs, so-called info-stations. Due to its flexibility, we claim that our mechanism can be applied in any location-dependent information system.

1 Introduction

With the increasing pervasiveness of mobile computing devices the need for mobile information access grows continuously. A large variety of mobile information systems already exists, e.g. map/navigation systems [10] or mobile guides [4]. Many of these systems are location-aware, i.e. they consider the users' locations in order to improve the service they offer. For example, location information, which is gathered by a GPS sensor, can be used to determine the information items that are probably of interest for the user. Since the same basic functionalities are useful in almost all location-aware information systems, we currently develop an infrastructure for such systems, which provides these functionalities [6]. One of these functionalities is the location-aware hoarding mechanism described in this paper.

Hoarding tries to overcome the drawbacks of wireless WANs, in particular the low bandwidth, high delay, and frequent disconnections. It aims at providing mobile information access for the users that can not be distinguished from an information access through a wired network. The idea is to transfer information, which is probably needed by the user in the near future, in advance, so that it is already stored on the user's mobile device when it is actually accessed. It is even possible to access hoarded information in areas where no network is available at all, e.g. within buildings or tunnels. The problem with hoarding is to predict, which information the user will need. In our mechanism the decision about what information to hoard (hoarding decision) is primarily based on predictions of

K.-L. Tan et al. (Eds.): MDM 2001, LNCS 1987, pp. 145–157, 2001.

a user's future movement. In addition, we consider the number of information items that the user will probably access at each of his future locations.

The remainder of this paper is structured as follows: In Section 2 we present our mechanism in detail. Afterwards, we analyze the efficiency of our algorithm in Section 3 and discuss the related work in Section 4. Finally, we conclude our paper in Section 5.

2   Hoarding Mechanism

In this section we describe our hoarding mechanism in detail. We begin with a description of the system environment. We also show how we gather and maintain the knowledge on which the hoarding decision is based and how this knowledge is finally used for the hoarding decision.

2.1   System Environment

We consider information systems that provide access to a set of discrete information items. The users access these items through mobile devices. We assume that the information access is location-dependent, i.e. it depends on the users' locations, which items they preferably access. Therefore, it is possible to use knowledge about a user's future location in order to predict the information items he will most probably request.

An example for a strongly location-dependent information access is the access to a map server in order to get a map of a user's current environment. Here, we exactly know, which parts of a map belong to each location. Thus, we can easily predict which information items will be accessed, if we know the user's future location. Further examples are the access to situated information [5] or to information provided by mobile guides.

For the communication infrastructure we use the info-station concept proposed in [2]. There, a number of high-bandwidth wireless LANs with a typically low range, so-called info-stations, are placed in an area otherwise only covered by a wireless WAN (see Figure 1). In our approach, the hoarding is exclusively performed at the info-stations. Each info-station has an associated proxy server, which coordinates the hoarding processes for the mobile clients arriving at the info-station. In the remainder of this paper we use the term info-station for the entirety of the wireless LAN and the associated proxy server.

Each info-station serves a geographically limited area, its so-called hoarding area. In reasonable configurations the hoarding area of an info-station will be bigger than the area covered by its wireless LAN. Each hoarding area is logically separated into non-overlapping zones, e.g. equally sized squares (see Figure 2).

2.2   Overview

The hoarding process for each user is performed in a cyclic manner. Every time a user visits an info-station, a new hoarding cycle begins. The cycle ends when he reaches the next info-station. Every cycle consists of the following three steps:

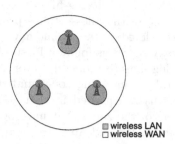

Fig. 1. The info-station infrastructure.

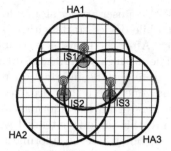

Fig. 2. Info-stations (IS), their hoarding areas (HA), and zones.

1. Download: During this step, the information items that the user will probably need before reaching the next info-station are transferred to his mobile device. The decision about what information items should be hoarded is based on predictions of the user's future movement. The total number of items that are transferred to the user's device depends on the memory size of the device and the time the user is willing to wait for the download process to finish.

2. Inter info-station movement: This step begins after the user has left the info-station. During this period, the information system can not be accessed through a wireless LAN. The user's information requests are primarily answered with the information hoarded at the previous info-station. Only in the case of hoard misses a connection to the information system has to be established through the wireless WAN. Ideally, the wireless WAN has not to be used at all. Actually, we can even rely on an infrastructure without a wireless WAN. However, then the user has to accept that in case of a hoard miss, his information request can not be answered. During the inter info-station movement, the identifiers of all visited zones are logged in a file on the user's mobile device. Additionally, the identifiers of all requested information items are logged together with the zones where they occurred.

3. Upload: When the user reaches the next info-station, the movement step ends and the upload step starts. The main task during this step is to propagate the information gathered in the log-file to the corresponding info-stations.

After the upload step has been terminated, the cycle restarts with the subsequent download step. In order to realize this hoarding mechanism we have to gather, maintain, and use knowledge about the users' information requests and their movement patterns. How we do this, is described in the following subsections.

2.3   Evaluation of Log-Files

The primary source of information about the users' behavior are the log-files, which have been written to their mobile devices during the period of inter info-station movement. In this subsection, we show how these log-files are evaluated during the upload period.

When a user arrives at an info-station, the evaluation of the log-file stored on his mobile device starts with the transfer of the file to the info-station's proxy server. After the transfer is completed, the file is deleted on the mobile device.

The log-files are further processed on the proxy server as follows: First, the reports about the information requests in the log-file are grouped, according to the zone where they occurred. So we get a table containing zones and the identifiers of all the information items that the user requested in that zone. Second, this table is extended with the identifiers of the zones that have been visited, but where no information request occurred. We end up with a table, which contains pairs (z, l) of zone identifiers z and lists l of information items requested in zone z. Each list l contains each information item at most once.

Finally, the proxy sends a report message to every info-station whose hoarding area covers at least one of the zones z_i in the table. To every info-station s at most one report message is sent, which includes all pairs (z, l) of the table for which the zone z belongs to the hoarding area of s. Although it would be more efficient to draw the required information directly from the log-file, we assume, for simplicity, that the evaluating proxy also sends a report message to itself.

To find out which info-stations serve a certain zone, the proxy asks a directory server which knows the hoarding area of every info-station. The log-files are transferred anonymously from the users' mobile devices to the proxy servers. However, the info-stations have to know the address of a user's device in order to communicate with it. Thus, information about a user's behavior might be mapped to the address of his mobile device. This leads to privacy problems that are comparable to those that appear when a user accesses a standard web server.

2.4   Knowledge

Every info-station maintains three different types of knowledge about each zone within its hoarding area: knowledge about which items are preferred at each zone, the probability with which each zone is visited, and the average number of information items that are requested at each zone.

Hot Spot Tables The knowledge about the preferred information items is stored in so-called hot spot tables. For every zone in an info-station's hoarding area the proxy server maintains a separate table. The tables contain pairs (i, c), where i is the identifier of an information item and c is a hit counter. The tables are sorted by the values of the hit counters.

In order to keep their hot spot tables up to date, the proxy servers process each incoming report message. Let us assume that a report message contains an entry that tells the proxy that information item i has been accessed in zone z. Then, the hot spot table of zone z will be updated in the following way: if there is already an entry for item i, the according hit-counter c is increased by one. Otherwise, a new entry for item i is added to the table. In this case, the according counter is initially set to one. To avoid that the hot spot tables become too big, all hit-counters are periodically decreased by one. If a hit-counter has been decreased to 0, the according entry is removed from the hot spot table. A further advantage of decreasing the counters is that the hot spot tables dynamically adapt to changes in the users' information request patterns.

Probability Maps The second source of information, which is used to select the items to hoard, is knowledge about the visit probabilities of each zone in an info-station's hoarding area. This knowledge is stored at each info-station in so-called probability maps.

Formally, a probability map is a function $p : Z \mapsto [0, 1]$, where Z is the set of zones located in the info-station's hoarding area. The function p assigns to every zone z in the hoarding area the probability with which the zone is visited. We call these functions probability maps because of their graphical representations. Such a representation is depicted in Figure 3. The brighter a square is depicted, the higher is the visit probability of the according zone.

Fig. 3. A probability map.

Like the hot spot tables, the probability maps are continuously updated. For this purpose each info-station maintains a visit counter v_z for every zone z within its hoarding area. Every time a configurable time period Δ has elapsed an update is performed. At the beginning of each time period Δ, all visit counters are set to 0. During a period Δ the visit counter v_z of a zone z is increased by one, every time a report message is received, which contains an entry for z. At the end of the time period Δ the visit probability $p_\Delta(z)$ of zone z during the time period Δ can be calculated as follows:

$$p_\Delta(z) = \frac{v_z}{n},$$

where n is the total number of report messages received during the time period Δ. Finally, the probability map p is updated by assigning new values $p'(z)$ to each zone z according to the following formula:

$$p'(z) = \alpha \cdot p(z) + (1 - \alpha) \cdot p_\Delta(z)$$

The parameter α determines how strong former time periods are reflected in the new probability map.

Request Maps Each info-station also maintains a request map of its hoarding area. Like the probability maps, the request maps are functions. A request map

$r : Z \mapsto [0..\infty)$ assigns to every zone z in the info-station's hoarding area, the average number of different information items, a user requests during a visit of zone z.

The update algorithm for the request maps, works quite similar to the one for the probability maps. For the time between two subsequent updates, the same interval Δ is chosen as for the update of the probability maps. In addition to the visit counters v_z, the update algorithm for the request maps uses request counters r_z. They are also set to 0, at the beginning of every time period Δ. The request counter r_z of zone z is increased, every time a report message is received that contains an entry for zone z with a non-empty list of information items. It is always increased by the number of information items in the list. At the end of an observation period Δ, the average number $r_\Delta(z)$ of information items a user requested during a visit of zone z is determined. This is done by using the counters v_z and r_z:

$$r_\Delta(z) = \frac{r_z}{v_z}$$

Finally, the new values $r'(z)$ for the probability map are determined as follows:

$$r'(z) = \beta \cdot r(z) + (1 - \beta) \cdot r_\Delta(z)$$

β is again a parameter to determine how strong former time periods are reflected in the new values.

2.5   Selection Algorithm

The selection algorithm uses the knowledge available at the info-stations, in order to determine the information items a user will most probably need before he reaches the next info-station. The algorithm is executed at the beginning of every download step.

In the following, we describe one of two different variants of our selection algorithm. It performs well, as long as the hot spot tables of different zones do not have many items in common. If there are items which appear in two or more hot spot tables, the performance of this variant decreases. The reason for this is that the same item is selected repeatedly for the download, and therefore resources are wasted. This problem is solved in the second variant, which is not described here due to space limitations. However, this second variant requires more calculations than the first one. Therefore, it should only be used if a significant number of information items appear in more than one hot spot table.

In the variant described here, the selection algorithm begins with the calculation of a hoarding score $h(z)$ for each zone z in the info-station's hoarding area. Since we want to transfer the most information items for the zones that are visited with the highest probabilities and where the highest number of different information items are accessed, we calculate the hoarding scores as follows:

$$h(z) = \frac{p(z) \cdot r(z)}{\sum\limits_{j \in Z} p(j) \cdot r(j)} \tag{1}$$

Basically, the hoarding score of a zone is the number of different information items, an average user requests in the zone, weighted with the zone's visit probability. In addition, these weighted request numbers are normalized, so that the sum of all hoarding scores within an info-station's hoarding area is 1.

Using the hoarding scores, the number $n(z)$ of information items that are hoarded for each zone z is determined as follows:

$$n(z) = N \cdot h(z), \tag{2}$$

where N is the maximum number of information items that can be transferred to the mobile client. Finally, for each zone z, the $n(z)$ information items that are most frequently accessed in z are hoarded on the user's mobile device. The information about what the most frequently accessed items are is drawn from the zone's hot spot table.

2.6   Enhancements

The main advantage of our mechanism is that we can easily exploit any kind of user-specific information about a user's future movement in order to improve the selection of the hoarded information items. In the following, we give two examples of such user-specific information and show how we use it for the hoarding decision. If no such information was available, our mechanism could be simplified to the use of only one zone covering the whole hoarding area. However, as we show in our analysis (see Section 3), it is highly beneficial to use user-specific information, what would then not be possible at all.

External Specifications In many cases the user or the application he runs, can provide information about where the user will go. For example, a navigation system can exactly predict the path on which the user will move.

To be able to use such information, we allow the applications and users to specify visit probability maps on their own. In contrast to the maps maintained by the info-station, such externally specified maps do not have to cover the whole hoarding area of an info-station. The externally specified maps are functions:

$$p_i : Z_i \mapsto [0..1], \text{where } Z_i \subseteq Z$$

If more than one external map is specified, we assume that $Z_i \cap Z_j = \emptyset$, if $i \neq j$. All externally specified maps and the info-station's map are integrated into one map $p' : Z \mapsto [0..1]$:

$$p'(z) = \begin{cases} p_i(z), \text{ if } z \in Z_i \\ p(z), \text{ if } z \notin \bigcup_{\forall i} Z_i \end{cases}$$

The definition of p' says that the info-station's map is only used in zones, where no external specification is available. We decided to do so, because the external information is user-specific, whereas the info-station's map only reflects the behavior of the average user. Therefore, it is expected to be less accurate than the external specification.

Masks A user moving towards a certain destination will probably not return to a zone that he has previously visited. To reflect this fact in the selection process, we offer the option to mask zones, which have already been visited. When masking is enabled, the selection algorithm uses a modified probability map $p' : Z \mapsto [0..1]$ instead of the original map p. For the modification of p, the log-file stored on the user's mobile device has to be analyzed. The log-file contains the identifiers of all zones, the user has visited, while encountering the info-station. We denote the set of these zones with V. The modified probability map is defined as follows:

$$p'(z) = \begin{cases} 0, & \text{if } z \in V \\ p(z), & \text{if } z \notin V \end{cases}$$

To use externally specified knowledge, the selection algorithm itself does not have to be modified. It just has to rely on the maps p' instead of p.

3   Analysis

In this section, we analyze our algorithm, especially the benefits that we get from the enhancements described in Section 2.6. The metric, we use to evaluate our algorithm, is the hit-ratio. The hit-ratio is the number of a user's information requests that can be answered with the hoarded information items divided by the total number of the user's information requests.

3.1   Model

In our model we assume that there are two different kinds of zones: preferred zones and normal zones. The preferred zones are those zones that are of special interest to the users. In a shopping guide system these might be the zones where malls and supermarkets are located. In contrast, the normal zones are not of interest for the average user and hence they are rarely visited.

Whether a zone belongs to the group of preferred zones or not, depends on whether its visit probability is higher than a given threshold or not. Although, in reality, each zone has its individual visit probability, we assume, for simplicity, that each zone is visited with the average visit probability of all zones within its group. We denote the average visit probability of the preferred zones with p_p and that of the normal zones with p_n. Thus, we assume, in the following, that each preferred zone is visited with the probability p_p and each normal zone is visited with the probability p_n.

Since the preferred zones are more interesting to the user, we assume that the average user requests more information items while he is located in a preferred zone than during his stay in a normal zone. The number of information items requested in a preferred zone is denoted with r_p, while the number of items requested in a normal zone is denoted with r_n. For the same reason we assume, that there is more information offered for the preferred zones and therefore more information items will be associated with them. The number of items associated with each preferred zone is denoted with a_p, whereas a_n denotes the number of items associated with each normal zone. We further assume that there are n_p preferred zones and n_n normal zones within the considered info-station's hoarding area.

3.2 Hoarding Scores

In the following, we calculate the hoarding scores that we get with the basic mechanism, the use of masking, and the use of an externally specified visit probability map.

Basic Mechanism If no user-specific knowledge is available at all, we get, according to equation (1), for the hoarding score h_p of a preferred zone and that of a normal zone h_n:

$$h_p = \frac{r_p \cdot p_p}{n_p \cdot r_p \cdot p_p + n_n \cdot r_n \cdot p_n} \qquad \text{and} \qquad h_n = \frac{r_n \cdot p_n}{n_p \cdot r_p \cdot p_p + n_n \cdot r_n \cdot p_n}$$

Masking If masking is used, we get different hoarding scores, since no information items are hoarded for the zones that a user visited before reaching the info-station. To calculate these hoarding scores, we first have to determine how many zones actually are visited before reaching the info-station. Therefore, we assume that each info-station is located in the center of its hoarding area. Thus, one half of the zones that a users visits while crossing a hoarding area will be visited before reaching the info-station and the other half will be visited thereafter. We can calculate the average number of preferred zones v_p, which a user visits during a trip through an info-station's hoarding area, and the average number of visited normal zones v_n as follows:

$$v_p = n_p \cdot p_p \qquad \text{and} \qquad v_n = n_n \cdot p_n$$

For the hoarding scores of the unmasked zones, i.e. zones that have not been visited previously, we then get:

$$h_{p/n} = \frac{r_{p/n} \cdot p_{p/n}}{\left(n_p - \frac{v_p}{2}\right) \cdot r_p \cdot p_p + \left(n_n - \frac{v_n}{2}\right) \cdot r_n \cdot p_n}$$

The hoarding score of a masked zone is 0. However, we assume that the user will not visit these zones. Thus, the masked zones must not be considered in the calculation of the average hit-ratios in the subsequent section.

External Specification For the analysis of the potential of external specifications, we chose a scenario where the user or the application is able to specify the whole path on which the user will move after visiting the info-station. This means that the hoarding mechanism gets an externally specified visit map p_1 that covers the whole hoarding area. The visit probability $p_1(z)$ of a zone z lying on the specified path is 1, that of all other zones is 0.

Since only the zones visited after reaching the info-station are considered for hoarding, we get for the zones lying on the specified path the following hoarding scores:

$$h_p = \frac{r_p}{\frac{v_p}{2} \cdot r_p + \frac{v_n}{2} \cdot r_n} \qquad \text{and} \qquad h_n = \frac{r_n}{\frac{v_p}{2} \cdot r_p + \frac{v_n}{2} \cdot r_n}$$

The hoarding scores of all other zones are 0, since their visit probabilities are 0. As with the masked zones, we assume that these zones are not visited and therefore must not be considered in the calculation of the average hit-ratios.

3.3   Hit-Ratios

With the hoarding scores the number of items t_p transferred for each preferred zone and the number of items t_n transferred for each normal zone can be determined according to equation (2):

$$t_p = h_p \cdot N \qquad \text{and} \qquad t_n = h_n \cdot N$$

If we assume that each of the items associated with every zone is accessed with the same probability, we can calculate the hit-ratios hit_p and hit_n for the average user in a single preferred zone and a normal zone as follows:

$$hit_p = \frac{t_p}{a_p} \qquad \text{and} \qquad hit_n = \frac{t_n}{a_n}$$

If the access probabilities are not equally distributed, the hit-ratios will be higher, since then the items with the highest access probabilities are hoarded. Finally, the average hit-ratio hit that a user achieves, while he is crossing an info-station's hoarding area, is:

$$hit = \frac{v_p \cdot r_p \cdot hit_p + v_n \cdot r_n \cdot hit_n}{v_p \cdot r_p + v_n \cdot r_n}$$

3.4   Results

In the following, we illustrate the hit-ratios that we get from the formulas introduced above. As long as a parameter is not varied for the calculation of a plot, we used the default settings summarized in Table 1. We assumed that 80 information items can be hoarded on a user's mobile device.

In our first set of calculations, we varied the number of preferred and normal zones. Figures 4 and 5 show the results for the basic algorithm and the algorithm using knowledge about the user's path. The number of preferred zones is shown on the x-axis, the number of normal zones on the y-axis, and the hit-ratio on the z-axis. If knowledge about the user's path is used, we get significantly higher hit-ratios. The results do not differ that much, when comparing the hit-ratios achieved without masking of previously visited zones to those achieved with masking. However, the hit-ratios achieved with masking are still up to 10% higher than those achieved without it.

Table 1. Default values of the used parameters.

Parameter	Value	Parameter	Value
r_p	10 items	r_n	1 item
n_p	10 zones	n_n	50 zones
a_p	20 items	a_n	2 items
p_p	0.5	p_n	0.1

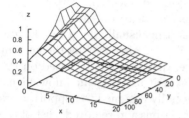

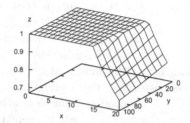

Fig. 4. Hit-ratios for different numbers of preferred zones and normal zones (no external knowledge).

Fig. 5. Hit-ratios for different numbers of preferred zones and normal zones (externally specified path).

We also found that the hit-ratios get higher, when the visit probability of the preferred zones is increased. In contrast, the hit-ratios decrease, when the visit probability of the normal zones is increased.

Figures 6 and 7 show the effect that the average number of information requests in each zone have on the hit-ratios. The x-axes show the average number of information items that the users request while they are located in a normal zone. The y-axes show the same for preferred zones. For graphical reasons, we interchanged the x- and y-axes in the two figures. Differing from the default value, we set the number of information items associated with a normal zone to 10.

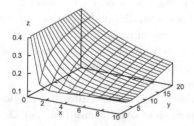

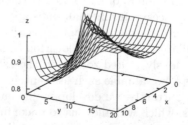

Fig. 6. Hit-ratios for different numbers of requests at preferred and at normal zones (no external knowledge).

Fig. 7. Hit-ratios for different numbers of requests at preferred and at normal zones (externally specified path).

4   Related Work

In this section we reflect the work on mobile information access done so far. We evaluate the usability of the existing approaches in the context of location-dependent information systems and compare them to our solution.

In [3] an asynchronous information access is proposed, i.e. if an information request occurs while no or only a low bandwidth is available, it is delayed until a high bandwidth network connection is available. The problem with this approach is that the users might then not be interested in the requested information anymore, as in the meantime they moved on to another location.

Other approaches, like [1] or [7], are based on broadcast dissemination of information. Broadcast-based dissemination mechanisms usually do not make any predictions on the information items the users will need after leaving the current broadcast cell for another location. Furthermore, they are mainly based on the access patterns of the average user and do not exploit user-specific knowledge.

The first hoarding approaches that were especially designed to support users during disconnections, e.g. [9], relied on user interactions and required a list of the user's preferred information items. This is not applicable in our scenario, because the users do not know in advance which information items they will access. Automated hoarding mechanisms, like [8], use semantic relationships between files in order to predict which files a user will need. In contrast to our approach the user's location is not considered there.

In [10] the user's position and movement pattern is considered for the determination of the items to be hoarded. This approach is focused on a map application for people driving on roads and can not be used as a generic mechanism for different types of location-dependent information systems. For example, the considered request patterns are restricted to the driving scenario. It is also assumed that the start and end point of the users' trips are known. With our mechanism this is not necessary, since it can rely on the internal knowledge to determine the direction a user will probably follow.

5   Conclusion

In this paper, we presented a map-based hoarding mechanism that uses location information in order to predict the information items that a user will most probably access. Our mechanism is applicable in any location-dependent information system. Its main advantage is that it can easily use any kind of additionally available, user-specific location information. For two examples, the masking of previously visited zones and the external specifications, we showed in our analysis how valuable such user-specific information can be.

Currently, we develop a simulation environment for mobile information access, which will allow us to make further evaluations of our mechanism. For the near future we plan to investigate how the selection process can be improved, e.g. by considering user profiles or hyperlinks between information items. We also plan to integrate the mechanism in our platform for location-aware applications [6].

References

1. S. Acharya and S. Muthukrishnan. Scheduling on-demand broadcasts: New metrics and algorithms. In *Proceedings of the Fourth Annual International Conference on Mobile Computing and Networking (MobiCom '98)*, pages 43–54, Dallas, Texas, USA, October 1998. 156
2. B. R. Badrinath, T. Imielinski, R. Frenkiel, and D. Goodman. Nimble: Many-time, many-where communication support for information systems in highly mobile and wireless environments.
   http://www.cs.rutgers.edu/~badri/dataman/nimble/, 1996. 146
3. H. Chang, C. Tait, N. Cohen, M. Shapiro, S. Mastrianni, R. Floyd, B. Housel, and D. Lindquist. Web browsing in a wireless environment: Disconnected and asynchronous operation in artour web express. In *Proceedings of the Third Annual ACM/IEEE International Conference on Mobile Computing and Networking (MobiCom '97)*, pages 260–269, Budapest, Hungary, September 1997. 156
4. K. Cheverst, K. Davies, K. Mitchell, and A. Friday. Experiences of developing and deploying a context-aware tourist guide: the guide project. In *Proceedings of the Sixth Annual International Conference on Mobile Computing and Networking (MobiCom 2000)*, pages 20–31, Boston, MA, USA, August 2000. 145
5. G.W. Fitzmaurice. Situated information spaces and spatially aware palmtop computers. *Communications of the ACM*, 36(7):39 49, July 1993. 146
6. F. Hohl, U. Kubach, A. Leonhardi, K. Rothermel, and M. Schwehm. Next century challenges: Nexus – an open global infrastructure for spatial-aware applications. In *Proceedings of the Fifth Annual International Conference on Mobile Computing and Networking (MobiCom '99)*, pages 249–255, Seattle, WA, USA, August 1999. 145, 156
7. Q. Hu, D. L. Lee, and W.-C. Lee. Performance evaluation of a wireless hierarchical data dissemination system. In *Proceedings of the Fifth Annual International Conference on Mobile Computing and Networking (MobiCom '99)*, pages 163–173, Seattle, WA, USA, August 1999. 156
8. G.H. Kuenning and G.J. Popek. Automated hoarding for mobile computers. In *Proceedings of the 16th ACM Symposium on Operating Systems Principles (SOSP '97)*, pages 264–275, St. Malo, France, October 1997. 156
9. M. Satyanarayanan, J.J. Kistler, P. Kumar, M.E. Okasaki, E.H. Siegel, and D.C. Steere. Coda: A highly available file system for a distributed workstation environment. *IEEE Transactions on Computers*, 39(4):447–459, April 1990. 156
10. T. Ye, H.-A. Jacobsen, and R. Katz. Mobile awareness in a wide area wireless network of info-stations. In *Proceedings of the Fourth International Conference on Mobile Computing and Networking (MobiCom '98)*, pages 109–120, Dallas, TX, USA, 1998. 145, 156

Session V: Coping with Movement

Hashing Moving Objects

Zhexuan Song[1] and Nick Roussopoulos[2]

[1] Department of Computer Science,
University of Maryland,
College Park, MD 20742, USA,
zsong@cs.umd.edu
[2] Department of Computer Science &
Institute For Advanced Computer Studies,
University of Maryland,
College Park, MD 20742, USA,
nick@cs.umd.edu

Abstract. In many real-life applications, objects need to be both spatially and temporally referenced. With the advancements of wireless communication and positioning technologies, the demand for storing and indexing moving objects, which are the objects continuously changing their locations, in database systems rises. However, current static spatial index structures are not well suited for handling large volume of moving objects due to massive and complex database update operations.

In this paper, we propose a new idea based on hashing technique: using buckets to hold moving objects. The database does not make any change until an object moves into a new bucket; therefore, the database update cost is greatly reduced. Then, we extend the design of existing system structure by inserting a filter layer between the position information collectors and the database. Based on the new system structure, we also present two indexing methods. Finally, different aspects of our indexing techniques are evaluated.

1 Introduction

Traditionally, database management systems adopt a "static" model which assumes that data stored in database remain stable until being explicitly changed through update operations. This model serves well if the properties of the objects rarely change. However, in reality, many objects change their properties continuously. One example of such applications is to maintain an air-traffic control system. In this application, the objects we studied are flying airplanes. The location property of the objects is dynamic. To maintain such dynamic location data under the "static" model, a "naive solution" is to update the location information of the objects in the database after every certain period of time.

The "naive solution" fails when the number of moving objects becomes increasingly large. Supposedly a database management system can process up to N_t transactions per second, and the number of objects is N_o. At each time interval, in the "naive solution", the location information of all objects needs to

K.-L. Tan et al. (Eds.): MDM 2001, LNCS 1987, pp. 161–172, 2001.
© Springer-Verlag Berlin Heidelberg 2001

be refreshed in the database. Thus, there are N_o update operations per cycle. It takes at least N_o/N_t seconds to finish. When N_o is small, for example several thousands in an air-traffic control application, the "naive solution" may still be acceptable. However, when N_o is large, for example, hundreds of thousands in a traffic monitoring system, or even more in mobile communication scenarios, each update cycle takes tens of minutes or even longer to finish. The location information of an object stored in database may be the location of that object more than ten minutes ago! Obviously, the query result based on these data is unacceptable.

Our main focus in this paper is to efficiently index large number of moving objects without generating high volume of database updates. For the most part, we discuss how to quickly respond to range queries over the objects' current location because range queries serve as basic operations for other queries such as nearest neighbor queries [CG99,SK98].

The paper is organized as the following: in part 2, we discuss related works in spatiotemporal database area. Subsequently in part 3, we propose the basic idea of our bucketized hashing technique and the system structure to implement it. In the next part, we present two specific methods. The experiment results are given in part 5 and the last part includes the conclusions and future research directions.

2   Related Work

Recently, many researchers have been focusing on indexing the locations of moving objects. The works has been mostly concentrated on point data. Various attempts can be classified into two categories, depending on the type of information being stored in the database.

The first approach stores the moving object location information, which is obtained by periodical sampling. The location of an object at a time between two consecutive sampled positions is estimated using interpolation. The movement of one object in d-dimensional space is described as a trajectory in a $(d+1)$-dimensional space after combining time into the same space [TUW98]. The methods which adopt this approach mainly focus on trajectories indexing.

In [PTJ99], the authors defined a R-tree-like structure called STR-tree. They used linear interpolation method, so that the trajectory of an object was a set of line segments. In a STR-tree, the line segments within the same trajectory were more likely to be stored together. Later, the authors proposed another structure called TB-tree, which totally preserved the trajectories[PTJ00]. They claimed that these two novel tree structures worked better than traditional R-tree family for range searches over trajectories.

The drawback of this approach is that for large amount of objects, too many database update operations may be triggered after each sampling. For example, in a STR-tree, each sampling period generates n line segment insertions in the database, where n is the population of objects. Due to the limited database processing capability, sampling can not occur too often for a large n. In addition, the uncertainty factor reduces query accuracy [WCD+98].

The second approach uses functions to describe the movement of objects and stores the functions in the database. In [KGT99], the authors used linear functions to describe the trajectories of objects. Since it was very hard to index a line in most spatial databases, the authors mapped a line into a point in the dual plane. The duality transformation formulated the problem in a more intuitive manner. However, it is worth noting that a rectangle query range becomes a polygon in dual space thus the query turns to be more difficult to execute.

Sistla, et.al. proposed a data model called MOST [SWC+97]. In that model, each object has a special attribute called *function*. This attribute is a function of time. Without explicit update, the position of each object can be found by combining the *function* attribute with others such as *position* and *time*. The model allows the DBMS to execute instantaneous, continuous and persistent queries. The idea is also later used in TPR-tree [SJL+00].

This approach can partially solve the overwhelming database update problem if the objects' movements follow some descriptive rules. However, in real life, a good movement description function hardly exists.

3   Hashing Techniques

One of the differences between moving objects and static objects is that the location of moving objects varies over time. In the database, if we want to store the exact location information of objects, it is inevitable to employ a large volume of database updates. Therefore, we apply a "fuzzy" view: we do not update the location of objects in database unless it leaves its original position very far.

There is some uncertainty in the query result. In range queries, given a query range R, the result includes two parts: some objects are definitely in the query range and some may or may not be and need further validation. The uncertainty causes the idea less useful in cases when exact answers are needed.

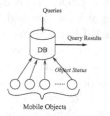

Fig. 1. The structure of other methods

In order to solve the problem, we design a new system structure. Before we present our design, we first review the structure of the other methods. In the traditional structure (see Fig. 1), moving objects send their latest statuses (such as location, function, velocity etc.) directly to the database. The database then updates the corresponding records. Different index structures (STR-tree, TPR-tree) are used in the database to accelerate the update procedures. All the queries are answered based on the information stored in database.

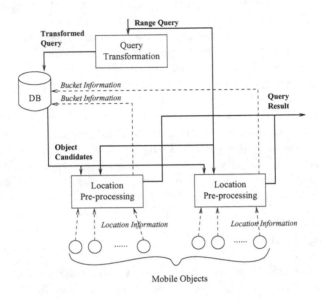

Fig. 2. The structure of hashing technique

Our method (Fig. 2), which is called *Hashing Technique*, works in a different way. We first introduce a hash function which uses objects' statuses as input. From this function, the system is able to find out which bucket each object belongs to. Only bucket information is stored in database, such as how many objects are in each bucket, which bucket each object is currently in, etc. Between the database and moving objects, we add a filter layer called "Location Pre-processing Layer (LP)". Each LP monitors a small set of objects and uses an array to store the latest status of those objects. When an object changes its location and generates an update request, the request first goes to the corresponding LP. The LP updates object's status locally, then it applies the hash function to the object's latest status to see whether the object is still in the same bucket. If so, the request is ignored. When the object moves into a new bucket, the request is translated into a bucket update request and sent to the database.

In our structure, most work is done in LPs. There are many benefits in doing so. Firstly, each LP only monitors a small set of objects and all the LPs are working in parallel. After sampling, the system can finish the corresponding LP update and computation quickly. Hence, the sampling can be performed more frequently. Secondly, the scalability of the system is high. When the object number increases, we only need to add more LPs and do not need to make changes in database.

Each bucket in the database contains all the objects which, by using hash function, have the same return value. The bucket can be viewed as a union region of all possible locations with the same hash value. For the rest of the paper, without confusion, the term region and bucket will be used interexchangably.

To answer range queries in our system, when a range query arrives, it first goes to a "query transformation module (QT)". QT translates the range query into a bucket query. For example, if a query is to "Find all the objects in range R", after translation, the query becomes: "Find all the buckets that intersect with R". Each bucket in the database belongs to one of the following three cases:

1. The bucket does not intersect with the query range. In this case, the objects in the bucket can not be the answer.
2. The query range encloses the bucket. Then, the objects in the bucket must be the answer.
3. The bucket intersects with the query range. Based on the information in database, the system can not distinguish which objects in the bucket are in the range and which are not. There are two possible solutions. The database could either give a statistically approximated result as suggested by [PIH+96,APR99], or retrieve all the objects in bucket and sends their id's to LPs. In the second case, LPs then check the objects' latest positions, filter out the "false alarms", and report the results. In our experiment, we adopt the later approach.

4   Hash functions

This section presents two different hash functions and gives detail description of corresponding methods.

4.1   Overlap-free Space Partition Method

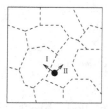

Fig. 3. Example of object moving

The first step of this method is to partition the space into many small zones. In Fig. 3, the square is the working space. The dashed lines divide the space into 12 zones. The region covered by each zone can be viewed as a bucket in database. A perfect partition makes each bucket contain almost the same number of objects all the time. However, the partition is done beforehand and we have no clue about the objects' movement, it is very hard to find such a perfect partition. But in some special case, a perfect partition can be simulated. For example, if objects are uniformly distributed and move randomly, an equally-sized partition is almost perfect. Or if we know that objects are moving close to some predefined locations, we could use Vorronoi diagram to partition the space.

In the next step, we give each zone a unique id number. The hash function now is: $f(p) = i$ where p is an object and i is the id of the bucket where p is currently in.

At time t, an object leaves from one zone to another one, like path I in Fig. 3, the LP which monitors this object sends an update request to database. The request has the form: $update(zone\_id, old\_bucketid, new\_bucketid, t)$. Sometimes, after an object changes its location, it still stays in the same zone, like path II in Fig. 3. According to our design, the database does not make any change.

The query execution is very intuitive after f is defined. For an *ad hoc* query, the database passes the query to the LP which monitors the object. The LP fetches the object's current location and returns the result. For a range query, the procedure is just like what we discussed in the last section.

It is worth noting that the bucket information is static. The information (size, location, etc.) of the buckets never changes once the hash function f is given. This allows us to use existing spatial index structures (R*-tree, Quad-tree) to manage the buckets in the database. Static bucket configuration also accelerates query execution procedure.

4.2   Augmented Space Partition Method

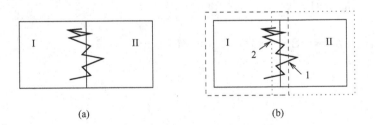

(a)   (b)

Fig. 4. An object moves along the border

In overlap-free space partition method, objects zigzagging along the bucket borders can cause big trouble. As showed in Fig. 4(a), I and II are two buckets. An object moves along the border. Anytime when it crosses the border (from bucket I to bucket II or vice versa), an update request is generated by the LP. The object is originally in bucket I. When it finishes the path, eight database updates are requested.

In order to solve the problem, we increase the size of each bucket slightly so that there is some overlapping between two buckets. An update request is generated only when an object leaves the augmented area. Showed as Fig. 4(b), the dashed square and dotted square are two augmented buckets. The object is at first in bucket I (the dashed square). At point 1, it leaves bucket I and goes into bucket II (the dotted square), then it moves in bucket II and at point 2, it goes back to bucket I. Now, following the same path, there are only two database updates being submitted.

The augmented space partition method works as following. At first we generate an overlap-free space partition, then we hash objects into buckets according to their original positions. After that, each bucket makes a δ-expansion. A δ-expansion means that the center of each bucket does not change, but the covered area increases a small length δ on all sides. For example, if a bucket covers a rectangle $[(x_0, y_0)(x_1, y_1)]$, after the δ-expansion, the bucket covers $[(x_0 - \delta, y_0 - \delta)(x_1 + \delta, y_1 + \delta)]$.

The next step is to find an appropriate hash function. Only using the current location information of objects as input is not sufficient: when an object moves into an area covered by more than one bucket, the function can hardly decide which bucket the object should be in. So we introduce an extra attribute called *previous_bucketid*. This attribute keeps track of which bucket an object is previously in and is sent to the hash function along with the current location information. After each time period, if an object currently stays in an area covered by only one bucket, everything is fine. Otherwise, i.e., if the area is covered by more than one bucket, the LP first checks if the object previously stayed in any of these buckets (using *previous_bucketed*). If so, the LP sends no update request to the database. If not, the system randomly picks one of these buckets for that object, then makes the change in database as well.

The index and query procedures are the same as in overlap-free space partition method.

5   Experiment Results

To access the merit, we implemented a simulation program and performed some experimental evaluation on different methods.

5.1   Experimental Setup and Data Generation

Since there are very few real data sets available in this field, we adopt a famous benchmarking environment called "Generate Spatio-Temporal Data (GSTD)" [NST99].

We use Java programming language in our experiments due to its strong thread support. In our test system, there are two LPs. Each LP monitors half of the objects. At the end of each time period, both LPs check the latest status of the moving objects and send the filtered update requests to the database. The database collects the requests and reports the experiment results.

The experiments are running on a Pentium II 300MHz machine with 128M memory. We use 20 bytes to represent each two dimensional object (2 doubles for location information and 1 integer for object id). The disk page size is 4K bytes. Each page can hold upper to 204 2-d objects.

Most other methods index the history information of each object, which makes them impossible to index large number of objects. So it is unfair to compare our method with them. Besides our four methods, we also implemented the R-tree method. The R-tree method works in traditional static way. It maintains a R-tree in database which stores the latest location information of objects.

The notation used in this section and abbreviations of algorithms are summarized in Table 1 for easy reference.

v	Speed of an object
$\bar{v}$	Average speed of all objects
$\sigma(v)$	Standard deviation of speed
S	Bucket size
$DU\#$	Number of database update
$\sigma(D)$	Standard deviation of initial distribution
RT	R-tree method
SP	Overlap-free space partition method
ASP	Augmented space partition method

Table 1. Notation and Algorithm abbreviations used in our experiment

The dataset consists of 100,000 moving objects in working space which is a unit square $[0,1]^2$. We study the performance of various methods on two initial object distributions and two movement patterns, which are described below:

Two initial distribution types: The first one is uniform distribution. In this case, objects are uniformly distributed in working space. the second one is Gaussian distribution. This time, objects are clustered around one or several central points. When we use Gaussian distribution, we set $\sigma(D)$ to be 0.1.

Two movement types: We defined two movement types for our experiment: random movement and directed movement. The second movement type is illustrative when we study cars' movement during rush hours. The settings are showed in Table 5.1. The detailed meaning of each parameter can be found in [NST99].

	$\bar{v}$	$\sigma(v)$	$max_x(speed)$	$max_y(speed)$	$min_x(speed)$	$min_y(speed)$
Random movement	0	0.005	0.005	0.005	-0.005	-0.005
Directed movement	0.005	0.005	0.01	0.01	0	0

Table 2. Settings for two movement patterns

The query sets consist of 1000 rectangles residing within the working space. We choose the centers of the rectangles randomly. The size of the query rectangle is 1% of the total area. At the end of each time interval, one query is randomly picked from the query set and applied to the current object distribution.

5.2   Experiment Results

Experiment 1: Impact of Bucket Size In this section, we want to study the index performance under different S and $\bar{v}$ in SP method.

We define the hash function to be $f(x, y) = i * int(y * i) + int(x * i)$. This function divides the working space into $i \times i$ equally-sized square buckets. Then we fix $\bar{v}$ to be 0.005 and record the performance under different i values. The result in Fig. 5 shows that the total number of database updates is proportional to i. When we fix i and change $\bar{v}$, as showed in Fig. 6, we find that the number of database updates is also proportional to $\bar{v}$. From the results obtained, we can conclude:

$$DU\# \propto \frac{\bar{v}}{\sqrt{S}}$$

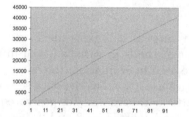
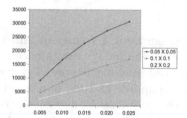

Fig. 5. Performance vs. S, $\bar{v} = 0.005$ **Fig. 6.** Performance vs. $\bar{v}$

Experiment 2: Impact of Overlapping Size In this experiment, we study the impact of overlapping size in ASP method. This time, the bucket size is fixed as 0.1×0.1. Fig. 7 shows the average number of database updates for different overlapping size. The x-axis is the size of expansion on each side, and the y-axis is the total number of database updates. Two curves illustrate the results under different $\bar{v}$.

At a first glimpse, it is clear that allowing overlapping between buckets helps considerably. This can filter many database updates requested by objects near the bucket borders. Note that the curve values decrease very fast at the beginning, then they decelerate in both cases. When $\bar{v}$ is slow, this pattern is even more obvious.

When the bucket expands on each side, the actual size of each bucket increases too. Thus, given a query range, the possibility for each bucket to intersect with that range increases and it degenerates the query performance. Therefore, to find a good overlap size is an important task for an ASP algorithm. From this experiment, we find that the best selection of the overlap size is $\bar{v}$. For example, if $\bar{v}$ is 0.005 in one case, in ASP, we should make a 0.005-expansion on each bucket. The benefit obtained from an expansion over that point is marginal.

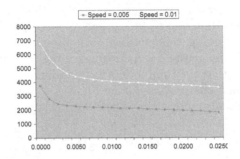

Fig. 7. Impact of overlapping size

Experiment 3: Study of index performance In this experiment, we want to observe the index performance of different methods in various initial distribution and movement types. Two metrics are used in evaluation: the number of database update and the number of disk pages used to store the data set. The number of database updates includes two parts: database updates generated by LPs and updates generated in bucket merges and splits. Fig. 8 and 9 show the results.

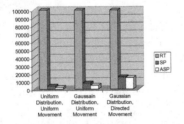   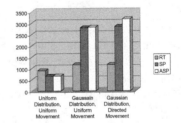

Fig. 8. Number of database updates   **Fig. 9.** Number of disk pages used

RT method updates the locations of all the objects at the end of each time period. Therefore, the number of database updates at each time period is the same as the number of objects. The other two methods are much better than RT method in this respect. In ASP method, the overlapping area is set to be $\bar{v}$. We find that the total number of database updates is about 60% to 70% of that in SP. There is significant improvement.

Experiment 4: Comparison on Query Performance In this part, we want to test the query performance for both of our two methods. We collect two sets of data in experiments: disk pages accessed and objects checked in LPs.

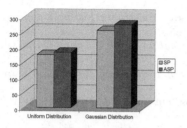 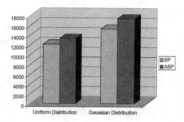

Fig. 10. Number of disk pages checked **Fig. 11.** Number of objects checked in LPs

ASP is a little worse than SP because after expanding the buckets, the possibility for each node to intersect with the query area increases a little bit. This results in extra query cost. However the difference is minor.

Discussion and Method Selection The first discussion is whether we should expand the buckets, i.e., using ASP instead of SP. Our answer is yes. The benefit of doing so is remarkable: about 30% - 40% of the database update requests are filtered. And the cost is small: the query is a little slower after that. The best overlapping size is the same as $\bar{v}$, which, in most cases, is very small too.

Another discussion is about the bucket size. In our experiment, we show that the following function can be used to describe the number of database updates: $DU\# = K\frac{\bar{v}}{\sqrt{S}}$ where K is a constant. Suppose a system can finish up to N_t update operations within a given time period, the selection of S should follows:

$$S \le (\frac{N_t}{K\bar{v}})^2$$

6   Conclusion and Future Works

In this paper, we studied moving object indexing problem. The technique we used is called hashing technique which saves the bucket information of each object instead of the object's exact location. A system structure and two hashing methods are suggested to support the application of this hashing technique. This work makes it possible to index and manage large number of moving objects.

Future researches include the following. Firstly, we want to find a way to index rectangle objects and the objects whose shapes change over time (such as forest fire, etc). Secondly, we plan to perform research on spatial distance join between moving objects. Finally, we want to find more hash functions based on our system structure.

Acknowledgments: The authors would like to thank Dr. Samir Khuller, Lusheng Ji, and Sherwood Yao for their helpful advice.

References

APR99.   S. Acharya, V. Poosala, S. Ramaswamy. *Selectivity Estimation in Spatial Databases* Proc. of SIGMOD 1999. 165

CG99.   Surajit Chaudhuri, Luis Gravano. *Evaluating Top-k Selection Queries* Proc. of VLDB, 1999. 162

Gut84.   A. Guttman. *R-Trees, A Dynamic Index Structure for Spatial Searching* Proc. of the ACM SIGMOD, 1984.

KGT99.   G. Kollios, D Gunopulos, V. J. Tsotras. *On Indexing Mobile Objects* In Proc. of PODS, 1999. 163

NST99.   M. A. Nascimento, J. R. O. Silva, Y. Theodoridi. *Evaluation of Access Structures for Discretely Moving Points* Intl. Workshop on Spatio-Temporal Database Management (STDBM'99), Edinburgh, UK, September 1999. 167, 168

PIH+96.   V. Poosala, Y. E. Ioannidis, P. J. Haas, E. J. Shekita. *Improved Histograms for Selectivity Estimation of Range Predicates* Proc. of SIGMOD 1996. 165

PJ99.   D. Pfoser, C. S. Jensen. *Capturing the Uncertainty of Moving-Object Representations* Advances in Spatial Databases, 6th International Symposium, SSD'99, Hong Kong, China, July 20-23, 1999.

PTJ99.   D. Pfoser, Y. Theodoridis, C. S. Jensen. *Indexing Trajectories of Moving Point Objects* Chorochronos Technical Report, CH-99-3, October, 1999. 162

PTJ00.   D. Pfoser, Y. Theodoridis, C. S. Jensen. *Novel Approaches in Query Processing for Moving Objects* Chorochronos Technical Report, CH-00-3, February, 2000. 162

Sam90.   H. Samet. *The Design and Analysis of Spatial Data Structures* Addison-Wesley, Reading, MA, 1990.

SK98.   Thomas Seidl, Hans-Peter Kriegel. *Optimal Multi-Step k-Nearest Neighbor Search* Proc. of SIGMOD 1998. 162

SR00.   Zhexuan Song, Nick Roussopoulos. *Hashing Moving Objects* Technical Report, CS-TR-4143, University of Maryland, 2000.

SJL+00.   S. Saltenis, C. S. Jensen, S. T. Leutenegger, M. A. Lopez. *Indexing the Positions of Continuously Moving Objects* Proc. of SIGMOD 2000. 163

SWC+97.   A. P. Sistla, O. Wolfson, S. Chamberlain, S. Dao. *Modeling and Querying Moving Objects* Proc. of ICDE 1997. 163

TJ98.   Nectaria Tryfona, Christian S. Jensen. *A component-Based Conceptual Model for Spatiotemporal Applications Design* CHOROCHRONOS project, technical report CH-98-10, 1998.

TUW98.   J. Tayeb, O. Ulusoy, O. Wolfson. *A Quadtree Based Dynamic Attribute Indexing Method* The Computer Journal, 41(3), 1998. 162

WCD+98.   O. Wolfson, S. Chamberlain, S. Dao, L. Jiang, G. Mendex. *Cost and Imprecision in Modeling the Position of Moving Objects* In Proc. of ICDE, 1998. 163

Storage and Retrieval of Moving Objects *

Hae Don Chon, Divyakant Agrawal, and Amr El Abbadi

University of California, Santa Barbara
Santa Barbara, CA 93106, USA
{hdchon,agrawal,amr}@cs.ucsb.edu

Abstract. We investigate the problem and provide a data model storing, indexing, and retrieving future locations of moving objects in an efficient manner. Each moving object has four independent variables which allow us to predict its future location: a starting location, a destination, a starting time, and an initial velocity. To understand the underlying complexity of the problem, we investigate and categorize the configurations where two variables can vary. Based on that understanding, we choose a configuration which is to some extent restrictive, but still can be used in a wide variety of realistic settings. A performance study shows that our model has much less overhead in processing range queries compared to other proposed approaches.

1   Introduction

Imagine you are driving a car equipped with an intelligent computer system that can communicate with a control center via a wireless network. While you are on a highway approaching a city area, you decide to stop for a cup of coffee and your car computer tells you that there are several upcoming exits on the road which have a coffee shop nearby. You ask the computer which one to choose to avoid traffic congestion in such a way that if you stop at the one after passing the city area, then you would avoid the upcoming congestion or if you stop at the one before the city, then existing congestion would disappear during your stopover. Alternatively, imagine that you have a flight scheduled at 11 a.m. at the airport two hours from your home and there is a highway control center which guarantees you the two hours travel time if you notify the control center of your schedule in advance. Then you do not have to leave your home earlier than necessary. There has been significant research in the area of Advanced Transportation Systems [4,7] in the past decade and the next generation of wireless communication will soon be able to make these scenarios real [3,1].

In order to develop enabling technologies to realize the above scenarios, a crucial component is to maintain up-to-date information about the location of moving vehicles on the road. There could be thousands of cars on a small segment of a highway at any given time of a day. And of course, they are moving continuously unless there is an accident or heavy traffic congestion on their paths.

---

* This research was partially supported by the NSF under grant numbers EIA98-18320, IIS98-17432 and IIS99-70700.

K.-L. Tan et al. (Eds.): MDM 2001, LNCS 1987, pp. 173–184, 2001.
© Springer-Verlag Berlin Heidelberg 2001

Updating their current locations once per second causes thousands of update transactions per second, not to mention the query transactions. Therefore, keeping track of each and every car's current location in real time is very hard to achieve if not impossible. However, instead of updating continuously, if we have a way of predicting the current locations of moving objects using some static information they provide either when they enter into the highway system or when they decide to get on the highway sometime in the future, then answering queries such as the above may become feasible.

Although we use cars on a highway as an example, any objects with some intelligent equipment such as airplanes or cellular phone users fall into the same category so that we can apply this technology to other applications. In this paper, we analyze the problem and propose a data model which abstracts moving objects as line segments and develop an efficient indexing technique explicitly designed for moving objects. The paper is organized as follows: Section 2 formalizes and reviews related work. In Section 3, we categorize all possible configurations so that we can pinpoint the best possible configuration on which we can build an efficient index structure. In Section 4, we give the performance results. Lastly, Section 5 gives conclusions and future work.

2   Problem Statement and Related Work

Objects such as automobiles, cellular phone users, and air planes change their locations continuously; we will use the term *moving objects* to refer to such entities. The problem we analyze and solve in this paper is the following: how to model moving objects so that we can store, index, and retrieve their future locations in an efficient manner. In particular, we are interested in answering a typical range query such as: $Q = $ *return all moving objects which would be in a section of a highway at some time in the future.* Each moving object in a one dimensional space has four independent variables which allow us to predict its future location: a starting location(s), a destination(e), a starting time(t_s), and an initial velocity(v_0). We assume that a moving object will notify the database system whenever it changes one of these four variables. Updating the database will be done by deleting first and inserting it again.

We can think of a moving object as a point in a four dimensional space. However, modeling a moving object this way is not appropriate for our purpose since first, they do not necessarily preserve the proximity in the real world meaning that two objects near each other in the real world may not be close in the four dimensional space. Second, indexing in a higher dimensional space is not as efficient as in a lower dimensional space.

Another way of modeling moving objects is to draw its expected trajectory in a two dimensional space with time and location as the two axes, and its trajectory becomes a line segment. Thus, we can also model a moving object as a line segment in two dimensional space. Then a typical query Q becomes a range query with range $[t_1, t_2] \times [y_1, y_2]$, in other words, find all moving objects that are between the location y_1 and y_2 during the time t_1 and t_2. The query can be stated as follows: from a line segments database, find all line segments which intersect the query rectangle $R([t_1, t_2] \times [y_1, y_2])$.

One critical assumption that affects the definition of the problem is the notion of registration (or reservation) meaning that before you actually get a service whether it is a highway or an airplane, you need to tell the system your schedule. Without registration, predicting congestion would be difficult. For instance, if we predict traffic congestion only based on the current information, then there would be no congestion whatsoever if the prediction is based on the information that exists in the database at 5 a.m. With the assumption of registration, we can use the result set of this query to predict traffic congestion or to guarantee the fixed travel time. Without it, we can predict at least how long and until which exit the congestion stays so that we can flexibly open or close exits in between.

Jagadish [10] considered the problem of indexing line segments that (i) go through a specified point or (ii) intersect a specified line segment. He first extends a line segment to an infinite line, gets the line equation, and uses the slope and y-intercept to transform a line into a point in a two dimensional space called the dual space. The transformation is known as Hough transformation [9]. It seems to have good storage utilization, however, when a line segment is transformed to a point in a dual space, half of the information is lost because a line segment has four parameters whereas an infinite line has only two parameters. Hoel and Samet [8] used PMR Quadtrees [13] to store and index line segments. They focused on queries such as finding a nearest line segment from a specified point. In many cases, they have to store information for a line segment over and over again which leads to significant storage overhead.

In [16], Sistla et al. proposed a data model called Moving Objects Spatio-Temporal(MOST) for representing moving objects. In the MOST data model, the concept of dynamic attributes is introduced, which consists of three sub-attributes, update value, update time, and function. Each moving object is assigned a dynamic attribute which is used to get its current location. They also proposed Future Temporal Logic as the query language for the MOST data model which is built on top of existing DBMS and takes advantage of the dynamic attributes. Wolfson et al. [19] addressed the uncertainty issues which determine the frequency with which the database has to update the locations of moving objects to provide a bound on the error. Erwig et al. [6] described an approach to model moving and evolving spatial objects introducing data types for moving points and moving regions together with a set of operations on such entities. They do not propose a specific design of such types and operations or a formal definition of their semantics. Instead, they give an outline of the work that should be done. They also developed an SQL-like query language with some new types of operators. However, their work concentrates on the queries for the current and the past information. Pfoser and Jensen [14] assumed that the positions of moving objects are tracked by using Global Positioning System and discussed sampling errors and uncertainty. As proposed by Erwig et al. [6], they only handled current and past information.

To the best of our knowledge, [17] is the first work that addresses the issue of indexing moving objects to query their future positions. They present a method to index moving objects using the PMR quadtree which shares the same drawbacks as the method proposed by Hoel et al. [8]. Kollios et al. [11] have proposed two methods that index moving objects in one dimensional space, and they have developed extensions for indexing moving objects in two dimensional space. One of the two methods uses a point access method. The other is a query approximation algorithm that uses multiple B^+-Trees. We will be comparing the methods proposed in this paper with those in [11]. Recently, Saltenis et al. [15] proposed a variant of R^*-Tree [2], Time-Parameterized R-Tree(TPR-Tree) to index the current and future positions of moving objects. Minimum Bounding Rectangles(MBR) of TPR-Trees grow or shrink to enclose containing moving objects. A moving object is assigned to an MBR so that the size of the MBR is minimum in some point of time when most of the queries will arrive.

3   Models

As stated earlier, a moving object has four independent variables, $\langle s, e, t_s, v_0 \rangle$. In this section, we investigate and categorize the configurations where two variables can vary so that we can choose the best possible configuration on which we can build an efficient indexing structure. The configurations where only one variable can vary are quite simple and not realistic [5].

3.1   Moving Objects with Two Degree of Freedom

In this section, we consider scenarios in which two of the four parameters are constants. With four parameters, there are 6 different combinations to consider. Due to the space limit, we enumerate only three of them with the figures(Figure 1) in the original space as well as in the dual space. In the figure, the upper graph shows the line segments in the original space and the shaded area of the lower graph is the result set of the range query. The reader can find all the enumerations and the figures in [5]. Since the y location starts from zero, the contraint on s and e is that they should be greater than or equal to zero.

The first combination (A) is the case where s and e can vary, in other words, all moving objects start at the same time with the same velocity. First, check the conditions on s. Define y_{lr} as the y-intercept of the line which passes through (t_2, y_1) and y_{ul} as the y-intercept of the line which passes through (t_1, y_2). Then for a line segment to intersect with the query rectangle R, the y-intercept of the line should be greater than or equal to y_{lr} and less than or equal to y_{ul}. The equation of the infinite line extended from the line segment which passes through (t_1, y_2) is $y = v_0 t + y_{ul}$. If we substitute (t_1, y_2) for (t, y), we get $y_{ul} = y_2 - v_0 t_1$. In the same fashion, we can get $y_{lr} = y_1 - v_0 t_2$. The y-intercept of the line segment which passes through (t_1, y_1), say y_{ll}, is $y_1 - v_0 t_1$. Second, check the conditions on e. For the line segment which passes the horizontal line between $[t_1, t_2]$, the destination(e) being greater than or equal to y_1 is enough to intersect with the query rectangle R. However, that is not enough for one whose y-intercept is in between y_{lr} and y_{ll}. It should cross the vertical line at t_1. The e value of such a line at t_1 is $v_0 t_1 + s$ for a fixed s. Therefore, we have one more condition on e, $s + v_0 t_1 \leq e$. See Figure 1(A). In summary, a moving object $\langle s, e, t_s, v_0 \rangle$ where s and e can vary should satisfy the following conditions to be included in the result set for the query $R([t_1, t_2] \times [y_1, y_2])$:

$$y_1 - v_0 t_2 \leq s \leq y_2 - v_0 t_1,$$

$$e \geq \begin{cases} y_1 & \text{if } y_1 - v_0 t_2 \leq s \leq y_1 - v_0 t_1, \\ s + v_0 t_1 & \text{if } y_1 - v_0 t_1 < s \leq y_2 - v_0 t_1 . \end{cases}$$

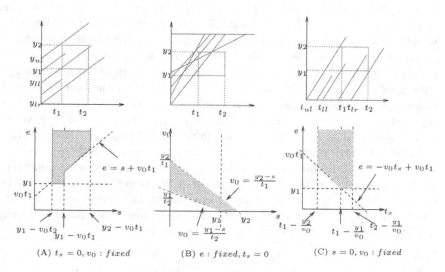

Fig. 1. Two parameters vary

The next combination (B) is the case where s and v_0 can vary. In this combination, all moving objects start at the same time to the same destination, but with different starting locations and different velocities. Suppose s is fixed, and define v_{lr} as the slope of the line which passes through (t_2, y_1) and whose y-intercept is s. Likewise, v_{ul} as the slope of the line which passes through (t_1, y_2) and whose y-intercept is s. Then, for a line segment with s less than y_1 to intersect with the query rectangle R, its slope should be greater than or equal to v_{lr} and less than or equal to v_{ul}. The equation of the line which passes a fixed s is $y = v_0 t + s$, and the slope of such line which passes through (t_1, y_2) is $\frac{y_2 - s}{t_1}$, and the slope of such line which passes through (t_2, y_1) is $\frac{y_1 - s}{t_2}$. Therefore, we have $v_{lr} = \frac{y_1 - s}{t_2}$ and $v_{ul} = \frac{y_2 - s}{t_1}$. For s greater than y_1, the slope being less than or equal to $\frac{y_2 - s}{t_1}$ is enough to intersect with the query rectangle R, assuming the slope should be greater than zero. See Figure 1(B). In summary, a moving object $\langle s, e, t_s, v_0 \rangle$ where s and v_0 can vary should satisfy the following conditions to be included in the result set for the query $R([t_1, t_2] \times [y_1, y_2])$:

$$\frac{y_1 - s}{t_2} \leq v_0 \leq \frac{y_2 - s}{t_1} \quad \text{if } s \leq y_1,$$

$$v_0 \leq \frac{y_2 - s}{t_1} \quad \text{otherwise} \ .$$

In combination (C) where e and t_s can vary, all moving objects start from the same location with the same velocity. Define t_{ul} as the t-intercept of the line which passes through (t_1, y_2) and t_{lr} as the t-intercept of the line which passes through (t_2, y_1). For a line segment to intersect with the query rectangle R, their t-intercept(t_s) should be greater than or equal to t_{ul} and less than or equal to t_{lr}. The equation of the infinite line extended from the line segment which passes through (t_1, y_2) is $y - y_2 = v_0(t - t_1)$. If we substitute $(t_{ul}, 0)$ for (t, y), we get $t_{ul} = t_1 - \frac{y_2}{v_0}$. Similarly, we can get the t-intercept of the line which passes through (t_2, y_1), $t_{lr} = t_2 - \frac{y_1}{v_0}$. Besides, t-intercept of the line which passes through (t_1, y_1) is $t_1 - \frac{y_1}{v_0}$, say t_{ll}. Now, let us consider the bounds on e. For a line segment whose t-intercept is greater than t_{ll} and less than t_{lr}, i.e. the line segment which passes the horizontal line between t_1 and t_2, e being greater than y_1 is enough for it to intersect with the query rectangle R. However, the line segment for which t-intercept is in between t_{ul} and t_{ll} should cross the vertical line at t_1. The equation of the infinite line which passes through a point (t_1, e) is $y - e = v_0(t - t_1)$. If we substitute $(t_s, 0)$ for (t, y), we get the e value of the line at t_1, $e = -v_0 t_s + v_0 t_1$. See Figure 1(C). In summary, a moving object $\langle s, e, t_s, v_0 \rangle$ where e and t_s can vary should satisfy the following conditions to be included in the result set for the query $R([t_1, t_2] \times [y_1, y_2])$:

$$t_1 - \frac{y_2}{v_0} \leq t_s \leq t_2 - \frac{y_1}{v_0},$$

$$e \geq \begin{cases} -v_0 t_s + v_0 t_1 & \text{if } t_1 - \frac{y_2}{v_0} \leq t_s \leq t_1 - \frac{y_1}{v_0}, \\ y_1 & \text{if } t_1 - \frac{y_1}{v_0} < t_s \leq t_2 - \frac{y_1}{v_0} \ . \end{cases}$$

We have considered three of six possible combinations and summarized them in Figure 1. An interesting thing to note is that in the dual space the shapes of the result sets of the range query differ from each other, and the shapes are irregular, meaning that they are not rectangular or circular. The reason we care about the shape being rectangular or circular is that most popular multidimensional index structures such as R^*-Trees [2] or SS-Trees [18] are based on the fact that the shape of the range queries is either rectangular or circular.

3.2 SV Model

In this section, we analyze each of the parameters(s, e, t_s, and v_0) and choose the most suitable configuration for building an efficient index structure and realistic combination of the six possible cases as our data model.

We start by considering a simple transformation that can be used to generalize the problem from one with fixed starting location s to one with variable s. We can transform an object with variable nonzero s and t_s into one with $s = 0$ and new t_s as follows,

$$newT_s = -s/v_0 + t_s .\tag{1}$$

With Transformation (1), we represent a moving object with any starting point as one that starts from the origin. Therefore, solving the limited problem where $s = 0$ is the same as solving the general problem where s could be anywhere, meaning that we can have constant s and variable t_s without restricting the problem. If we visualize the conversion, it corresponds to extending a line segment to the t axis and getting the new t_s coordinate. This conversion introduces some overhead if we ask a query about the past. For example, if a moving object, m, starts to move from $s = 10$ at time $t_s = 10$ with velocity $v_0 = 1$, then the $newT_s$ by Transformation (1) is 0. Next, if we ask a query about the vehicles in the time period between 3 and 5, m would come up as a result, although m does not exist at that time. This is an example of the overhead that we could have avoided if we do not convert t_s to $newT_s$. However, this is not a significant problem since we need the filtering when we query the past. In this case, quick response time is not as important as in the real time system.

Next, consider the destination parameter e. When e varies, there are two ways to convert the variable e to some fixed e. One is to set it to some constant and apply some filtering technique at the end of every query, which could introduce significant overheads. The other is to move the line segment so that the y coordinate of the right end point(e) of the line segment becomes a fixed constant. In this case, two other parameters(s and t_s) change correspondingly, which could make the problem more complex. In any case, converting variable e to some fixed constant is not helpful to solve the problem. Therefore, e should be a variable, which leaves us no choice except v_0 being constant. However, requiring constant v_0 is actually not a significant constraint. In real world highways with vehicles equipped with discrete speedometers, the number of different velocities is actually not so large. We can therefore easily create multiple instances of fixed velocity models for any given stretch of a highway under consideration. The more instances we have, the more precision we would gain. However, for a moving object whose velocity does not match one of the instances, we can insert it into the one which has the closest velocity and make it update more often than other objects whose velocity match exactly an instance.

Among the six combinations, (C) fits in with our purpose of choosing a configuration that has the most realistic assumptions and at the same time captures the abstraction of the problem well. Since (C) assumes $s = 0$, we can apply Transformation(1) without restricting the problem. Secondly, as we have discussed above, (C) assumes variable e and constant v_0. We call this combination SV model(fixed s, v) and claim that this model captures the abstraction of the problem well. In the next section, we support this claim by considering an experimental evaluation with realistic database workloads.

4 Performance

In this section, we introduce the SS-Tree [18] as the underlying index structure, explain experimental settings, and show the result of a performance study.

We use the SS-Tree [18] as the underlying index structure. The SS-Tree is a high-dimensional search tree proposed by White and Jain [18] for similarity searches such as k-nearest neighbor query. It has been shown to outperform the R^*-Tree [2] in high-dimensional k-nearest neighbor query. We expect the SS-Tree to perform better also for range queries than the R^*-Tree due to the same reasons.

As discussed earlier, we can cluster moving objects with the same velocity by associating them with an instance of the SS-Tree. Another benefit of using the SV model is that the shape of the result set in the SV model is close to rectangular (as shown in Figure 1(C)) which is easier to handle since many index structures(e.g., R^*-Tree variants) use it as a result set of a range query.

The SV model requires an index structure for a fixed velocity and we assume that there are only 5 different velocities, therefore we need 5 SS-Trees for the SV model. Each SS-Tree for the SV model is associated with a fixed velocity, $v = 0.8, 0.9, ..., 1.2$. The Dual transform model does not require multiple instances of an index structure, therefore, only one SS-Tree is used.

4.1 Experimental Setting and Uniform Data Distribution

In this section, we describe the experimental setting, the data sets and the metrics used. We first generate N objects, where $N = 10000, 20000, ..., 80000$. Each object has 5 variables: a unique ID(id), a starting location(s), a destination(e), a starting time(t_s), and a velocity(v_0). We assign a sequence number to each object as its ID and set the starting location to zero. After randomly generating two numbers in the range [0,500], we assign one to the destination and the other to the starting time. We maintain two lists, one sorted based on t_s and the other sorted on the time when a moving object reaches the destination and is supposed to remove itself from the system. The time to remove is $t_e = \frac{e-s}{v_0} + t_s$. The system starts the clock running from 0 to 500. At each tick, it inserts the objects which are supposed to start at that time, and deletes the objects which are supposed to reach their destinations by that time. To start with, the system is run for the first 20% of the time. A new object is inserted into the SV model by inserting into the SS-Tree corresponding to the same velocity as the object's together with (id, t_s, e). In the Dual transform model, the object is inserted into the SS-Tree with id, the velocity, v_0, and the y-intercept, $-v_0 \times t_s$. After that, at every other tick, we run 5 random queries ($[t_1, t_2] \times [y_1, y_2]$) against the two models and collect the results. If the width($t_2 - t_1$) is 5, we call the query a 1% query and if it is 50, a 10% query. t_1 should be greater than the current tick value. For a given query, the SV model first converts the rectangle to another rectangle as follows(See Figure 2(a)): $(t_1, t_2) \rightarrow (t_1 - \frac{y_2}{v_0}, t_2 - \frac{y_1}{v_0})$, $(y_1, y_2) \rightarrow (y_1, y_{max})$. With the converted rectangle, the SV model runs the query against the 5 SS-Trees and merges all the results. The Dual transform model also converts the

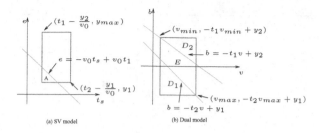

(a) SV model   (b) Dual model

Fig. 2. Two Models

rectangle to another one as follows (See Figure 2(b)): $(t_1, t_2) \rightarrow (v_{min}, v_{max})$, $(y_1, y_2) \rightarrow (-t_2v_{max} + y_1, -t_1v_{min} + y_2)$.

The overhead of the SV model is the number of objects for which (t_s, e) satisfies $e < -v_0t_s + v_0t_1$, where v_0 is the velocity of the corresponding SS-Tree, i.e., the number of objects which are in the area A in Figure 2(a). We refer to this as the *SV overhead* . The rest of the objects are the exact answers.

Before we identify different overheads in the Dual transform model, we need to take a closer look at [11] in which Kollios et al. propose a query approximation algorithm using multiple B^+-Trees. Kollios et al. noticed that depending on where the origin is considered, the y-intercept of the corresponding line segment can be different, resulting in the areas D_1 and D_2 in Figure 2(b). Multiple B^+-Trees are kept, which contain the same information about the moving objects but use different origin values. When a query arrives, the sizes of the area $D_1 + D_2$ are computed from all indices to choose the one with the minimal size, and process the query against that index structure. In this fashion, the overhead associated with the areas D_1 and D_2 is minimized. We call this the *index overhead* which is the number of objects that would not have been retrieved if the rectangle is not used to retrieve the answer set. Since we use one multidimensional index structure the size of the areas D_1 and D_2 that is generated is an upper bound of what is incurred in [11]. For the comparison, we define another kind of overhead that cannot be avoided even if the size of the area $D_1 + D_2$ is reduced to 0 by using multiple B^+-Trees. That overhead is the number of objects that are inside E but not the exact answer. We call this the *dual transformation overhead* . This *dual transformation overhead* is introduced because the Dual transform model loses half of the information of the object when it transforms the original space to the dual space.

We now compare the percentage of the three kinds of overheads as we vary the size of the objects or the width of the query rectangle. As observed in Figure 3(a), the percentage of the *SV overhead* is less than 1% in any size of the data when the width is 5(1% query), and less than 4% in any size of the data when the width is 50(10% query). The *dual transformation overhead* is around 25% in 1% query and around 22% in 10% query.

Figure 3(b) shows that as the width gets larger, the *SV overhead* becomes bigger and the overheads due to the Dual transform model become smaller. The

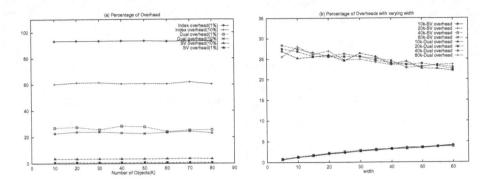

Fig. 3. Percentage of overheads with varying data size

reason is that as the width grows, the number of objects in the exact answer set also grows, so does the size of the area A. The result set of the Dual transform model also grows as the width grows, however, it already includes too many false hits to start with so that the rate at which it introduces the new false hits to the growing result set is a lot less than the rate at which previous overhead becomes exact answers. Even if we have an ideal algorithm that returns the objects in the area E without any extra work in terms of the I/O, the Dual transform model would still have 20% overheads compared to less than 4% as in the case of the SV model. In any case, the SV model outperforms the Dual transform model in terms of additional I/O.

4.2   Simulated Realistic Data

In 1990, the Santa Barbara County Association of Governments published the document [12] that is a study of Route 101 from the Hollister exit to the county line in the Santa Barbara area which is about 30 miles long. The purpose of the study is to review existing conditions and programmed improvements and to forecast travel for the year 2000. Directly from the document are the name of the exits, the lengths between exits, the annual growth of the sections until the year 2000, approximate traffic volume per lane per hour, and the number of lanes in each section. From that information, we calculate the projected traffic volume at the year 2000 and multiply the number of lanes and get the numbers for the traffic per segment per hour at peak time. The average speeds are roughly around 30 miles per hour. What we need for simulating the SV model are each car's starting time and destination along with its velocity. We also need to take its starting location into account although the SV model assumes that it is zero. Therefore, we have to use our knowledge about the neighborhoods and highway exits of the area. First, we assign a *getoff* and a *geton* rate to each exit. It is a combination of our experience and the data from [12]. If the traffic becomes less at an exit, then more cars get off than get on the exit and vice versa. We distribute the cars which get on an entry to the upcoming exits based on the *getoff* rates of each exit. And we make some number of cars get on an exit based on the *geton* rates and randomly choose the starting times of each car from one hour interval. After applying this scheme, the numbers we derive is similar in the sense that when the exact numbers change, they also change with similar rate. The readers can find the numbers in [5]. The test setup is identical to the previous subsection. Figure 4 shows the results. Although the exact numbers are a little bit different from the uniformly distributed data, the general trend of the results complies with earlier findings.

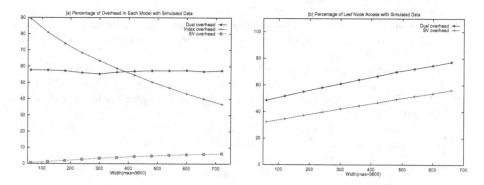

Fig. 4. Performance with realistic data distribution

5   Conclusion and Future Work

A moving object moves with four independent parameters, $\langle s, e, t_s, v_0 \rangle$. We considered the scenarios where not all parameters are variables. There are 6 different combinations when two parameters can vary, and we analyzed all of them. Among them, we chose the SV model where $s = 0$ and v_0 is fixed and t_s, e can vary because it offers the most realistic setting for moving objects and we can build an efficient multidimensional index structure on it. The performance test showed that the SV model has significantly lower overhead when compared to the Dual transform model [10,11]. Although we used the SS-Tree as the underlying index structure, any other index structure would work because the SV model does not depend on the underlying index structure.

References

1. I. Akyildiz, J. McNair, J. Ho, H. Uzunalioglu, and W. Wang. Mobility Management in Current and Future Communications Networks. *IEEE Network*, pages 39–49, 1998.   173
2. N. Beckmann, H. Kriegel, R. Schneider, and B. Seeger. The R^*-Tree: An Efficient and Robust Access Method for Points and Rectangles. In *Proc. ACM SIGMOD Int. Conf. on Management of Data*, pages 322–331, 1990.   176, 178, 180

3. K. Buchanan, R. Fudge, D. McFarlane, T. Phillips, A. Sasaki, and H. Xia. IMT-2000: Service Provider's Perspective. *IEEE Personal Communications*, 1997. 173

4. CalTrans.   Advanced   Transportation   Systems   program   Plan. *http://www.dot.ca.gov/hq/newtech*, 1996. 173

5. H. Chon, D. Agrawal, and A. El-Abbadi. Storage and Retrival of Moving Objects. Technical Report TRCS00-21, Department of Computer Science, University of California, Santa Barbara, 2000. 176, 176, 183

6. M. Erwig, R. H. Güting, M. Schneider, and M. Vazirgiannis. Spatio-Temporal Data Types: An Approach to Modeling and Querying Moving Objects in Databases. In *GeoInformatica*, volume 3, 1999. 175, 175

7. B. Foreman. A Survey of Wireless Communications Technologies for Automated Vehicle Control. In *Future Transportation Technology Conf. and Exposition*, Costa Mesa, CA, 1995. 173

8. E. Hoel and H. Samet. Efficient Processing of Spatial Queries in Line Segment Databases. In *Advances in Spatial Database - 2nd Symposium*, 1991. 175, 176

9. P.V.C. Hough. Method and Means for Recognizing Complex Patterns. *U.S. Patent No. 3069654*, 1962. 175

10. H. V. Jagadish. On Indexing Line Segments. In *Proceedings of the Int. Conf. on Very Large Data Bases*, Brisbane, Australia, 1990. 175, 183

11. G. Kollios, D. Gunopulos, and V. J. Tsotras. On Indexing Moving Objects. In *Proceedings of ACM Symp. on Principles of Database Systems*, 1999. 176, 176, 181, 181, 183

12. G. Lorden, J. Kemp, D. Daskal, A. Terry, and N. Ramirez. *South Coast route 101 corridor study*. Santa Barbara County Association of Governments, 1990. 182, 182

13. R. Nelson and H. Samet. A Consistent Hierarchical Representation for Vector Data. In *ACM SIGGRAPH*, pages 197–206, 1986. 175

14. D. Pfoser and C. S. Jensen. Capturing the Uncertainty of Moving-Object Representations. In *Proc. of the SSDBM Conf.*, pages 111–132, 1999. 175

15. S. Saltenis, C. Jensen, S. Leutenegger, and M. Lopez. Indexing the Positions of Continuously Moving Objects. In *Proc. ACM SIGMOD Int. Conf. on Management of Data*, pages 331–342, Dallas, Texas, 2000. 176

16. A. P. Sistla, O. Wolfson, S. Chamberlain, and S. Dao. Modeling and Querying Moving Objects. In *Proceedings of the Int. Conf. on Data Engineering*, 1997. 175

17. J. Tayeb, O. Ulusoy, and O. Wolfson. A Quadtree Based Dynamic Attribute Indexing Method. In *Proceedings of ACM Symp. on Principles of Database Systems*, 1998. 176

18. D. White and R. Jain. Similarity Indexing with the SS-Tree. In *Proceedings of the Int. Conf. on Data Engineering*, 1996. 178, 180, 180, 180

19. O. Wolfson, B. Xu, S. Chamberlain, and L. Jiang. Moving Objects Databases: Issues and Solutions. In *Proceedings of the 10th International Conference on Scientific and Statistical Database Management*, 1998. 175

A Mobility Framework for Ad Hoc Wireless Networks *

Xiaoyan Hong, Taek Jin Kwon, Mario Gerla, Daniel Lihui Gu and Guangyu Pei

Department of Computer Science
University of California, Los Angeles, CA 90095, USA
{hxy, kwon, gerla, gu, pei}@cs.ucla.edu

Abstract. Mobility management in ad hoc wireless networks faces many challenges. Mobility constantly causes the network topology to change. In order to keep accurate routes, the routing protocols must dynamically readjust to such changes. Thus, routing update traffic overhead is significantly high. Different mobility patterns have in general different impact on a specific network protocol or application. Consequently the network performance will be strongly influenced by the nature of the mobility pattern. In the past, mobility models were rather casually used to evaluate network performance under different routing protocols. Here, we propose a universal mobility framework, Mobility Vector Model, which can be used for recreating the various mobility patterns produced in different applications. Case studies on optimal transmission range as a function of mobility and on network performance under various mobility models are presented in the paper. Simulation results show that excessively large transmission range will not improve network performance significantly because of the increased collisions. There is an optimal range between $1.5 - 2$ times the mean node distance for free space channel. Also, simulation results show that different mobility models will have different impact on the network performance for a variety of routing protocols (AODV, DSR, FSR). When choosing routing protocols for ad hoc network applications, performance studies under multiple mobility models are recommended. The Mobility Vector model can provide a realistic and flexible framework for reproducing various models. . . .

1 Introduction

Multi-hop wireless networks are an ideal technology to establish an instant communication infrastructure for civilian and military applications. Target applications range from collaborative, distributed mobile computing to disaster recovery (such as fire, flood, earthquake), law enforcement (crowd control, search and rescue) and tactical communications. However, as the members of an ad hoc network move, the performance tends to degrade. One reason of such degradation is the traffic control overhead required for maintaining accurate routing tables in

---

* This work was supported in part by NSF under contract ANI-9814675, in part by DARPA under contract DAAB07-97-C-D321 and in part by Intel.

K.-L. Tan et al. (Eds.): MDM 2001, LNCS 1987, pp. 185–196, 2001.

the presence of mobility. Different mobility patterns will affect the performance of different network protocols in different ways. Therefore, it is very important to study the impact of mobility patterns on different network protocols in order to achieve the best performance in each scenario.

Many mobility models have been proposed for ad hoc wireless networks. Each one of them was designed to produce a particular motion behavior. A popular scheme is the Random Walk model [3]. In this model, a mobile host moves from its current position to the next with memoryless, randomly selected speed and direction. Many mobility models were derived from this one. Among them, is the Random Waypoint mobility model [6]. The model breaks the entire movement of a mobile host into a sequence of pause and motion periods. A mobile host stays in a location for a certain time then it moves to a new random-chosen destination at a speed uniformly distributed between [0, MaxSpeed].

The above mobility models apply to individual motion behaviors. However, in a real environment, a group of mobile hosts tend to move with a common objective (e.g., military deployment). Therefore, the group motion behavior is also important in some applications. To this end, the Reference Point Group Mobility (RPGM) model was proposed [4]. In this model, there is a logical "center" for each group. The center's motion summarizes the entire group's behavior. Each node is assigned a reference point (i.e., relative position with respect to the center) which follows the center movement. The random displacement in the neighborhood of the reference point represents the individual random motion component for each node.

One of the major applications of ad hoc wireless networks is the digital battlefield. In the tactical environment, mobile nodes could be individual soldiers, artilleries, SAM launchers, trucks, helicopters, support vehicles, UAVs in the sky and even satellites at higher elevations. Each different entity has different communication capabilities. So, it is reasonable to assume that the whole network is a heterogeneous environment. In this environment, different types of mobile nodes will have different types of motion behavior. Therefore, a flexible mobility framework is needed to model this hybrid motion patterns. The Mobility Vector model [5] is suitable for this need. Even in a homogeneous environment, the Mobility Vector model can be used to advantage, for example to avoid some unrealistic random movements such as sudden stops, turn backs, sharp turns, etc. The Mobility Vector model will be described in the next section. The ability of representing versatile models suggests that the model can be used as a mobility framework for various simulation.

The paper is organized as follows. In Section 2, the Mobility Vector framework is described. Section 3 discusses average speed and transmission range issues related to mobility models. Section 4 presents the performance results using various mobility models. Section 5 concludes the paper.

2   Mobility Vector Model

In this section, we introduce a new mobility framework, which can simulate natural and realistic mobility for various applications, especially in heterogeneous network applications. Most of the existing mobility models allow random movements, such as sudden stops, turn backs, sharp turns, and etc., which are physically impossible in the real world. By "remembering" mobility state of a node and allowing only partial changes in the current mobility state, we can reproduce natural motions. With this scheme, it is possible for us to imitate almost any existing mobility model. As we will see, the advantages of this model are: simplification of position updates, ease of implementation and opportunity for mobility prediction.

2.1   Mobility Vector Model

The mobility of a node is expressed by a vector (x_v, y_v), which represents 2-dimensional velocity components of the node. The 3-dimensional extension is straight forward. The scalar value (norm) of a mobility vector is the speed, computed as the distance between the current position of a node and the next position after a unit time. The mobility vector $\overrightarrow{M} = (x_m, y_m)$ or (r_m, θ_m) is the sum of 2 sub vectors: the Base Vector, $\overrightarrow{B} = (bx_v, by_v)$ or (r_b, θ_b) and the Deviation Vector, $\overrightarrow{V} = (vx_v, vy_v)$ or (r_v, θ_v). A Base Vector defines the major direction and speed of a node. A Deviation Vector stores the mobility deviation from the base vector. The model shows that $\overrightarrow{M} = \overrightarrow{B} + \alpha \times \overrightarrow{V}$, where α is an acceleration factor. By properly adjusting the acceleration factor and make the speed varing in the range [Min, Max], it is possible to generate a smoother trajectory and eliminate the chance of unrealistic node motions. This is an important feature of the new mobility vector model. For radian coordination, the Min/Max steering angle and the steering factor also can ensure more natural direction change.

2.2   Mobility Vector Model as a Framework

Gravity Model In some wireless communication systems, receivers may tend to move towards the signal source, looking for a better signal. For example, in a cellular system, if a user experiences a low quality of communication and can move around, he may try to move towards a Base Station. The Gravity Model reproduces the above mobility patterns. Every mobile node in this model is assigned a charge. Some of them have positive charges, others have negative charges, and the rest of them are not charged. The latter are free from gravity. For example, in the above cellular system, the Base Station has a negative charge and some of the mobile nodes have positive charges. Nodes with the same polarity repel each other; and nodes with opposite polarity attract each other. The force between any two nodes can be modeled by base vector using the Mobility Vector model. It is a function of distance and charges.

Location Dependent Model This model represents a collective mobility pattern in a specific area. For example, if a node is on a freeway, its mobility vector has a common component which represent the direction and the allowed speed of the freeway. If we have a digitized map and traffic pattern based on the map, we can use the base vector to implement the collective mobility. When a node moves around the area, it acquires the location dependent base vector specified at the current position.

Targeting Model Targeting is a common pattern of mobility, where nodes move towards a target. Given the target coordinate, it is simple to calculate a proper base vector. When a node approaches a target, it reduces its velocity using negative acceleration factor and then pause when the mobility vector is adjusted to zero. This is an improved implementation of Random Waypoint model which avoids sudden stops.

Group Motion Model In ad hoc networks, communications are often among teams which tend to coordinate their movements (e.g., a firemen rescue team in a disaster recovery situation). To support this kind of communications and movements, the Mobility Vector model can provide efficient and realistic group mobility models. Different group patterns can be represented using base vectors while deviation vectors show the individual behaviors of members in a group. Thus the model can provide flexible group motion patterns for heterogeneous networks, such as those including UAVs (Unattended Airborne Vehicles). UAV backbone nodes and ground nodes typically will exhibit different motion behavior.

3   Calibration of Mobility Parameters

3.1   Average Speed and Distance Traveled

As we mentioned in Section 1, many models adopt random motion. With random motion, when an average speed is given, the actual traveled distance may be larger than the geographical displacement over a given time interval. For example, a node may just bounce around its initial location in a certain period where the traveled distance is large but the geographical displacement is near zero. The reduced displacement will lessen the impact of mobility on the applications using random mobility models. Here we analyze different mobility effect under the traveled distance and the geographical displacement.

In simulation, the average speed is defined as the actual traveled distance over simulation time. This measure is conceptually and computationally simple and commonly used. Here we also measure the geographical displacement. We measure the two types of distances over a small time interval. After averaging the two measures over all the intervals in simulation and over all nodes, we normalize actual traveled distance by geographical displacement. The result is the extra distance traveled in order to achieve a certain geographical displacement.

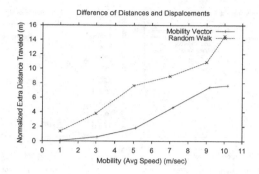

Fig. 1. Displacement Measure

Figure 1 reports the extra distance traveled as a function of average speed for two mobility models, i.e., Random Walk and Mobility Vector. The figure shows that Random Walk model produces more extra traveled distance than Mobility Vector model. Which means that given the same instantaneous speed, the Random Walk produces less geographical displacement. This lessens the impact of mobility at instantaneous speed on topology change. The positive influence of this phenomenon to routing protocol will be seen further in Section 4.

3.2   Transmission Range and Link Changes

An advantage of the limited simulation space is that it can maintain a certain degree of node distribution density, which is necessary for keeping a node's connection to its neighbors, given the transmission ranges of nodes are limited. However, when nodes are mobile, the distribution of nodes can not keep as uniform as the initial time. To what degree this will affect the network connecting topology and in turn, affect the performance of routing protocols and upper layer protocols will depend on many factors, such as, transmission range and mobility speed, as we will study in this section.

From intuition, it is understood that in order to get a good performance, the choice of transmission range is related to mobility. As the battery power is a critical constraint for mobile wireless communications, we want to choose the minimum possible range which yet provides adequate connectivity in the face of mobility.

In this section, we use four mobility models to study the link change rate. The models we choose are Random Walk, Random Waypoint, Reference Point Group Mobility (RPGM) model and the Mobility Vector. Every model requires specific parameters to define the motion it will produce. In order to compare them on an equal base, we choose the parameters in such a way that they provide the same average speed (measured through traveled distance as defined in Section 3.1).

We monitor the change of link status (up, down) caused by the motion of nodes. The rate of the change is used as an indicator of topology change. We

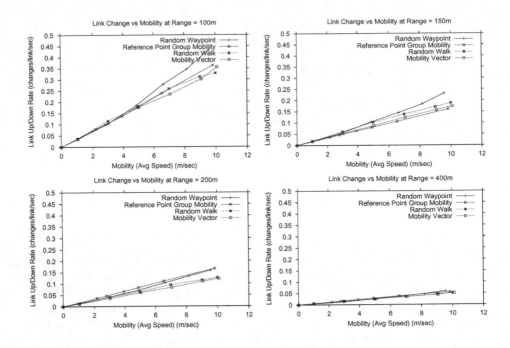

Fig. 2. Link Change vs Mobility at Various Transmission Ranges

evaluate the effect of mobility to the link change rate under various transmission ranges from 100m to 400m. The simulation area is 1km × 1km with 100 nodes uniformly distributed at initialization. The mean distance between nodes is 100m. Free space channel model is used to calculate the transmission range. We initialize our topology with same density and same scatter pattern for every model for each set of parameters. We run three experiments using the same initial density but different scatter pattern. The final results are the average over of all the executions. For RPGM, a rectangular group motion trajectory is used.

The experiment results given in Figure 2 show that in terms of the link change rate, for the same transmission range, the four models do not present great differences. Small differences exist. For example, Random Waypoint has higher rate at high mobility when transmission range is small. When the transmission range is large, every model has very small link change rate. When mobility increases, the link change rate increases for all the mobility models.

As the models behave similarly under different transmission ranges, we only show results from Mobility Vector model to investigate how the link change rate reacts to the change of transmission range at different mobility. Figure 3 illustrates that when transmission range is equal to the mean distance between nodes (i.e., 100m), the change rate is very high - about 35% for mobility = 10; However, when the transmission range increases to 1.5 times of the mean distance, the change rate reduces to a half of the 35%; And when the transmission range increases to 2 times of the mean distance, the change rate decreases to almost one third (about 12%). Further increasing of transmission range decreases the change rate continuously, but does not create dramatic effect. This property holds for all the mobility. Thus, for the sake of minimizing energy consumption, choosing transmission range at a range of 1.5 - 2 time of mean distance is a good solution in free space channel environment.

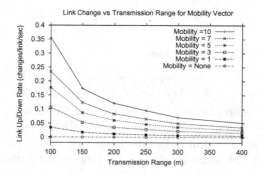

Fig. 3. Link Change Using Mobility Vector

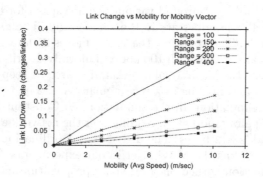

Fig. 4. Link Change Using Mobility Vector

Figure 4 gives another view of the relation between link change rate and mobility. The increase of mobility increases the changing rate.

4   Impact on Network Performance

In a multi-hop network, even relatively small node movements can cause noticeable changes in network topology and thus affect the performance of upper layer protocols, such as throughput and delay. An example of ranking of routing protocols for various scenarios is given in [4]. Exploiting the observations in previous sections regarding the relationship between transmission range and link dynamics, we study in this section the impact of mobility on routing performance.

We will not conduct a complete comparison across "all" routing protocols. Good surveys in this subject can be found in [9,10,11,12]. Here we study a restricted set of routing protocols to which we apply various mobility models with varying transmission ranges.

4.1 Experimental Configuration

The routing protocols used are Dynamic Source Routing (DSR) [6], Ad hoc On Demand Distance Vector Routing (AODV) [7], and the Fisheye State Routing (FSR) [8]. They are all provided within the GloMoSim library [1]. The GloMoSim library is a scalable simulation environment for wireless network systems using the parallel discrete-event simulation language PARSEC [2]. The packet delivery ratio – the ratio between the number of packets received and those originated by the sources, is used as a performance metric.

We use previous mobility models, they are: Mobility Vector, Random Waypoint, Reference Point Group Mobility (RPGM) and Random Walk. The parameters of the four models are set so as to achieve the same average speed. For Mobility Vector model, the acceleration factor is set to zero and for Random Waypoint, the pause time is fixed to 10 seconds. The Min/Max speeds for both model are set to be ± 1 around various average speed for experiments. For RPGM model [4], all the nodes are in the same group. The group's trajectory is a rectangular cycle. The center of the group moves 250m on each edge. The simulation area is 1km × 1km with 100 nodes uniformly distributed at initialization. The RPGM has 1.25km × 1.25km simulation area to keep nodes spreading in 1km × 1km field and moving in a rectangular cycle. The transmission range will change in our simulation. In the simulation, 50 Constant Bit Rate (CBR) source-destination pairs randomly spreading over the network are used. The size of the data payload is 512 bytes. The distributed coordination function (DCF) of IEEE 802.11 is used as the MAC layer in our experiments. The radio model has the capture function turned on. Free space propagation model is used. The channel capacity is 2 Mbits/sec.

4.2 Results

Figure 5 gives the simulation results for AODV in high mobility (10m/sec) and low mobility (2m/sec) respectively. Figure 6 gives the results for DSR, and Figure 7 for FSR.

In general, no matter what mobility models are in use, increase of transmission range increases the delivery ratio. Increasing transmission range from one to twice the mean distance (i.e., from 100 to 200m) shows larger improvement with high than low mobility. These results are constant with those in Section 3.2, i.e.,

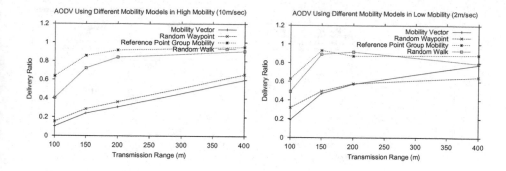

Fig. 5. Packet Delivery Ratio for AODV

link up/down statistics. This effect is particular evident in RPGM and Random Walk model.

A further increase of the transmission range to 4 times the mean distance, however, has different effects on different routing schemes. When transmission range increases, the density of neighboring nodes is increased. Thus more collisions occur. At high mobility, increased density will increase the chance for finding new routes when an old route is broken. The final effects of increased transmission range are mixed with these factors. Mobility Vector and Random Waypoint benefit from the increase in radio range. However, RPGM and Random Walk show little improvement and in some cases, throughput drops. The reason is that RPGM and Random Walk suffer from more collisions because they are more topology stable than the other two models at a given average speed.

The increase in transmission range has different effects on different routing schemes as well. In particular, FSR (Figure 7) has large degradation of delivery ratio from 200m to 400m. This is because at large transmission range, there will be too many nodes within the fisheye scope. Then, the increased routing table size and corresponding periodic update traffic overhead degrades the packet delivery capability.

In spite of these differences, we can still conclude that transmission range from 1.5 – 2 times the mean distance will produce uniformly the best improvements in delivery ratio. This appears to be the optimal range for a free space channel.

The four mobility models have different impact on routing protocols. Our most realistic model, the Mobility Vector model, produces the worst case routing performance, with the widely used Random Waypoint model coming the second worst. The Waypoint model produces a straight line motion pattern between pauses. Its impact on routing, thus, is more like that of the Mobility Vector, which moves on a smooth trajectory. In the RPGM model, the coordinated motion behavior among group members and the swing around reference points tends to produce a smaller over all topology change, and thus better delivery ratio, though the link change performance is compatible to all others. For

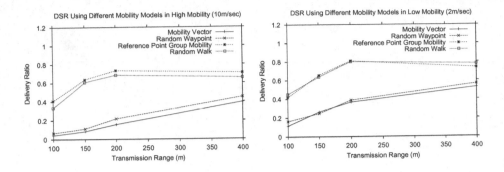

Fig. 6. Packet Delivery Ratio for DSR

Random Walk, recall from subsection 3.1 that nodes also tend to swing forward which leads to mobility underestimation and thus higher packet delivery ratio is observed.

Simulation results thus show that the choice of the mobility model makes a difference in the study of network performance. The results also suggests that a realistic mobility model is not necessarily producing better routing performance. In a contrary, given a realistic mobility model, studying how well a routing protocol can perform will help in evaluating routing protocols for applications of ad hoc networks. Performance studies among various models are necessary.

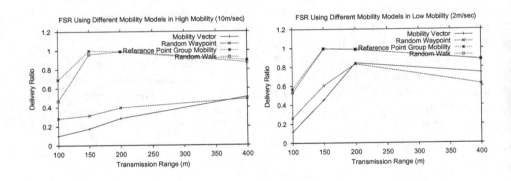

Fig. 7. Packet Delivery Ratio for FSR

5   Conclusion

In this paper we have proposed a mobility framework - Mobility Vector model. The model uses sub vectors for keeping current mobility information and providing partial changing in motion. Mobility Vector model provides realistic and flexibility for reproducing various models within a single framework in various simulations. The study of link dynamics shows different mobility models do not produce remarkably different behavior. However, the simulation results show that a transmission increase from 1.5 – 2 times the mean node distance will drastically reduce link change rate, which, as a consequence, will generate larger packet delivery ratio no matter what routing protocols are used. The effect of further increasing the transmission range is positive for Mobility Vector and Random Waypoint, but is neutral or even negative (in the FSR case) for RPGM and Random Walk.

In summary, the choice of the mobility models makes a difference in the study of network performance. Mobility Vector and Random Waypoint models provide "lower bound" type performance while Random Walk and RPGM produce top performance. These results show that, prior to deploying ad hoc network in a real environment, it is not sufficient to test its performance with a single mobility model since the choice of motion pattern can have major impact on performance.

References

1. M. Takai, L. Bajaj, R, Ahuja, R. Bagrodia and M. Gerla. GloMoSim: A Scalable Network Simulation Environment. *Technical report 990027*, UCLA, Computer Science Department, 1999. 192
2. R. Bagrodia, R. Meyer, M. Takai, Y. Chen, X. Zeng, J. Martin, and H.Y. Song. PARSEC: A Parallel Simulation Environment for Complex Systems. *IEEE Computer*, vol. 31, no. 10, Oct. 1998, pp.77-85. 192
3. M. M. Zonoozi and P. Dassanayake. User mobility modeling and characterization of mobility patterns. *IEEE Journal on Selected Areas in Communications*, 15(7):1239–1252, September 1997. 186
4. X. Hong, M. Gerla, G. Pei, and C.-C. Chiang. A Group Mobility Model for Ad Hoc Wireless Networks. In *Proceedings of ACM/IEEE MSWiM'99*, Seattle, WA, Aug. 1999, pp.53-60. 186, 192, 192
5. T. J. Kwon and M. Gerla. Clustering with Power Control. In *Proceedings of IEEE Military Communications (MILCOM'99)*, Atlantic City, NJ, Oct. 1999. p.1424-8, vol.2. 2 186
6. D. B. Johnson and D. A. Maltz. Dynamic Source Routing in Ad Hoc Wireless Networks. In *Mobile Computing*, edited by T. Imielinski and H. Korth, Chapter 5, Kluwer Publishing Company, 1996, pp. 153-181. 186, 192
7. C. Perkins and E. Royer. Ad hoc on-demand distance vector routing. In *Proceedings of the 2nd IEEE Workshop on Mobile Computing Systems and Applications*, pages 90–100, Feb 1999. 192
8. A. Iwata, C.-C. Chiang, G. Pei, M. Gerla, and T.-W. Chen. Scalable Routing Strategies for Ad-hoc Wireless Networks. In *IEEE Journal on Selected Areas in Communications*, Aug. 1999, pp. 1369-1379. 192
9. J. Broch, D. A. Maltz, D. B. Johnson, Y.-C. Hu, and J. Jetcheva. A performance comparison of multi-hop wireless ad hoc network routing protocols. In *ACM/IEEE International Conference on Mobile Computing and Networking (Mobicom98)*, pages 85–97, 1998. 192
10. P. Johansson, T. Larsson, N. Hedman, B. Mielczarek and M. Degermark. Scenario-based Performance Analysis of Routing Protocols for Mobile Ad-hoc Networks. In *Proceedings of ACM/IEEE MOBICOM'99*, pp. 195-206, Aug. 1999. 192

11. S.-J. Lee, M. Gerla and C.-K. Toh. A Simulation Study of Table-Driven and On-Demand Routing Protocols for Mobile Ad Hoc Networks. In *IEEE Network*, vol. 13, no. 4, Jul/Aug 1999, pp.48-54. 192
12. S. R. Das, C. E. Perkins and E. M. Royer. Performance Comparison of Two On-demand Routing Protocols for Ad Hoc Networks. In *Proceedings of IEEE IN-FOCOM 2000*, Tel Aviv, Israel, Mar. 2000. 192

Session VI: Networks and Systems Issues

Operating System and Algorithmic Techniques
for Energy Scalable Wireless Sensor Networks

Amit Sinha and Anantha P. Chandrakasan

Massachusetts Institute of Technology, Cambridge, MA 02139

{sinha,anantha}@mtl.mit.edu

Abstract. An system-level power management technique for massively distributed wireless microsensor networks is proposed. A power aware sensor node model is introduced which enables the embedded operating system to make transitions to different sleep states based on observed event statistics. The adaptive shutdown policy is based on a stochastic analysis and renders desired energy-quality scalability at the cost of latency and missed events. The notion of algorithmic transformations that improve the energy quality scalability of the data gathering network are also analyzed.

1 Introduction

Massively distributed, ad-hoc, wireless microsensor networks have gained importance in a wide spectrum of civil and military applications [1]. Advances in MEMS technology [2], combined with low power, low cost DSPs and RF circuits have resulted in cheap and wireless microsensor networks becoming feasible. A distributed, self-configuring network of adaptive sensors has significant benefits. They can be used to remotely monitor inhospitable and toxic environments. A large class of benign environments too require the deployment of a large number of sensors such as intelligent patient monitoring, object tracking, assembly line sensing, etc. Their massively distributed nature provides wider resolution as well as increased fault tolerance than a single sensor node. Several projects that demonstrate the feasibility of sensor networks are underway [3][4].

A wireless microsensor node is typically battery-operated and is thus energy constrained. To maximize the lifetime of the sensor node after its deployment all aspects including circuits, architecture, algorithms and protocols have to be made energy efficient. Once the system has been designed, additional energy savings can be obtained by using dynamic power management concepts [5] whereby the sensor node is shutdown if no interesting events occur. Such event driven power consumption is critical to obtaining maximum battery-life. In addition, it is highly desirable that the node has a graceful energy-quality (E-Q) scalability [6] such that if the application so demands, the user is able to extend the mission lifetime at the cost of sensing accuracy. Energy scalable algorithms and protocols are required for such energy constrained situations.

Sensing applications will present a wide range of requirements in terms of data rates, computation, average transmission distance, etc. As such protocols and algorithms will have to be tuned to each application. Therefore, embedded operating systems and software will be critical ingredients in such microsensor networks as programmability will be a necessary requirement. In this paper we propose an Operating System directed Power Management technique to improve the energy efficiency of the sensor nodes. *Dynamic Power Management* (DPM) is an effective tool to reduce system power consumption without significantly degrading performance. The basic idea is to shut down devices when they are not needed and wake them up when necessary. DPM in general is a non-trivial problem. If the energy and performance overheads in transitioning to sleep states were negligible then a simple greedy algorithm which makes the system go into the deepest sleep state as soon as it is idle would be perfect. However, in reality, transitioning to a sleep state has the overhead of storing the processor state and shutting off the power supply. Waking up too takes a finite amount of time. Therefore, implementing the right policy for transitioning to the sleep state is critical for the success of DPM. A power-aware model for sensor nodes is also introduced. We also

K.-L. Tan et al. (Eds.): MDM 2001, LNCS 1987, pp. 199-209, 2001.
© Springer-Verlag Berlin Heidelberg 2001

demonstrate how the algorithm can be used to provide desirable E-Q characteristics in sensing applications. Finally, we introduce the concept of energy scalable algorithms. The principal notion being that computation be done is such a fashion that a drop in energy availability should result in minimum possible quality degradation.

2   System Models

2.1   Sensor Network and Node Model

The fundamental idea in distributed sensor applications is to incorporate sufficient processing power in each node such that they are self-configuring and adaptive. Fig. 1 illustrates the basic sensor node architecture. Each node consists of the embedded sensor, A/D converter, a processor with memory (which in our case will be the StrongARM SA-1100 processor [7]) and the RF circuits. Each of these components are controlled by the micro Operating System (μ-OS) through micro device drivers. An important function of the μ-OS is to enable Power Management (PM). Based on event statistics, the μ-OS decides which devices to turn off/on.

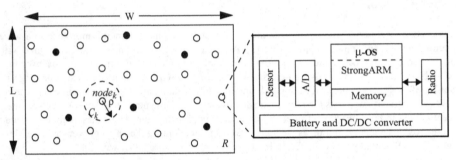

Fig. 1. Sensor network and node architecture

Our network essentially consists of η homogeneous sensor nodes distributed over a rectangular region R with dimensions WxL with each node having a visibility radius of ρ (shown by the region C_k). Three different communication models can be used for such a network. (i) Direct transmission (every node directly transmits to the basestation), (ii) Multi-hop (data is routed through the individual nodes towards the basestation) and (iii) Clustering. If the distance between the neighboring sensors is less than the average distance between the sensors and the user or the basestation, transmission power can be saved if the sensors collaborate locally. Further its likely that sensors in local clusters share highly correlated data. Some of the nodes elect themselves as 'cluster heads' (as depicted by nodes in black) and the remaining nodes join one of the clusters based on a minimum transmit power criteria. The cluster head then aggregates and transmits the data from the other cluster nodes. Such application specific network protocols for wireless microsensor networks have been developed [8]. It has been demonstrated that a clustering scheme is an order of magnitude more energy efficient than a simple direct transmission scheme.

2.2   Power Aware Sensor Node Model

A power aware sensor node model essentially describes the power consumption in different levels of node-sleep state. Every component in the node can have different power modes, e.g. the StrongARM can be in active, idle or sleep mode; the radio can be in transmit, receive, standby or off mode. Each node-sleep state corresponds to a particular combination of component power modes. In general, if there are N components labelled (1, 2, ..., N) each with k_i number of sleep states, the

Table 1. Useful sleep states for the sensor node

	StrongARM	Memory	Sensor, A/D	Radio
s_0	active	active	on	tx, rx
s_1	idle	sleep	on	rx
s_2	sleep	sleep	on	rx
s_3	sleep	sleep	on	off
s_4	sleep	sleep	off	off

total number of node-sleep states are $\prod k_i$. Every component power mode is associated with a latency overhead for transitioning to that mode. Therefore each node sleep mode is characterized by a power consumption and a latency overhead. However, from a practical point of view not all the sleep states are useful. Table 1 enumerates the component power modes corresponding to 5 different useful sleep states for the sensor node. Each of these node-sleep modes correspond to an increasingly deeper sleep state and is therefore characterized by an increasing latency and decreasing power consumption. These sleep states are chosen based on actual working conditions of the sensor node e.g. it does not make sense to have the A/D in the active state and everything else completely off. The design problem is to formulate a policy of transitioning between states based on observed events so as to maximize energy efficiency. The power aware sensor model is similar to the system power model in the Advanced Configuration and Power Interface (ACPI) standard [9]. An ACPI compliant system has five global states. SystemStateS0 (working state), and SystemStateS1 to SystemStateS4 corresponding to four different levels of sleep states. The sleep states are differentiated by the power consumed, the overhead required in going to sleep and the wakeup time. In general, the deeper the sleep state, the lesser the power consumption, and the longer the wakeup time. Another aspect of similarity is that in ACPI the *Power Manager* (PM) is a module of the OS.

2.3 Event Generation Model

An event is said to occur when the a sensor node picks up a signal with power above a pre-defined threshold. For analytical tractability we assume that every node has a uniform radius of visibility ρ. In real applications the terrain might influence the visible radius. An event can be static (e.g. a localized change in temperature/pressure in an environment monitoring application) or can propagate (e.g. signals generated by a moving object in a tracking application). In general, events have a characterizable (possibly non-stationary) distribution in space and time. We will assume that the temporal behavior of events over the entire sensing region, R, is a Poisson process with an average rate of events given by λ_{tot} [10]. In addition we assume that the spatial distribution of events is characterized by an independent probability distribution given by $p_{XY}(x,y)$. Let p_{ek} denote the probability that an event is detected by $node_k$, given the fact that it occurred in R.

$$
P_{ek} = \frac{\int\limits_{C_k} p_{XY}(x, y) dx dy}{\int\limits_{R} p_{XY}(x, y) dx dy}
\tag{1}
$$

Let $p_k(t, n)$ denote the probability that n events occur in time t at $node_k$. Therefore, the probability of no events occurring in C_k over a threshold interval T_{th} is given by

$$
P_k(T_{th}, 0) = \sum_{i=0}^{\infty} \frac{e^{-\lambda_{tot}T_{th}}(\lambda_{tot}T_{th})^i}{i!}(1 - P_{ek})^i = e^{-P_{ek}\lambda_{tot}T_{th}}
\tag{2}
$$

Let $p_{th,k}(t)$ be the probability that at least one event occurs in time t at $node_k$.

$$
P_{th, k}(T_{th}) = 1 - P_k(T_{th}, 0) = 1 - e^{-P_{ek}\lambda_{tot}T_{th}}
\tag{3}
$$

i.e. the probability of at least one event occurring is an exponential distribution characterized by a spatially weighted event arrival rate $\lambda_k = \lambda_{tot} p_{ek}$.

In addition, to capture the possibility that an event might propagate in space we describe each event by a position vector, $\mathbf{p} = \mathbf{p_0} + \int \mathbf{v}(t)dt$. Where $\mathbf{p_0}$ is the coordinates of the point of origin of the event and $\mathbf{v}(t)$ characterizes the propagation velocity of the event. The point of origin has a spatial and temporal distribution described by Equation 1 to Equation 3. We have analyzed three distinct classes of events: (i) $\mathbf{v}(t) = 0$, the events occur as stationary points, (ii) $\mathbf{v}(t) = const$, the event propagates with fixed velocity (e.g. a moving vehicle), and, (iii) $|\mathbf{v}(t)| = const$, the event propagates with fixed speed but random direction (i.e. a random walk).

3   Shutdown Policy

3.1   Sleep State Transition Policy

Assume an event is detected by $node_k$ at some time and it finishes processing it at t_1 and the next event occurs at time $t_2 = t_1 + t_i$. At time t_1, $node_k$ decides to transition to a sleep state s_k from the active state s_0 as shown in Fig. 2. Each state s_k has a power consumption P_k, and the transition time to it from the active state and back is given by $\tau_{d,k}$ and $\tau_{u,k}$ respectively. By our definition of node-sleep states, $P_j > P_i$, $\tau_{d,i} > \tau_{d,j}$ and $\tau_{u,i} > \tau_{u,j}$ for any $i > j$.

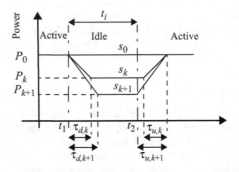

Fig. 2. State transition latency and power

We will now derive a set of sleep time thresholds $\{ T_{th,k} \}$ corresponding to the states $\{ s_k \}$, $0 \le k \le N$ (for N sleep states) such that transitioning to a sleep state s_k from state s_0 will result in a net energy loss if the idle time $t_i < T_{th,k}$ because of the transition energy overhead [12]. This assumes that no productive work can be done in the transition period, which is invariably true, e.g. when a processor wakes up the transition time is the time required for the PLLs to lock, the clock to stabilize and the processor context to be restored. The energy saving because of state transition is given by

$$E_{save,k} = P_0 t_i - \left(\frac{P_0 + P_k}{2}\right)(\tau_{d,k} + \tau_{u,k}) - P_k(t_i - \tau_{d,k}) \tag{4}$$

$$= (P_0 - P_k)t_i - \left(\frac{P_0 - P_k}{2}\right)\tau_{d,k} - \left(\frac{P_0 + P_k}{2}\right)\tau_{u,k}$$

and such a transition is only justified when $E_{save,k} > 0$. This leads us to the threshold

$$T_{th,k} = \frac{1}{2}\left[\tau_{d,k} + \left(\frac{P_0 + P_k}{P_0 - P_k}\right)\tau_{u,k}\right] \tag{5}$$

which implies that the longer the delay overhead of the transition $s_0 \rightarrow s_k$, the higher the energy gain threshold, and the more the difference between P_0 and P_k, the smaller the threshold. These observations are intuitively appealing too. Table 2 lists out the power consumption of a sensor-node described in Fig. 1 in the different power modes. Since the node consists of off the shelf components, its not optimized for power consumption. However, we will use the threshold and power consumption numbers detailed in Table 2 to illustrate our basic idea. The steady state shutdown algorithm is as follows

```
if( eventOccurred() == true ) {
    processEvent();
    ++eventCount;
    lambda_k = eventCount/getTimeElapsed();
    for( k=4; k>0; k-- )
        if( computePth( Tth(k) ) < pth0 )
            sleepState(k);
}
```

When an event is detected at $node_k$, it wakes up and processes the event (this might involve classification, beamforming, transmission etc.). It then updates a global eventCount counter which stores the total number of events registered by $node_k$. The average arrival rate, λ_k, for $node_k$ is then updated. This requires use of an μ-OS timer based system function call getTimeElapsed() which returns the time elapsed since the node was turned on. The μ-OS then tries to put the node into sleep state s_k (starting from the deepest state s_4 through s_1) by testing the probability of an event occurring in the corresponding sleep time threshold $T_{th,k}$ against a system defined constant P_{th0}.

Table 2. Sleep state power, latency and threshold

State	P_k (mW)	τ_k (ms)	$T_{th,k}$
s_0	1040	-	-
s_1	400	5	8
s_2	270	15	20
s_3	200	20	25
s_4	10	50	50

3.2 Missed events

All the sleep states, except state s_4 have the actual sensor and A/D circuit on. Therefore if an event is detected (i.e. the signal power is above a threshold level) the node transitions to state s_0 and processes the event. The only overhead involved is latency (worst case being about 25ms). However, in state s_4, the node is almost completely off and it must decide on its own when to wake up. In sparse event sensing systems (for example vehicle tracking, seismic detection etc.) the inter-arrival time for events is much greater than the sleep time thresholds $T_{th,k}$. Therefore, the sensor node will invariably go into the deepest sleep state s_4. The processor must watch for pre-programed wake-up signals. These signal conditions are programmed by the CPU prior to entering the sleep state. To be able to wake up on its own the node must be able to predict the arrival of the next event. An optimistic prediction might result in the node waking up unnecessarily while a pessimistic strategy will result in some events being missed.

Researchers have tried to model the interarrival process of events in reactive systems. In [11] the distribution of idle and busy periods is represented by a time series and approximated by a least square regression model. In [12] the idleness prediction is based on a weighted sum of past periods where the weights decay geometrically. The authors of [13] use a stochastic optimization technique based on the theory of Markov processes. All the above techniques result in a performance penalty.

However, in our context, being in state s_4 results in missed events as the node has no way of knowing if anything significant occurred. What strategy gets used is a pure design concern based on how critical the sensing task is. We discuss two possible approaches.

- Completely disallow s_4 - If the sensing task is critical and any event cannot be missed this state must be disabled.
- Selectively disallow s_4 - This technique can be used if events are spatially distributed and not totally critical. Both random and deterministic approaches can be used. In the protocol described in [8] the 'cluster heads' can have a disallowed s_4 state while the normal nodes can transition to s_4. Alternatively, the scheme that we propose is more homogeneous. Every $node_k$ that satisfies the sleep threshold condition for s_4 goes to sleep with a system defined probability p_{s4} for a time duration given by

$$t_{s4,k} = -\frac{1}{\lambda_k}\ln(p_{s4}) \tag{6}$$

Equation 6 describes the steady state behavior of the node and the sleep time is computed such that the probability that no events occur in $t_{s4,k}$ i.e. $p_k(t_{s4,k}, 0) = p_{s4}$. However, when the sensor network is switched on and no events have occurred for a while, λ_k is zero. To account for this we disallow transition to state s_4 until at least one event is detected. We can also have an adaptive transition probability p_{s4}, which is zero initially and increases as events are detected later on. The probabilistic state transition is described in Fig. 3.

The advantage of the algorithm is that efficient energy tradeoffs can be made with event detection probability. By increasing p_{s4}, the system energy consumption can be reduced while the probability of missed events will increase and vice versa. Therefore, our overall shutdown policy is governed by two implementation specific probability parameters, (i) p_{th0} and (ii) p_{s4}.

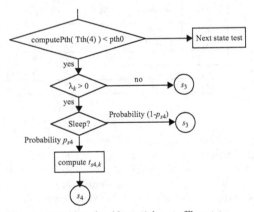

Fig. 3. Transition algorithm to 'almost off' s_4 state

3.3 Results

We have simulated a $\eta=1000$ node system distributed uniformly and randomly over a 100m x 100m area. The visibility radius of each sensor was assumed to be $\rho=10$m. The sleep state thresholds and power consumption are shown in Table 2. Fig. 4 shows the overall spatial node energy consumption over for an event with a gaussian spatial distribution centered around (25, 75). The interarrival process is Poisson with $\lambda_{tot} = 500$ s^{-1}. It can be seen that the node energy consumption tracks the event probability. In the non-power managed scenario we would have a uniform energy consumption in all the nodes.

One drawback of the whole scheme is that there is a finite and small window of interarrival rates λ_{tot} over which the fine- grained sleep states can be utilized. In general, the more the differentiated the power states (i.e. the greater the difference in their energy and latency overheads) the wider the range of interarrival times over which all sleep states can be utilized. Fig. 5(a) shows the range of event arrival rates at a node (λ_k) over which the states s_1 - s_3 are used significantly. If $\lambda_k < 13.9$ s^{-1}, transition to state s_4 is always possible (i.e. at least the threshold condition is met, actual transition of course occurs with probability p_{s4}). Similarly, if $\lambda_k > 86.9$ s^{-1}, the node must always be in the most active state. These limits have been computed using the nominal $p_{th0} = 0.5$. Using a higher value of p_{th0} would result in frequent transitions to the sleep states and if events occur fast enough this would result in increased energy dissipation associated with the wake-up energy cost. A smaller value of p_{th0} would result in a pessimistic scheme for sleep state transition and therefore lesser energy savings.

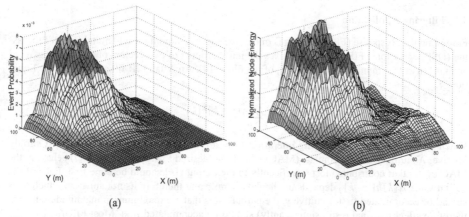

Fig. 4. (a) Spatial distribution of events (gaussian) and (b) Spatial energy consumption in the sensor nodes

Fig. 5(b) illustrates the Energy-Quality trade-off of our shutdown algorithm. By increasing the probability of transition to state s_4 (i.e. increasing p_{s4}) energy can be saved at the cost of increased possibility of missing an event. Such a graceful degradation of quality with energy is highly desirable in energy constrained systems.

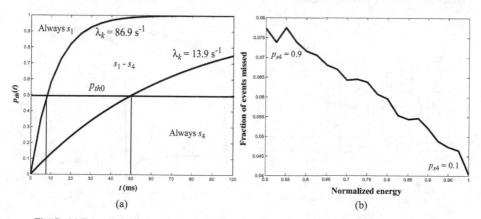

Fig. 5. (a) Event arrival rates at a node (b) Fraction of events missed versus energy consumption

4   Energy Scalable Algorithms

It is highly desirable that we structure our algorithms and systems in such a fashion that computational accuracy can be traded off with energy requirement. At the heart of such transformations lies the concept of incremental refinement. Consider a scenario where the distributed sensor network is being used to monitor seismic activity from a remote basestation. Sensor nodes are energy constrained and have a finite lifetime. It would be highly desirable to have energy scalable algorithms and protocols running on the sensor network such that the remote basestation could dynamically reduce energy consumption (to prolong mission lifetime if uninteresting events have occurred) by altering the throughput and computation accuracy. This type of behavior necessitates algorithmic restructuring so that every computational step leads us incrementally closer to the output. We now illustrate the algorithmic restructuring notion using two examples of popular signal processing algorithms in the context of sensor based computation.

4.1   Filtering Application

Finite Impulse Response (FIR) filtering is one of the most commonly used Digital Signal Processing (DSP) operations. FIR filtering involves the inner product of two vectors one of which is fixed and known as the impulse response, $h[n]$, of the filter [14]. An N-tap FIR filter is defined by Equation 7.

$$y[n] = \sum_{k=0}^{N-1} x[n-k]h[k] \tag{7}$$

When we analyze the FIR filtering operation from a pure inner product perspective, it simply involves N multiply and accumulate (MAC) cycles. For desired Energy-Quality (E-Q) behavior, the MAC cycles that contribute most significantly to the output $y[n]$ should be done first. Each of the partial sums, $x[k]h[n-k]$, depends on the data sample and therefore its not apparent which ones should be accumulated first. Intuitively, the partial sums that are maximum in magnitude (and can therefore affect the final result significantly) should be accumulated first. Most FIR filter coefficients have a few coefficients that are large in magnitude and progressively reduce in amplitude. Therefore, a simple but effective *most-significant-first transform* involves sorting the impulse response in decreasing order of magnitude and reordering the MACs such that the partial sum corresponding to the largest coefficient is accumulated first as shown in Fig. 6(a). Undoubtedly, the data sample multiplied to the coefficient might be so small as to mitigate the effect of the partial sum. Nevertheless, on an average case, the coefficient reordering by magnitude yields a better E-Q performance than the original scheme.

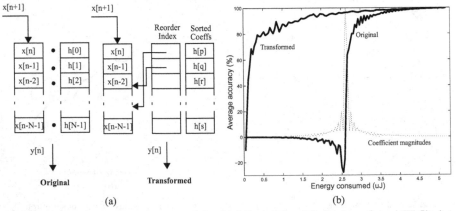

Fig. 6. (a) FIR filtering with coefficient reordering (b) E-Q graph for original and transformed FIR filtering

Fig. 6(b) illustrates the scalability results for a low pass filtering of speech data sampled at 10kHz using a 128-tap FIR filter whose impulse response (magnitude) is also outlined. The average energy consumption per output sample (measured on the StrongARM SA-1100 operating at 1.5V power supply and 206MHz frequency) in the original scheme is 5.12μJ. Since the initial coefficients are not the ones with most significant magnitudes the E-Q behavior is poor. Sorting the coefficients and using a level of indirection (in software that amounts to having an index array of the same size as the coefficient array), the E-Q behavior can be substantially improved. The energy overhead associated with using a level of indirection on the SA-1100 was only 0.21μJ which is about 4% of the total energy consumption. The basic characteristic of an energy scalable algorithm is illustrated in Fig. 6(b). It is obvious that if the available energy per sample/task is reduced by 50% the quality degradation in the transformed system is only 10% as opposed to 100% degradation in the original filtering algorithm.

4.2 Image Decoding Application

The Discrete Cosine Transform (DCT), which involves decomposing a set of image samples into a scaled set of discrete cosine basis functions, and the Inverse Discrete Cosine Transform (IDCT), which involves reconstructing the samples from the basis functions, are crucial steps in digital video [15]. The 64-point, 2-D DCT and IDCT (used on 8x8 pixel blocks in of an image) are defined respectively as

$$X[u, v] = \frac{c[u]c[v]}{4} \sum_{i=0}^{7} \sum_{j=0}^{7} x[i,j] \cos\left(\frac{(2i+1)u\pi}{16}\right)\cos\left(\frac{(2j+1)v\pi}{16}\right) \tag{8}$$

$$x[i,j] = \frac{1}{4} \sum_{u=0}^{7} \sum_{v=0}^{7} c[u]c[v]X[u,v] \cos\left(\frac{(2i+1)u\pi}{16}\right)\cos\left(\frac{(2j+1)v\pi}{16}\right) \tag{9}$$

DCT is able to capture the spatial redundancy present in an image and the coefficients obtained are quantized and compressed. Most existing algorithms attempt to minimize the number of arithmetic operations (multiplications and additions) usually relying on the symmetry properties of the cosine basis functions (similar to the FFT algorithm) and on matrix factorizations [16]. The E-Q behavior of these algorithms are not good as they have been designed such that computation takes a minimal yet constant number of operations. The Forward Mapping-IDCT (FM-IDCT) algorithm, proposed in [17] can be shown to have an E-Q performance with is much better than other algorithms. The algorithm is formulated as follows

$$\begin{bmatrix} x_{0,0} \\ x_{0,1} \\ \vdots \\ x_{8,8} \end{bmatrix} = X_{0,0} \begin{bmatrix} c_0^{0,0} \\ c_1^{0,0} \\ \vdots \\ c_{64}^{0,0} \end{bmatrix} + X_{0,1} \begin{bmatrix} c_0^{0,1} \\ c_1^{0,1} \\ \vdots \\ c_{64}^{0,1} \end{bmatrix} + \dots + X_{8,8} \begin{bmatrix} c_0^{8,8} \\ c_0^{8,8} \\ \vdots \\ c_{64}^{8,8} \end{bmatrix} \tag{10}$$

where $x_{i,j}$ are the reconstructed pels, $X_{i,j}$ are the input DCT coefficients, and $[c_k^{i,j}]$ is the 64x64 constant reconstruction kernel. The improved E-Q behavior of the FM-IDCT algorithm can be attributed to the fact that most of the signal energy is concentrated in the DC coefficient ($X_{0,0}$) and in general in the low-frequency coefficients as shown in Fig. 7(a). Instead of reconstructing each pixel by summing up all its frequency contributions, the algorithm incrementally accumulates the entire image based on spectral contributions from the low to high frequencies.

Fig. 7(b) and Fig. 8 illustrate the E-Q behavior of the FM-IDCT algorithm. It is obvious from Fig. 7(b) that almost 90% image quality can be obtained from as little as 25% of the total energy consumption. In terms of the overhead requirement, the only change that is required is that we now need to store the IDCT coefficients in a transposed fashion (i.e. all the low frequency components first and so on).

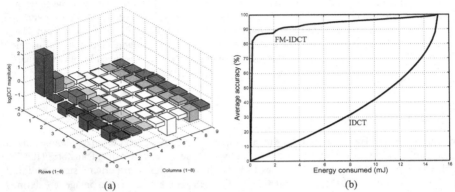

(a)   (b)

Fig. 7. (a) 8x8 DCT coefficients averaged over a sample image (b) E-Q graph for FM-IDCT vs normal IDCT

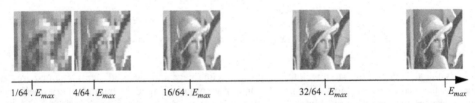

Fig. 8. llustrating the incremental refinement property with respect to computational energy of the FM-IDCT algorithm

5   Conclusions

We have proposed a system level power management scheme for distributed wireless data acquisition sensor networks using a two fold approach for energy scalability viz. event driven shutdown and algorithmic restructuring. For event driven shutdown, we explicitly characterize the meaningful power states of a node and uses a probabilistic technique to make predictive transitions to the low power modes based on observed event statistics. The scheme is simple to implement and has negligible memory overhead. The technique we have proposed is fairly general and can be used for power management in any system characterized by different levels of power consumption in various stages of shutdown. We have also demonstrated the feasibility of a graceful energy-quality tradeoff using our shutdown strategy. In energy constrained sensor nodes, it is desirable to have energy scalable algorithms. We have demonstrated the basic idea of algorithmic restructuring for improved energy-quality behavior using two popular signal processing examples.

ACKNOWLEDGEMENTS

This research is sponsored by the Defense Advanced Research Project Agency (DARPA) Power Aware Computing/Communication Program and the Air Force Research Laboratory, Air Force Materiel Command, USAF, under agreement number F30602-00-2-0551. The U.S. Government is authorized to reproduce and distribute reprints for Governmental purposes notwithstanding any copyright annotation thereon[1].

REFERENCES

[1]   A. P. Chandrakasan, et. al., "Design Considerations for Distributed Microsensor Systems", Proceedings of Custom Integrated Circuits Conference, San Deigo, CA, May 1999, pp. 279-286
[2]   MEMS Technology Applications Center, http://mems.mcnc.org
[3]   The MIT µAMPS Project, http://www-mtl.mit.edu/research/icsystems/uamps/
[4]   The WINS Project, http://www.janet.ucla.edu/WINS
[5]   L. Benini and G. D. Micheli, Dynamic Power Management: Design Techniques and CAD Tools, Norwell, MA, Kluwer 1997
[6]   A. Sinha, A. Wang and A. P. Chandrakasan, "Algorithmic Transforms for Efficient Energy Scalable Computation", International Symposium on Low Power Electronics and Design, Italy, July 2000
[7]   http://developer.intel.com/design/strong/sa1100.htm
[8]   W. Heinzelman, A. Chandrakasan and H. Balakrishnan, "Energy Efficient Routing Protocols for Wireless Microsensor Networks", Proceedings of 33rd Hawaii International Conference on System Sciences (HIC-SS '00), January 2000
[9]   Advanced Configuration and Power Interface, http://www.teleport.com/~acpi/
[10] E. R. Dougherty, Probability and Statistics for Engineering, Computing and Physical Sciences, Prentice Hall 1990
[11] M. B. Srivastava, A. P. Chandrakasan and R. W. Broderson, "Predictive System Shutdown and Other Architectural Techniques for Energy Efficient Programmable Computation", IEEE Transactions on VLSI Systems, vol. 4, no. 1, March 1996, pp. 42-54
[12] C.-H. Hwang and A. Wu, "A Predictive System Shutdown Method for Energy Saving of Event Driven Computation", Proceedings of the International Conference on Computer Aided Design, 1997, pp. 28-32
[13] L. Benini, et. al, "Policy Optimization for Dynamic Power Management", IEEE Transactions on Computer-Aided Design of Integrated Circuits and Systems, vol. 18, no. 6, June 1999, pp. 813-833
[14] A. V. Oppenheim and R. W. Schafer, Discrete Time Signal Processing, Prentice Hall, New Jersey, 1989
[15] N. Ahmed, T. Natarajan and K. R. Rao, "Discrete Cosine Transform", IEEE Trans. on Computers, vol. 23, Jan 1974, pp. 90-93
[16] W. H. Chen, C. H. Smith and S. C. Fralick, "A Fast Computational Algorithm for the Discrete Cosine Transform", IEEE Trans. on Communication, vol. 25, Sept 1977, pp. 1004-1009
[17] L. McMillan and L. A. Westover, "A Forward-Mapping Realization of the Inverse Discrete Cosine Transform", Proceedings of the Data Compression Conference (DCC '92), March 1992, pp. 219-228

---

1. The views and conclusions contained herein are those of the authors and should not be interpreted as necessarily representing the official policies or endorsements, either expressed or implied, of the Defense Advanced Research Project Agency (DARPA), the Air Force Research Laboratory, or the U.S. Government.

Towards a Programmable Mobile IP[*]

Alvin T.S. Chan[1], Dan He[2], Siu Nam Chuang[1], Jiannong Cao[1]

[1]The Hong Kong Polytechnic University
Department of Computing
Hung Hom, Kowloon
Hong Kong, SAR, China
cstschan@comp.polyu.edu.hk

[2]INRIA/IRISA
Campus de Beaulieu
35042 RENNES CEDEX
France

Abstract. This paper describes the design and implementation of a highly configurable and robust Mobile IP framework that employs active networking principles. Through the provision of open programmable interfaces and execution environment, new mobile services or application-specific customized services can be rapidly developed and deployed within the Mobile IP networking environment. ANTS [11] is being employed as the baseline active network execution environment for the implementation of our programmable Mobile IP framework. In particular, we have extended ANTS considerably to export mobile IP native interfaces to support mobile specific functionalities. The design of our active Mobile IP framework is currently implemented over the Linux operating system. The programmable framework is applied to the Mobile IP agent nodes namely, the mobile node, foreign agent, home agent and correspondent node. To demonstrate the ease of designing and deploying new mobile services, this paper describes the setup of an experiment to implement an active route optimization service.

1. Introduction

While mobile computing has created a new paradigm shift in providing anywhere, anytime and anyplace computing environment, it has raised important technical challenges that are often non-trivial. In particular, there is a need to address the contrasting quality of service (QOS) delivery between the mobile and stationary environments. Existing networking infrastructure dominated primarily by Internet connectivity is designed around a fixed network concept. The primary assumptions of reliable connectivity, large available bandwidth, stationary end hosts and resource-rich operating environment have greatly motivated the design of existing fixed network protocols [1].

In mobile computing environments, the end systems and intermediate components participating in an end-to-end communication are required to deal with the scarce and dynamically varying resources. Such requirements translate to the need for research into mobile-enabling of existing and new networking infrastructure to better support mobile computing.

To support mobility in an Internet environment, the Mobile IP has been designed to provide the necessary mechanisms to enable correspondent node (CN) to conveniently locate a mobile node, even it is away from its home network. This is achieved by having the mobile node

---

[*] This project is supported by the Hong Kong Polytechnic Central Research Grant G-YB76 and GV-893.

K.-L. Tan et al. (Eds.): MDM 2001, LNCS 1987, pp. 210–221, 2001.
© Springer-Verlag Berlin Heidelberg 2001

(MN) acquire a new care-of-address (COA) when it is visiting a new point of attachment on the Internet [2]. The care-of-address obtained from the participating foreign agent (FA) forms the new physical contact IP address for the mobile node. This care-of-address is communicated to the mobile node's home agent so that subsequent packets destined for the mobile node will be forwarded to the mobile node care-of-address via the home agent, as shown in Fig. 1.

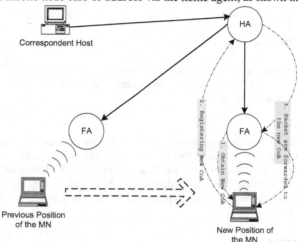

Fig. 1. Mobile IP Operation

While Mobile IP provides the necessary mechanisms to support point-of-attachment mobility, it lacks of the protocol features and architectural characteristics to support adaptive and mobility specific processing to better react to the intrinsically dynamic operating environment of mobile computing. The need to support and provide adaptiveness and mobile-aware processing stems from the fact that mobile and wireless environments are subjected to changing operating and resource constrains. As a result, protocols operating in such constrained environment are required to adapt to these changes with the ultimate objective of optimizing the use of scarce computing resources.

Active and programmable networking technology represents an attractive solution to provide rich programming interfaces to support dynamic and adaptive processing on existing mobile computing platform. Programmable and active networking is a relative new concept that has met with great interests in the networking research community [3, 4]. While much of the active networking concept has been successfully applied to the fixed networking environments, very little work has been focused on applying active network to mobile computing. Research in [5] has focused on applying active network principles for the development of adaptive mobile networking solutions based on the Mobiware toolkit. Mobiware is an open programmable mobile network that uses CORBA to provide distributed object programmability to mobile capable devices across an end-to-end communication link.

In this paper, we present our approach to realizing a highly configurable, composable and programmable mobile network architecture by applying active networking concepts to the mobile Internet environment. In particular, instead of extending Mobile IP in terms of defining new syntax and semantics to existing packet formats, and to add new adaptive algorithms, our research work focuses on applying composable active services on existing Mobile IP framework. The design work aims to minimize any modification done on the IP level of protocol control, but instead focus on the important aspects of abstracting the programmable functionality. The abstraction provides a level of programmable interfaces over the existing Mobile IP framework in which active services can be rapidly designed and deployed to modify or augment new protocol behaviors. The approach ensures that traditional networking functionality will continue to interoperate with or without active enabling the Mobile IP specifications. In addition to opening up the programming interface to the Mobile IP, a significant part of our work deals with the important formulation of a set of common programmable services that are mobile-specific. These services are designed to augment functionality that are notably missing in existing Mobile IP specifications to support wireless and mobile communication environments.

2. Design Approach

The section describes the important design principles that have guided and motivated the creation of a new class of Internet-based active mobile networking architecture to support rapid service creation and deployment.

Mobile Internet

Despite Mobile IP and Internet poor support for truly configurable and adaptive mobile computing environment, we envision that the Internet will continue to play an important role in providing an integrative and robust networking environment. In particular, it is an important decision that we design the framework that leverages on the existing Internet infrastructure, while providing extensible and rapid deployment of mobile services to enhance the overall end-to-end quality of service.

Seamless Integration

While applying active technologies to extend and develop new approaches to programming mobile network services, it is important to define a mobile programming model that seamlessly integrates to the existing Internet. The programming model describes the environment in which active services can be readily created, composed, communicated and deployed using protocols and mechanisms supported by the Internet framework. In the context of Mobile IP, new services can be deployed into home agent node, foreign agent node, mobile node, and intermediate active-enabled devices. These services are designed to seamlessly operate and leverage on the Internet for moving service-specific programs to the destined agent nodes, while collectively interacting to achieve a mobile network service.

Cross Layer Processing

In the context of OSI reference model, previous works in active networking have primarily focused on applying programmable network for specific layer and for specific functions. For example, active networking has been successfully applied within the IP layer for improving on the multi-cast performance [6], as well as for enhancing congestion control [7]. However, mobile computing presents technological challenges that are not easily resolved by focusing on specific layer functionality design to better support mobile communications. In recent years, as mobile computing continues to gain prominence, research works have been directed to look into various approaches to improving performance from within various protocol layers [8], including physical, datalink, network, transport and application layer. Each layer of the protocol processing serves to enhance the performance across mobile communication environment by offering augmented mobile specific services that are designed to mask away the imperfections and issues pertaining to mobile computing. In our work, we view the challenges of mobile computing as spanning across multiple protocol layers, such that optimum performance can be derived from cross layer processing (CLP). Cross layer processing (CLP) represents the divergence away from the traditional implementation of a progressive layered protocol stack processing, in which protocol functions are executed from layer n to layer $n+1$ fashion (or vice-versa). Such protocol processing technique requires a strict conformance to the protocol stack arrangement and does not permit "cut-through" layer processing along the path of communications. Fig. 2 shows a traditional layered protocol processing architecture across a mobile IP environment. The idea of CLP is to allow protocol architectural layering flexibility by providing mechanisms for cross layers protocol processing. The objective is to permit non-sequential layer processing by allowing layer n to proceed to layer m. Layered Protocol Processing   **Fig. 3** shows the protocol processing architecture across a mobile IP environment based on CLP approach. By designing and implementing CLP on our active Mobile IP framework, it provides us with the utmost flexibility in programming and deploying new services on a robust protocol processing architecture. It can be shown through examples that CLP forms a highly robust and powerful paradigm for deploying new services in the mobile Internet environment. The first example represents a protocol known as Snooping-TCP [9] that was designed to alleviate the poor end-to-end performance of unmodified TCP in the wireless medium. In the context of CLP, the Snooping-TCP implementation residing at the access point represents a cross layer processing scenario in which data packets at the access point are allowed to cross the datalink layer boundary to process transport-specific functionality. The protocol involves filtering of frames that are bypassing the datalink layer at the access point and to process these frames by examining the transport layer specific fields for possible loss of packets and acknowledgment information. The aim here is to mask away any non-congestion-related losses from the TCP sender that are instead caused by losses in the wireless link. In this case, the Snooping-TCP operating at the access point is responsible to perform cross layer filtering of transiting frames and to perform localized error recovery due to losses in the wireless link. The next example demonstrates the use of CLP to dynamically regulate the quality of service at the foreign agent node to changing operating conditions in a wireless environment [10]. In this scenario, *application-specific* service such as multi-level video transcoding agent can be deployed at the foreign agent node to dynamically monitor the environment and to react to the changing link quality by down sampling the video quality transiting across the wireless medium. In short, the two examples represent only a snapshot of the rich benefits of CLP to support a truly robust and programmable mobile network architecture.

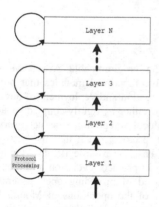

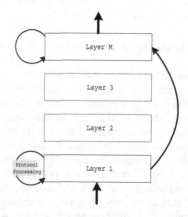

Fig. 2. Layered Protocol Processing   **Fig. 3.** Cross Layered Protocol Processing

Packet Snooping

In addition to providing programmable interfaces to Mobile IP functionality, there is also a need to extend the architecture to support implementation of cross layer processing. Such provision will provide the necessary mechanisms to allow new service agent to capture cross layer(s) packets, which are not necessary derived from the usual layer-to-layer protocol stack processing. Packet filtering represents an attractive solution to provide cross layers capturing of transiting packets by specifying the necessary filtering rules to indicate packets that are of interests to the service agent. New mobile service agents implementing flow-based processing along the communication path can employ the packet filtering service to capture layer specific packets, and to inject new protocol behaviors along the flow. Fig. 4 shows a typical flow-processing model in which a packet filter object is pre-programmed to route transiting packets to the respective service codes, which represent new active mobile service. Examples of such flow-based processing include local error recovery between wireless links, congestion control, video transcoding, Snooping TCP, buffering and etc.

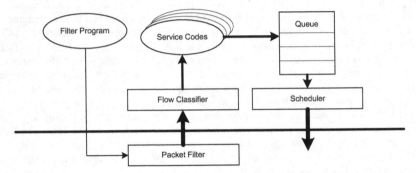

Fig. 4. Packet Filter Flow Process Operation

3. Architectural Overview

Shown in Fig. 5 is the architectural overview of the programmable Active Mobile IP framework. The architectural design is comprised of five functional modules that provide a collection of open programmable interfaces for design, creation and deployment of new active services. New services can be developed and deployed either as tightly-coupled or loosely-coupled protocol integration. In a tightly-coupled protocol integration, the new service is designed to tightly integrate to the existing Mobile IP protocol, such that the new service effectively changes the basic protocol behavior of the baseline Mobile IP. The facilities to enable tightly-coupled service deployment, allow for rapid protocol evolution and innovation. The requirement of such facilities translates to the need of providing open programming interfaces to directly program and change the behavior of the operations of Mobile IP. An example of a tightly-coupled service is the development and deployment of the route optimization protocol, which eliminates the so-called triangular routing. In this case, the new service is required to directly modify the tunneling and routing facilities of the original Mobile IP procedures, such that active service codes residing on the respective agent nodes can co-ordinate to provide a optimize routing facility. In the loosely-coupled protocol integration, the new service does little or no modification to the existing Mobile IP implementation. Instead, the service is implemented in a flow processing model, such that it is transparent to the underlying Mobile IP. One or more flow processing services can be implemented along an existing end-to-end Mobile IP link. An excellent example of deploying such kind of services is the Snooping TCP service. In this case, the Snooping TCP does no modification to the Mobile IP but provides masking of loss of packets along the wireless links by introducing local error recovery. The following sections describe in detail the functions of each module and how it contributes to the realization of a truly configurable and programmable Mobile IP architecture.

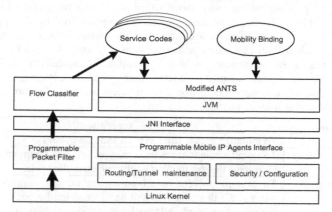

Fig. 5. Active Mobile IP Architecture

3.1   Execution Environment

Instead of developing a service creation and execution environment for the active node from scratch, we have taken the decision to adopt the ANTS approach [11] and extend it to support programmable Mobile IP functionality. In particular, we make use of the ANTS capsule programming model to create and deploy new agent services. Our model, however, does not inherit ANTS approach of generalizing a capsule as a basic replacement for a packet and using it to dynamically control and deploy services on-the-fly. To deploy a new agent service, we make use of ANTS abstraction of a service protocol that is comprised of a code group, which in turn is comprised of a collection of related capsules types whose forwarding routines are transferred as a unit by the code distribution system. The service agent, comprising of collection of capsules, is transferred as an autonomous unit of service codes. Importantly, the Mobile IP active-enabled nodes continue to offer routing and tunneling functionality of transferring data packets between the correspondent node, home agent, foreign agent and mobile node. Capsules do not replace transiting packets found in normal networks. The code distribution system of ANTS provides the necessary mechanisms to automatically transfer active codes between the agents to deploy new mobile network services. The active code distribution adds new services and functionality to nodes out-of-band from the normal packets process by Mobile IP. To enable peer-to-peer communications and control between active nodes, capsules are also used as signaling agents to co-ordinate distributed service functionality. In this case, the capsule can contain service-specific control data as well as instructional codes in which the destination active node can process and execute.

3.2   Programmable Packet Filter Interfaces

Packet filter is an effective mechanism for implementation of user-level protocols and services [12]. It provides the necessary facilities for user-level packet capturing of transiting packets at the datalink layer. The filter acts as a monitoring agent for packets arriving from the link and decides if a packet should be accepted, and if so, pass on the packets to the listening service agents at the next level. Traditionally, the use of packet filter requires that the application agent to setup the filter rules and executes it during program startup. In order to provide dynamic customization of filter rules even while active services is in operation, we have extended the packet filter mechanism to provide on-the-fly control and management of filter capturing process. In particular, we have adopted high-level filter specification language from *libpcap[1]* as the baseline filter rule description language. Shown below are some function calls to control and manage the packet filtering process.

Function	Operation
initFilter()	To initialize packet filter system and rule queues
*setRule(char *rule)*	To install a rule to filter incoming packets and return an integer which represents the slot number of the corresponding rule.
getPacket(slot, block)	To capture packets based on the rule's slot number. If block is *true(i.e. '1')* this function will be blocked until a packet that matches the rule is returned. Alternatively, if block is *false (i.e. '0')*, then the call is non-blocking.
deleteFilter(slot)	To remove the slot rule and free rule queue.

Based on these rich interfaces provided by the node operating system, it is possible to design and program a customized classifier for flow specific processing. These interfaces are all exported to Java interface via JNI to access *libpcap's* native method implementation.

The question still remains on how to specify a filter rule script. To facilitate rapid prototyping of the architecture and to avoid the need to develop a new filter description language, we have taken the decision to employ *tcpdump* high-level filter description language for programming the packet filter. For example, a simple rule such as, *"ip src host 158.132.11.141"* means to capture all packets from host with IP address of *158.132.11.141*. A flow processing service can use the *getPacket()* primitive to read all incoming packets from host *158.132.11.141*. More complex rules to access different levels of protocol data can similarly be programmed depending on the needs of the underlying mobile network service.

3.3   Programmable Mobile IP Agents Interfaces

Mobile IP supports mobile node changing point-of-attachment in the Internet by extending the routing and tunneling functionality of traditional IP with the co-ordination of distributed agent services. The agent services, which include the home agent, foreign agent and mobile node agent, collectively collaborate to perform re-routing and tunneling of packets arriving at the home agent to the foreign agent's care-of-address, which forms the proxy IP address to contact the mobile node. In order to provide programmability options to change, modify or add new services to existing Mobile IP functionality, there is a need "open" the interfaces to the basic agents that help to co-ordinate the implementation of Mobile IP routing and tunneling. Shown below are the Java classes that export open interfaces for programming the Mobile IP agents.

---

[1] *libpcap* is a library for access of BSD Packet Filter (BPF) resource.

The home agent API class provides a set of methods to probe the status and operating conditions, retrieve mobile node's care-of-address, tunneling information and destroying tunnel operation.

```
class jhaapi {
        public native Tunnel_count jHaGetTunnelCount( int timeout);
        public native Tunnel_ID jHaGetTunnelID( int timeout);
        public native JTunnelInfo jHaGetTunnelInfo(String id, int timeout);
        public native int jHaDestroyTunnel(String id, int timeout);
        public native JhaStatus jHaGetStatus( int timeout);
        public native int jHaEnableMobile(String mobile_addr, int enable,int timeout);
        public native Care_of_addr jHaGetCareOfAddr(String mobile_addr, int
timeout);
}
```

The foreign agent API class provides a set of methods to access the status and operating conditions, retrieve tunneling information and destroying tunnel operation.

```
class jfaapi {
        public native Tunnel_count jFaGetTunnelCount( int timeout);
        public native Tunnel_ID jFaGetTunnelID( int timeout);
        public native JTunnelInfo jFaGetTunnelInfo(String id, int timeout);
        public native int jFaDestroyTunnel(String id, int timeout);
        public native JFaStatus jFaGetStatus( int timeout);
}
```

The mobile node provides interface access to the status and operating conditions, tunneling information, create and destroy tunnel operations, and retrieve foreign agent information.

```
class jmnapi {
public native Care_of_address jMnGetCareOfAddr(int timeout);
public native Tunneling_mode jMnGetTunnelingMode(int timeout);
public native JMobileStatus jMnGetStatus(int timeout);
                    public native int jMnConnect(int tunneling_mode, int timeout);
public native int jMnDisconnect(int timeout);
public native JMobileFaList jMnGetFaList(int timeout);
public native JMobileFaInfo jMnGetFaInfo(int timeout);
    }
```

3.4   Routing and Tunnel Interfaces

The routing and tunnel interfaces provide programmable access to the native routing table residing inside the operating system kernel. In particular, service agents can leverage on such interfaces to construct IP-to-IP tunneling between communicating entities, provide modifications to the IP routing table entries, add/delete route entries and request for interface and binding information within the IP operating environment. Shown below are some primitives that are exposed as Java programming interfaces:

Method	Description
TunnelAdd()	Add a tunnel to remote host
TunnelDestroy()	Remove tunnel
TunnelConnect()	Connect mobile node to high level tunnel
TunnelUnconnect()	Tear down the tunnel connection
RouteAddTable()	Add a route entry

RouteDelTable()	Remove a route entry from Table
RoutetoHost()	Get routing entry from a given host
RouteReplace()	Replace a routing entry
RouteAddNet()	Add subnet routing entry
RouteDelNet()	Delete subnet routing entry
RouteReplaceNet()	Replace subnet routing entry
RouteGet()	Find out the correct Interface from the destination address
RouteAdd()	Add the destination address to the interface
RouteDel()	Delete the routing entry
GetIfName()	Get interface na me
GetIfAddr()	Get binding address of interface
GetInterfaceMap()	Return all interfaces in this host
GetLocalAddr()	Get local address.

4. Implementation

As described earlier, ANTS is being employed as the baseline active network execution environment for the implementation of our programmable Mobile IP framework. In particular, we have extended ANTS considerably to export Mobile IP native interfaces to augment the existing functionality already provided by the ANTS execution environment. Since ANTS essentially uses Java as the baseline operating environment, the extended interfaces specific to Mobile IP operations are required to be exported to Java method calls using the Java Native Interface (JNI). In which case, JNI forms a layer of abstraction in which the Java-based service agents uses to invoke the native active Mobile IP services. The Mobile IP implementation is modified and extended from [2] to support active programming interface. The implementation supports hierarchical ordering of foreign agents with hop-by-hop building of IP tunnels across the participating entities.

The implementation of the active Mobile IP is primarily written in native C language and compiled to the native x86 machine code to optimize processing speed. To provide programmability at the Java interface level, JNI is used to switch Java call flow to native Linux *sendmsg* and *recvmsg* system calls to access and control the operations of the participating Mobile IP agents, including the home agent, foreign agent(s) and the mobile node agent.

4.1 Experimental Setup

We have selected to implement the active route optimization service to demonstrate the functionality and extensibility of our active Mobile IP in introducing and implementing new services to the mobile environment. It is important to note that the active optimization service implemented on our active Mobile IP platform is not compliant to the Mobile IP standard as described in [13]. We believe that the inefficient behavior of a non-optimized mobile IP triangular routing scenario serves as an ideal experiment to demonstrate how active mobile service can be easily developed and deployed in an active network environment.

The experiment was performed on a testbed network consisting of three Linux workstations connected by dedicated 100Mbps Fast Ethernet network links, as shown in Fig. 6. The Linux-implemented router is based on an x86 PC Pentium II/400Mhz installed with two 100Mbps cards and 128M RAM. The router is configured to only use Linux kernel forwarding services. The foreign agent and home agent are running on two Pentuim 233Mhz, 64M RAM and they are located on two separate subnets interconnected via the router. All executing nodes are running Linux 2.2.10. Except for the router, all nodes are installed with ANTS active network transfer system.

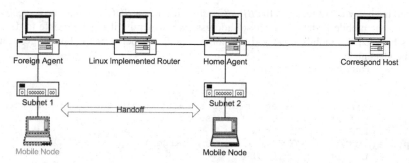

Fig. 6. Experimental Setup

Triangle routing is a well-known issue of Mobile IP. It is mainly determined by mobile IP architecture. When a mobile node is visiting some subnet, even datagrams from correspondent node on the same subnet must be routed through the Internet to the mobile node's home agent, only then to be tunneled back to the original subnet for final delivery. This indirect routing mode is called triangle routing. It delays the delivery of datagrams to the mobile nodes and burdens on the network. A scheme of optimization has been proposed[13]. The idea is to cache the binding of a mobile node and to then tunnel their own datagrams directly to the care of address indicated in that binding, bypassing the mobile nodes' home agent.

According to the scheme described in [13], the document defines four message formats to optimize mobility binding. In our active service implementation, we have developed three capsules types to manage tunneling from the mobile node to the correspondent node. The three capsules are defined as binding update message (implemented as *BUCapsule*), binding warning message (implemented as *BWMCapsule*) and binding request message (implemented as *BRMCapsule*). At the mobile node, an active service object running under the ANTS environment is responsible for monitoring the mobile node agent daemon to check whether it's Care-of-Address has been changed. If so, it sends a *BWMCapsule* to the home agent. Upon receiving the capsule, the home agent then sends the *BUCapsule* to the correspondent node. The home agent subsequently removes the mobility binding between the mobile node and the home agent.

A portion of the mobile agent execution flow is shown below:

```
while(true){
    //get status of Mobile Node
    if (mn.jMnGetStatus(100) == (new jmip.apiconst().API_SUCCESS))
        { // is Mobile node in Home Net?
        try{
        if (CoA !=NodeAddress.fromString(mn.status.co_addr))
            {//if mobile node has changed it's Care-of-Adddress,
            // sent out a BWMCapsult to home agent.
            BWMCapsule c = new BWMCapsule(port,port,home,cshost);
            c.MNAddr = mobile;
            c.target = cshost;
            c.CoA = CoA;   //we extend RFC2000 to add CoA in Binding
            //warning Message // send a BWM capsule to HA.
```

```
            System.out.println("Sent Warning Message to Home Agent");
            send(c);
        }
    } catch( Exception e){
        e.printStackTrace();
    }
}
```

When the home agent receives the *BWMCapsule*, it sends a *BUCapsule* to the correspondent node with the mobile node's new care-of-address. Subsequently, it is responsible to delete the tunnels between the mobile node and the home Agent, and between the home agent and the correspondent node.

```
if (cap instanceof BWMCapsule)
    {
        System.out.println("Get BU Capsule");
        // when home agent gets a warning message from mobile node
        // it sends it to Coresspondent node.
        BUCapsule bu = new
BUCapsule(port,port,((BWMCapsule)cap).target);
        bu.lifetime =1000;
        bu.MNAddr = ((BWMCapsule)cap).MNAddr;
        bu.CoA = ((BWMCapsule)cap).CoA;
        send(bu);
    }
```

A portion of the correspondent node execution flow is shown below:

When the correspondent node receives a *BUCapsule* from the home agent, a tunnel is established between the correspondent node and the mobile node's new position. If a tunnel exists between the entities, that tunnel will be deleted before establishing a new tunnel to reflect the change in mobile node's new position based on the contents of *BUCapsule*.

```
if (cap instanceof BUCapsule)
    {
        if (cs.IpTunnelExist(CoA, cshost)!= null) // delete the old
tunnelling.
        cs.IpTunnelDel("TUNEL"+NodeAddres.toString((BUCapsule)cap.CoA));
        cs.jIpTunnelAdd("TUNEL"+(BUCapsule)cap.CoA, (BUCapsule)cap.CoA,
NodeAddress.toString(cshost)); // add a new tunneling
    }
```

5. Conclusions

This paper describes the design and implementation of an active mobile IP framework that supports highly configurable and rapid deployment of active mobile services. While traditional mobile IP provides primitive support of point-of-attachment mobility, it lacks the protocol features and architectural characteristics to support the dynamic operating environment of mobile computing. The mismatch in the protocol features of mobile IP that is designed specifically to operate in static wired environment, and the dynamic varying quality of service (QOS) environment of wireless mobile computing motivates the need to revisit the design of mobile IP. Instead of re-engineering mobile IP from bottom-up, the project proposes the extension of mobile IP to support active networking concepts. By applying active networking principles to the development of adaptive mobile IP, we are able to create a highly extensible and configurable framework that supports rapid deployment of new mobile services over existing mobile IP environment. Importantly, the active extension of mobile IP provides us with the unique opportunity to implement and deploy new mobile services while leveraging on existing Internet infrastructure.

The design of our active mobile IP framework is currently implement over the Linux operating system, using ANTS as the baseline active execution environment. The programmable framework is applied to the mobile IP agent nodes namely, the mobile node, foreign agent, home agent and correspondent node. To demonstrate the ease of designing and deploying new mobile services, we have setup an experiment to implement an active route optimization service. It is important to note that in our implementation, we have not discussed security issues pertaining to active service deployment. In general, this problem represents an exciting challenge not only for this project but active networking on the whole. We believe that security and programmability are orthogonal functionality. In this regard, we are currently working to implement a security framework that employs service reflection mechanism to capture capsule invocation to active interfaces before authorizing a service call. This work is in progress and will be the subject of our future publication.

Acknowledgements

We would like to thank the members of TSE-Institute of the Helsinki University of Technology for their help and provision of the detail implementation of the Dynamic-HUT Mobile IP, in which our work is based on. Also, we would like to thank MIT Laboratory for Computer Science for the provision of the ANTS toolkit.

References

1. R.H. Kartz, "Adaptation and Mobility in Wireless Information Systems," IEEE Personal Communications, vol. 1, no. 1, 1994.
2. C. Perkins et. al., "IP Mobility Support," RFC2002, Oct 1996.
3. D.L. Tennenhouse et. al. "A Survey of Active Network Research," IEEE Communications Magazine, vo. 35, no. 1, Jan. 1997, pp. 80-86.
4. Michael Hicks, et. al. "PLAN: A Packet Language for Active Networks," *Proc. Of the third ACM SIGPLAN International Conference on Functional Programming Languages*, 1998, pp. 86-93, ACM.
5. A.T. Campbell, "Mobiware: QOS-aware Middleware for Mobile Multimedia Communications," 7th IFIP International Conference on High-Performance Networking, White Plains, NY, Apr. 1997.
6. H. Li-Wei, H. Lehman, S.J. Garland, and D.L. Tennenhouse, "Active Reliable Multicast," Infocom 1998, San Francisco, California, 1998.
7. Williamson, B.; Farrell, C., "Active Congestion Control," IEEE Globcome 1998, vol. 3, 1998 , pp. 1509 -1514.
8. J. Jing, A. Helal and A. Elmagarmid, "Client-Server in Mobile Environments," ACM Computing Surveys, vol. 31, no. 2, Jun 1999, pp. 117-157.
9. H Balakrishnan, S. Seshan and R. Kartx, "Improving Reliable Transport and Handoff Performance in Cellular Wireless Networks," Wireless Networks.
10. Bharadvaj, H.; Joshi, A.; Auephanwiriyakul, S., An Active Transcoding Proxy to Support Mobile Web Access", Reliable Distributed Systems, 1998. Proceedings. Seventeenth IEEE Symposium on , 1998 , pp.118 -123.
11. David. J. Wetherall, J.V. Guttag, D.L. Tennenhouse, "ANTS: A Toolkit for Building and Dynamically Deploying Network Protocols," IEEE OPENARCH'98, San Francisco, California, April 1998.
12. Steven McCanne and Van Jacobson, "The BSD Packet Filter: A New Architecture for User-level Packet Capture", 1993 Winter USENIX conference, Jan 25-29, 1993, San Diego, CA.
13. Perkins C et al. Route Optimization in Mobile IP. Internet Draft, Feb 2000.

Adaptive Call Admission Control in Wireless Multimedia Network

Marjan Bozinovski and Liljana Gavrilovska
Institute of telecommunications
Faculty of Electrical Engineering
Karpos II b.b., P.O.B. 574
91000 Skopje, R.Macedonia
bmarjan@dazhbog.etf.ukim.edu.mk, liljana@cerera.etf.ukim.edu.mk

Abstract. There is a tremendous growth of broadband multimedia services in mobile cellular networks. Call admission control (CAC) is the most significant issue in quality of service (QoS) provisioning for these services. We propose an adaptive CAC, which upgrades the upper limit (UL) scheme and is verified through the simulation. The proposed algorithm allows each cell to accept a new call if the estimated average differential of each multiclass handoff failure probability is non-positive. The generic form of the algorithm is independent of cellular network structure.

1 Introduction

Recently, the mobile communication technologies have exhibited a rapid progress. This progress leads to introduction of many different classes of high-speed multimedia traffic in wireless cellular networks. Also an adaptation of the existing voice-oriented personal mobile communication network is required in different domains. One of the domains that need adaptation for multimedia traffic is the domain of the *call admission control* (CAC). The CAC is responsible for providing acceptable quality of service (QoS) for all types of multimedia traffic.

The new call blocking probability P_{nb} and *the forced call termination probability P_{fct}* are the most important performance measures in connection-level QoS [1], [2]. The new call blocking probability is the probability that a new call request is blocked. The forced call termination probability is the probability that an ongoing call is forced to terminate due to handoff failure. The forced call termination probability is approximately a linear function of the *handoff failure probability P_{hf}* [3], which is the probability that a handoff attempt is not succesful because the destination cell has no free channels. *The carried traffic T_c* is another important QoS parameter. This parameter represents the average number of ongoing calls per cell. In multimedia case, the above-defined performance parameters can be divided into two classes:

- *particular class performance parameters* defined for each traffic class;
- *total performance parameters* defined for the total traffic.

In the further text, we will introduce a convention for referring to multimedia calls that belong to multiple and different types of classes. They will be referred to as *multiclass* calls. There are several CAC schemes applicable to multimedia networks. The most frequently used CAC policies in wireline networks are *complete sharing*

K.-L. Tan et al. (Eds.): MDM 2001, LNCS 1987, pp. 222-230, 2001.

(CS), *complete partitioning* (CP) and *threshold*. In the first scheme, calls of every class share the bandwidth pool. In the CP policy, bandwidth for each class is exclusively reserved. In the threshold policy, a newly arriving call is blocked if the number of calls of each class is greater than or equal to a predefined threshold. The threshold policy is optimal in two-class networks [4]. Previously mentioned policies form a so-called *coordinate-convex policy*. Several CAC schemes have been proposed within this policy [4], [5] and [6].

In wireless multimedia network, the threshold scheme is known as *upper limit* (UL) scheme. UL scheme gives very good performance, while the parameter P_{fct} is concerned, but it degrades the parameter P_{nb}. In general, the consequence is reduction of the carried traffic. Therefore, the UL CAC scheme is suboptimal in some implementations. The special form of UL scheme in single-class case is well-known *conventional guard scheme* (CGC), which is one of the widely used priority schemes in a single-class mobile cellular network [7].

In [8], analytical models were developed for a cellular mobile environment consisting of mixed platform types with different classes of channel and resource requirements. Handoff calls are prioritized over new calls and quotas are incorporated for each type of resources. Performance parameters like carried traffic, new call blocking and forced call termination probabilities for each platform and call type are numerically evaluated from the analytical models.

A bandwidth reservation algorithm that guarantees QoS to multimedia traffic is proposed in [9]. If the traffic is real-time, the call is admitted only if the requested bandwidth can be reserved in the call-originating cell and all its neighbors. For non-real time traffic, the requested bandwidth is reserved only in the originating cell. This scheme guarantees QoS, but it has two general drawbacks: (*i*) bandwidth is reserved redundantly since the user moves only to one of the six neighboring cells (assuming hexagonal cell geometry), and (*ii*) the stringent call admission procedure might not admit many real-time requests in a highly overloaded system.

A history-based call admission strategy that works in one-class system (e.g. mobile telephony) is proposed in [10]. The algorithm upgrades CGC scheme and a new call request is accepted if the estimated handoff failure rate for the actual system state is not higher than a predetermined QoS value for handoff failure probability. The estimation is made using the past system statistics. Also, this scheme can be generalized to function in multimedia mobile network, and then the number of conditions that should be satisfied in order to accept or reject a new call request, is equal to the number of traffic classes.

Our proposed scheme, together with [10], falls into the class of adaptive policies whose admission decisions depends on the past system behavior. The algorithm is used as extension of the UL scheme and its primary goal is to improve the parameter P_{nb} of UL, with insignificant affection of P_{fct}.

The rest of the paper is organized as follows. Section 2 describes the cellular model used in the simulation and gives the analytical expressions used for evaluation of the performance parameters. Section 3 describes the CAC algorithm. Section 4 presents the numerical results, and the summary and conclusion are presented in section 5.

2   Simulation Model

2.1 Cellular Model

One-dimensional (1-D) cellular system is simulated in our model. This cellular model is deployed in streets and highways [11]. Fig. 1 shows that it consists of N cells. Streets are assumed to be with zero width and the length of each cell is d.

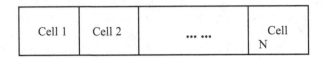

Fig. 1. One-dimensional cellular structure

We assume that there are K classes of calls in a mobile cellular network. Let b_i denote the number of channels of a class-i call, required to set up the call.

The new call arrivals of class-i ($i=1,2, ..., K$) follow a Poisson process with mean λ_i. Also, we assume exponential distribution for the service time of a class-i calls, with mean value of $1/\mu_i$. The finite service area in the simulation, causes the edge effects, and they are partially eliminated, assuming neighboring relations among the outermost cells. So, if a user reaches the left edge of the highway, he will re-enter the highway from its west edge.

In microcellular networks, fast moving users cause a great amount of handoff blocking. Therefore, we assume that the speed has a normal truncated probability density function ($v\in[0$ km/h, 100 km/h]), with mean v_m and standard deviation σ_v.

The channel allocation scheme applied in the cells is fixed channel assignment (FCA). The total number of channels (minimum bandwidth units) allocated to each cell is C. The simulation model assumes UL CAC scheme implementation and as previously said, the proposed algorithm is an extension of this scheme. The UL scheme is defined by vector $n_{ul}=[n_{ul}[1], n_{ul}[2], ..., n_{ul}[K]]$, where $n_{ul}[i]$ ($i=1,2,...,K$) is the threshold for class-i calls and a newly arriving class-i call will be accepted only if the number of class-i ongoing calls is lower than parameter $n_{ul}[i]$.

2.2 Evaluation of the Performance Parameters

Several important performance parameters were presented in the previous section. The new call blocking probability and forced call termination probability are significant to the service users, while the service provider is concerned with the efficient network utilization, represented by carried traffic per cell. The actual evaluation of the parameters of interest is as follows:

1)   New call blocking probability (for class-i $P_{nb}[i]$) is determined as:

$$P_{nb}[i] = \frac{\text{total number of blocked new class-}i\text{ calls in all cells}}{\text{total number of new class-}i\text{ call requests in all cells}}$$

2)   Forced call termination probability (for class-i $P_{fct}[i]$) can be obtained from:

$$P_{fct}[i] = \frac{\text{total number of blocked class-} i \text{ handoff attempts in all cells}}{\text{total number of admitted new class-} i \text{ calls in all cells}}$$

3) Carried traffic per cell (for class-i $T_c[i]$) is given by [12]:

$$T_c[i] = T_{off}[i] \frac{t_{dur}[i] / NCA[i]}{t_\mu[i]}$$

where $T_{off}[i]$ is the offered traffic to the network of class-i, normalized to a single cell. In fact, $T_{off}[i] = \lambda_i / \mu_i$, where λ_i is the average arrival rate of class-i, and μ_i is the average call service rate of class-i. $t_{dur}[i]$ is a cumulative duration of all class-i calls that were admitted in the whole network. $NCA[i]$ is the total number of new class-i call attempts in all cells. $t_\mu[i]$ is the mean service time of class-i and $t_\mu[i] = 1/\mu_i$. $t_{dur}[i]$ and $NCA[i]$ are obtained as outputs from the simulation.

3   Call Admission Control

This proposed CAC is dynamic algorithm. The base station in each cell constantly monitors the rate of each multiclass handoff failure occurrences as a function of time $P_{hf}(i,t)$ (i is a multiclass index and t is a time istant), which represents the class-i probability of handoff failure within its area. When the number of class-i calls in the observed cell is greater than or equal to $n_{ul}[i]$ and when new class-i call request is posed to the corresponding base station, the algorithm turns on and it begins the admission decision process. Generally, the admission decision will be positive for the call, if such decision in the past had not forced positive average differential of any multiclass handoff failure rate. Only new calls are of interest to this algorithm, since handoff calls are accepted whenever there is/are a free channel/s in the destination cell.

The cellular structure can be viewed as a one-dimensional array. Each cell can be represented by its corresponding index. As shown in Fig.1, the cell with index n, is denoted by C_n. Let the scalar $N_n(t)$ represent the number of occupied channels in the cell C_n at the instant t. It is also assumed that the system is capable to register the direction of a mobile movement. We only consider the mobiles from the neighboring cells that move towards the cell C_n, because the others will not affect the state of the cell. So, let the other scalar, $A_n(t)$ denote the total number of channels in the cells that are adjacent to C_n, occupied by mobiles moving to the cell C_n at the time t. Thus, *the state of a cell C_n at the moment t* can be defined as a vector:

$$S_n(t) = [N_n(t) \ \ A_n(t)] \tag{1}$$

$N_n(i, t)$ is another scalar that represents the number of ongoing class-i calls in the cell C_n at the moment t. When a new class-i call request arrives at the cell C_n and $N_n(i, t) < n_{ul}[i]$, the network unconditionally accepts it. The algorithm starts to work at the moment when a new class-i call request appears and $N_n(i, t) \geq n_{ul}[i]$. It makes an estimation of the *threshold parameter*, and decides whether to accept the new call or not, depending upon given criterion.

Let the new class-i call request arrive at C_n when the cell is in the state $S_n(t_0) = [N_n(t_0) \ \ A_n(t_0)]$, $N_n(i, t_0) \geq n_{ul}[i]$. The admission decision will be based on threshold parameter, written in the database record. This record corresponds to the latest state from the past, which is identical with the previously defined state. Each database record contains $5+2K$ elements (data); $4+K$ elements are related to the past and $1+K$ elements are related to the actual moment t_0 that should be written at the same moment (note that K is the number of traffic classes). The elements of a database record are:

1. The cell identifier (integer; in this case it is n);

2. i: numerical (integer) value that defines the class

   of the new call (in this case let it be the i-th class)

3. $S_n(t_1) = [N_n(t_1)\ A_n(t_1)]$: the state of the cell C_n at the instant t_1, $t_1 < t_0$, $S_n(t_0) = S_n(t_1)$;

4. m : Number (integer) of occurrences of the same state (in fact, the cell at the instant t_0 is by $m+1$-th time in the same state);

5. *Class-1 threshold parameter*: the numerical value of the average elementary change of class-1 handoff failure rate defined in the following way:

$$\overline{\Delta P_{hf}(1,T,m)} = \frac{\sum\limits_{j=1}^{m} \Delta P_{hf}(1,T,j)}{m} \tag{2}$$

$\vdots$

4+K. *Class-K threshold parameter*: the numerical value of the average elementary change of class-K handoff failure rate defined in the following way:

$$\overline{\Delta P_{hf}(K,T,m)} = \frac{\sum\limits_{j=1}^{m} \Delta P_{hf}(K,T,j)}{m} \tag{3}$$

$\Delta P_{hf}(i,T,j)$ is the elementary change of a class-i handoff failure rate after elementary time T from the instant when a new call request has appeared and the system was found in the same state by j-th time. The detailed determination of this metric for each multiclass will be described later in the text.

Now, the new call request is accepted only if

$$\overline{\Delta P_{hf}(i,T,m)} \le 0 \qquad \forall\, i = 1,...,\ K \tag{4}$$

Otherwise, it is rejected.

In order to reduce the required memory resources, one possible solution was found in concerning the total (aggregate) traffic in the analysis. It reduces the number of elements in each database record and accordingly the complexity of the algorithm. This strategy will be further referred to as *estimated total handoff failure differential* (ETHFD) scheme. In ETHFD, the only condition for a new call request to be accepted is the average estimated change of the total handoff failure probability to be non-positive. Thus, we obtain a less rigid scheme that accepts more new calls than the scheme in this paper. We will compare these two schemes with UL and comment the results in Section 4.

Then, the last few elements of the database record related to the actual state are updated:

4+K+1. $P_{hf}(1, t_0)$: this is the value of class-1 handoff failure rate of the cell C_n at the moment t_0;

.

.

.

5+2K-1. $P_{hf}(K, t_0)$: this is the value of class-K handoff failure rate of the cell C_n at the moment t_0;

5+2K. $t_0 + T$: it is the moment in the future when new data should be updated into the same record. T is a predefined elementary estimation interval, and by changing it, we can influence on performance of the strategy.

One of the last steps in this procedure is monitoring the handoff failure rates after T time units from the moment t_0, and updating a new data into the record. At the instant $t_0 + T$, the algorithm is again automatically turned on and it should record the actual class-i handoff failure rates in the cell C_n. Let these values be denoted by $P_{hf}(i, t_0 + T)$ ($i=1,...,K$). Then, the elementary change of class-i handoff failure rate occurred in the interval $[t_0, t_0+T]$ is determined:

$$\Delta P_{hf}(i, T, m+1) = P_{hf}(i, t_0 + T) - P_{hf}(i, t_0) \tag{5}$$

The final step is computing the average elementary change of each class-i handoff failure rate:

$$\overline{\Delta P_{hf}(i, T, m+1)} = \frac{\sum_{j=1}^{m+1} \Delta P_{hf}(i, T, j)}{m+1} = \frac{m \cdot \overline{\Delta P_{hf}(i, T, m)} + \Delta P_{hf}(i, T, m+1)}{m+1} \tag{6}$$

Finally, the numerical values $m+1$, $\overline{\Delta P_{hf}(1, T, m+1)}$,...,$\overline{\Delta P_{hf}(K, T, m+1)}$ are updated into the above-defined database record as 4-th, 5-th,...,(4+K)-th element, respectively.

This criterion guarantees that allocation of a reserved channel/s to a new call request will not cause the multiclass handoff failure probabilities to exceed the corresponding values of these probabilities determined with UL scheme. Even if it happens, that would be a consequence of an extensive traffic load.

As it was emphasized, the goal of the new strategy is: when the vector n_{ul} is fixed, to reduce multiclass probabilities $P_{nb}[i]$ ($i=1,...,K$) of implemented strategy relative to that of UL, and to keep $P_{fcr}[i]$ of the new strategy unchanged or negligible increased (relative to the corresponding $P_{fcr}[i]$ of UL).

The algorithm is not restricted only to one dimensional environment, because the only relevant factor from the neighboring cells is the total number of channels within them, occupied by mobiles moving to that cell. If implemented in other cellular models, this factor could be, for instant, the total number of occupied channels within them. Thus, the proposed call admission strategy could be applied to arbitrary cell topology.

4   Numerical Results

Three performance parameters have been compared: new call blocking probabilities $P_{nb}[i]$, forced call termination probabilities $P_{fct}[i]$ and carried traffic $T_c[i]$ for two traffic classes ($K=2$; $i=1, 2$). Fig. 2 shows $P_{nb}[i]$, $P_{fct}[i]$, $T_c[i]$ as functions of the total offered traffic for UL, ETHFD and the proposed strategy, for UL threshold vector $n_{ul}=[11, 3]$, while the number of channels allocated to each cell is $C=20$. The bandwidth requirements of each class are: $b_1=1$, $b_2=3$. The total offered traffic is $T_{off}=\lambda/\mu$, where $\lambda=\lambda_1+\lambda_2$, $\lambda_1=3\cdot\lambda_2$ and $\mu=\mu_1=\mu_2=1/120$ s^{-1}. The time interval T is taken as $T=k\cdot(d/v_m)$, where d is the cell length ($d=100$ m), and v_m is the mean speed of the vehicle's motion ($v_m=30$ km/h). The coefficient k has to be variable parameter for different values of T_{off}, in order to achieve best performance ($k\in(0,1]$). The standard deviation of vehicle's speed is $\sigma_v=30$ km/h. The number of cells in the system is $N=10$. The number of elements in each database record is $5+2K=5+2\cdot2=9$.

The figures show that the system parameters are improved, i.e. $P_{nb}[1]$, $P_{nb}[2]$ are reduced, $T_c[1]$, $T_c[2]$ are increased and $P_{fct}[1]$, $P_{fct}[2]$ are negligibly increased, when the new strategy is applied.

When compared to ETHFD, the proposed strategy shows better performance, regarding forced call termination probabilities, but the new call blocking probabilities are better in ETHFD. This can be explained by the fact that in ETHFD, admission decision is only based on a single condition, while in the proposed strategy, the admission decision is a logical AND function of K conditions. Consequently, in the first case, new calls are accepted more frequently than in the second scheme. Thus, ETHFD avoids more blockings of new calls, improves more successfully the network utilization, but it causes more forced call terminations than the new strategy.

5   Conclusion

This paper describes an adaptive algorithm for call admission control in a multimedia wireless cellular network. UL gives good performance as far as P_{fct} is concerned, but it deteriorates P_{nb}. Therefore, the goal of the proposed policy is to reduce P_{nb}, while leaving P_{fct} unaffected. The algorithm upgrades the UL scheme, where decisions whether to reject a new multiclass call request are based on past experience i.e. multiclass handoff failure. The experimental results show that our scheme improves the network performance. The drawback of this scheme is that it strongly depends on UL scheme, since the QoS criteria are not implemented through predefined upper bound values. A step forward would be the expression of these criteria in terms of predefined thresholds.

The proposed algorithm is quite general, because it does not depend on the type of cellular structure, and it can adapt itself to any dynamic changes of a mobile traffic.

References

[1] Stephen S. Rappaport, "The Multiple-Call Hand-off Problem in High-Capacity Cellular Communications Systems," *IEEE Transactions on Vehicular Technology*, Vol. 40, No. 3, pp. 546-557, Aug. 1991.

[2] Mahmoud Naghshineh and Mischa Schwarz, "Distributed Call Admission Control in Mobile/Wireless Networks", *PIMRC '95*, pp. 289-293, 1995.

[3] B. Jabbari, "Teletraffic Aspects of Evolving and Next-Generation Wireless Communication Networks", *IEEE Personal Communications,* pp. 4-9, Dec. 1996

[4] Keith W. Ross and Danny H. K. Tsang, "The Stochastic Knapsack Problem", *IEEE Transactions on Communications*, Vol. 37, No. 7, pp. 740-747, July 1989.

[5] Scott Jordan and Pravin P. Varaiya, "Control of Multiple Service, Multiple Resource Communication Networks", *IEEE Transactions on Communications*, Vol. 42, No. 11, pp. 2979-2988, Nov. 1994.

[6] Chi-chao Chao and Wai Chen, "Connection Admission Control for Mobile Multiple-class Personal Communication Networks", *IEEE Journal on Seleted Areas in Communications*, Vol. 15, No. 8, pp. 1618-1626, 1997.

[7] D.Hong, S.S. Rappaport, "Traffic model and performance analysis for cellular mobile radio telephone systems with prioritized and nonprioritized handoff procedures", *IEEE Trans. Vehic. Teh.*, vol. VT-35, no.3, Aug.1986

[8] S. Rappaport, C. Purzynski, "Prioritized resource assignment for mobile cellular communication systems with mixed services and platform types", *IEEE Transactions on Vehicular Technology*, vol. 45, no.3, pp. 443-457, Aug. 1996.

[9] C. Oliveira, J. B. Kim, T. Suda. "Quality-of-Service Guarantees in High-Speed Multimedia Wireless Networks", *IEEE International Communications Conference 1996,* Dallas Texas, pages 728-734.

[10] Marjan Bozinovski, Petar Popovski and Liljana Gavrilovska, "Novel Strategy for Call Admission Control in Mobile Cellular Network", *Vehicular Technology Conference (VTC'2000)*, Fall, Boston, USA, 24-28 September 2000.

[11] David A. Levine, Ian F. Akyildiz and Mahmoud Naghshineh, "A Resource Estimation and Call Admission Algorithm for Wireless Multimedia Networks Using the Shadow Cluster Concept", *IEEE/ACM Transactions on Networking*, Vol. 5, No. 1, pp. 1-12, Feb. 1997.

[12] M. D. Kulavaratharasah and A. H. Aghvami, "Teletraffic Performance Evaluation of Microcellular Personal Communication Networks (PCN's) with Prioritized Handoff Procedures," *IEEE Trans. Veh. Technol.*, vol. 48 no.1 pp. 137-152, Jan. 1999.

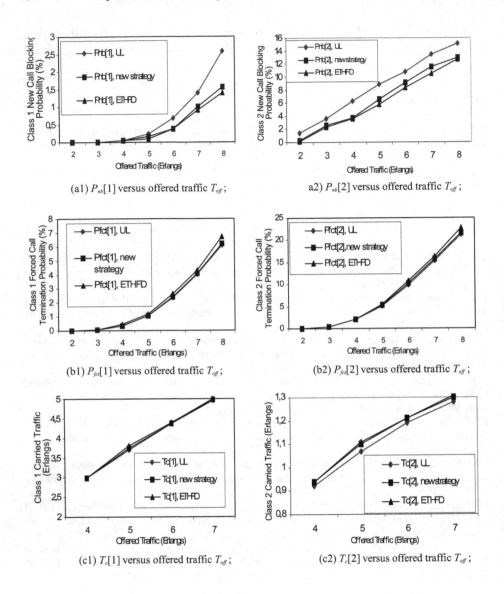

(a1) $P_{nb}[1]$ versus offered traffic T_{off};

a2) $P_{nb}[2]$ versus offered traffic T_{off};

(b1) $P_{fct}[1]$ versus offered traffic T_{off};

(b2) $P_{fct}[2]$ versus offered traffic T_{off};

(c1) $T_c[1]$ versus offered traffic T_{off};

(c2) $T_c[2]$ versus offered traffic T_{off};

Fig.2. Comparison of UL, ETHFD and new strategy for C=20 and n_{ul}=[11, 3].

Industrial Papers

Soft Mobile Ad-Hoc Networking

Tao Zhang, Wai Chen

Telcordia Technologies
445 South Street
Morristown, New Jersey 07960, U.S.A.
{tao,wchen}@research.telcordia.com

Abstract. Today's mobile ad-hoc networking approaches require nodes to maintain network topology and routing tables, which limits network scalability. This paper proposes *soft mobile ad-hoc networks* in which nodes do not maintain network topology and routing tables. We show that soft networks are feasible, have less overhead than existing approaches under many conditions, and may achieve the best possible end-to-end delay performance among all known ad-hoc networking approaches with little scalability degradation.

1 Introduction

In a mobile ad-hoc network, any node may be mobile and may route packets for other nodes. Today, three categories of routing methods exist for mobile ad-hoc networks: pre-computed routing, on-demand routing, and flooding. Pre-computed routing computes routes to all destinations *a priori* and keeps the routes up-to-date at all times. Pre-computed routing can be flat or hierarchical. Flat routing requires each node to maintain a routing table containing all other nodes in the network and hence does not scale to large networks. Hierarchical routing organizes nodes into a hierarchy of clusters and is highly scalable for fixed networks [1]. Unfortunately, today's hierarchical routing mechanisms do not scale well in mobile ad-hoc networks. Locating mobile nodes, maintaining consistent location databases on mobile nodes and maintaining rapidly changing clusters have proven difficult to do and cause prohibitively heavy signaling loads in large mobile ad-hoc networks. On-demand routing discovers a route only when needed, by flooding a query to all the nodes [2],[3],[4],[5]. The query packet remembers the intermediate nodes. Nodes that know how to reach the destination send the route information accumulated in the query packet back to the source. Routes are kept up-to-date for the duration of a packet flow. Today, on-demand routing has the highest scalability potential, but its scalability is still seriously limited by query flooding and route maintenance.

The primary cause of the limited scalability of today's ad-hoc networking approaches is that they generate *"hard"* networks that require nodes to maintain network topology and routing tables. These mechanisms also create a dilemma: they cannot achieve high scalability and low latency at the same time.

This paper proposes a new approach for ad-hoc networking – *soft mobile ad-hoc networking* – which eliminates the need for nodes to discover and maintain network

K.-L. Tan et al. (Eds.): MDM 2001, LNCS 1987, pp. 233-238, 2001.
© Springer-Verlag Berlin Heidelberg 2001

topology or routing tables. This paper shows that soft networking is feasible, may provide significantly higher scalability than existing approaches and generate the best optimal delay performance with little sacrifice in network scalability.

2 Soft Mobile Ad-Hoc Networks

In a soft mobile ad-hoc network, nodes do not have to maintain any state on network topology at any time. They do not have to determine or maintain end-to-end paths before, during, or after delivering data packets. Instead, unless the destination is a neighbor (a node within direct radio contact), each node uses a *function F* to determine, locally and independently of other nodes, where to send a packet. This paper will show that soft networks are feasible even when *F* is a function of only the number N of nodes in the network. This suggests that mobile ad-hoc nodes could use the number of other available nodes alone (without knowing the network topology or end-to-end paths) to determine where to send a packet so that their collective decisions lead the packet to its destination.

Soft networks can be realized by an innovative application of the theories of random graphs. A random graph is a graph created according to a probability distribution [6][7]. Random graphs have predictable properties and can be used to solve challenging networking problems that cannot be easily solved by other methods.

A soft ad-hoc network is formed by *evolving* a random graph hop-by-hop from a source to a destination as a packet travels from one node to another. Function *F* maps each neighbor of a node into *1* or *0*, where *1* means that a copy of the packet should be sent to the neighbor and *0* otherwise. A specific implementation of *F* is that it maps a neighbor to *1* with a *properly selected* probability *p* (called the *edge probability*). If the packet is actually sent from node *A* to its neighbor *B*, we say that there is a *soft link* between *A* and *B*. This soft link may stay alive only for the duration of that packet transmission from A to B. All soft links that have been used for delivering a packet forms a soft ad-hoc network. The network is *soft* because nodes do not need to memorize the network topology or paths taken by a packet. The network is an *evolving network* in that all its soft links do not have to exist at the same time. It *evolves* as a packet travels from node to node. Different packets between the same source and destination may be delivered over different soft networks.

3 Feasibility Analysis

We show, in Theorem 1, that a soft ad-hoc network is feasible in that it can virtually guarantee that a packet reaches its destination in a single *try* if the value of *p* is chosen properly. A *try* is to give a packet once to a network for delivery.

Theorem 1: The probability that a packet reaches its destination in a single try approaches *1* when the number N of nodes increases if *p* satisfies Eq. 1.

$$p = c \frac{\log N}{N} \tag{1}$$

where c can be *any* constant real number that is larger than one.

Proof: Consider a packet that needs to be sent from node S to node D. Starting from S, a random graph evolves as soft links are added when the packet is sent from one node to another. It is sufficient to show that this random graph will evolve into a connected graph with probability approaching *1* when N increases if p satisfies Eq. 1. Theory 4.3.1 in Reference [7] states that any random graph evolved by adding one link at a time with a probability p that satisfies Eq. 1 will be connected with probability approaching *1* when N increases.

Theorem 1 suggests that nodes in mobile ad-hoc networks may use only the number of other available nodes to determine where to send a packet in order to virtually ensure that the packet will reach its destination in just a single try.

Theorem 1 assumes that a node has zero knowledge about which neighbors are better candidates for delivering a packet. In a real network, a node may have more information (e.g., energy level and signal strength) to help decide where to send a packet so that the probability of successful packet delivery may be increased.

When N≠∞, the proposed approach does not guarantee that every packet reaches its destination in a single try. Successful delivery of every packet is not our objective, nor is it achievable by any existing approach. Instead, soft networking is a scalable method that delivers each packet with a high probability of success.

Theorem 1 assumes that the link probability p is the same for every pair of nodes, which may not be true in a real network. The probability of successful packet delivery under non-identical values of p needs further study.

4   Overhead Analysis

This section compares the overheads of the proposed soft ad-hoc networking approach with today's most scalable alternative, on-demand routing. Overhead will be measured by the number of packet transmissions for delivering the same number of user packets from a source to a destination. One packet transmission occurs when a packet is sent from one node to another. Point-to-point data delivery is often a preferred mode of operation in mobile ad-hoc networks. It can save energy, generate lower radio interference, and have longer radio reach than broadcasting.

Existing on-demand routing methods broadcast route discovery packets to *all* nodes to discover a path to the destination. The path is then used by user packets and kept up-to-date by exchanging routing updates among the nodes and replacing failed paths with new ones. For these methods, our overhead calculation will include only packet transmissions for path establishment, which can significantly underestimate their overheads. At any time t, if we draw an edge between every two nodes that are within direct radio contact of each other and denote the resulting graph by $G_h(V,E)$, the average number of packet transmissions for path discovery at time t will be approximately $H+2|E|$. The first term, H, is the average hop-count distance between two nodes in G_h and represents packet transmissions for sending a response to the source. The second term represents packet transmissions incurred by the path discovery packet. It results from the fact that every node (except the destination) has to broadcast at least one path discovery packet to each of its neighbors (except the one from which the packet comes) and that nodes on both ends of a link could broadcast to each other simultaneously. Suppose that an average of K user packets are delivered each time an end-to-end path is set up on demand. The average total number M_1 of packet transmissions each time a path is established becomes $M_1=2|E|+(K+1)H$.

Using the proposed soft networking approach, the average number of packet transmissions for delivering K user packets at time t will be proportional to the average number of soft links in the soft network, which will be a subset of the edges in G_h. Since each edge in G_h may become a soft link with probability p, the average number of packet transmissions for delivering one packet is approximately $2p|E|$. The average number M_2 of packet transmissions for delivering K packets becomes $2Kp|E|$. Fig.1 shows M_2/M_1 assuming $|E| \cong N(N-1)/20$, $H \cong log_2N$, and $c=0.01$.

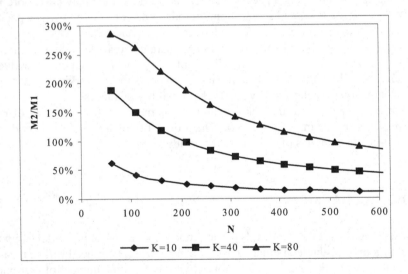

Fig. 1. Scalability comparisons with existing on-demand routing for ad-hoc networks.

One can observe from the above results that the proposed soft networking approach incurs lower overhead than existing on-demand ad-hoc routing regardless network size if most packet flows are not extremely long. When most packet flows are very long, the overhead of the proposed approach may be higher. In such a case, soft networking may be used for on-demand path establishment only and a path may be kept alive for sending more packets as in today's on-demand routing. Route discovery overhead using soft networking is approximately $100p\%<100\%$ of the overhead of today's on-demand routing because each node, using soft networking, sends a route discovery packet to each of its neighbors with probability p.

5   Delay Performance Analysis

We show, in Theorem 2, that the proposed soft networking approach could, by choosing a proper edge probability p, provide the best possible end-to-end delay among *all* known ad-hoc networking approaches. It achieves such performance using a new p (defined in Eq. 5) which is slightly higher than the p specified in Eq.1, suggesting that there is little degradation of its scalability. When the network grows larger, the delay performance of the proposed approach gets closer to the optimal while, in contrast, the delays of today's ad-hoc networking approaches typically get farther away from the optimal. In other words, the proposed soft networking approach could solve the dilemma between high scalability and low delay.

Theorem 2: Consider N nodes. Let $\Delta \geq 3$ be the maximal node degree of a soft network. Let D be the number of hops a packet has to traverse to reach its destination in the worst-case in a soft network. Let D_{min} be the minimum number of hops a packet has to traverse using *any* ad-hoc networking technique if the degree of every node is at most Δ. Then, D can be arbitrarily close to D_{min} in a large network. More precisely, if $N \to \infty$, D is asymptotically optimal, i.e., for any fixed $\varepsilon > 0$, we have

$$\lim_{N \to \infty} P\left(1 \leq \frac{D}{D_{min}} < 1 + \varepsilon\right) = 1 \tag{2}$$

Proof: First, according to the Moor Bound [6], we have

$$D_{min} \geq \frac{\log(N-1)}{\log(\Delta)} \tag{3}$$

Second, we have the following random graph theorem from [6]: if $\Delta \geq 3$ and d is the smallest integer for which

$$(\Delta - 1)^{d-1} \geq (2 + \rho)N\Delta \log N \tag{4}$$

holds for any fixed $\rho \geq 0$, then almost every Δ-regular graph on N vertices has diameter less than or equal to d.

Third, according to Theorem 5.1.3 in [7], if $N\Delta$ is an even number, every random graph will have a Δ-regular spanning sub-graph if p satisfies Eq. 5,

$$p = \frac{\log N}{N}\left(1 + (\Delta + 1)\frac{\log \log N}{\log N} + \frac{\omega_N}{\log N}\right) \tag{5}$$

where $\omega_N \to \infty$ arbitrarily slowly when $N \to \infty$. In other words, if p is chosen to satisfy Eq. 5, the diameter D of each random network generated by the proposed approach should also be no more than d as specified in Eq.4. Therefore, we have

$$D \le d \le \frac{\log N}{\log(N-1)} + O\left(\frac{\log\log N}{\log \Delta}\right) \tag{6}$$

Combining Eq. 3, Eq.4, and Eq. 6, we arrive at

$$1 \le \frac{D}{D_{\min}} \le \frac{\log N \log \Delta}{\log(N-1)\log(\Delta-1)} + O\left(\frac{\log\log N}{\log N}\right) \tag{7}$$

If $N \to \infty$, the upper bound in Eq. 7 becomes smaller than $1+\varepsilon$ for any fixed $\varepsilon > 0$.

6   Conclusions

This paper proposes *soft ad-hoc networks* in which nodes do not have to maintain network topologies and routing tables. The approach is shown to be feasible and could provide high scalability and optimal end-to-end latency at the same time.

References

1. Sharony, J.: An Architecture for Mobile Radio Networks with Dynamically Changing To-pology using Virtual Subnets. ACM Journal of Mobile Networks and Applications (1996) 75-86
2. Pearlman, M.R., Haas, Z.J.: Determining the Optimal Configuration for the Zone Routing Protocol. IEEE Journal on Selected Areas in Communications, Vol. 17, No. 8, August 1999
3. Perkins, C. et al: Ad Hoc On-Demand Distance Vector (AODV) Routing. IETF Draft, Oc-tober 1999
4. Park, V. Corson, S.: Temporally-Ordered Routing Algorithms (TORA) Version 1 Func-tional Specification. IETF Draft, October 1999
5. Broch, J., *et al*: The Dynamic Source Routing Protocol for Mobile Ad Hoc Networks. IETF Draft, October 1999
6. Bollobas, B.: Random Graphs. Academic Press Inc., London, UK (1985)
7. Palmer, E.M.: Graphical Evolution: An Introduction to the Theory of Random Graphs. John Wiley & Sons, New York, Chichester, Brisbane, Toronto, Singapore (1985)

CC/PP for Content Negotiation and Contextualization

Lalitha Suryanarayana[1] and Johan Hjelm[2]

[1] Senior Member of Technical Staff, SBC Technology Resources,
9505 Arboretum Blvd., Austin, TX 78759, USA
lalitha@tri.sbc.com
[2] Former W3C Fellow at the World Wide Web Consortium (W3C)
Currently Senior Research Project Manager, Ericsson Nippon KK,
YRP Center Ichiban-kan, 3-4 Hikarino-oka, Yokosuka, 239-0847 Kanagawa, Japan
Johan.hjelm@era-t.ericsson.se

Abstract. The proliferation of Internet-enabled devices supporting a variety of user-interface paradigms and modalities motivates the need to create presentations of content that are optimized for the specific configurations that they must be rendered on. As a result, there is also a need for a standardized capabilities-and-content negotiation mechanism that will allow clients accessing the web to assert their capabilities to the server serving the content. This paper discusses Composite Capabilities/ Preferences Profile (CC/PP), a protocol-independent extensible framework that can be used for communicating any meta data information such as device and document profiles. We describe WAP User Agent Profiles as a use case and recommend the architecture for conveying contextualized information to enable context based environmental adaptation in the future.

1 Introduction

The presentation mechanisms in the current web are designed for users with large screens and high-end computers. With more device types than ever proliferating the online space[1], there is an emerging need for content to be suitably formatted for rendering to these devices. Mobile devices especially, have varied user interface paradigms and can present content in different modalities such as text, sound or a combination of the two. Further more, key characteristics in terms of hardware and layout as well as the software application environment supporting the browsers are as heterogeneous as the device and device types themselves. In addition, presentation preferences vary between individual users. In order for the content on the current World Wide Web to then be usable from such terminals, there is a need for the application server to be aware of the context[2] in which the information is being presented.

---

[1] According to International Data Corporation (2000), by year 2002, data capable mobile terminals (WAP) will be the device of choice for web access, with almost 1.3 billion web-capable phones by 2004 as compared to about 700 million wired terminals [1].

[2] Here we use the term "context" to imply both, the user's frame of reference as well as the user agent/ browser context.

K.-L. Tan et al. (Eds.): MDM 2001, LNCS 1987, pp. 239-245, 2001.

Current techniques involve either explicitly using different URLs for different versions/ formats of the content or the use of HTTP1.1 User Agent headers to assert a limited set of information about the client [2]. In the former case, users must remember and use different URLs for the same site, depending on the method and means of access. While the User Agent header fields are sufficient for selecting a representation from a set of variants, they do not enable a richer description of the characteristics of the device, such as its screen size or position information. The granular details of the client capabilities are critical for creating an optimal presentation, especially when this presentation involves filtering or transformation of the content from one format to another. Such granularity in capabilities description also supports the emerging notion of separating content from presentation, which results in a higher degree of customization than ever before.

This paper describes a framework that enables communication and negotiation of device and user agent capabilities and user preferences in the context of a web session. The framework in itself is generic and can be used to assert meta data information (profile), about any element on the web, such as device capabilities, intermediate proxy services and web documents. The model supports a machine understandable environment, allowing web servers and proxies serving content to dynamically adapt and tailor the content based on the parameters presented by the requesting client.

2 Composite Capabilities/ Preferences Profile

Such a framework was first proposed by the Mobile Access Interest Group in the World Wide Web Consortium (W3C). Composite Capabilities/ Preferences Profile (CC/PP) [3], [4] is based on Resource Description Framework [5], [6], a semantic meta data application encoded in XML. The CC/PP architecture model uses RDF to define schemas upon which vocabularies can be independently developed and implemented. In the case of HTTP, a user agent generates, encodes and appends a profile[3] onto an outgoing HTTP request at the requesting end [7]. Intermediate proxies or gateways along the path of the request can append additional descriptions of the services they provide. At the origin server, the profile is dynamically composed from these and other fragments (RDF documents) such as collected from CC/PP repositories, then parsed and interpreted to determine the features of the presentation environment. The content can be generated either by using filtering techniques specific to device or user's preferences, or by selecting an appropriate presentation format that maintains the content intact. Depending upon the application, a suitable variant of the content itself may also be selected (from a set) or dynamically generated. This is returned in the HTTP response, possibly further transformed by the intermediate network elements and finally rendered to the client. See Figure 1.

---

[3] Profile is simply a collection of properties that describe the capabilities of the client and its environment.

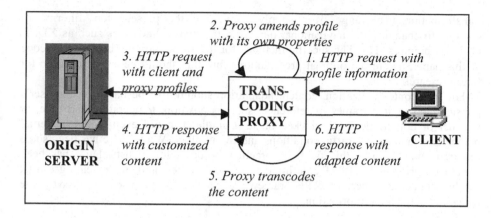

Fig. 1. Architecture for CC/PP, illustrated over HTTP

CC/PP is well suited for devices connecting from low bandwidth, high latency networks. By using both, RDF for profile transmission and XML namespaces, it inherently supports vocabulary extensions for emerging terminals or applications. The ability to assert user preferences[4] along with support for a *"split-client-split-server"* web architecture by means of dynamic profile composition makes CC/PP extremely compelling for use in contextualization.

3   Content Adaptation and Contextualization

If the presentation of the content is too tightly bound to the markup of the content itself, it may become impossible to display it on some terminals. Given the variations in terminal types and access methods, it is in the content author's best interests to separate the actual content from the presentation to the extent possible. In other words, abstracting the markup or style from the semantics allows for multiple styles to be associated and rendered with the same content. One such enabler is Cascading Style Sheets [8] on the World Wide Web, which enables the declaration of the content rendering to be separated from the content markup. Tailored style sheets can then be sent to the terminal, enabling a precise adaptation of the presentation. However the customized presentation for mobile devices may involve a change in the application paradigm or modality itself. For instance, the "deck of cards" paradigm in WAP enabled small-screen devices is substantially different from the "infinite scroll" model of web pages. The optimal solution therefore is to model the navigation of the content in a device-independent way and then adapt the content based on the device profile [9]. The content adaptation can be carried out using a transformation process, one for each type of device, through the use of XSLT [10] on XML documents. The

---

[4] For example, a user driving her car may wish to receive content in audio (voice) form when she docks her device in the hands-free cradle of her car, as opposed to a graphical (visual) presentation which might be preferable when she is walking to a train station.

transformation may range from simply converting the presentation, filtering of content, to changing the navigational paradigm through technologies such as XDNL [11] or Xpointers [12]. The specific methods for transformation are beyond the scope of this paper, as are the optimal presentations, but this should be a fruitful topic for future research.

For true contextualization, content adaptation should also be based on the user's physical and logical frames of reference, such as position, temperature and time, or whether or not the device is docked on to a cradle. It could even include external parameters such as the traffic conditions and the weather. While there has been some research undertaken in this field, no practical solution for industrial use has been developed prior to CC/PP. By defining new vocabularies, and implementing a trust mechanism[5], the generic CC/PP framework can easily be used to convey the necessary contextual information.

4   User Agent Profiles – The WAP Use Case

An example of CC/PP in actual use is the WAP User Agent Profiles (UAProf), specified by the WAP Forum as part of its WAP1.2.1 specifications [13]. WAP UAProf extends CC/PP to mobile WAP terminals. Since a WAP user agent (micro browser) transmits binary encoded XML over a Wireless Session Protocol (WSP) session between the WAP client and the WAP gateway, the specification defines CC/PP headers over WSP that can be translated into CC/PP headers over HTTP, based on the CC/PP Exchange Protocol [7]. The WAP Forum has defined its own profile vocabulary and associated WAP binary encoding that include assertions for hardware and software characteristics, WAP specific features and transport network capabilities. The specifications also recommend optimization mechanisms over the air, such as the caching of CC/PP-WSP headers for the duration of the WSP session. A sample user agent profile supported by a WAP terminal is illustrated in RDF below.

WAP User Agent Profiles and CC/PP are critical to next generation architectures that will support the convergence of the mobile web technologies with that of the classic web. Vendors of WAP gateway and browsers have already begun to offer commercial implementations of User Agent Profiles as a step towards enabling this convergence. In fact, the Mobile Execution Environment group within ETSI has agreed to adopt UAProf for asserting device capabilities in future mobile devices[6].

Sample RDF Listing of a User Agent Profile for a fictitious WAP device.

```
<?xml version="1.0"?>

<rdf:RDF xmlns:rdf="http://www.w3.org/1999/02/22-rdf-
syntax-ns#"
xmlns:prf="http://www.wapforum.org/UAPROF/ccppschema-
19991014991014#">
```

---

[5] The W3C CC/PP working group is currently developing a trust model for the framework.

[6] MExE is part of the 3rd Generation Partnership Project, a joint initiative by standards bodies including the European Telecommunications Standards Institute (ETSI), ARIB and the IT, set up to design the future mobile network environment, including mobile client devices.

```
<rdf:Description ID="MyProfile">

<prf:component>

   <rdf:Description ID="TerminalHardware">

      <rdf:type
resource="http://www.wapforum.org/UAPROF/ccppschema
19991014#HardwarePlatform" />

      <prf:Defaults
rdf:resource="http://www.thissite.com/thisdev/thismodel
" />

            <!-- Override the ImageCapable property -->

      <prf:Imagecapable>Yes</prf:Imagecapable>

   </rdf:Description>

</prf:component>

</rdf:Description>

</rdf:RDF>

<!—Sample default properties at
http://www.thissite.com/thisdev/thismodel -->

<?xml version="1.0"?>

<rdf:RDF xmlns:rdf="http://www.w3.org/1999/02/22-rdf-
syntax-ns#"
xmlns:prf="http://www.wapforum.org/UAPROF/ccppschema-
19991014#">

   <rdf:Description about =
"http://www.thissite.com/thisdev/thismodel">

      <prf:Vendor>UniqThisDev</prf:Vendor>

      <prf:Model>thismodel9786</prf:Model>

      <prf:TextInputCapable>Yes</prf:TextInputCapable>

      <prf:ImageCapable>No</prf:ImageCapable>

      <prf:ColorCapable>No</prf:ColorCapable>

      <prf:ScreenSize>600x400</prf:ScreenSize>

      <prf:OutputCharSet>

         <rdf:Bag>

            <rdf:li>US-ASCII</rdf:li>

         </rdf:Bag>
```

```
        </prf:OutputCharSet>
      </rdf:Description>
    </rdf:RDF>
```

5   Summary

We have described Composite Capabilities/ Preferences Profile as a simple yet powerful framework for communicating the client capabilities and user preferences to a web server that aims to render customized content to mobile devices. With the evolution of web technologies such as XHTML [16], the framework is expected to gain broader foothold as the primary mechanism for conveying document profiles. CC/PP is currently being standardized under the auspices of the W3C, and with User Agent Profiles already specified in the WAP context, the technology has already begun to gain industry wide acceptance and adoption as a core technology in the evolution of the Internet architecture.

6   Acknowledgements

The authors gratefully acknowledge the contribution of all the members of the W3C CC/PP Working Group and the WAP Forum User Agent Profile Drafting Committee, as well as their employers (SBC Technology Resources, Ericsson Research and the W3C) for continued support in this activity.

References

1. Borland, "Technology tussle underlies the wireless web", CNETNews.com, 04/00.
2. Singhal, Bridgman, Suryanarayana, et. al., "WAP – Writing Applications for Mobile Devices", Addison Wesley, to be published, Sept 2000.
3. Composite Capabilities/Preferences Profile, Franklin Reynolds, et. al.,. W3C Note November 1998. http://www.w3.org/TR/NOTE-CCPP-19990527
4. The CC/PP Working Group home page, http://www.w3.org/Mobile/CCPP/
5. Lassila and Swick, "Resource Description Framework (RDF) Model and Syntax Specification", W3C Recommendation, 02/99, http://www.w3.org/TR/REC-rdf-syntax/
6. Brickley and Guha, "Resource Description Framework (RDF) Schema Specification 1.0", W3C Candidate Recommendation, 03/00. http://www.w3.org/TR/PR-rdf-schema
7. Ohto and Hjelm, "CC/PP Exchange Protocol using HTTP 1.1 Extension Framework" W3C Note 06/99. Available at http://www.w3.org/TR/NOTE-CCPPexchange
8. Cascading Style Sheets, http://www.w3.org/Style/CSS/
9. Hjelm, "Designing Wireless Information Services", John Wiley and Sons, 06/00.
10. Clark, "XSL Transformations Version 1.0", W3C Recommendation, 11/99, http://www.w3.org/TR/xslt

11. Ito and Manabe, "XML Document Navigation Language", W3C Note, 03/00, http://www.w3.org/TR/xdnl
12. The W3C XML pages, at http://www.w3.org/XML/
13. Specifications for Wireless Application Protocol (WAP) Version 1.1, http://www.wapforum.org
14. Raggett, Stark and Wugofski, "XHTML Document Profile Requirements", W3C Working Draft, 09/99, http://www.w3.org/TR/xhtml-prof-req/
15. Fielding, J. Gettys, J. Mogul, H. Frystyk, L. Masinter, P. Leach, T. Berners-Lee, Hypertext Transfer Protocol -- HTTP/1.1. IETF Draft Standard RFC, June 1999. http://www.rfc-editor.org/rfc/rfc2616.txt
16. "XHTML1.0: The Extensible Hypertext Markup Language", W3C Recommendation, 01/00, http://www.w3.org/TR/xhtml1/

Serving Spatial Location Information over the Internet

Haitao Tang, Mari Korkea-aho, Jose Costa-Requena, and Jussi Ruutu

Nokia, P.O. Box 407, FIN-00045 NOKIA GROUP, Finland
Haitao.Tang@nokia.com

Abstract. This paper proposes a concept of serving spatial location information over IP networks. It clarifies and explores the requirements and solutions to realize the concept. The crucial issues elaborated with solutions are: definitions of target and its location, its naming requirements and mechanisms, its roaming among location servers, acquiring spatial location information over IP networks. Recently, issues of location-based applications have been raised in the IP community. This paper contributes to a cutting edge effort for supporting such applications over IP networks.

1   Introduction

Finding the spatial location of any object associated to a physical entity has been a crucial need to people for a very long time. With increasing accessibility of spatial location information via IP networks, the need to use such information by various applications grows. The increasing mobility of different devices is also accelerating the need.

For example, some of the applications/services (e.g., [4]) proposed are: IP-based emergency call, rescue applications, navigation, remote control, property management, delivery tracking, critical health monitoring, location specific resource announcement and discovery, location sensitive billing, various networking and protocol optimizations, management of equipment in the field, etc.

In order to obtain the spatial location of the object (called target), we need to have the following capabilities. First, there must be methods available to position the targets. Second, there must be a way to know from where and how the location of a target can be requested. Third, there must be methods to send the requested spatial location information of the targets to the legitimate requesting parties.

Usually, the targets belong to people or organizations. Therefore, the availability of their spatial location information is constrained by the privacy needs of their owners as well as the mechanisms needed to identify the requesting parties who are allowed to use the spatial location data. The location data may be further filtered (e.g., modifying the accuracy and presentation format) before its sending according to the data access policies associated to the identified parties.

There are several different ways available for positioning targets. These include, e.g., GPS positioning [1], local positioning [2], cellular positioning [3], cell

K.-L. Tan et al. (Eds.): MDM 2001, LNCS 1987, pp. 246–251, 2001.

ID based positioning [4], etc. The positioning accuracy varies from meter level (GPS and local positioning) to kilometer level (cell ID based positioning).

However, there is no standard way for an application to get the information over the Internet, although there are many methods to determine the spatial locations of resources. In addition, there is no existing way (except that via specific configuration) for the application to find out where and how the location information of a target can be requested.

The motivation of this paper is thus to introduce and further explore the requirements needed to solve the problem: How can an application acquire the spatial location of an identifiable resource over/represented on the Internet in a reliable, secure, and scalable manner? In addition, this paper introduces the results obtained so far by the IETF effort [5] and further explore the crucial aspects and solutions on target naming, roaming, etc., which are needed to fully solve the problem.

2   Target and Their Locations

A target is a physical entity in the existing space/time reference frame or a logical entity that in turn is hosted by a physical entity in the existing space/time reference frame. A target may be stationary or in motion. A location is a place where a target is "physically" situated in the existing reference frame, i.e., the location of the physical target itself or the location of its hosting entity.

Spatial location (our focus) is the location of a physical object in this real world, expressed via a coordinate system (e.g. latitude, longitude, and altitude) using a certain geographic reference system (e.g. WGS-84). In addition to the coordinates themselves, the location information generally also incorporates, at least, the time of determination of the location and its estimation accuracy.

3   Service Architecture

The service of spatial location information over the Internet is based on the simple client-server model. There are four elements related to the system, i.e., target, client, server, and proxy server, where client and server (including proxy server) are well-known.

A target is a physical entity in an existing space or a logical entity given it is hosted by a physical entity in that space. A target is only the entity whose spatial location a client requests and a server provides. Targets are not system elements in the service architecture - here, they are only the entities whose spatial location information the clients and servers address.

4   Target Naming and Roaming

4.1   Naming Targets via Uniform Resource Identifiers

In order to obtain the spatial location of a target, there must be a method to identify and refer to the target. This paper proposes two identifiers to a target: (1) Target information ID (TID) and (2) Target record Accessing iD (TAD).

The TID serves as a persistent, location-independent, resource identifier, even valid after the existence of the target. On the other hand, TAD is generally made of contact information, handling procedure(s), etc., for the repository of the target's location information. TAD can only tell you where/how to get the location information of a given target. There can be more than one TAD for a given TID. It can be time/place dependent, non-persistent, etc.

A TID can be very well named with a Uniform Resource Name (URN) [7,8]. For example, the URN based TID of Mike Lee's car can be:

urn:namespace-xyz:car=abc-888,registration-state=nnn,owner=mike.lee,nationality=
xyz,id=221068-3355,email=mike.lee@hardcom.com,pstn=+358405021988

A TAD can be very well named with a Uniform Resource Identifier (URI) [6]. Take Mike's car as the case. Its URI based TADs can be dependent on where the car is located currently. For example,

slop:car=abc-888,registration-state=nnn@car1.find.gov:5888;valid-till=31.8.2000

slop:abc-888@vehicle.monitoring.eu:transport=tcp:2008

where, "slop" is the protocol or scheme for accessing the location information.

4.2   Target Roaming between Location Servers via TAD

The target is not a network entity. It is only an entity represented by a spatial location server in the network to serve for the target's location information. A target needs to register its TID (or a subset of it) to a spatial location server in order to make the target's location information accessible over the network via the server. A TAD is then allocated for the target and registered with its TID (or a subset of it), by the location server.

"Target roaming between location servers" means that a target can change its current representing location server from one location server to another because of time, geographic location, service relationships, and/or other reasons. The current representing location server of a target knows and serves the current spatial location information of the target according to the policy requirements set for the target by the target itself or its owner.

A target should have a default TAD that serves as a relatively persistent or default record accessing ID. A target can roam from its default location server to a visited location server. When a visited location server serves the location information of the roaming-in target, the visited location server is the current representing location server for the target. After mutually authenticating each other on the target's TID (or a subset of it) and the visited server ID, the visited server allocates a visiting TAD for the target and informs its default location server of the target's current visiting TAD. The default location server of the target can then bind the two TADs (the default and the visiting).

When a client requests the location information of the target via the default TAD to the default location server, the server will reply the client with the current visiting TAD of the target. The client can then request the location information via the current visiting TAD to the target's visited location server.

5   Acquire Spatial Location Information

When a client knows the TAD of a target already, the remaining task is: How can the client acquire the location information from the server over the Internet? This section introduces requirements for the feasible solution, called as Spatial Location Protocol (SLoP). Some details can be found in [9].

5.1   Spatial Location Representations

There are various existing location data representations/expressions [10]. SLoP thus needs to support those different location data representations/ expressions. For interoperability reasons, it needs to have an absolute location system as the supported format by all SLoP speakers. Its data format should be selected as such, e.g., longitude, latitude, and altitude, with timestamp and accuracy, etc. When needed by a SLoP end, SLoP should be able to select and use any of all other supported absolute location systems and their data formats. It is also needed for SLoP to be capable of adding and supporting new location systems and data formats. In addition, when needed, SLoP should be able to carry descriptive locations.

5.2   Representation Negotiation Mechanism

Due to various location data representations/expressions used, two SLoP speakers may not understand each other, on certain given data representation/ expression. Therefore, SLoP needs to have a representation negotiation mechanism designed. The mechanism must be able to support the selection of the wanted location system and data format between two SLoP speakers.

5.3   Security Mechanisms

Spatial location information can be very sensitive and its owner may want to prevent any unwanted party from the information. Therefore, there must be an authentication mechanism selected/defined between SLoP speakers to guarantee the integrity/authenticity/accessibility (e.g., no spoofing attacks) of the involved parties. There must be an encryption system selected/defined to guarantee the privacy/confidentiality of the transferred information between SLoP speakers. In addition, it would be preferred to select/define a mechanism to guarantee availability (preventing Denial of Service (DOS) attacks to a SLoP speaker).

Use of the authentication and/or the encryption mechanisms should be setable by the SLoP endpoint (user may enable or disable the use of the mechanisms). It is done per session or per SLoP endpoint. The primary design for security in SLoP must be end-to-end. When end-to-end security is not possible for certain cases, then hop-by-hop security associations could be used between the server and the client if allowed by the related policy for a target.

5.4   Policy Mechanisms

Owners/servers of spatial location information usually set specific rules to regulate the accesses to the spatial location information, due to their privacy needs or other reasons. There are four basic sets of policies, i.e., security policy, locatability policy, accuracy policy, and explicitness policy, while any new policy set or individual rule can be added if needed.

Security policy tells what are the mechanisms and parameters for the authentication of the SLoP speakers, for the guarantee of the integrity/ authenticity/accessibility for the involved parties, as well as for confidentiality of the transferred information between SLoP speakers. Locatability policy defines who can access certain location information under what conditions. Accuracy policy tells what accuracy of the location information is for what group/individual given they are allowed to have that information. Explicitness policy defines, with what specificity, the location information is presented to what group/individual, such as "at home", "in Helsinki", "in Europe", etc., when needed. Privacy policy is in fact built from the combination of the four policy sets.

The policy instance for a target should be available to the server representing the target, where the policy instance tells how a server shall serve the spatial location of the target.

5.5   Transmission and Reliability Mechanism

There are two major requirements for the transmission, i.e., involved overhead and transport reliability of the transmission method. A balance is needed to achieve both requirements.

The design of a reliability mechanism is affected by the transport protocol below SLoP. Various transport protocols have different reliable levels. If TCP is selected, there is no need to have this extra mechanism. However, TCP seems too heavy for some SLoP speakers. UDP is thus likely to be selected. If UDP is used, a reliability mechanism must be designed into SLoP. One needs to add a retransmission timer to SLoP speaker, as a lightweight solution.

5.6   SLoP Message Coding Mechanism

Message coding can be binary-based coding or text-based coding. Binary coding is a good choice for the protocols of the transport layer and the lower. However, it is difficult to extend new information types to the protocols. SLoP is designed to be an application space protocol. There are various information types that can be carried via SLoP for various local or global purposes of the applications over it. We thus need a globally acceptable text-based coding mechanism (e.g., with XML syntax) selected/designed for encoding/decoding SLoP messages. All SLoP speakers must support the coding mechanism.

6   Conclusions

Spatial location information relates to many aspects, especially when it is served through a communication network. This paper has introduced the problem scope for serving spatial location information over IP networks. It has explored the requirements and solutions for solving the problem. Serving spatial location information over IP networks is not an easy task. Some issues still need to be further clarified, such as the location request routing.

Acknowledgments

The authors are deeply grateful to all those who have contributed to the IETF Spatial Location effort (http://www-nrc.nokia.com/ietf-spatial/).

References

1. Hofmann-Wellenhof, B., Lichtenegger, H., and Collins, J.: Global Positioning System - Theory and Practice, Fourth edition. SpringerWienNewYork (1997). 248
2. Mettala, R.: Bluetooth Protocol Architecture, 1.C.120/1.0, Bluetooth White Paper. http://www.bluetooth.com/developer/download/download.asp?doc=175   (1999). 248
3. Rantalainen, T., Ruutu, V., Saleh, B., and Hasting, J.: Point-to-point Signaling Messages for E-OTD and GPS Capable GSM Mobile Stations, T1P1.5/99187-r0. Technical Subcommittee T1P1 (1999). 248
4. ETSI: Digital cellular telecommunications system (Phase 2+); Location Services (LCS); (Functional description) - Stage 2, GSM 03.71 version 7.3.0 Release. ETSI (1998). 248, 249
5. Tang, H.: Charter Proposal of Spatial Location Working Group. http://www-nrc.nokia.com/ietf-spatial/charter-items-v031.txt (2000). 249
6. Berners-Lee, T., Fielding, R., Irvine, U., and Masinter, L.: Uniform Resource Identifiers (URI): Generic Syntax. RFC2396, IETF (1998). 250
7. Moats. R.: URN Syntax. RFC2141, IETF (1997). 250
8. Daigle, L., van Gulik, D., Iannella, R., and Faltstrom, P.: URN Namespace Definition Mechanisms. RFC2611, IETF (1999). 250
9. Rosen, B., Costa-Requena, J., Korkea-aho, M., Ylianttila, M., Mahy, R., Takahashi, K., and Farrell, S.: Spatial Location Protocol Requirements. draft-rosen-spatial-requirements-00.txt, IETF (2000). 251
10. WGS84: WGS 84 Implementation Background. http://www.wgs84.com/wgs84/wgs84.htm. 251

On-Line Service Adaptation for Mobile and Fixed Terminal Devices

Jari Korva [1], Johan Plomp [1], Petri Määttä [1], Maija Metso [2]

[1] VTT Electronics, Kaitovayla 1, FIN-90570 Oulu, Finland
{jari.korva, johan.plomp, petri.maatta}@vtt.fi
[2] University of Oulu, MediaTeam, P.O. Box 4500, FIN-90014 UNIVERSITY OF OULU,
Finland
maija.metso@ee.oulu.fi

Abstract. This paper reports on the dynamic adaptation of multimedia services for both mobile and fixed terminal devices. The adaptation is done based on the device features and includes both the adaptation of the presentation format (e.g. HTML, WML, SMS, E-mail, and speech-driven browsers) and the multimedia contents. The services are defined in XHTML with some extensions. In this paper, we mainly focus on the considerations involved in the development of the adaptation methodology. The architecture of the system is also described briefly. The research is part of the Princess project, a joint project of Oulu University and VTT Electronics.

1 Introduction

Service providers have had to reconsider the architecture of their Web-based services because of the growing diversity of the terminals used to access their services. Not only do portable devices like PDA's set their own requirements to the scalability of the services, but particularly mobile devices open up a whole new dimension for the services. Since mobility is for the time being coupled with small displays, alternative input methods and slow data transfer in addition to alternative standards for contents description, traditional HTML services will not suffice without major revisions.

There are several options for how to tacle the problem of providing a service for a diversity of clients with varying features: in addition to manually authoring several versions of the same service, there are also client-, server- and proxy-based approaches for dynamic adaptation [4]. The last one is also referred to as automatic re-authoring [3] or Web intermediaries [1]. Thus, because the term 'proxy' refers strongly to Web proxies, we prefer the concept 'intermediary', which is more general.

An example of the client-side adaptation is the World Wide Web: its basic principle was to be universality of access irrespective of hardware, software, network and user characteristics [2]. In this approach, services are authored using a format that is not dependent on specific terminal characteristics – it is a task of the client terminal to decide how to present the user interface and the content to the user. Therefore, this approach requires some level of homogeneity within the clients support for protocols and presentation formats.

K.-L. Tan et al. (Eds.): MDM 2001, LNCS 1987, pp. 252–259, 2001.

In server-based approach content and (possibly) application logic are authored platform independently too, but the service provider creates platform dependent converters or gateways. Lately there has been a proliferation of this category of tools especially from database vendors. These new tools are often based on XML technologies, particularly using XSLT transformation features. It is also possible to implement server-side adaptation using a more traditional multi-tiered architecture.

Intermediary-based approach is suitable for highly heterogeneous environments where service providers and client terminals are not capable or willing to perform the adaptation. This approach introduces an additional mediating component, an adapter (Figure 1), which allows the implementation of services independent of accessing terminal types. These adapters may work at multiple levels: they may perform content transcoding, or in more complex cases, link different network protocols or user interface interaction styles together.

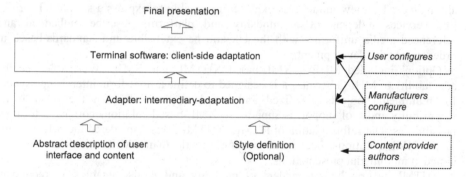

Fig. 1. Using client and/or intermediary-adaptation

The intermediary approach has benefits both from content provider and user point of view. Abstracting a variety of client terminals from the content provider reduces service development costs and makes it possible that content providers do not have to follow developments in terminal devices that closely. For the user, this approach allows anytime, anywhere and any terminal access independent of the service. Changing from one terminal to another is also smoother as user preferences are contained in the mediator, not in the terminal device.

On the other hand, the intermediary approach also has inherent drawbacks: it does not allow end-to-end security as the mediator must be able to influence the interaction between the client and the server. Also, it limits the possibilities of optimising the content, functionality and appearance for different client terminals compared to manually authoring different versions for different terminals.

This paper reports on the progress in the Princess project, which aims to develop a system for providing multi-media services to different terminals (HTML, WML, SMS, E-mail and a simple speech-driven Java browser) using the intermediary approach. There are also other commercial products and research demonstrations in this category [5], but many of them are focused on a more limited area, like image transcoding on the Web. The platform adapts to the user's terminal and the user's preferences and performs the necessary scaling of the media as well as the conversion to the required contents format (HTML, WML, etc). The scaling of the multimedia contents has been reported in earlier papers [6] and [7].

2   Adaptation of Services

The selected intermediary-based approach involves a requirement of a modality and platform independent or redundant format that is required in order to present the service user interface and content to the adapter (this requirement is common to the client-based approach). Redundant in this context means that presentation may contain several alternative representations for different modalities (e.g. a picture and an alternative textual presentation for it). [9] During the first phase of the Princess project, a proprietary object-oriented format was used to describe the user interface of the service. The actual content (media) was either embedded in, or referenced by this presentation. This approach was very limiting because user interface and content are often inseparable: consider, for example, hypertext links and image maps.

To overcome the limitations of the object model, we started looking for alternatives. The new model was expected to be able to express a simple UI for on-line services independent of modality and platform, describe embedded and referenced media uniformly with the UI, and be extensible and standards-based in order to ease the development.

Options included MHEG, XML-based XHTML and SMIL. We challenged the adaptability of MHEG because it is designed to define a final-form interchange syntax for multimedia objects via fixed and broadcast networks. On the other hand, extensibility and tool support is superior in XML-based solutions compared to other possibilities. The reformulation of HTML, XHTML, was considered the better choice of the XML solutions, because it is more generic than SMIL, which is primarily aimed at multimedia presentations.

XHTML is greatly independent of modality and it also enables a redundant (alternative) content. To make extensions to the XHTML markup, we defined our own XML Namespace. By this mechanism we defined a priority-attribute, which may get integer values that denote the relative relevance of the content of that part of the document. This is the simplest possible way to eliminate an irrelevant content from presentations for limited displays.

In the following chapters, we define the actual implementation of a Princess platform in more detail.

2.1   Architecture

Figure 2 presents the architecture of the Princess-platform. ServiceBroker is the container for user agents and service catalogue. The adaptation is performed in two components: DMS and gateway. The gateway takes care of session handling and user interface adaptation. It contains several modules: protocol handlers, which perform protocol level operations (including recognition of terminal and network characteristics), UI Adapters that do the adaptation from the internal presentation model (XHTML) to the terminal-specific format, and internal services which provide generic services for session control and configuring user preferences. The DMS (digital media server) is for media adaptation and content provider interface.

The gateway architecture has been designed to be modular, so that the inclusion of new terminal types is easy. For example, WAP and WWW-terminals use the same protocol (HTTP) and session tracking technologies – the only component that needs to be implemented separately is the UI Adapter.

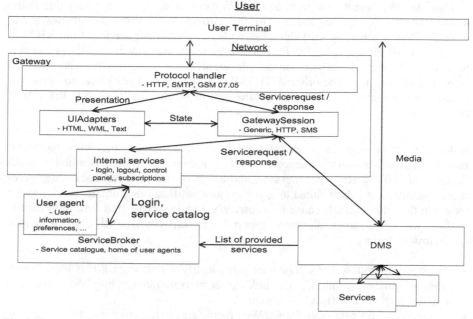

Fig. 2. Princess platform architecture (gateway described in detail)

2.2 Terminal Specific Implementations

WWW. Because of the internal presentation model, the only adaptation that is required for the WWW is accounting for the older browsers that are not directly capable of displaying XHTML. To accomplish this we chose to convert XHTML to HTML, which is a straightforward process. Another alternative would have been to follow the HTML compatibility guidelines (see [10]).

WAP. The WAP protocol stack is a set of mobile terminal specific protocols defined by the WAP Forum consortium (http://www.wapforum.org). The need for such a protocol stack arose, since existing protocols meant for fixed networks are not suitable for wireless connections, e.g. GSM or GPRS.

The speed of a typical WAP connection, the maximum size of the WAP presentation and the small screen size of mobile WAP-enabled terminals encompass the main limitations for WAP services. On the other hand, WAP redefines many issues in current standards, which makes its adoption more difficult.

In Princess, the conversion from the internal presentation model (XHTML) to WML is implemented by using the XSLT transformation language. Currently none of the multimedia components, including images, audio, and video, is transmitted to the

WAP-enabled devices because of the limited support for images and the absence of provisions for audio or video in the WML standard.

From the implementation point of view, WAP-development is not easy due to the incompatibility and incompleteness of the current WAP products, gateways and devices. Thus, a generally workable solution for conversion of services from XHTML format to WML format is hard to find. At the moment, one way around the problem is to make the adapted presentation simple enough, i.e. filter all but the essential information away from the original XHTML presentation. In principle, however, the idea is to maintain the same temporal structure of service that is used in the WWW browsers.

SMS. A short message as a user interface has severe usability problems: bare text-based command-response interaction with a minimal keyboard, limited transfer capacity of 160 characters per message, and a lack of real-time feedback. Because of these limitations, it is best suited to asynchronous notifications from the service to the user. On the other hand, because it is currently a widely supported feature in mobile phones, we decided to create some support for interactivity as well. Thus, we added the following features:

- Possibility to follow links. The user can identify a link from a text like: "Show more information ($link1)". The link can be activated by sending back a message containing the link id (link1 in this case).
- Possibility to use data input forms. Web forms are difficult to present to the user in a short message and using them is very demanding, since the user cannot usually see the template he receives from the service while he writes the response message. Therefore, we decided not to present forms to the user in any way. Instead, we implemented a possibility for advanced users to access them using a specific notation: for example, "&name john" equals the case where the user inputs john to the name-field in a WWW-browser.

The most appropriate services for SMS use are stateless and have a simple interaction (not many messages sent back and forth). Also, the service provider should both mark the most relevant information so that the amount of text does not exceed 160 characters and name resources (e.g. links) intuitively so that they are easy to remember.

The implementation of the SMS gateway differs significantly from the other gateways. For example, the generic bi-phased user authentication and service selection process was replaced by a single-phased approach, because compared to username and password, the user can be authenticated more comfortably from his phone number. The system also provides the administrator an opportunity to define shortcuts to often-requested information. In the future, this option could be provided for the user, too.

Speech-driven. An earlier version of the Princess platform allowed for the generation of a Java GUI representation (mostly using AWT elements) from the generic content presentation. A methodology for controlling the resulting Java GUI by speech was implemented and reported in an earlier paper [8]. The speech interface utilised the names of the elements to allow for a limited and dynamically changing vocabulary, improving the recognition performance. The speech recogniser was designed for the Finnish language.

After the adoption of XHTML as the generic service description language, generating a Java GUI presentation was not regarded desirable (though not impossible). Instead, a Java HTML browser was used to display the service and a swing-based control element extraction mechanism (Java Accessibility API) was deployed for deriving the speech actions. Subsequently, the speech actions were matched to inputs obtained by off-the-shelf speech recognition software.

3   Media Adaptation

Media adaptation needs processing power when compressing video or scaling other multimedia presentations and this task is delegated to the Digital Media Server, DMS (Figure 2). The DMS receives parameters, such as the user terminal capability and network bandwidth, from the gateway, and the adaptation is based on these parameters together with the user's preferences and service provider's choices.

The adaptation taxonomy used is presented in [6]. The adaptation taxonomy is a two-tiered approach for adapting multimedia presentations: it is composed of optimisation, or semantic adaptation, and scaling, the physical part of the adaptation.

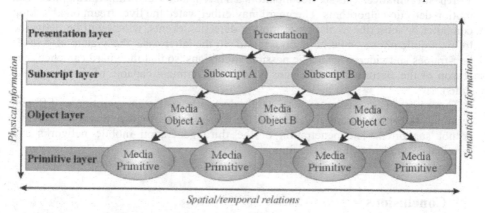

Fig. 3. Content model for multimedia adaptation

Original multimedia presentations are described by the media content model depicted in Figure 3 [7]. In the media content model, the presentation is divided into four semantic layers. The topmost layer describes the presentation as an entity. This layer can be divided into two or more subscripts, which describe the logical entities (indexes) within the presentation, e.g. pages or files in a multimedia presentation stream. The object layer consists of media objects, which are defined as logical entities of the subscript layer, e.g. images, headlines, or audio clips. Finally, the primitive layer defines the properties of the actual physical data in the form of headers and bodies.

This multimedia presentation adaptation concept is used together with the UI adaptation to deliver the most suitable presentation to the end user's terminal as fast as possible. Rough adaptation is done near the service provider and the adapted presentations are stored into a database, from which they can be retrieved when the user requests the service.

4   Pilot Services

The implemented Princess-platform has been verified by a few pilot services. This chapter briefly describes these services and how adaptivity affects each of them.

Information Services. The implemented information services deliver contact information, stock prices and weather forecasts to the user. We consider this category an ideal demonstration of adaptivity for two reasons: firstly, the simplicity of the user interface makes it possible to use this category of services even through short messages. Secondly, the information can be naturally expressed using different modalities (e.g. stock prices can be expressed as both text and graphs).

Video Surveillance. This service monitors a surveillance video camera equipped with motion detection algorithms. The guard may either watch the live stream on a desktop computer or subscribe to alarms of motion detection events, which will be delivered to his mobile phone while he is on a round. In the latter case, the system also saves key-frames and video clips of the possible incursions, so that the guard can check the reason of the alarm when he regains access to a terminal capable of displaying the video.

Currently, this service more successfully demonstrates the co-operation of different terminals rather than adaptivity, because the transmission of video to wireless devices is not supported. The penetration of the third generation mobile networks and terminals may change this in the future.

5   Conclusions

The Princess system has successfully shown its abilities to adapt services based on the properties of the client terminal. It is able to support terminals ranging from SMS via WML to full-fledged HTML-capable browsers with a variety of sizes and colour properties. The approach allows for extension by new future technologies and currently provides already rudimentary support for speech control.

During the selection of the presentation model, we noticed that the requirements were conflicting or at least challenging – supporting adaptation to simple devices while allowing the development of versatile user interfaces implementing attractive services is not an easy task. However, the choice of an XML-based presentation format has definitely worked out well in spite of the fact that the used standards (XHTML, XSLT) were under development during the project.

In this paper, we presented considerations relevant to the adaptation process. A distinction was made between different approaches to adaptation based on the location where the adaptation is performed. A brief description of the architecture was also given. Adaptation considerations for the different supported technologies were outlined and the paper was concluded by references to the media adaptation and the pilot projects.

Further research includes the addition of user profiling support and the related adaptation features. Also, the speech driven interface will be improved. The system has been tested under laboratory conditions by the project personnel. More elaborate pilot services are being developed, and they will be evaluated by a larger audience.

6 Acknowledgements

We gratefully acknowledge the support of TEKES and our industrial partners.

7 References

1. Barrett, B., Maglio P. P.: Intermediaries: New Places for Producing and Manipulating Web Content. Proceedings of the 7th WWW Conference (WWW7), 1998.
2. Berners-Lee,   T.:   Web   Architecture   from   50,000   feet. http://www.w3.org/DesignIssues/Architecture.html. Referenced on 30.4.1999.
3. Bickmore, T. W., Schilit, B. N.: Digestor: Device-Independent Access to the World Wide Web. Proceedings of the 6th WWW Conference (WWW6), 1997.
4. Fox, A., Gribble, S. D., Chawathe, Y., Brewer, E. A.: Adapting to Network and Client Variation Using Infrastructural Proxies: Lessons and Perspectives. IEEE Personal Communications, Vol. 5, No 4, 1998.
5. Ma, W-Y., Bedner, I., Chang, G., Kuchinsky, A., Zhang, H.: A Framework for Adaptive Content Delivery in Heterogeneous Network Environments. Proceedings of the Multimedia Computing and Networking 2000 (MMCN00).
6. Metso, M., Koivisto, A., Sauvola, J.: Multimedia Adaptation for Dynamic Environments. Proceedings of the 2nd IEEE Workshop on Multimedia Signal Processing, p. 203-208, 1998.
7. Metso, M., Koivisto, A., Sauvola, J.: Content Model for Mobile Adaptation of Multimedia Information. Proceedings of the 3rd IEEE Workshop on Multimedia Signal Processing, p. 39-44, 1999.
8. Peltola, J., Plomp, J., Seppänen, T.: A dictionary-adaptive speech driven user interface for a distributed multimedia platform. Euromicro workshop on Multimedia and Telecommunications, Milan, Italy, 1999.
9. Vanderheiden, G.: Anywhere, Anytime (+Anyone) Access to the Next-generation WWW. Computer Networks and ISDN Systems. Vol 29, p. 1439-1446, 1997.
10. W3C (World Wide Web Consortium): XHTML™ 1.0: The Extensible HyperText Markup Language. W3C Working Draft, http://www.w3.org/TR/xhtml1.

Multicast Micro-mobility Management

Vincent Magret, Vinod Kumar Choyi

1201 E.Campbell Road, M/S 446-310
Network Strategy Group
Alcatel USA
Richardson, TX 75081
{vincent.magret, vinod.choyi}@usa.alcatel.com

Abstract. Mobile IP [RFC 2002] offers a neat support to mobile users, in order
that mobile nodes can roam from one network to another quite easily. The
concept suffers from a major drawback when the user's movement imposes a
high frequency of handoffs. Mobile IP requires the mobile node to inform its
home agent of its new location every time it changes its point of attachment.
The concept, which is sometimes referred to as macro-mobility is not suitable
when there are frequent handoffs because of the latency that is incurred due to
the exchange of registration messages between the Base Station and the Home
Agent. The term micro-mobility defines an extension to the base concept, by
hiding the exact location of the mobile node from the home agent. The mobile
node's exact location is kept local within the wireless domain it has visited.
This document presents a new protocol designed to address micro-mobility.

Introduction

In a world where wireless networking is becoming a predominant solution to offer
access to customers from anywhere, it is important to have a design that allows
smooth mobility. The user needs to be able to move along his/her path without
suffering from connectivity disruptions. Mobile IP defines a protocol with which the
mobile node retains its home address regardless of the network it is connected to. But
when handoffs become too frequent, it poses major problems. The registration process
requires exchange of messages between the mobile host, the foreign agent and the
home agent. This is the basic behavior of a mobile node implementing Mobile IP. We
can note that the interaction with the foreign agent may be bypassed if the mobile
node is capable of obtaining a care-of address by some means like DHCP [RFC2131].

The first section of the document introduces the concept of micro-mobility, with
the aim of providing a definition for it. The two following sections present two
different approaches currently available in regard of micro-mobility support. The third
section introduces the protocol defined by Alcatel. Finally we conclude this document
with future studies which could improve the multicast micro-mobility (MMM)
protocol.

K.-L. Tan et al. (Eds.): MDM 2001, LNCS 1987, pp. 260-268, 2001.
© Springer-Verlag Berlin Heidelberg 2001

Micro-mobility

The booming evolution of wireless communication, which now offers a "wireless Internet", creates a new requirement on Internet protocols: support of mobility. Mobile IP offers a base concept on which the Internet Engineering Task Force [IETF] leverages to define the architecture of tomorrows Mobile Internet. Mobile IP defines three entities: the home agent, the foreign agent and the mobile host collaborating together in order to provide the forwarding services to the current location of the mobile host. The mobile host can use the foreign agent advertisement message to obtain a so-called care-of address (temporary address). The mobile host registers with its home agent to create a binding that defines the parameter of the forwarding service. The home agent is then in charge of capturing the packets that are sent to the mobile host. The home agent then forwards the packets to the mobile host's visited network, using tunneling protocols [RFC2003][RFC2004]. There is a consensus to define Mobile IP as a protocol offering macro-mobility or inter-domain mobility. To introduce the concept of micro-mobility, we must define the notion of wireless domain. A wireless domain is a structured network administrated by a single entity (e.g. an operator or service provider). The domain interconnects different networks and the edge or leaf routers to be connected to the base stations. An illustration of such a topology is depicted in Figure 1.

Micro-mobility allows a mobile host to move within a wireless domain from the coverage of one base-station to another without having to notify its home agent whenever it performs a handoff. Basically, when the mobile host moves within a foreign domain, the network must be able to modify its routing configuration in order to route packets to the mobile host. Depending on the protocol design the mobile host can either participate in the modification process or leave it up to the routers within the domain to do it. Ideally the mobile host should not be impacted by the micro-mobility protocol.

Hop-by-Hop Protocol

There are currently two protocols that have been submitted to the Mobile IP working group that uses the hop-by-hop technique. Using the hop-by-hop approach, routing decisions are performed at each hop. The next hop is determined by performing a table lookup which determines the interface to be used. The two protocols are Handoff Aware Inter-domain infrastructure [HAWAII]and Cellular IP [CIP].

HAWAII

HAWAII defines the *Domain Root Router* (DRR) as the connecting device between the Internet and the wireless domain. A domain as defined in [HAWAII] can contain several hundred base stations, thereby increasing the probability that the mobile host, after having registered with its home agent, remains in the same wireless domain. In such a scenario the home agent's role is very much reduced.

The mobile node or mobile host uses the usual Mobile IP concepts when moving for the first time into a foreign domain. The protocol requires that the mobile node use a co-located care-of address, an address that is not given by the foreign agent. The address can be obtained for instance via DHCP [RFC2131]. The mobile node appends a Network Address Identifier Extension [RFC2794] so that the domain can differentiate between a visiting mobile node from a mobile node administrated by the domain. For a visiting node, the base station (i.e. the router that is connected to the base station) creates an entry in the routing cache for the mobile node and forwards the registration request to the home agent of the mobile node. Each node along the path realizes the same operation (i.e. creation of a routing cache's entry) until the message reaches the DRR, where the registration request is forwarded to the home agent.

The mobile node must be able to memorize the address of the current base station, so that it can provide the IP address along with its registration request when performing a handoff to a new base station. The presence of the Previous Foreign Agent Node Extension [ROUTEOPT] helps the base station to determine if the mobile node had previously registered via another base station from within the same wireless domain. When the base station detects this extension, it triggers the route update algorithm. Two possibilities are defined depending on the capacity offered by the wireless technology used. If the mobile node can receive packets from two base stations simultaneously, the routing update process goes until the crossover router (i.e. the router that has one interface leading to the old base station and the other one leading towards the new one); this scheme is also called the non-forwarding scheme. In the forwarding scheme wherein the mobile nodes are not capable of simultaneously listening to multiple base stations the route update message is sent till it reaches the old base station. This scheme allows the old base station to forward the packets intended for the mobile node to the mobile node's new location

If there is no traffic and the mobile node is not yet idle, the mobile is required to transmit path update messages. These messages are propagated towards the DRR and at each router in its path the routing entries are refreshed. .

Correspondent nodes send packets to the home address of the mobile node. The home agent intercepts these packets and creates a tunnel using the co-located care-of address of the mobile node. When the packets arrive at the DRR, the hop-by-hop process takes over from regular routing algorithm. At this point each hop uses the routing entries previously updated by the mobile host. The protocol is extended with a support for paging [HAWAII PAGING]

CIP

Cellular IP [CIP] is similar to HAWAII as it relies on a hop-by-hop principle to handle the traffic within the wireless domain. The protocol differs on the terminology used, the messages and its interaction with Mobile IP. The protocol is not very clear as to how it interacts with mobile IP and the only reference made states that the CIP protocol must be realized prior to Mobile IP. The Domain Root Router is called a CIP gateway. The CIP gateway includes two sub-components: the gateway controller and the gateway filter. The Gateway Controller (GC) receives packets that are usually update packets that are used by the Gateway to update the locations of the MN and are then dropped. The Filter (GPF) checks to see if packets coming from within the domain are to be sent to the GC or forwarded on to the Internet.

A Few Words on Hop-by-Hop Protocols

Both solutions offer a routing protocol allowing support of micro-mobility. HAWAII requires the mobile node to receive an agent advertisement as defined in Mobile IP before being able to update the routing entries along the path from the DRR to the last router. This principle does not allow a very efficient handoff as required by "real-time" applications such as Voice over IP. The protocol also imposes that the router, which acts as "pseudo" foreign agent, to respond directly to the mobile node by sending a Mobile IP registration reply. This behavior is not in line with Mobile IP because it imposes the router to know the secret key normally shared between the mobile node and the home agent to compute the authentication extension required by Mobile IP. CIP imposes modifications to Mobile IP at the mobile node and the implementation of CIP at every mobile node, which are stringent restrictions and a drawback of the solution. Both protocols may face scalability problems if they are deployed over cellular infrastructure, where the number of users could easily be over a million.

Protocol Overview

For the definition of the protocol, we are taking the hypothesis that base stations are not simply passive bridges, as they have an active participation in the protocol. We believe that efficient handoffs can only be obtained if there is a tight liaison between the link and the network layers. The second hypothesis is that several base stations are connected to the same base station router (BSR), as this design allows a more efficient behavior.

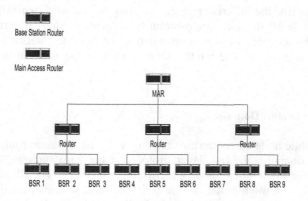

Figure 1 Home or foreign domain topology

The Main Access Router (MAR) supports Mobile IP. The MAR may serve as a foreign agent and/or a home agent. The MAR also implements part of the protocol extensions described in this document. The MAR processes the BSR extension that are appended to every registration request. The MAR allocates and inserts the multicast address extension before forwarding the registration reply.

The routers within the wireless domain support IP multicast routing.

The Base station Routers (BSR) implement the extensions described in this document. The BSR appends the BSR extension to each Mobile IP registration request. The BSR processes the multicast address extension appended to the Mobile IP registration reply. The BSRs periodically send a neighbor binding update to every BSR surrounding it. This message is used by the neighboring BSRs to manage their own probable cache. This cache contains the information of the mobile nodes that are located within the vicinity of the BSR.

As mentioned earlier, the topology is well known, and each BSR knows the IP address of other BSRs that are located in its neighborhood. For instance BSR 4 knows the IP addresses of BSR 3 and BSR 5, as these BSRs are its neighbors. Each base station router knows the IP address of its Main Access Router.

The protocol extends the current Mobile IP protocol with a set of messages designed so that:

- A BSR may communicate with its neighboring BSRs, the list of mobile node's information that are currently under the BSR's coverage area. This message is called the **neighbor binding update extension**. This message is sent from BSR to BSR.
- A BSR can inform its MAR the IP address of the BSR that has forwarded the Mobile IP registration request. This message is called the **BSR extension**. This message is appended to the mobile IP registration request.
- A MAR can inform the BSR of the multicast address assigned to a particular mobile node when a mobile node is granted access to the network. This message is called the **multicast address extension**. This message is appended to the Mobile IP registration reply.
- BS informs the BSR with the link layer characteristics of a mobile node entering its cell. This message is called the **mobile node advertisement extension**. The message MAY contain more than one mobile node's information.

We now describe the different phases, detailing how these extensions contribute in extending mobile IP to offer micro-mobility support. A short description is given below about the sequence of operations when a mobile node enters a foreign domain. This protocol takes the assumption that there is a single operator managing the foreign network.

Entering the Foreign Domain

When a mobile node enters the coverage area of a base station router (or any other router in this domain), the link layer protocol at the base station (BS) serving the mobile node triggers a mobile node advertisement message. The BS informs its BSR of the entrance of a mobile node in the cell. The base stations periodically send the mobile node advertisement message to the BSR with the list of mobile nodes located in the base station cell.

The BSR will take an action based on the presence of the link layer information of the mobile node in its caches. If there is an entry for the mobile node in its binding cache, then the BSR refreshes the entry. If there is an entry in its probable cache, then the BSR joins the multicast group and transfers the entry from the probable cache to the binding cache. If there are no entries in either of its caches then the BSR sends a mobile IP agent advertisement message to the mobile node.

Upon receiving the advertisement the mobile node sends a registration request to the base station router. The BSR adds its IP address (i.e. BSR extension) to the mobile node registration request and forwards it to its MAR. The MAR after having performed all the required checks necessary for granting the registration request (AAA protocol, challenge/response, and key exchange, NAI...) forwards the registration request without the BSR extension (this extension is stripped by the MAR) to the home agent.

The MAR creates an entry in the pending cache for the mobile node with its address and the address of the BSR serving the mobile node. For the home agent the MAR is apparently hosting the mobile node. The home agent, based on its policy, grants or denies the registration request. Considering that the home agent grants the request, it sends its reply to the foreign agent (i.e. the MAR).

If the mobile node initiates the first registration request and moves towards a new cell connected to a new BSR, the mechanism previously described will trigger a second registration request. The new BSR processes the registration request as described in the previous paragraph (i.e. the BSR appends the BSR extension to the registration request). The MAR receiving the mobile node registration checks in its pending cache. If the cache is hit, the MAR will conclude that the mobile node has moved under another BSR's coverage area while the mobile node's home agent processes the previous registration request. The MAR updates the pending cache to reflect the new BSR address.

When the MAR receives the registration reply it moves the entry for the mobile node from the probable cache to the binding cache and assigns a multicast address to the mobile node. The registration reply is forwarded to the BSR preceding the multicast address extension. The BSR removes the multicast address extension and forwards the registration reply to the mobile node. It also creates a binding entry associating the multicast address to the mobile node.

The current BSR of the mobile node periodically informs its neighboring BSRs of the newly created bindings with a neighbor binding update message. This message includes the mobile node address, the care-of address, the home agent address, the multicast address, the link layer information and the lifetime of the registration for each mobile node within its coverage. The neighbor binding update message refreshes partially the probable cache entries. It is a partial refresh, because the cache will be entirely refreshed only after the BSR has received every neighbor binding update message from each of its neighboring BSRs.

If the mobile node remains under the coverage area of a base station, then the base station sends periodic refresh message (mobile node advertisement) to its BSR (periodicity needs to be defined). The mobile node advertisement message refreshes partially BSR's binding cache entries. It is a partial refresh, as the cache will be entirely refreshed after the BSR has received every mobile node advertisement message from each of the base stations.

If the mobile node moves to another base station connected to the same BSR, the base station immediately sends a mobile node advertisement message with the link layer information of the mobile node.

If the mobile node moves to a cell that is connected to a different BSR than the one serving it, then the BS informs the new BSR of the presence of the mobile node by sending a mobile node advertisement message. If the BSR has an entry in its probable cache associating the link layer information given by the BS to the one found in the probable cache then it sends a message asking the MAR to join the multicast group. Meanwhile, the old BSR, which does not receive a mobile node advertisement message from at least one of its BSs refreshing the binding cache entry of the mobile node, then moves the entry to its probable cache presuming that the mobile node has moved to its neighbor.

If the mobile node can receive and transmit via several base stations the mobile node will receive the same message from these base stations.

Care-of Address

The proposed protocol does not make any special requirement on the type care-of address used by the mobile node. This address can either be a foreign agent care-of address or a co-located care-of address.

The MAR should initially require that all the BSRs set the 'R' bit in the agent advertisement message they send after receiving a mobile node advertisement message.

Apart from the above requirement the principle remains identical. If the mobile node registers with a co-located care-of address, the BSR appends the BSR extension to the registration request. The MAR processes the registration and removes the BSR extension. The MAR allocates a multicast address for the mobile node and appends the multicast address extension to the registration reply. The only difference resides in the traffic management, i.e. which node removes the tunnel and forwards the packet to its mobile destination.

Traffic Flow

If the correspondent node is located outside the foreign wireless domain, packets sent to a mobile node will be addressed to the home network. The home agent captures and tunnels the packets to the care-of address of the mobile node. This address corresponds to the MAR's IP address. The MAR upon receiving the tunneled packets checks to see if there is a valid binding cache for the mobile node. If the MAR has a valid binding cache for the mobile node, it then de-tunnels the packet and creates a new tunnel. The IP address of the MAR is set as the source address of the tunneled packet, the destination address is the multicast address assigned to the mobile node, and then the packet is sent through the tunnel. . Each BSR that has subscribed to the diffusion group receives a copy and de-tunnels the packets and the BSR that has a binding entry for the mobile node forwards the packets to the mobile node.

Moving within the Foreign Domain

The main advantage of the protocol is the low latency required before receiving packets on outgoing connections. The protocol, as it relies on link layer, allows such performance to be achieved.

If the mobile node enters a new cell, the base station MUST inform the BSR of the presence of the mobile node. It MUST send a mobile node advertisement message including the link layer information of the mobile node. Two scenarios can be foreseen. The mobile node has moved to another base station but remains under the coverage of the same BSR (i.e. the mobile node is served by a BS linked to the same BSR), then no action is needed.

If the mobile node is not among the ones served by the BSR (i.e. the BSR does not have a binding cache), but the BSR has an entry in the probable cache, the BSR must immediately subscribe to the multicast group.

Make before Break Option

The "make before break" option requires that the surrounding BSRs of a serving BSR subscribe to the diffusion group as soon as they receive the neighbor update message. This option also requires that all the BSRs not currently serving the mobile node (i.e. the mobile node's entry is in the probable cache) to filter and discard all the incoming multicast packets. The filtering is removed when the BSR receives a mobile node advertisement from one of its base station.

This option is intended to reduce the latency incurred because of the join messages that have to be sent to the MAR and the processing delay at the MAR. Using Make Before Break, the neighboring BSRs would have joined the group prior to the entry of the mobile node within its cell and therefore does not incur the latency. The processing is then limited to the removal of the filtering feature associated with this particular multicast address.

Conclusion

The protocol described in this document offers a new solution to the challenging micro-mobility issue. The are a number of advantages this protocol offers when compared to the other solutions mentioned. This protocol is completely transparent to the mobile node, which is not aware of the wireless domain and see the BSR as a "pseudo" foreign agent. The use of multicast allows the deployment of a "make before break" feature presenting advantages in case of "real-time" traffic such as voice over IP, although it is important to note that the advantage has its associate drawback. The drawback is the "useless" traffic generated to the BSRs that do not serve the mobile host at this point in time.

We are building a simulation platform to validate the concept and measure the performance of the protocol. We need to be sure that the handoff latency is sufficiently reduced to offer an efficient quality of service for the end user. We also need to investigate the issues related to multicast routing, however since the communication profile is a strict one-to-few, we are convinced that the protocol could take advantage of protocol such as explicit multicast. There are still several optimizations that can be done to the base protocol, however they require further studies.

References

[IETF]: Internet Engineering Task Force, http://www.ietf.org.

[RFC2131]: *"Dynamic Host Configuration Protocol"*, R. Droms, RFC 2131, March 1997, Obsolete RFC 1541, http://www.ietg.org/rfc.

[RFC2002]: *"IP Mobility Support"*, C. Perkins (Editor), RFC 2002, October 1996, http://www.ietf.org/rfc.

[RFC2003]: *"IP in IP encapsulation"*, C. Perkins, RFC 2003, October 1996, http://www.ietf.org/rfc.

[RFC2004]: *"Minimal encapsulation within IP"*, C. Perkins, RFC 2004, October 1996, http://www.ietf.org/rfc.

[RFC2794]: *"Mobile IP Network Access Identifier Extension for IPv4"*, P. Calhoun, C. Perkins, RFC 2794, update RFC 2290, March 2000, http://www.ietf.org/rfc.

[RFC2236]: *"Internet Group Management Protocol, Version 2"*, W. Fenner, Xerx Parc, RFC 2236, update RFC 1112, November 1997, http://www.ietf.org.

[HAWAII]: *"IP micro-mobility support using HAWAII"*, R. Ramjee, T. La porta, S. Thuel, K. Varadhan, L. Salgarelli, Lucent Bell Labs, draft-ietf-mobileip-hawaii-00.txt, work in progress.

[HAWAII-PAGING]: *"Paging support for IP mobility using HAWAII"*, R. Ramjee, T. La porta, Lucent Bell Labs, T. Li, Cornwell University, draft-ietf-mobileip-hawaii-paging-00.txt, work in progress.

[CIP]: *"Cellular IP"*, A. Campbell, J. Gomez, C-Y Wan, S. Kim, Columbia University and Z. Turanyi, A. Valko, Ericsson, draft-ietf-mobileip-cellularip-00.txt, work in progress.

[ROUTEOPT]: *"Route optimization in Mobile IP"*, C. Perkins, Nokia Research and D. Johnson Carnegie Mellon University, draft-ietf-mobileip-optim-09.txt, work in progress.

[MULTICAST]: *"Seamless IP Multicast Receiver Mobility Support"*, Jiang Wu, The Royal Institute of Technology KTH/IT in Kista Sweden, draft-jiang-msa-00.txt, work in progress.

Posters

Personal Workflow Management in Support of Pervasive Computing

San-Yih Hwang, Jeng-Kuen Chiu, Wan-Shiou Yang

Department of Information Management
National Sun Yat-Sen University, Taiwan
{syhwang,jack,ryang}@mis.nsysu.edu.tw

1. Introduction

With the advent of new wireless technologies, mobile personal computers (MPCs) are quickly gaining their popularity. Concurrently an increasingly number of services for MPCs have been developed. However, current services view PMCs as a vehicle to perform individual activities. No attempt has been made to provide *process services* that reach mobile users via their PMCs. In the real world, many personal applications are process-oriented, e.g., planning a trip, holding a party, applying a new job, etc. We expect PMCs to help manage and execute these processes in the future, serving the role of planning, coordinating, and reminding task executions so as to accomplish predefined personal goals. On the other hand, traditional workflow management systems are mainly used to coordinate business processes in enterprises. These processes must be repetitive and have well-formed structures. Personal processes differ from their business counterparts in that they are subject to change and rigid regulations on control flow are seldom imposed. As a result, personal activities are related mainly due to their data dependencies and their coordination must be flexible. These differences demand a new personal workflow model as well as the innovative design of a personal workflow system (PWFS).

2. The Process Model

We model a process as a set of tasks, each of which is associated with several attributes such as name, input data, output data, the durations and places in which this task can be executed. We can view a PWFS as a function that, when time and place allow, maps a set of input data and a set of tasks into a set of output data. Formally, this function can be specified as

$$2^{D_{data}} \times 2^{D_{task}} \rightarrow 2^{D_{data}} \cup \{\bot\}, \text{ where} \bot \text{indicate invalid execution}$$

Viewing a PWF as a function described above allows us to place the following inquiries:

1.   Given a set of input data items and a set of tasks to be executed, what data items can be generated?
2.   Given a set of input data, what tasks should be executed in order to produce a specific set of output data?
3.   To execute a specific set of tasks, what input data items are needed?

K.-L. Tan et al. (Eds.): MDM 2001, LNCS 1987, pp. 271-272, 2001.
© Springer-Verlag Berlin Heidelberg 2001

Therefore, we propose the following three operations that intend to answer the above three queries:

ProduceData: inputset × taskset → outputset

InvolvedTask: inputset × outputset → taskset

RequiredData: taskset × outputset → inputset

With the above three operations, many queries about the execution of a personal process can be specified. For example, suppose the user would like to identify the set of tasks that can be co-executed with C after both A and B complete, the following SQL statement is specified:

SELECT   t.name

FROM   TASK t, c

WHERE   t **IN** InvolvedTask(ProduceData(avail,('A','B')),ANY)

AND   c.name = 'C'

AND   t.time **OVERLAPS** c.time

AND   t.place **OVERLAPS** c.place;

3. Implementation Issues

We propose to adopt metagraphs [1], a formal model designed to express data dependencies of processes in model bases community, to specify personal processes. The analytical capability of metagraphs paves the way for efficiently implementing the proposed operations. Besides, implementing a personal workflow system involves many issues. To name a few: the storage of personal processes, the design of graphical interface, the presentation of worklist, the development of triggering system, the design of temporal and spatial operations, and so forth. These issues will be investigated when we come to stage of implementation.

A unique feature about business processes is its flexibility. It is quite often that mobile users execute tasks that produce unexpected results or even engage in some totally unplanned tasks. In this case, rather than rejecting this change, the PWFS can do nothing but to accept the consequence. In return, the PWFS examines the impact of this change and adjusts the unexecuted part of the task definitions according to user's decision. For example, the execution of a task may generate fewer data items than expected. As a result, some subsequent task may become unexecutable due to the lack of required input data. However, while the entire task may not be executed, part of the task may still be executable, resulting in the splitting of a task. On the other hand, executing a task may sometimes produce extra data items. These extra data items may in turn enable the early execution of some tasks or make others obsolete. Operations for measuring the effect of unexpected task execution have been proposed but are not presented here due to space limitations.

References

[1] A. Basu and R.W. Blanning, "A Formal Approach to Workflow Analysis," *Information Systems Research*, 11(1), 2000, pp.17-36.

An Agent Based Architecture
Using XML for Mobile Federated Database Systems

Carlos Sanchez[1], Le Gruenwald [2]

[1] The RiskMetrics Group, 341 W. Chestnut Noble OK, 73068 USA,
Carlos.Sanchez@riskmetrics.com
[2] The University of Oklahoma, Computer Science Department, Norman, OK 73019 USA
ggruenwald@ou.edu

Abstract. We advocate the use of agents to model a system that allows us to integrate and protect information stored in both mobile and fixed devices, while trying to preserve a consistent authorization state. We propose a system called HAFS, which makes use of an object oriented access control data model to enforce security across the mobile federation and XML as a language to represent and exchange the common meta-data among agents.

1   Introduction

Having interoperability among information structures has become increasingly important for the research and industry communities to compete in a world where demand for new technology, services and information is growing. These information structures include database systems, data repositories and hardware devices. Unfortunately, many of these data repositories are still not widely accessible due to many unresolved security issues. In addition, new technological advances in mobile computing outpace the development of solutions for secured data sharing among users of these new technologies. We believe that these issues can be addressed in an environment where data sources (databases, devices and operating systems, etc.) can be connected and used without violating their security policies with the addition of a common distributed and Highly Available Federated System (HAFS).

2   HAFS

HAFS is proposed as an agent-based system whose main task is to enforce established security policies and protect the information found in different data sources. Agents are used because they are entities capable of carrying out goals, perform a great variety of activities and make part of a larger community of agents that have mutual influence of each other [1]. In addition, HAFS employs object-oriented paradigm not only to describe security guidelines (i.e. policies, access controls, etc.) of the different Component Database Management Systems (CDBMS), but also to cope with the

K.-L. Tan et al. (Eds.): MDM 2001, LNCS 1987, pp. 273-274, 2001.

heterogeneity of them. Finally, HAFS makes use of the eXtensible Markup Language (XML) for the description of access control policies and the exchange of relevant data such as database schemas and messages.

3   Architecture

Each data source in HAFS (i.e. a fixed or mobile) is assigned to a security agent, - whose main function is to enforce security over the objects store in the data source. Each device that provides support or holds an agent is called an *agent server*. In mobile environments, agent servers would usually run on base stations and fixed hosts. However, in some occasions such as in ad-hoc networks, some mobile devices could host/run agents as well. In addition, an agent may protect one or more data sources. This allows the data stored in small and/or power constraint devices to be protected without requiring these devices to run their security agents. Finally, *agent servers* not only allow inter-agent communication through the use of an *information space*, but also provide functionality to locate and dynamically load agents on behalf of [mobile] users.

4   Conclusions

XML and Agent technologies in the recent years have created an environment where new ideas can be put together to create solutions for many problems in the database area. We believe that these tools in conjunction with the Object-Oriented Database Security framework can allow us to model a security mechanism for database federations that include mobile hosts.

References

1. Hayes C.: Agents in a Nutshell: A Very Brief Introduction. IEEE Transactions on Knowledge and Data Engineering, Vol. 11, No. 1, January/February 1999
2. Imielinski T., Badrinath B.R.: Mobile Wireless Computing Solution and Challenges in Data Management. Communications of the ACM (CACM), Volume 37, 1994
3. Jonscher D.: Access Control in Object Oriented Federated Database Systems. Infix 1998 (ISBN 3-89601-449-8)
4. Klush M.: Intelligent Information Agents in Cyberspace. Intelligent Information Agents, Springer-Verlag Berlin, 1998 book preface
5. W3C: Extensible Markup Language. REC-xml-19980210 file, W3C Recommendation 10-Feb-98. Available via www.w3c.org

Designing Electronic Forms in Web Applications: Integration of Form Components

Soroush Sedaghat

Management Information Analyst, Executive Information Management
University of Western Sydney, Australia
s.sedaghat@uws.edu.au

Abstract.

This paper suggests an innovative and practical approach for designing electronic forms (e-forms) to assist user-friendly collection of accurate data in Web environments.

Key Words

Web Form Design, Web Applications, Data Management, Web Components, e-form

1. Introduction

Traditional paper-based forms, which are used for data collection, has two distinct problems: not being user-friendly by not providing warning to users when they are filling out incorrect information and also contributing to introduction of some data errors into the systems when collected information is transcribed into such systems. Similarly their equivalent electronic forms (e-forms), common in Web systems, would suffer the same problems if they were not properly designed. In this paper, we propose harmonious integration of Web-form components into small sets for collecting accurate pieces of information from users.

2. E-Form Design

Web-based electronic forms (e-forms) are normally composed of form components such as push buttons, text boxes, select lists, check boxes, radio buttons, drop down menus and a series of hyperlinks which all in connectivity with relational databases display, update or collect the required information from users. The normal trends for designing such forms is to populate the page with a series of form components that work independent of each other and sometimes perform simple data validation tasks. This may not be a suitable method when e-forms are to be used in complex web applications. Therefore we propose designing forms by constructing small sets of integrated components such that not only the components within each set would interact with each other in a synchronized fashion, but also each set can interact with other sets in the same form, or the linked forms, to cross-validate the relationship of

K.-L. Tan et al. (Eds.): MDM 2001, LNCS 1987, pp. 275-276, 2001.

one piece of information with the other. This would assist users to navigate and to fill out the required information easily. It would also prevent errors by turning off operation of certain components when they are not required. Hence the overall results would lead to better *data management* and ensuring the accuracy and consistency of the information being collected. Each set is designed to suit gathering one or a few related data items and it contains the type of components that can assist such data collection. The operation of components in the set are synchronized and their relationships are properly defined, so that, when one or more *related* components in a set are selected, then the response of the other components, in the same set, to mouse or keyboard input are automatically disabled. Figure 1 shows a section of a Web-form comprising two component sets: set one uses radio buttons and check boxes, while set two uses just radio buttons. These two sets also work together so that completing one without the other does not allow the user to proceed with the rest of the form. In set one, checkboxes are operational if the "yes" radio button in the same set has been selected other wise they remain inactive to the "no" radio button.

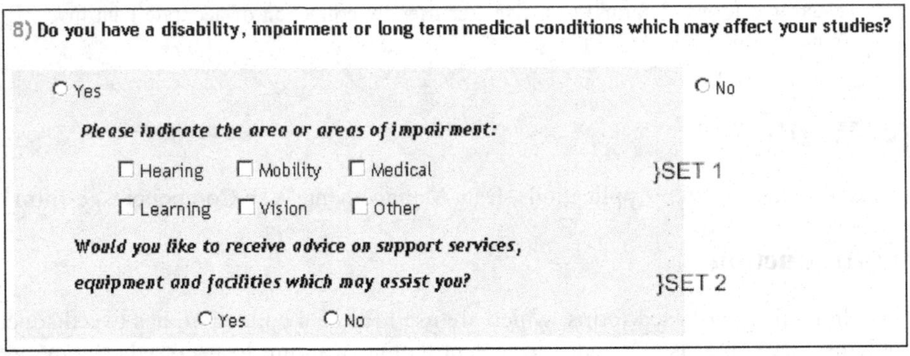

Figure 1: Integration of Web form components in two sets

Figure 2 shows a set comprising three subsets of drop-down lists and radio buttons. Here, selecting one radio button in a sub-set will deactivate the operation of drop down lists belonging to other radio buttons.

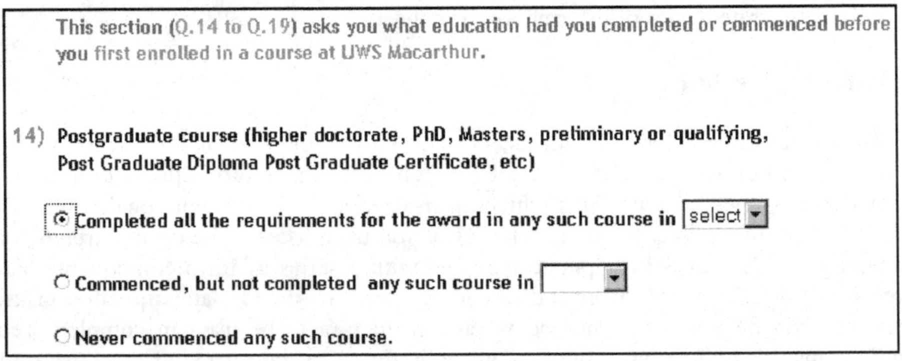

Figure 2: Integration of Web form components in three sub- sets

These can be incorporated in design using scripting languages such as Java and Javascript and they can be executed on the client's machine for speed and efficiency.

Increasing Concurrency of Transactions Using Delayed Certification in Mobile DBMSs

IlYoung Chung and Chong-Sun Hwang

Dept. of Computer Science and Engineering, Korea University
5-1, Anam-dong, Seongbuk-Ku, Seoul 136-701, Korea
{jiy, hwang}@disys.korea.ac.kr

Abstract. As the server in mobile environments may not have any information about the state of its clients' cache(stateless server), using broadcasting approach to transmit the list of updated data to numerous concurrent mobile clients is an attractive approach. In this paper, a new concurrency control protocol is proposed to reduce aborts of concurrent transactions. The proposed protocol can improve the throughput of transactions by increasing the number of transactions which can be committed by the server during the same broadcasting interval. For this, with the proposed protocol, the server delays the certification of transactions until the next broadcasting point. The protocol adopts adaptive broadcasting as the way of sending invalidation reports, which shows stable performance by choosing appropriate broadcasting strategy between synchronous and asynchronous broadcastings.

In broadcast based optimistic concurrency control, mobile clients send commit requests of transactions to the server, when they completes all operations of transactions. Then the server decides commit or abort of transactions based on *serializability*, using the lists of data items that are read and written by the transactions[1]. In order to improve the throughput of transaction processing, the proposed protocol tries to increase the number of transactions which can be committed during the same broadcasting interval. We propose this concurrency control protocol based on the *adaptive broadcasting* environment[2], which is a hybrid of the synchronous and asynchronous broadcasting strategy. With the adaptive broadcasting approach, the proposed protocol can dynamically adjust the broadcasting method according to the system workload[2].

When it is time to broadcast the result of transactions(i.e. commit or abort) according to the adaptive broadcasting strategy, the server should determine which transaction can be committed and which should be aborted, among those which have requested commit after the last broadcasting point. In traditional optimistic concurrency control, if two transactions requesting commit show conflicts within the same broadcasting interval, the one whose commit request has arrived earlier has the priority, as a result, transactions which requested commit later than a conflicting transaction should be aborted[1]. With this approach, the decision of commit or abort is made against previous conflicting request, whenever a commit request message arrives.

K.-L. Tan et al. (Eds.): MDM 2001, LNCS 1987, pp. 277–278, 2001.
© Springer-Verlag Berlin Heidelberg 2001

We can consider the situation when the throughput is degraded with the traditional strategy, due to an early arrived transaction which shows conflicts with many transactions. Let's consider the following example. In this example, $r_i(x)$ and $W_i(x)$ denote a read and write operation performed by a transaction T_i on data item x.

$$T_1 : r_1(x)\ w_1(x)\ r_1(y)\ w_1(y)$$
$$T_2 : r_2(x)\ r_2(y)$$
$$T_3 : r_3(y)\ r_3(z)$$
$$T_4 : r_4(z)\ r_4(x)$$

If we assume that commit requesting messages of these transactions arrive within the same period of broadcasting, and as the order of T_1, T_2, T_3 and T_4. With the existing concurrency control algorithms, when the server receives the commit request of T_1, since the server has received no conflicting commit requesting of other transactions before T_1 during the same period (checking against transactions in the previous period will be discussed in the following section). However, the rest of transactions, T_2, T_3 and T_4, cannot be committed as they have accessed the common data item x which is updated by T_1 which is already determined to commit. If the server does not give priority to T_1 (selects T_1 as a victim), other three transactions can be saved, and the number of aborted transactions can be reduced to one. Let us consider another example:

$$T_1 : r_1(x)\ r_1(y)\ r_1(z)$$
$$T_2 : r_2(x)\ w_2(x)$$
$$T_3 : r_3(y)\ w_3(y)$$
$$T_4 : r_4(z)\ w_4(z)$$

Also in this example, if the commit request of T_1 arrives earlier than others, T_2, T_3 and T_4 should be aborted, as they show conflicts with T_1.

The throughput of the transaction processing can be improved, if the server considers the number of conflicts with the committing transaction, by delaying the certification process until the broadcasting point which is determined by adaptive broadcasting strategy. In the delayed certification protocol, the more conflicts does a transaction incur, the lower priority does the server give to the transaction. With this strategy, the protocol can increase the concurrency of transactions when there exist many conflicts among transactions.

References

1. D.Barbara, "Certification Reports: Supporting Transactions in Wireless Systems," in *Proceedings of IEEE International Conference on Distributed Computing Systems*, 1997, pp.466-473.
2. I.Chung, J.Ryu, and C.-S.Hwang, "Efficient Cache Management Protocol Based on Data Locality in Mobile DBMSs," in *Concurrent Issues in Databases and Information Systems, Proceedings of ADBIS-DASFAA*, LNCS 1884, Springer Verag, 2000, pp.51-64.

Multi-resolution Web Document Browsing in a Distributed Agent Environment*

Stanley M.T. Yau[1], Hong Va Leong[1], and Antonio Si[2]

[1] Department of Computing, Hong Kong Polytechnic University, Hong Kong.
{csmtyau,cshleong}@comp.polyu.edu.hk
[2] Oracle Corporation, 500 Oracle Parkway, Redwood Shores, CA 94065.
asi@eng.sun.com

A mobile environment is characterized by low communication bandwidth and poor network connectivity. Accessing web documents in a mobile environment is inefficient and ineffective. To address this, we have developed a multi-resolution transmission and browsing mechanism for web documents [3]. In this mechanism, a web document is modeled as a hierarchy of levels of detail (LOD), which include Document, Section, Subsection, Subsubsection, and Paragraph. An organizational unit at the Document LOD is composed of several organizational units at the Section LOD, each of which is in turn, composed of several organizational units at the Subsection LOD, and so on. Using information retrieval techniques, we associate each organizational unit with an information content, indicating the degree to which the unit captures the content of the document. A user could request a document to be transmitted at various LODs. When transmitted at the Document LOD, the whole web document is considered as a single unit and all its sections will be transmitted in sequence. When transmitted at the Section LOD, the section with the highest information content will be transmitted first, with its subsections transmitted in sequence. In general, all descendants of the chosen organizational unit will be transmitted in sequence. This multi-resolution transmission and browsing mechanism enables a mobile user to explore the more content-bearing portion and terminate the transmission of an irrelevant document earlier, providing a means to deal with the low bandwidth problem.

In this paper, we realize the multi-resolution transmission mechanism within the design and implementation of a *Distributed Agent Environment* (DAE). The concept of DAE is to create a logical boundary to divide up different agents and resources into manageable and distinct entities [2,4]. We refer to each logical boundary of entities and resources as a DAE. Our DAE architecture is illustrated in Figure 1, where the system functionalities are supported by agents.

Depending on the mobility requirement, we distinguish between two different types of agents, namely, static and mobile agents. Static agents provide resources and facilities to mobile agents. Mobile agents migrate among DAEs by taking advantage of the locality and resources to satisfy their goals. In general, a static agent belongs to the type of *residential agent*. All residential agents stay within an execution environment, which is referred to as a Domain. A mobile agent belongs to the type of *visiting agent*. All visiting agents execute in an execution

* This research is supported in part by the Hong Kong Polytechnic University research grant numbers 350/922 and G-T040.

K.-L. Tan et al. (Eds.): MDM 2001, LNCS 1987, pp. 279–281, 2001.

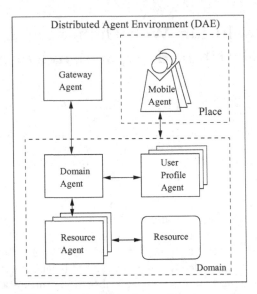

Fig. 1. A distributed agent environment

environment at their visiting host, which is referred to as a Place. The Place provides the appropriate environment for incoming agents to execute as guest processes, under certain constraints on access privileges on resources.

A typical DAE is composed of Domain, Place, and a dedicated static agent, called Gateway Agent, which provides a firewall functionality to prevent unauthorized mobile agents that fail the security check from penetrating into the DAE to access resources. Within a Domain, there are a number of agents executing. The Gateway Agent also acts as the communication proxy for information flow between different DAEs. The static Domain Agent coordinates the activities occurring in the domain [1] and provides a migration service to mobile agents. If the migration of a mobile agent is rejected by a remote host, it will be the duty of Domain Agent to restart the mobile agent for it to travel to a new destination. In DAE, Domain Agent acts as a central manager, which registers all information resources provided by the resource agents in the domain. It advertises public information resources and provides an inquiry service for all mobile agents from both inside and outside of the DAE. Mobile agents inquire Domain Agent to ensure that there are sufficient compatible resources within the DAE for the mobile agents to achieve their goals. This is the mechanism used by mobile agents to interrogate the contents of a particular DAE before actual migration.

Static Resource Agents provide public access interface to particular information resources such as databases. The resources and their structures are encapsulated and hidden from all other agents, so that replacement of resources and their agents becomes transparent to the rest of the DAE. Static User Profile Agents are associated with visiting mobile agents as surrogates during their stay in their Place. They helps to maintain user profiling information about mobile agents, including group of user preferences and to customize the results returned to mobile agents accordingly. Finally, visiting mobile agents perform services at remote Places on behalf of agents from their originating host. They ask local Domain Agent for candidate list of domains and migrate to the appropriate host after proper negotiation.

Based upon our DAE, we build an application for multi-resolution mobile web browsing. The application is implemented as a collection of Java classes. In this application, a web client will specify the goal, defining the web document to be browsed and how it is being browsed by configuring the appropriate properties of a mobile agent that will be sent off from the client DAE. Before the mobile agent is physically launched to a Place in the DAE of the selected base station, preliminary negotiation may take place such as finding the best base station among a set of potential base stations, with resources compatible with the task carried by the agent. Once the mobile agent is migrated to the Place of a base station DAE, the agent enjoys a better network connectivity and can perform web document retrieval, information content computation, scheduling and order transmission on behalf of the mobile client. Migration of agents to another base station upon the physical movement of the mobile client to elsewhere can also be achieved readily.

Upon successful negotiation and dispatching of the mobile agent to base station DAE, the visiting agent will reside at a Place of the base station DAE. The visiting agent could contact the Domain to determine the transmission ordering of various organizational units of a document depending on the information content of the document and the required LOD as specified in the visiting agent. Since the actual document resources may reside on remote hosts other than the base station, communication is required. In our design of DAE, we advocate interoperability and system integration by adopting CORBA to serve as the wired network infrastructure. Finally, the Domain would transfer the requested document in a sequence as specified by the transmission order to the mobile client. As mobile web browser of the mobile client is receiving the document, the document would be stored as an internal document resource and rendered to the browser. Preliminary experiments have shown that our DAE performs reasonably well, through the use of mobile agents.

References

1. Jonathan Dale and David C. DeRoure. A Mobile Agent Architecture for Distributed Information Management. In *Workshop on the Virtual Multicomputer*, 1997. 280
2. Lars Hagen, Markus Breugst, and Thomas Magedanz. Impacts of Mobile Agent Technology on Mobile Communication System Evolution. *IEEE Personal Communications*, pages 56–69, August 1998. 279
3. H.V. Leong, D. McLeod, A. Si, and S.M.T. Yau. Multi-resolution Transmission and Browsing in Mobile Web. In *CIKM Workshop on Web Information and Data Management*, pages 13–16, 1998. 279
4. OMG. Mobile Agent System Interoperability Facilities Specification. Technical report, Object Management Group, Framingham, Mass, 1997. Available at ftp://ftp.omg.org/pub/docs/orbos/97-10-05.pdf. 279

Dynamic Remote Update
Adapting Wireless Network Connection States

SungHun Nam   and   Chong-Sun Hwang

Dept. of Computer Science and Engineering, Korea University
5-1, Anam-dong, Seongbuk-Ku, Seoul 136-701, Korea
{shnam, hwang}@disys.korea.ac.kr

Abstract. To maintain cache consistency at mobile clients, server broadcasts updated information. The broadcasting information is invalidation or propagation. However, invalidation of frequently accessed data causes many cache requests. Although propagation can reduce cache requests, it is easily damaged by outer interference under unstable connection state of wireless network. The larger message, the higher probability of damage has. To resolve these problems, we suggest remote update algorithm that dynamically selects invalidation or propagation for an updated data item according to wireless network connection states.

Caching of frequently accessed data in a mobile client can be an effective approach to reduce contention on narrow network bandwidth. However, once caching is used, there is required to transmit information of updated data to ensure cache consistency between mobile clients and server.

Broadcasting approach is widely accepted to maintain cache consistency, and to control the concurrent transactions in mobile environments [1,2,3,4]. Broadcasting information is generally classified into two, invalidation and propagation message.

In pull-based approach, invalidation is generally used to maintain cache consistency of mobile clients [2,3,4]. And it can be divided into two approaches according to when invalidation message transmitted, synchronous (periodic) [1,2,3] and asynchronous [4]. The synchronous approach broadcast invalidation report periodically, and the asynchronous approach broadcast invalidation report whenever update transaction committed. However, in both approaches, invalidation of frequently accessed data causes contention on narrow network bandwidth with increasing cache requests. Thus, the data transmission due to cache requests is main reason of wireless network bottleneck. Although propagation can reduce the cache requests, propagation of all updated data also can cause wireless network contention. And wireless transmissions are subject to interference from outside source, absorption, scattering, fading, and inter-symbol interference. Moreover, since conditions change over time(due to mobility or intermittent interference sources) the error environment will also change. The larger message is more easily affected by outer interference. Thus, propagation increases error rate of transmitting data.

When broadcasting message broken by outer interference, since the most of stateless server in mobile environments do not require acknowledgement, some mobile clients may not receive the broadcasting message. So, mobile client cache may be in inconsistent state. But, in case of synchronous approach, since mobile client receive invalidation report periodically, can recognize the broadcasting message be lost. Thus, mobile client refreshes his cache whenever invalidation report doesn't arrive in certain period. However, in any approach, if the losing probability of broadcasting message increases, performance can be degraded. In asynchronous approach, since the number of stale data item in mobile client cache increases, abort rate of transaction at server increases. In synchronous approach, since the mobile client refresh his cache whenever broadcasting message doesn't arrived in certain period, it degrades system performance.

To reduce cache requests of invalidation approach and adapt a variable and high error environment, we suggest adaptive broadcasting message selection algorithm. In our approach, server always watches the amount rate of transmitted message on down link and we assume all mobile clients in cell uniformly communicate with server. If the amount rate decreased, the reason is increasing of message retransmission due to high error rate. If the amount rate of transmitted message keeps over certain level, we can say the connection states between server and mobile clients are stable. Otherwise, the connection states are unstable. When the connection states keeps stable state, if server receive commit request of transaction from mobile client and the transaction is committed, server contain updated contents in broadcasting message for a data item that has certain degree of access frequency and sharing among mobile clients to reduce cache requests. However, if the connection states are in unstable state, server broadcast just invalidation report to decrease error rate of broadcasting message. Thus our approach resolves the problems of invalidation and propagation used solely in mobile environment.

References

1. D.Barbara, "Certification Reports: Supporting Transactions in Wireless Systems," *Proceedings of IEEE International Conference on Distributed Computing Systems*, 1997.
2. D.Barbara and T.Imielinsky, "Sleepers and Workaholics: Caching in Mobile Environments," *Proceesings of ACM SIGMOD International Conference on Management of Data*, 1994.
3. S.Lee and C.-S.Hwang, "Supporting Transactional Cache Consistency in Mobile Database Systems," *Proceedings of ACM International Workshop on data engineering for wireless and mobile access*, 1999.
4. S.Khurana and A.Kahol, "An Efficient Cache Maintenance Scheme for Mobile Environments," *Proceedings of IEEE International Conference of Distributed Conputing Systems*, 2000.

Performance Modeling of Layered-Data Delivery for Mobile Users through Broadcast/On-Demand Hybrid Communication

Kenya Sato*, Soichi Hasegawa, Shigeaki Tagashira, Keizo Saisho, Akira Fukuda

Graduate School of Information Science
Nara Institute of Science and Technology
8916-5 Takayama, Ikoma, Nara, 630-0101, Japan

Abstract. We have proposed an efficient layered-data delivery system through multiple heterogeneous networks, which are on-demand and broadcast [1]. It is considered that layered data, such as map data, are composed of (1) common parts available or useful to many clients, and (2) personalized parts for individual clients. The system sends the personalized parts through on-demand networks and the common parts through broadcast networks. In this paper, we implement and evaluate a performance model of the system consisting of a client and two servers (broadcast and on-demand). The evaluation results show that our proposed system works effectively under certain conditions.

1   Implementation of Performance Modeling

Although there are many proposals, such as [2], for broadcast and on-demand data delivery, we have proposed an efficient layered-data delivery system through on-demand and broadcast multiple heterogeneous networks, as the target applications to deliver map databases to mobile users. The model consists of a broadcast server, an on-demand server and a client connected to two Ethernet segments, A and B. The broadcast server broadcasts data items with a data carousel policy through a UDP datagram on the segment A, and the on-demand server sends data items requested by the client through TCP connection on the segment B.

The broadcast server reads the broadcast program table, which includes the number of UDP packets (1400Bytes/packet) in each data item. The size of all data items is 70k (1400*50) Bytes. The server sends data items an unlimited number of times following the broadcast program to a broadcast channel on the Ethernet segment with a flat broadcasting policy. The on-demand server receives requests from a client, and sends the requested data items. A TCP connection is created for each request between a server and a client. The on-demand server can receive many requests at the same time.

Data items are sent with three kinds of methods; only the broadcast method, only the on-demand method, and the broadcast/on-demand hybrid method. The parameters refer to the condition to send geographic map data to mobile users.

---

* Currently with Harness System Technologies Research Ltd., Suzuka, Japan

K.-L. Tan et al. (Eds.): MDM 2001, LNCS 1987, pp. 284–285, 2001.

The map data are composed of mesh data items whose size is 50k to 100k Bytes. In this evaluation, the size of data items is supposed to be 70kbytes. The bandwidth of broadcast and on-demand is restricted for bandwidth Ethernet (10Mbps). This would be wider than that of a mobile communication, however; the future mobile communication can approach to the current Ethernet speed. Broadcast data ratio of a server is 20%, and on-demand is 80%. The total number of data items are 10, 20, and 30, which is much smaller than the real number of users. The reason for this restriction is because the number of users depends on the number of processes that can be created on the evaluation platform. Therefore, we have adjusted the period (3sec.) between each request to decrease it. Six data items requested by a user corresponds to the number of mesh data items of the geographic map while a vehicle needs (three) and a user requires (three) facility data items. We presume a facility data item is located on a mesh data item.

2   Evaluation Results

Figure 1 shows that latency for the broadcast method is constant for the number of users. In the case that the number of users on the on-demand method is ten or more, latency increases considerably. This means that the required bandwidth (6 x 70kBytes x 10 / 3sec. $\simeq$ 10.9Mbps) exceeds the usable bandwidth (10Mbps). By using the hybrid method we propose, the rate of increasing latency is alleviated in comparison with the on-demand method. For example as shown in Figure 1(b), when there are fewer than five, the latency of the on-demand method is smaller than the hybrid method. When more than five, the hybrid method is smaller. Compared with the broadcast method, the hybrid method is smaller in the case the number of users is small. This means the number of data items for broadcast is dominant when the broadcast data items is 20% of the total data items, so the latency of the hybrid method is much smaller than the broadcast method. Therefore, the important thing is to determine which data items are broadcasted. When the number of users is small, the on-demand method is effective, and when the number of uses is large, the broadcast method is effective. However, the hybrid method is useful unless the network bandwidth is not overflowed with on-demand communications.

References

1. K. Sato, K. Hirano, K. Saisho, and A. Fukuda: "Proposal of an Algorithm for Transmission and Cache of Location Dependent Data for In-Vehicle Computer System", Proc. the 6th World Congress on Intelligent Transpoft Systems (CD-ROM), Paper Number 3157, 1999. 284
2. S. Acharya, M. Franklin, and S. Zdonik: "Balancing Push and Pull for Data Broadcast", Proc. ACM SIGMOD, Vol.26, No.2, pp.183–194, 1997. 284

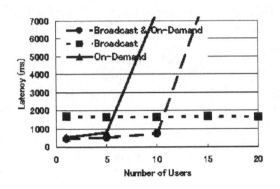

(a) 10 data items

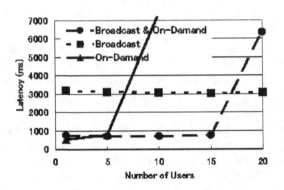

(b) 20 data items

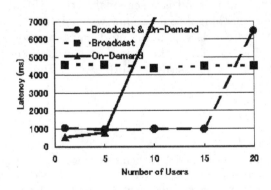

(c) 30 data items

Fig. 1. Number of Users v. Latency Time with 30 Data Items.

Energy-Efficient Transaction Management for Real-Time Mobile Databases in Ad-hoc Network Environments

Le Gruenwald, Shankar M. Banik

University of Oklahoma
School of Computer Science
Norman, OK 73019
{ggruenwald, smbanik}@ou.edu

Abstract. In an ad-hoc mobile network architecture, all the mobile hosts (MHs) are connected with each other through a wireless network that has a frequently changing topology. This type of architecture is used in many applications such as battlefields and disaster recovery where it is difficult or not feasible to depend on a static wired communication infrastructure. These applications are usually time-critical where many of their transactions must not only be executed correctly but also within their deadlines. In addition, the MHs in this environment are not connected to unlimited power supplies and may store data that can be shared by other MHs. Existing mobile database transaction management techniques do not consider the ad-hoc network characteristics, real-time constraints and energy limitation. This paper identifies the issues that need to be addressed in this new environment and proposes approaches for solutions.

1 Introduction

The Transaction Manager of a Mobile Multi-Database Management System (MMDBMS) is responsible for providing reliable and consistent units of computing to its users, and must address the issues of disconnection and migration of users. This paper provides a transaction management technique that considers energy consumption and real time requirements for an ad-hoc network MMDBMS. In this environment all MHs are roaming and the network that interconnects these MHs is a wireless network with a frequently changing topology.

2 Proposed Solution Approaches

MHs in our architecture can be classified into two groups: 1) computers with reduced memory, storage, power and computing capabilities which we will call Small Mobile Hosts (SMHs) and 2) classical workstations equipped with more storage, power, communication and computing facilities than SMHs which we will call Large Mobile

K.-L. Tan et al. (Eds.): MDM 2001, LNCS 1987, pp. 287-288, 2001.

Hosts (LMHs). Every MH will have a radius of influence. The MHs will operate in three modes to reduce the energy consumption: active, doze and sleep mode.

Transactions are classified into two categories: firm and soft [3]. Firm transactions must be aborted if they miss their deadlines while soft transactions still can be executed after their deadlines have expired.

In our transaction management technique, we have considered time as the most important factor in handling firm transactions and energy in handling soft transactions. So the SMH will submit a firm transaction to the nearest LMH and a soft transaction to the LMH which has the highest available energy. Now if the LMH is in the active mode, it will receive the transaction and start processing the transaction. If the LMH is in the doze mode, and the transaction is firm, it will wake up and start processing the transaction. But if the LMH is in the sleep mode, it will not be able to receive the transaction. In this case the requesting SMH will wait for some time period. If it does not receive the result of the transaction in this time period, it will again check its local database to find the next nearest LMH (for firm transactions) and submit the transaction.

Each LMH will have three components: Transaction Scheduler (TS), Transaction Coordinator (TC) and Transaction Manager (TM). The LMH after receiving a transaction from an SMH will pass the transaction to TS which will use a real-time energy-efficient dynamic scheduling algorithm to schedule transactions. The scheduling algorithm will organize the transactions in a queue that reflects their priorities of execution. Then the first transaction from the queue will be taken by the TC. The TC will check the required data items for this transaction after consulting the 'Global Schema'. If all the data items required by the transaction are available in this LMH, it will pass the transaction to its TM. If all the data items are not available in this LMH, the TC will find the LMHs which contain the required data items from the 'Global Schema'. Then it will divide the global transaction into sub-transactions and submit the corresponding sub-transactions to the participating LMHs. The participating LMHs after processing the sub-transactions will inform the coordinator LMH. The coordinator LMH will use PGSG algorithm [2] to verify Atomicity/Isolation properties of the global transaction. Then it will submit the result of the transaction to the requesting SMH. The requesting SMH after receiving the result of the transaction will send an acknowledgement to the LMH.

Detailed description of the transaction management technique can be found in [1].

References

1. Banik, Shankar M., L., Gruenwald.: Power Aware Management of Mobile Real-Time Database Transactions in Ad-hoc Networks. Technical Report, School of Computer Science, University of Oklahoma, October 2000.
2. Dirckze, R., L, Gruenwald : A Pre-serialization Transaction Management Technique for Mobile-Multi-databases. To appear: Special Issue on Software Architecture for Mobile Applications, MONET 2000.
3. Gruenwald, L., et al. : Database Research at The University of Oklahoma. ACM SIGMOD RECORD, Vol. 28, No. 3, September 1999.

Author Index

Lecture Notes in Computer Science

For information about Vols. 1–1894
please contact your bookseller or Springer-Verlag